3 8015 02039 5897

D1434860

FORGOTTEN EMPIRE
The world of Ancient Persia

FORGOTTEN EMPIRE
The world of Ancient Persia

EDITED BY JOHN CURTIS AND NIGEL TALLIS

WITH CONTRIBUTIONS BY

BÉATRICE ANDRÉ-SALVINI · BARBARA ARMBRUSTER · AGNÈS BENOIT

PIERRE BRIANT · VESTA SARKHOSH CURTIS · IRVING FINKEL

PETER HIGGS · ZAHRA JAFAR-MOHAMMADI · ANDREW R. MEADOWS

SHAHROKH RAZMJOU · ANN SEARIGHT · ST JOHN SIMPSON · NEAL SPENCER

MATTHEW W. STOLPER · ALEXANDRA VILLING

THE BRITISH MUSEUM PRESS

THE TRUSTEES OF THE BRITISH MUSEUM WISH TO THANK THE NATIONAL MUSEUM OF IRAN AND THE MUSÉE DU LOUVRE FOR THEIR LOANS, AND THOSE WHOSE GENEROSITY HAS MADE THIS EXHIBITION POSSIBLE.

Ancient Persia, located just beyond the world of Ancient Greece and the Near East, was a great influence on those civilizations from which we have directly drawn our own identity and culture. In today's mutually dependent and interconnected world, it is good to be reminded of the depth of the common human experience and heritage which we all share. BP is delighted to support this important exhibition which illuminates so much of this heritage and will, I hope, promote renewed interest in this remarkable region of the world, and admiration for its remarkable history and achievements.

bp

LORD BROWNE OF MADINGLEY
Group Chief Executive, BP

CROYDON LIBRARIES

LEN

02039589

Askews	22-Mar-2006
935 CUR ANC	£25.00

© 2005 The Trustees of the British Museum

J.E. Curtis and N. Tallis have asserted the right to be identified as the authors of this work

First published in 2005 by
The British Museum Press
A division of The British Museum Company Ltd
38 Russell Square
London WC1B 3QQ

Reprinted 2005

www.britishmuseum.co.uk

A catalogue record for this book
is available from the British Library

ISBN-13: 978-0-7141-1157-5

ISBN-10: 0-7141-1157-0

Designed by Harry Green
Printed in Spain by Grafos SA, Barcelona

THE IRAN HERITAGE FOUNDATION and its supporters

LORD ALLIANCE	FLORA FAMILY FOUNDATION	ARDESHIR NAGHSHINEH
BALLI GROUP PLC	SASSAN GHANDEHARI	SEDIGHEH RASTEGAR
CHILTERN GROUP PLC	HINDUJA FOUNDATION	ALI SATTARIPOUR
CREDIT SUISSE	ALIREZA ITTIHADIEH	ABOLALA SOUDAVAR
AMIR FARMAN FARMA	MEHDI METGHALCHI	

IRAN CULTURAL HERITAGE & TOURISM ORGANIZATION

BANK MELLI IRAN

NATIONAL PETROCHEMICAL COMPANY (NPC)

IN ADDITION THE BRITISH MUSEUM WOULD LIKE TO THANK

SIR JOSEPH HOTUNG for his generous contribution

CONTENTS

FOREWORD BY THE DIRECTOR

NEIL MACGREGOR
DIRECTOR, BRITISH MUSEUM

This exhibition focuses on one of the great periods of Iranian civilization when the kings of the Achaemenid dynasty established an empire that for over 200 years (550–330 BC) brought stability, prosperity and a flourishing civilization to what we now call the Middle East and beyond. Planned from the outset as a grand collaboration, the exhibition has involved several of the great European museums coming together with the national collections of Iran, furthering our ambitions of closer co-operation with our sister institutions in Europe and Iran. Our aspirations were shared by Dr Henri Loyrette, the Director of the Louvre, and I am most grateful to him and his colleagues for agreeing to lend so many important pieces. These come mainly from Susa, where French archaeologists worked with such distinction from 1884.

When I visited Iran in April 2003, Mr Mohammad-Reza Kargar, Director of the National Museum in Tehran, and the Iranian authorities reacted favourably to our proposal for an exhibition about Achaemenid Persia, and promised straightaway to lend many of their key pieces. They have been true to their word, and the material coming from the National Museum in Tehran and Persepolis Museum now forms the nucleus of this exhibition. We are honoured by and most grateful for this extraordinary generosity.

We value highly our links with Iran, and set great store by this collaboration with the National Museum. Another manifestation of this close relationship is the Sasanian coin project, which is aimed at publishing joint catalogues of the collections in the National Museum and in the British Museum. And in due course we hope to send a small exhibition to Iran centred on the Cyrus Cylinder.

For Iranians the cylinder symbolizes the achievements of Cyrus, the founder of the Achaemenid empire, who in 550 BC proclaimed himself king of the Medes and the Persians. He went on to defeat the last Babylonian king Nabonidus and to capture Babylon, now in Iraq, in 539 BC. The cylinder, which was inscribed in Babylonian cuneiform and buried in Babylon, describes the exploits of Cyrus and relates how he returned statues of gods to various shrines from which they had been seized and allowed deported peoples to return to their homes. It is sometimes called the first Bill of Human Rights. The Jews are not mentioned by name but it is assumed that it was as part of this programme of tolerance and reconciliation that they were allowed to return to Jerusalem and build the Second Temple. At any rate, Cyrus is especially revered by the writers of the books of Ezra-Nehemiah and Isaiah. Because of these biblical references, Cyrus was for centuries regarded as a proponent of religious tolerance and a champion of human rights. Political theorists like Machiavelli portray him as the model king and Europeans long revered him as the ideal ruler. Whatever the truth of these claims, the present exhibition, which is the first of its kind, provides an opportunity to reassess the achievements of the ancient Persian kings and their empire. They are remarkable, particularly in the fields of architecture, arts and crafts, and administration. At this difficult time when east–west relations and understanding are at a low ebb it is instructive to see what a remarkable contribution the ancient Near East has made to the cultural heritage of the world, and the exhibition clearly gives the lie to the common western perception that the Achaemenid empire was a nest of despotism and tyranny that was swept away by Alexander. On the contrary, in its acknowledgement of cultural differences within one coherent and effective state, it is perhaps more than ever a proper object of admiration and study.

FOREWORD

MOHAMMAD-REZA KARGAR

DIRECTOR, NATIONAL MUSEUM OF IRAN

برکسی پوشیده نیست که دانش باستانشناسی در راه شناخت تمدنها، بدون در نظر گرفتن مرزهای جغرافیایی پدید آمده است و جلوه های شگفتی آور تمدنهای دیرین، با تلاش و پویش دانشمندان باستان شناس از ژرفای تاریک و خاموش بستر کهن سر برون آورده و در برابر دید همگان گذارده می شود. امروز بخشی از فرایند آن همه تلاش به نام " امپراتوری فراموش شده، جهان هخامنشیان" در برابر شما است.

بعضی از تئوریها که سرآمد آن متعلق به هانتینگتون می باشد و در کتاب پرفروش و سیاسی او که با عنوان " برخورد تمدنها" نشر یافت، به برخورد احتمالی تمدنهای جهان اشاره دارد که بر پایه اعتقادات مختلف، جهان بینی های متفاوت ، یا بر اساس سنت های مختلف تاریخی شکل گرفته و بنابراین دارای مدلهای گوناگون نیز هست. موزه ملی ایران با برخورداری از ظرفیت های ژرف فرهنگ، هنر و تمدن ایران تلاش نمود تا راه دیگری که همانا گفتگوی تمدنها بود در آستانه ورود به هزاره سوم در پیش گیرد و بر همین اساس در نوامبر سال ۲۰۰۰ نمایشگاه " هفت هزار سال هنر ایران " را در کشور اتریش برپا نمود. تصور آن نمی رفت که پس از گذشت حدود ۵ سال در جایگاهی که تحقق این مهم را با این شتاب فزاینده شاهد باشیم. ما توانستیم مخاطبان زیادی را در اروپا جذب کنیم و با برنامه هایی که امروز در سراسر جهان دنبال می کنیم، امید وافر داریم که پنجره ای نو به سوی جهانیان بگشاییم. تمدن، هنر و فرهنگ اصیل ایران که با وجود تاثیر از دیگر تمدنهای همجوار خویش، در طول قرون متمادی پویایی خود را از دست نداده است ، به خلاقیت و دوام خویش ادامه داده است.

امیدواریم حاصل این تلاشها معرف نقش موزه ها و ثبات و صلح جهانی باشد که همانا لازمه آن شناخت عمیق و مثبتی است که بر پایه هنر حاصل می شود.

نمایشگاه حاضر معرف داشته های ارزنده اولین امپراطوری جهانی است که موفق شد با احترام به باورها و حقوق انسانی، دولتی فراگیر و یکپارچه را تشکیل دهد و سه قاره آسیا، اروپا و آفریقا را به هم پیوند دهد و هنری را پایه گذاری نماید که با استفاده از عناصر هنری همه ملتهای امپراتوری در شکل دادن به هنری که دارای هویت پارسی است و نمادی است از ساختار سیاسی، هنر و معماری ای خلق کند که در جهان بی نظیر بوده است و با بازکردن راههای مختلف دریایی و جاده هایی که در خشکی ادامه یافت و در تمامی امپراطوری گسترده شده بود، حیات اقتصادی سه قاره را در گرو خود داشته باشد و در نهایت موفق شد پایه گذار نظامی باشد که اساس آن بر تلاش در جهت نفی انسانی بود. متاسفانه تاریخ دوره هخامنشی بیشتر به خاطر جنگهایش معروف شده و چهره واقعی و هویت اصلی آن پنهان و فراموش شده است . امید است این نمایشگاه بتواند یاد آور همه فراموش شده های فرهنگ، هنر و تمدن امپراطوری هخامنشیان در تاریخ باشد. همکاری این چنینی دو کشور ایران و انگلستان در این نمایشگاه بعد از حضور ایران در نمایشگاه " جهان اسلام " که در سال ۱۳۵۵ برگزار شد، اولین همکاری جدی دو موزه بزرگ بریتانیا و ملی ایران است.

از زمانی که ایده یک نمایشگاه طرح می شود تا زمانی که تحقق می یابد زحمات و تلاش زیادی را طلب می کند که در این زمینه نیز باید قبل از هر کس از جناب آقای دکتر جان کرتیس، مدیر بخش خاورنزدیک باستان که این ایده را طرح نمودند تشکر کرد. همچنین همراهی و تلاش جناب آقای نیل مک گریگور رئیس محترم موزه بریتانیا که با سفر هایی که به ایران داشته اند تحقق آن را باعث شدند، که می بایست تشکر جدی خود را از ایشان داشته باشم. از تمامی همکارانم در موزه ملی ایران بخصوص از آقای شاهرخ رزمجو مسئول مرکز پژوهش های هخامنشی و سرکار خانم زهرا جعفرمحمدی مسئول نمایشگاههای بین المللی موزه، بخش تاریخی و همچنین از سرکار خانم گرجی و همکارانشان در بخش مرمت تشکر می کنم. همچنین از مهندس طالبیان مدیر بنیاد پژوهشی پارسه-پاسارگاد و همکارانشان برای همکاری همه جانبه شان تشکر می شود. از نمایندگی های سیاسی و فرهنگی دو کشور بخصوص از جناب آقای دکتر عادلی سفیر محترم کشورمان در لندن بخاطر حمایت های گسترده شان تشکر می شود. در آخر نیز از همه مراکز، موسسات، انجمن ها و سازمانهایی که در انجام این اتفاق یاری رسانده اند سپاسگزاری می گردد.

امید است این نمایشگاه بتواند پاسخی علمی و متقن به همه تفسیر ها و تحریف های این بخش از تاریخ که سهم زیادی در تمدن سازی بشری داشته است باشد.

محمدرضا کارگر
رئیس کل موزه ملی ایران

Archaeology has succeeded in identifying ancient cultures which take no account of present-day geographical boundaries. The amazing splendours of ancient civilizations have been revealed through the efforts of archaeologists who have retrieved treasures from the dark, silent places where they have been lying hidden since ancient times.

Today some of the results of these great efforts are in the British Museum's exhibition 'Forgotten Empire: the world of Ancient Persia'. The National Museum of Iran possesses examples of the culture and art of ancient Iran dating from the period discussed by Samuel Huntington in his bestselling book *Clash of Civilizations*. The National Museum has tried to develop a new dialogue between civilizations at the beginning of the third millennium AD. It was for this reason that in the year 2000 the exhibition '7,000 Years of Persian Art' opened in Austria. It was never imagined that after five years we would be in a position to witness the development of this exhibition with such speed and that it would attract so much interest in Europe, so much so that we would now want to open up a new window to the world. The traditional civilization, art and culture of Iran, despite contacts with other cultures throughout the centuries, has not lost its characteristic features and has continued to keep its own identity.

We hope that the results of these endeavours will reflect the role of museums today and help to maintain world peace, as in order to do this we need a deep knowledge of what the art is based on. The present exhibition shows how this first world empire succeeded in establishing a unified state that connected the three continents of Asia, Europe and Africa by respecting cultures, religious beliefs and human rights. It developed an artistic style that used the motifs of all nations in order to form an art that was characteristic of a political formation but that still had a Persian identity. The architecture created by the Ancient Persians was unique in the world. By opening up different sea routes and developing an extensive road network it improved trade and economic conditions in the three continents, and ultimately succeeded in creating an order that was based on achievement. Unfortunately, the history of the Achaemenid period is better remembered for its wars and its true character remains forgotten by many. It is hoped that this exhibition will serve as a reminder of all that has been forgotten about the culture, art and civilization of the Achaemenid Empire and its place in history.

This co-operation between the two countries of Iran and Britain is the first serious co-operation between the two museums – the British Museum and the National Museum of Iran – since Iran's presence in the 'The Arts of Islam' exhibition at the Hayward Gallery in 1976.

From the point that this exhibition was first mooted up to its completion much effort has been expended, and for this we thank first and foremost Dr John Curtis, Keeper of the Department of the Ancient Near East at the British Museum, who came up with the idea, but also Mr Neil MacGregor, the respected Director of the British Museum, for his co-operation and support. With the journeys he has undertaken to Iran, Mr MacGregor has made the project possible and I express my sincere thanks to him and to all my colleagues at the National Museum, particularly Mr Shahrokh Razmjou, in charge of the Centre for Achaemenid Research, and Mrs Zahra Jafar-Mohamadi, in charge of international exhibitions. My thanks also go to the Department of History, and Miss Mahnaz Gorji and her colleagues in the Department of Conservation. We are also grateful to Mr Mohammad Hassan Talebian, Director of the Parsa-Pasargadae Research Foundation and his colleagues for their co-operation in every respect. I am also grateful to the diplomatic and cultural representatives of the two countries, in particular Dr Adeli, the respected Ambassador of our country in London, for his extensive support. Finally, I would like to thank all centres, foundations, and institutions that have supported this event.

It is hoped that this exhibition will make a contribution to the study of this period of history which made such a great contribution to the development of human civilization.

PRÉFACE

HENRI LOYRETTE
PRÉSIDENT-DIRECTEUR DU LOUVRE

La coopération archéologique entre l'Iran et la France est plus que centenaire, elle a eu pour cadre principal l'exploration du palais de Darius le Grand à Suse.

Il est vrai que c'est à un savant britannique, W.K. Loftus que revient l'honneur d'avoir découvert le site de Suse et entamé la fouille en 1851. Mais les travaux de grande ampleur ont été véritablement entrepris par Marcel Dieulafoy à partir de 1885, mettant au jour les principaux éléments de l'Apadana. Cette activité s'est traduite par l'arrivée au musée du Louvre d'un décor architectural monumental de l'époque perse, frise des archers, frise des lions, chapiteau de l'Apadana. Installé dans une salle inaugurée en 1888, ce décor qui révéla au public parisien la splendeur des Achéménides constitue toujours un des points forts du musée. Puis Jacques de Morgan, en application de la convention archéologique signée entre la France et la Perse en 1895, ouvrit une longue ère de recherche.

A Téhéran, les autorités iraniennes confiaient à l'architecte André Godard, directeur du Service des antiquités depuis 1928, le soin de dresser le plan du musée Iran Bastan et d'y présenter les antiquités récemment mises au jour en Iran; dans la ville moderne de Sush, sur l'autre rive du Shaour, s'élevait bientôt un musée de site du plus grand intérêt.

Au Louvre, la longue amitié entre la France et l'Iran, moteur de cette coopération sur la longue durée, explique l'exceptionnelle richesse du Louvre dans le domaine de l'art achéménide. Les grandes rénovations des espaces ont été accompagnés ces dernières années par d'importantes opérations de restauration des œuvres. La célèbre frise des archers, les animaux mythologiques en terre cuite et en briques glaçurées, ont été patiemment nettoyés, de nouveaux remontages ont été possibles à partir de fragments, d'autres sont en cours. Chercheurs du monde entier, étudiants, restaurateurs continuent de se pencher sur ces œuvres.

L'exposition organisée par le British Museum et le Musée national de Téhéran est une entreprise internationale exceptionnelle, à laquelle le musée du Louvre se joint par un choix d'œuvres prestigieuses, vaisselle d'orfèvrerie, tous les bijoux de la tombe princière de Suse, un archer récemment restauré, dans un magnifique panorama de l'art perse achéménide.

EDITORS' FOREWORD AND ACKNOWLEDGEMENTS

There is no doubt that a major exhibition focusing on the empire of Ancient Persia is long overdue. Between 550 and 330 BC the Achaemenid kings of Iran controlled an empire that stretched from the River Indus to North Africa and from the Aral Sea to the Persian Gulf. It was the greatest empire the world had seen up until that time. In addition to building splendid palaces at Persepolis, Pasargadae, Susa and Babylon, the Achaemenid kings also introduced effective systems of administration and a good communications network. During this period exquisite works of art were produced, and scientific and cultural studies prospered in places such as Babylon. In many ways the Persian Empire was responsible for transmitting to Greece and the west the contributions made by the ancient Near East to the development of civilization, notably by the Assyrian and Babylonian Empires. In spite of the achievements of ancient Persia, however, there has never been a major exhibition on the subject. This has now become possible through the generosity of the Islamic Republic of Iran and its willingness to lend some of their most important and iconic Achaemenid pieces. This generosity of spirit has been matched by the authorities in the Louvre who have also been ready to lend some of their most outstanding objects. Furthermore, the present time, when the Middle East is under the spotlight as never before, seems to be a particularly appropriate moment to mount an exhibition on one of the great civilizations of antiquity and to show to the museum-going public in the west the splendours of the Ancient Persian civilization. Throughout, the project has received the enthusiastic support of Neil MacGregor, and without his encouragement the exhibition would hardly have been conceived, let alone brought to fruition.

The material in the exhibition comes from the National Museum in Tehran, the Persepolis Museum, the Louvre and the British Museum's own collections. With the exception of the Oriental Institute Museum at the University of Chicago, all the great collections of material from the Iranian heartland are therefore represented, and it has not been necessary to go further afield for more material. For Achaemenid-period material from outside Iran we have relied largely on the British Museum's own extensive collection, distributed over a number of different departments and never exhibited together before. From some parts of the empire there are extensive holdings of spectacular Achaemenid-period material in the countries where it has been found, notably Turkey, the Caucasus and Thrace; but the inclusion of this would have greatly enlarged the size of the exhibition and would not have been practical in present circumstances. The emphasis here, then, is on the central part of the Achaemenid Empire. In accordance with recent international guidelines, only unexcavated material that has a pre-1970 provenance has been included in the exhibition.

Ancient Persia is perhaps best remembered in the west for its war with Greece and for the later invasion by Alexander of Macedon in 334–330 BC, culminating in the gratuitous destruction of Persepolis. For the Persians, however, the Graeco-Persian Wars were probably little more than a troublesome frontier skirmish that took place nearly 2,000 miles away from Persepolis, and native Iranian sources are largely silent on this question. Instead, our information about the wars and about much else in connection with the ancient Persians comes from Greek authors such as Herodotus. These accounts are inevitably written from a Greek rather than a Persian perspective, and it is because of them that the conflict is often represented as a contest between freedom and democracy on the one hand, and tyranny and despotism on the other. One of the aims of the exhibition will be to redress this negative Eurocentric view of the ancient Persians.

A project of this size would not have been possible without the help and encouragement of many people whose assistance is recorded in the acknowledgements. A number of scholars have come together to produce this catalogue, and their contributions are credited as appropriate. They remain responsible for their own contributions, which the editors have not sought to change. In a subject as dynamic and complex as Achaemenid studies there are inevitably differences of opinion on some matters, and these will be reflected in the catalogue. In this way, the catalogue presents some of the latest thinking on much-debated issues such as religion, administration and warfare. Although the information has been drawn from a variety of sources, the catalogue entries remain the responsibility of the editors.

The publication of this catalogue has been supervised by Laura Brockbank, who has been a patient and conscientious editor. Thanks are also due to Harry Green, who designed the book, and Colin Grant, who read the proofs. Photographers that deserve special mention are Lisa Baylis (British Museum), Ebrahem Khadem-Bayat (Tehran), Goran Vranić (Zagreb) and Catarina Maria Gomes Ferreira (Lisbon). Ann Searight has produced the drawings with her customary skill. Claire Burton has helped greatly with the production of the text. Unless otherwise stated, the translations of Old Persian inscriptions and Greek texts are taken from R.G. Kent, *Old Persian Grammar, Texts, Lexikon* (Kent 1953), or after the various Loeb editions.

An exhibition project of this size with accompanying catalogue is dependent on the help and co-operation of many people. Foremost amongst them have been Neil MacGregor and Vesta Sarkhosh Curtis. To these names should be added the following:

IRANIAN CULTURAL HERITAGE AND TOURISM ORGANIZATION
His Excellency Seyyid Hussein Marashi, Mohammad Atrianfar, Seyyid Mohammad Behshti

NATIONAL MUSEUM OF IRAN, TEHRAN
Mohammad-Reza Kargar, Zahra Jafar-Mohammadi, Shahrokh Razmjou, Mahnaz Gorji, Souri Ayazi, Zahra Akbari

PERSEPOLIS
Mohammad Hassan Talebian, Maziar Kazemi, Hassan Rahsaz

MUSÉE DU LOUVRE
Annie Caubet, Agnès Benoit, Béatrice André-Salvini

BRITISH MUSEUM
Dean Baylis, Christopher Walker, Irving Finkel, Dominique Collon, St John Simpson, Jerry Baker, Wendy Adamson, Jane Newson, Theodora Georgiou, Herma Chang (Department of the Ancient Near East); Nicolas Bel (special assistant), Andrew R. Meadows (Department of Coins and Medals); Alexandra Villing, Peter Higgs, Dyfri Williams (Department of Greek and Roman Antiquities); Neal Spencer (Department of Ancient Egypt and Sudan); Andrew Burnett, Deputy Director (Collections); Carolyn Marsden-Smith, Alec Shaw, Caroline Ingham, Paul Tansey, Austin Barlow, Jenny Tither, Ted Wood (Department of Presentation); Michael Wilson (special adviser); Sam Moorhead (Department of Education and Information); Tracey Sweek, Denise Ling, Pippa Pearce (Department of Conservation, Documentation and Science); Sukie Hemming, Anneke Rifkin (Development Department); Joanna Mackle, Hannah Boulton (Department of Communications); Honor Wilson-Fletcher (Marketing).

IRANIAN EMBASSY IN LONDON
Seyyed Mohammad Hussein Adeli, Ali Akbar Rezaei

TEHRAN
Maryam Alaghband (Balli Group, Tehran), Varouj P. Samuelian (Unipack S.A.), Parvaneh Sattari (Pasargad Tours)

BRITISH COUNCIL, TEHRAN
Michael Wilson

IRAN HERITAGE FOUNDATION
Vahid Alaghband, Farhad Hakimzadeh

Some objects from Tehran illustrated in the catalogue may unfortunately not be exhibited due to conservation issues.

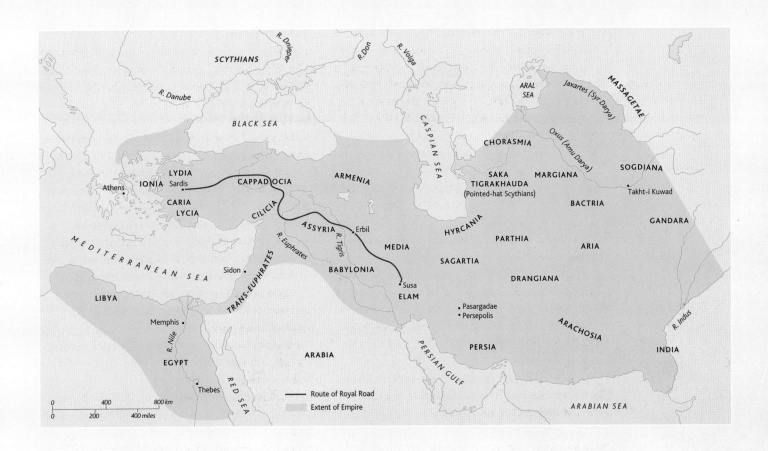

Map of the Persian Empire at its greatest extent showing the principal provinces and the route of the royal road from Susa to Sardis.

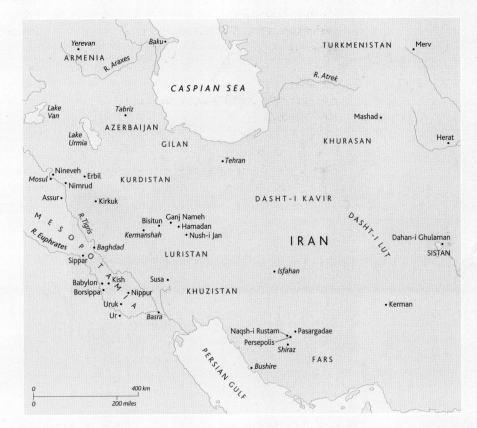

The central part of the Persian Empire showing the main sites occupied during the Achaemenid period.

1

HISTORY OF THE PERSIAN EMPIRE (550–330 BC)

Pierre Briant

The origins of the Persian people and the stages which led to the creation of the first ancient world empire remain shrouded in mystery, or at least beset by uncertainties. In spite of the progress made by archaeology and epigraphy, we remain inadequately informed about the first centuries of Persian history, between about 1000 and 600 BC.

The Classical texts are almost silent on this period, apart from the various descriptions of the heroic origins of the empire's founder Cyrus the Great, who became king of Persia around 557 BC. He was the son of Cambyses I and the grandson of Cyrus I, both of whom reigned over the

1 The Tomb of Cyrus at Pasargadae. The entrance to the tomb chamber is above the stepped platform. The chamber is now empty, but according to the Greek author Arrian, Cyrus was buried in a golden coffin.

country of Anshan, in the heart of the region which would take the name of Persia (Parsa). Cyrus himself testified to his genealogy in the famous Babylonian text known as the Cyrus Cylinder (cat. 6), which was written after the conquest of Babylon in 539 BC: 'I am ... the son of Cambyses, the great king, king of Anshan, grandson of Cyrus, the great king, king of Anshan, great-grandson of Teispes, the great king, king of Anshan ....' Together with what we know from Neo-Elamite tablets, and from the seal

of Kurash of Anshan (cat. 308), this title attests to close contacts between the first Persian kingdom and the kings of Susa. At the same time, we know that the Persians maintained a specific relationship with the Medes, both on a cultural and a political level.

It was this same Cyrus the Great (557–530 BC) and his army who around 550 BC conquered Ecbatana and the Median kingdom, and then, four years later, Sardis, the kingdom of Lydia and Asia Minor; in 539 BC Cyrus defeated the Babylonian king Nabonidus and entered Babylon. Following these conquests, all the kings and rulers of the Fertile Crescent came to prostrate themselves in front of their new master; at the same time Cyrus authorized the Jewish community that had been exiled to Babylon since 587 BC to return to Jerusalem and rebuild the Temple of Yahweh. Meanwhile, he probably launched an expedition across the Iranian plateau into Central Asia as far as Bactria-Sogdiana, where he established a series of forts on the left bank of the River Jaxartes (Syr Darya), which would be regarded as the northern border of the empire. He disappeared during this campaign, or a little later, and was buried at Pasargadae in the tomb that he had erected there not far from the main palaces (fig. 1).

By this time, the once small kingdom of Persia had become the centre of an impressive empire. However, it would extend further under Cyrus's immediate successors. On becoming king following the death of his father, Cambyses (530–522 BC) continued the work of conquest and in 525–522 BC launched an attack on the last large independent kingdom of the Middle East, pharaonic Egypt. From this point on, the empire stretched from the Syr Darya to the first cataract of the Nile, and from Samarkand to the Mediterranean.

It was during this period in 522–520 BC that the empire underwent its first serious crisis, though it was not destroyed by it. The episode, which is known from the long account by Herodotus and the explanation that Darius himself gave on the cliff at Bisitun (fig. 2), endangered both the dynastic line and Persian imperial domination.

2 The rock relief of Darius at Bisitun, 520–519 BC. Darius has his foot on the prostrate body of Gaumata (the false Smerdis) and in front of him are nine rebel kings roped together at the neck. The relief is surrounded by inscriptions in Old Persian, Elamite and Babylonian. See also fig. 6.

On the death of Cambyses on his way back from Egypt, a usurper (the Smerdis of Herodotus, or Bardiya/Gaumata of Darius) seized power in Persia. With the aid of the royal army, Darius launched a counter-attack and removed his rival. Although his own legitimacy was tenuous, he proclaimed himself king by linking himself to the royal line. But he soon had to take up arms again against a series of local revolts, which extended in particular to the central areas of the empire (Babylonia, Media and Persia itself), the countries of the Iranian plateau and to Central Asia. It took over a year for Darius and his generals to put an end to the uprisings. It was as a result of his victories that the king ordered the construction of the relief and the engraving of the trilingual inscriptions on the cliff at Bisitun in Media. The figure of the man whom Darius named the usurper (Gaumata) is depicted lying on his back under the feet of the king (see figs 2 and 6). Those rulers who had rebelled and finally been overcome are identified in short inscriptions, indicating that they were 'liar-kings': bound to each other by a cord passed around their necks, they are paraded in front of their triumphant victor. A little later Darius conducted a campaign into Central Asia against the Saka, during which he overthrew King Skunkha (recognizable on the extreme right-hand side of

the relief), and then in 518 BC he went on to annex the Indus valley to his empire (see map, p. 11 top).

During the reign of Darius (522–486 BC) the empire reached its peak. Indeed, in 513 BC, while his generals launched a campaign against Cyrenaica, Darius led his armies into Europe. He conquered the western coast of the Euxine Sea (the Black Sea), then crossed the River Danube (Istros) in pursuit of the Scythian armies. He soon had to turn back, but he was able to leave a strong army in Europe, charged to annex Thrace and Macedonia. The unprecedented power of the Great King is illustrated perfectly in the decision, taken undoubtedly soon after Darius's return from Europe, when he was staying in Sardis, to create an Achaemenid royal currency: the daric (gold coin) and the shekel (silver coin), on which was stamped the image of a warrior-king. The revolt of the Greek cities of Asia Minor in 499–493 BC did not spoil Darius's track record. What we term the first Persian War cannot simply be reduced to the defeat at Marathon in 490 BC, since another consequence was the subjugation of the Aegean islands. By this date the empire extended from the Indus to the Balkans (see map, p. 11 top).

The construction of the large royal residences at Susa and Persepolis is the most brilliant testimony to Persian imperial power. On the gold and silver tablets deposited in the foundations of the audience hall (the Apadana) at Persepolis (fig. 3), Darius expressed himself proudly as follows: 'Here is the kingdom that I possess, from the Sakas [Scythians] who are beyond Sogdiana to the land of Kush [Nubia], from India to Sardis.' In another famous inscription on the front of the tomb which he had cut into the cliff at Naqsh-i Rustam (fig. 4), located, like nearby Persepolis, at the heart of Persia, Darius addressed his subjects in similar terms, pointing out the sculptures which represented the conquered people: 'See these sculptured figures which carry the throne, then you will understand that the spear of the Persian warrior has travelled far, then you will understand that the Persian warrior has fought far from Persia' (DNa). There is a similar proclamation on the statue of Darius found at Susa: 'Here is the stone statue that Darius the king ordered to be made in Egypt so that whoever sees it in the future will understand that the Persian warrior governs Egypt' (DSab). Together with many other documents, these declarations express the idea that the Persians are a conquering people who rule from within their empire, and their king Darius is the 'king of kings, king of all races, king of this great land which extends so far, the son of Hystaspes, an Achaemenid, a Persian son of a Persian, an Aryan of Aryan stock' (DNa).

The defeats of Xerxes during the second Persian War (480–479 BC), followed by the creation of the Delian League under the control of Athens seriously threatened Persian positions in the eastern Aegean. It would, however, be wrong to conclude, as used to be the case, that the Achaemenid Empire entered a long period of decline starting from the reign of Xerxes (486–465 BC). Influenced by a vision centred on Athens and Greece, such an interpretation does not bear up to the analysis of Elamite documentation from Persepolis, Akkadian documentation from Babylonia, or Aramaic documentation from Egypt, not to mention the numismatic, archaeological and iconographic evidence.

The circumstances surrounding several royal successions illustrate one of the weaknesses of Persian power and one of the uncertainties associated with imperial power in general. When Xerxes was assassinated by plotters, several of his sons violently disputed power, until one of them took control under the name of Artaxerxes (465–424 BC). But on his death the family conflicts broke out again: it was only at the end of another war that one of his bastard sons seized power and took the name of Darius (424–404 BC). He was succeeded by one of his sons, Artaxerxes II. The beginning of Artaxerxes II's reign was marked in turn by serious dynastic disagreements, when his younger brother (Cyrus the Younger) raised an army and advanced as far as Babylonia to seize power. Artaxerxes II was victorious at Cunaxa, but the end of his long reign was marked again by plots at court. One of his many sons succeeded him (Artaxerxes III, 359/8–338 BC), before being assassinated by the eunuch Bagoas; he appointed to the throne Arses, one of the sons of the late king (Artaxerxes IV, 338–336 BC), before removing him and promoting Artashata under the name of Darius. When you consider that this same Darius (III) was assassinated in 330 BC by his close relations, it becomes clear that, since the death of Cambyses in 522 BC, the dynastic succession was very frequently called into question by plots and assassinations.

The explanation is simple: Persia was not a monarchy of the constitutional type, where the rules of succession are

3 Gold and silver plates with a foundation inscription of Darius written in Old Persian, Elamite and Babylonian. Pairs of these plates were discovered in foundation boxes buried beneath the southeast and northeast corners of the Apadana at Persepolis. For the silver example, see cat. 2.

4 The cliff at Naqsh-i Rustam with tombs of Artaxerxes I (left) and Darius. At the foot of the cliff are rock reliefs of the Sasanian period. See also figs 22 and 70.

fixed and unchanging, and where the final word does not rest with armed force. Even when, despite everything, the same family remained in power, this continuing uncertainty was to have unavoidable consequences for the survival of the empire. The Achaemenid king was not only the 'King of Persia', the intermediary between the Persian gods and the population of his country, but also the 'king of kings', 'the king of lands which extend so far'. The questioning of dynastic power thus often had repercussions in various subject countries.

One of the clearest examples of this is the succession of Artaxerxes II from Darius II. Even though Darius died in his bed and his elder son succeeded him in apparent peace, the subsequent rebellion of Cyrus the Younger had disastrous consequences for the state of the empire. Cyrus not only mustered Greek mercenaries, he also more importantly raised an imperial army in Asia Minor, according to the military powers which had been granted him by his brother the king. So, to some extent, the battle of Cunaxa was a confrontation between two royal armies: one raised by Artaxerxes in the central and eastern part of the empire, and another raised by Cyrus in the western areas. At the same time, the Persian nobility and the local dynasts around the empire had to choose between two loyalties – that which they owed to the legitimate king (Artaxerxes) and that which the rebel (Cyrus) required of them. The

question was solved by the defeat and the death of Cyrus, but what would have happened if Cyrus had been more astute, and if the result of the battle had been undecided?

Whatever the answer, the war between the two brothers did not fail to have detrimental consequences for imperial power itself. One sees this clearly in Egypt. The years between 404 and 400 BC were a time of trouble, which ended with the seizure of power by an Egyptian dynasty. It was the end of the first Persian domination of Egypt, which had started in 525 BC with the conquest by Cambyses. The central Persian government would try to reconquer Egypt during the fourth century BC, but it would fail on several occasions. It took until 343/2 BC for Artaxerxes III to succeed, after having subdued another revolt at Sidon in Phoenicia. A new revolt, provoked by the pharaoh Khababash, occurred in Egypt before the arrival of Alexander in 332 BC, as recounted in particular on the so-called 'Stela of the Satrap'.

Egypt does seem to have constituted a special case. In the Delta, Lower Egypt was in effect a Mediterranean country, largely open to the sea since at least the Saite dynasty. Greeks, Carians and Ionians of Asia Minor, as well as Aramaeans, were numerous in Naucratis and in other centres of the Delta, including the satrapal capital, Memphis. This is well illustrated by an Aramaic papyrus that probably dates back to Xerxes. It records the business of a customs station in the Delta, where commercial boats arriving from the Anatolian coast (Ionia) and from the Phoenician coast were inspected and taxed. For these reasons, the Delta was a theatre of confrontation between Athenians and Persians from the foundation of the Delian League in 478 BC. This certainly explains the long revolt in the year 460 BC, which was subdued by Megabyzus. But trouble had blown up before then, from the end of the reign of Darius I, and Xerxes had to conduct a campaign there. Other more endemic disturbances are attested to by Aramaic papyri from the reign of Darius II. One of these documents is dated to year 7 of the Egyptian king Amyrtaeus, who proclaimed himself pharaoh in the year 404 BC.

Egypt was the only country to regain its independence for a long period (400–343/2 BC), but it was not the only one to revolt against Persian domination. The great rebellions of the years 522/520 BC had already indicated the relative fragility of the empire. Other revolts are recorded on Babylonian tablets during the reign of Xerxes, but the references do not tell us anything about their origin or extent. There is also mention of a Bactrian rebellion at the beginning of the reign of Artaxerxes I and of an insurrection of Phoenician cities in the middle of the fourth century BC. Apart from these significant revolts, which obliged the central government to send an army and sometimes even forced the king to head a punitive expedition, there were also small local disturbances, which the governors of the provinces (satraps) and their subordinates were charged to repress.

To the dynastic disputes and the rebellions of the subjected peoples should be added the revolts of satraps. Appointed directly by the king, the satraps were representatives of great Persian noble families and had extremely significant powers and duties: to maintain law and order, raise and pass on taxes, and muster military quotas. They did not have the right to strike coins, a prerogative which rested with the king; in certain cases, they might be authorized to strike coins in order to lead military campaigns, but these were not strictly speaking satrapac coins. In addition, the satraps did not have power over all fortified towns or the Treasuries.

In spite of the extent to which they were monitored by central government, it was tempting for satraps to liberate themselves and assume a certain amount of autonomy. Some of these attempts in the course of the fifth century BC are recalled by the Classical texts, but they do not appear to have seriously endangered royal power. Traditionally called the 'great revolt of the satraps', the most serious incidents took place during the fourth century BC in Anatolia, between about 366 and 359 BC. According to the Greek author Diodorus of Sicily, several satraps from the western coastal areas united against the king Artaxerxes II and triggered off a secession (*apostasis*), which coincided with rebellions by several subject peoples of southernmost Asia Minor, and also by the Syrians and Phoenicians:

> Facing the significant communal force which had been formed against the Persians, Artaxerxes also made preparations for war: he had to go to war at the same time with the king of Egypt, the Greek cities of Asia Minor, the Lacedaemonians and their allies, and with the satraps and the strategists who controlled the coastal districts. (XV.90)

Other authors even make it clear that one of the rebellious satraps called Datames aimed to carry out an offensive against the heart of the empire, beyond the Euphrates. In short, the Persian Empire would have been at this point on the brink of complete implosion.

One should assess these facts objectively and methodically. That there were revolts and rebellions during this period is not in any doubt. However, it is extremely doubtful that all this activity was coordinated. According to the above-mentioned author Diodorus, the rebellion of the satraps ended pitifully: their leader, Orontes, reckoned that it would be more advantageous for him to betray his companions and deliver them to the royal government. Datames' end was similar: he was also betrayed by someone close to him, then speedily executed. Ultimately, whilst these satrapal revolts undoubtedly generated trouble, they never aimed to overthrow the Achaemenid dynasty, and the central government was never seriously endangered by them.

If one wishes to assess the track record of the empire following more than two centuries of Persian domination, it is instructive to examine the situation at the point when Darius III took power. It has been commonly believed for a long time, for various reasons, that the Persian Empire was by then in full decline: this viewpoint helps to explain the final victory of Alexander. But if one analyses the situation, it quickly becomes clear that the reality was in fact much more complex. The Great King's assets remained very significant. Far from being destroyed by the actions of the mercenaries, the imperial military reserves remained considerable and well prepared. In spring 334 BC, on the orders of Darius, Arsites, satrap of Hellespontine Phrygia, gathered the forces led by the satraps of Asia Minor, and faced the Macedonian army at Granicus. The Achaemenid navy was undeniably superior, even though, for little known reasons, it did not oppose the Macedonian landings.

During the following months Darius raised a considerable army in Babylon and led it towards Cilicia, where, once again, Alexander was victorious at Issus in November 333 BC. Finally, during the following two years Darius again made formidable preparations and chose a location for the forthcoming battle in Upper Mesopotamia (Gaugamela), where on 1 October 331 BC he was defeated by the Macedonian troops. The conclusion that can be drawn from these confrontations is two-fold: on the one hand, the empire always had at its disposal inexhaustible reserves of soldiers and money, but on the other hand, as far as one can tell, the Macedonians were tactically and strategically superior.

On a political level, in spite of the plots and assassinations which marked recent dynastic history, Darius's authority was not to blame: it was only at the point when the unstoppable successes of Alexander, from Gaugamela to Persepolis, had won over the satraps that the Great King was no longer able to oppose the Macedonian invasion. Such was not the case during the period 336–330 BC. Whatever mistakes he made, Darius still had many noble Persians, satraps and strategists all ready to serve him. Defections occurred only little by little. The first was that of Mithrenes, governor of Sardis, who joined the Macedonian king after the defeat at Granicus. The governor of Damascus did the same after the battle of Issos, which made it possible for the Macedonians, without encountering any opposition, to take hold of this important city that before the battle had sheltered the treasures and family of Darius. Then, more serious still, after Gaugamela another of the satraps, Mazaeus, approached Alexander: in exchange, he obtained the post of satrap of Babylon. His example was followed by the satrap of Susa, then by the commanders of Persepolis and of Pasargadae.

As regards the subject peoples, there is no evidence for general anti-Persian revolts, even after the first defeats by the Macedonians. Certain populations and cities even put up stubborn resistance: the most notable example is Tyre, which remained loyal to Darius; the same happened in Gaza. Whilst the Greek and Latin texts like to testify to the triumphal entry of Alexander into Egypt and Babylon, and to explain that the populations were delighted to be rid of their Persian oppressors, the situation was not like this in reality. In the course of his conquests, Alexander faithfully adopted the strategy followed by the Achaemenid kings since Cyrus: to make alliances with the local elites, to recognize the position and the privileges which they enjoyed in their own countries, and to respect their sanctuaries, gods and local cults. It is what Cyrus and his successors had done, and what Alexander did too. Due to these concessions by the victor the elites decided to join forces with Alexander, and to organize triumphal ceremonies on his entry into the cities. One sees this very clearly in Babylon in particular: the Babylonian tablets (astronomical diaries) do indeed show that after the battle of Gaugamela negotiations were opened between Alexander and the Babylonian authorities, and they imply quite clearly that an agreement of suitable form was concluded. In other words, the reception which Alexander received in various cities does not reflect how the people felt about Achaemenid domination.

But, finally, the clearest indication of the solidity of the construction of the Achaemenid Empire is offered by the many elements which Alexander himself borrowed. Not content to capture just the borders of the empire of the Great Kings, the Macedonian victor appealed not only to local elites (such as Egyptian and Babylonian), but also to the Persian and Iranian nobility, the true backbone of the empire. Conscious of the impossibility of controlling such an empire using only the Macedonian nobility, Alexander decided very early (from the capture of Sardis in 334 BC) to propose to the Iranian nobility that they work with him and in collaboration with the Greeks and the Macedonians. In order to symbolize this, in 324 BC a number of grand weddings between Macedonian nobles and heiresses of great Persian and Iranian families were celebrated at Susa in accordance with Persian ceremony.

Achaemenid imperial history does not stop abruptly in July 330 BC with the assassination of Darius III by Bessus and his accomplices. Presenting himself from that point on as an avenger of Darius, Alexander re-established the borders at the Syr Darya in the north and at the Indus in the east, before imposing a new imperial domination on the Persian Gulf. With this in mind, the true end of the Achaemenid imperial ideal should be dated not to 330 BC, but to 323 BC when Alexander died: after this fighting broke out between the *Diadochi* (the Successors), which eventually led to the creation of competing and hostile kingdoms (the Hellenistic kingdoms), instead of the united empire created by Cyrus and his successors, and then revived by Alexander.

2

ACHAEMENID LANGUAGES AND INSCRIPTIONS

Matthew W. Stolper

Early European visitors to the ruined palaces of Persepolis saw what seemed to be inscriptions in unknown writing using characters composed of wedge-shaped elements. Often the inscriptions were in three parts, and the characters in each part were different. When the three sorts of writing appeared together, the same sort was usually in the privileged place: at the top of a vertical array, or in the middle of a horizontal array. Some observers guessed that the inscriptions were in more than one language and more than one script, a guess that was the first step in deciphering the cuneiform writing systems.

Partial decipherment at the beginning of the nineteenth century confirmed that the monuments belonged to Darius, Xerxes and Artaxerxes, the kings of the Achaemenid dynasty whose names and histories had been handed down by Greek and Roman writers (fig. 5). The completed decipherment, more than forty years later, confirmed that the inscriptions were in three different languages, written with two different scripts. The language in the privileged position was that of the empire's rulers, now called Old Persian. The other two were languages of the empire's subjects: Elamite, spoken in southwestern Iran long before the Iranians arrived there, and Akkadian, the ancient language of Babylonia and Assyria. Old Persian used a script of its own. Akkadian and Elamite used two different forms of the same cuneiform writing that archaeologists and epigraphers found on tablets and monuments in Babylonia and Assyria, and eventually in other parts of western Asia.

These trilingual inscriptions were emblems of the Achaemenid Empire's immensity and complexity. These properties were sometimes expressed in Old Persian using the adjective *vispazana*, 'having all kinds (of people)'. The Elamite versions do not translate this word, but use a loan-word taken from another form of the same adjective. The Akkadian reinterprets the adjective with a phrase that means literally 'of all languages'. This portrayal of the Achaemenid Empire as a realm of many peoples and many tongues appears again and again in the records of Achaemenid history, ranging from the relief sculptures of tributaries carved on the royal palaces and tombs to Herodotus's description of the exotic contingents in the armies of Xerxes. The people of the Achaemenid Empire wrote more languages than these three, and they spoke still more, but the inscriptions represent the polyglot empire with languages that were not merely different, but linguistically unrelated to each other: Old Persian was an Indo-European language, Akkadian a Semitic language and Elamite an unaffiliated language.

The subjects of earlier empires had also spoken and written many languages, but the inscriptions in the palaces of the Assyrian and Babylonian kings were only in the language of the rulers. The Achaemenids departed from these imperial precedents to represent their own empire: hence, the particular languages of the Achaemenid inscriptions were unprecedented symbols of the relationship between rulers and ruled and between ancient history and the Achaemenid present. A closer look at the languages and inscriptions will bear this out, examining the nature of the languages, when and how they were used, the inscriptions, and for whom they were meant.

LANGUAGES
OLD PERSIAN

The language of the rulers, Old Persian, belongs to the Indo-European family, whose members include languages spoken from India (ancient Sanskrit, modern Hindi and others) to Europe (ancient Latin and Greek, modern Romance, Germanic and Slavic languages, and others). Indo-Iranian languages are a subgroup of Indo-European, and Iranian languages are a subgroup of Indo-Iranian. The ancient written Iranian languages are Old Persian, Avestan (the language of the Zoroastrian scriptures) and Pahlavi (the language of Sassanian inscriptions). Modern Iranian languages include modern Persian (Farsi, an indirect descendant of the language of the Achaemenid inscriptions), Kurdish, Pashto and others.

Much of the common vocabulary of Old Persian is easily recognizable from other Indo-European languages (for example, Old Persian *asti*, meaning 'is', cf. Latin *est*, German *ist*; Old Persian *pita^r-*, cf. Latin *pater*, English *father*). The grammatical forms (noun endings, verb tenses and moods, etc.) are few and simple in comparison to Avestan, Sanskrit or even Classical Greek. To a speaker of Akkadian or Elamite, Old Persian would have been an alien language. To speakers of Ancient Greek, the similarities must have made it easy to grasp, but the scanty grammatical forms must have made it difficult to speak. Still, when Themistocles, the Athenian commander of the defence against the armies of Xerxes, was sent into exile, he needed only a year of Persian study to impress the Achaemenid king.

Persian, however, was not the only Iranian language of ancient Iran, nor even the most common one. Speakers of Iranian languages had migrated into western parts of the region that became Iran before 1000 BC. As they spread out and settled among indigenous people, they developed distinct Iranian dialects. Inscriptions of the Assyrians called most of the Iranians Medes. Persians were at that time a smaller group, beyond the reach of Assyrian power. They settled among the Elamite population of what would become Persia proper, modern Fars, and they developed a distinct language. Even among the Iranian population of the Achaemenid Empire, therefore, Persian was the language of a ruling minority.

Persian was marked by sound changes that did not occur in the language of the Medes or in other Old Iranian languages. An example is the word that is translated into English as 'satrap'. The consonant cluster *-tr-* in the English word comes from an original ancient Iranian form with the cluster *-thr-*. But in Old Persian this Iranian cluster changed to a sibilant (an *s*-like sound) of uncertain quality, transcribed as *-ç-*. In Old Persian, therefore, the word is *xšaçapāva^n* (literally, 'protecting the kingdom'). The Greeks heard this word in a common Iranian form, but not in the distinctive Persian form, and this borrowing from the non-Persian form was transmitted in turn to other languages.

Most of the Iranians who took command in the Achaemenid provinces were non-Persians, so such non-Persian forms predominate among Iranian loan-words in Akkadian, Aramaic and other written languages of the provinces. Even in the heart of the empire the Old Persian of the royal inscriptions contained many non-Persian dialect forms. Some are political or religious terms loaded with affect and implication. The foremost

epithet of the rulers, 'great king', is composed of non-Persian forms. The grammatical construction of another epithet, 'king of kings', is non-Persian. Even the adjective *vispazana*, 'of all kinds (of people)', is non-Persian; the Persian form would be *visadana* – and that is in fact the form borrowed in the Elamite version. For some words, both Persian and non-Persian forms occur in the inscriptions (for example, both the Persian *asa* and non-Persian *aspa*, 'horse', etc.), doublets that testify to the coexistence of Iranian dialects at the Achaemenid courts. Some non-Persian forms may come from the dialects of pre-Achaemenid Iranian kingdoms, especially from the Median kingdom that had battled the Assyrian Empire. The Achaemenids adopted them to attach themselves to an older, glorious history, and to present themselves, as inscriptions of Darius I put it, not just as 'Persian, of Persian descent', but also as 'Iranian, of Iranian stock'.

A new writing system was invented for this language of elevated political expression. The elements of the signs are wedge-shaped, but the signs themselves have no formal connection with the cuneiform characters used to write Akkadian and Elamite. There are only forty-two Old Persian signs, used with almost perfectly consistent rules, but because the system was so parsimonious, it allowed much ambiguity. Thus, the five characters that spell the verb 'is' could be read, in theory, in any of seventy-two ways. To a speaker of Persian, seventy-one of them would be nonsense. To read the word correctly, as Old Persian *asti*, requires knowledge not only of the script, but also of the language.

Old Persian script was used only for the Old Persian language, and only on durable materials for sumptuary uses: prepared rock faces, stone blocks bonded into the walls of buildings or laid under their foundations, enamelled bricks that imitated carved stone panels, stone or metal plates, bowls, jars, blades, stone weights and stone cylinder seals. The rare Old Persian texts on clay tablets (cat. 1) are copies of texts that were also carved on stone. The Old Persian language and script were used only for the king's inscriptions, or else to identify objects or people connected with the king.

The written language of the empire's rulers that we call Old Persian was not what the kings and satraps spoke, or indeed what anyone spoke. It was an artificial idiom, drawing forms from several Iranian dialects, both contemporary and old, and using a grammar that was already archaic when the inscriptions were made. It was written with a script invented for these inscriptions and used for no other purpose. Old Persian writing and language together were not so much vehicles for communication among Persians as instruments for the great

5 The west pillar of the south portico of the Palace of Darius at Persepolis with inscriptions of Xerxes in Old Persian, Elamite and Babylonian.

king's display of his presence and power. The Persian texts present Darius and Xerxes at the centre of a larger Iranian world, and at the zenith of a longer Iranian history; accordingly, when Darius named this form of writing in his inscription at Bisitun, he did not call it *Pārsa*, 'Persian', but *Ariya*, 'Iranian'.

ELAMITE

When trilingual inscriptions are presented in vertical array, the second version, directly below the Old Persian, is in Elamite. Elamite is unrelated to Old Persian or to Akkadian. It has no certain relatives or descendants, though some scholars think it is distantly related to the Dravidian languages of South Asia. When the Achaemenid inscriptions were deciphered, it became possible to recognize older Elamite texts. Indeed, by the time of the Achaemenids, Elamite was already an ancient language, written in versions of Mesopotamian cuneiform script at least as early as 2200 BC in parts of modern Khuzestan and Fars.

The early Elamite variants of cuneiform script were similar to contemporary Mesopotamian cuneiform, but after about 600 BC the Elamite script developed separately, using distinctive sign forms, sign inventories and writing rules. By the time of the Achaemenids, Elamite cuneiform would have looked odd to a Babylonian, as difficult to make out as German *fraktur* writing is for a modern reader of printed English.

Elamite had been the primary language of successive ancient kingdoms in territories of western Iran. At their height, around 1800 BC, the Elamite kings wielded influence over political and military affairs in Mesopotamia. Rulers who struggled with Babylonian and Assyrian kings around 1400–1150 BC created the monumental buildings, brilliant works of art and royal inscriptions that came to define Elamite culture for modern archaeologists and historians. In about 750–640 BC the Elamites were implacable foes of the Assyrians, frustrating Assyrian efforts to subjugate Babylonia and the Iranian borderland, and eventually drawing frightful Assyrian reprisals that culminated in the devastation of Susa in 646 BC.

Two territories formed the heart of these Elamite kingdoms: facing Mesopotamia, the region around Susa, in modern Khuzestan; facing the interior high country of Iran, southeast of Susa, the region around Anshan, in modern Fars. When Iranian speakers spread out over western Iran, some of them came into these Elamite territories, and in Anshan they became the dominant population. Elamite Anshan thus became the kingdom of the Persians, and so when Cyrus II the Great described his royal lineage on the Cyrus Cylinder (cat. 6), he entitled himself and his forebears 'kings of Anshan'. This

was one reason for the use of Elamite as the second language of the Achaemenid inscriptions. Just as Old Persian, with its dialect forms and archaisms, expressed ties to a larger Iranian world and a deeper Iranian past, Elamite expressed a tie to the still deeper past of the territory that had become the Persian homeland.

Unlike Old Persian, Elamite was never limited to royal inscriptions and royal display. At Susa and at Anshan it had also been used to write incantations, works of scholarship and especially administrative records. The Achaemenids continued this long-established use of Elamite as a written language of administration. Two groups of Achaemenid Elamite administrative texts on clay tablets have been found at Persepolis, records of supplies and labourers in the reigns of Darius I, Xerxes and Artaxerxes I. Some of the people named in these texts have Elamite names, but most have Iranian names, from members of the royal family and provincial governors down to local supervisors and clerks. When the Iranians who operated the Achaemenid state recorded the day-to-day management of the great king's assets in the very heartland of Persia, they composed the records in the established written language of the place, Elamite. Nor was this practice confined to Persia. Isolated tablets imply that similar Elamite records were archived not only at Susa, but also at district centres in modern Afghanistan and Armenia, and so perhaps all across the Iranian interior. This was another reason for the use of Elamite in the Achaemenid inscriptions: Elamite was and remained the language of practical literacy in Iran. Indeed, most scholars believe that the first version of Darius's account of his rise to power was carved beside the relief at Bisitun before the Old Persian script was developed. It was composed, no doubt, in Darius's own language, but Darius had it written, read out to him, and first inscribed on the rock face in Elamite, because Elamite was how Iranians communicated in writing.

AKKADIAN

The third language of the trilingual inscriptions is a Babylonian dialect of Akkadian, a Semitic language related to Hebrew, Arabic and others. Akkadian texts were written in Mesopotamia as early as about 2400 BC, and continued to be written until about AD 75. Between about 1800 and 1200 BC Akkadian was the foremost written language of western Asia, used for commerce and diplomacy, and also to teach and preserve works of literature, religion and science – not only in Babylonia and Assyria, but at times also in Egypt, Syria-Palestine, Anatolia and even Elam.

By the time of the Achaemenids, however, the use of Akkadian was largely confined to Mesopotamia. It was in retreat and perhaps already in eclipse as a spoken language, displaced by Aramaic, but it was still flourishing as a written language. Babylonian scribes used an evolving contemporary dialect for letters, contracts and administrative records. Babylonian scholars used an established literary dialect for poetic, religious, philological, scientific and historical texts – the body of Mesopotamian learning accumulated over millennia – as well as for developing branches of learning such as mathematical astronomy and horoscopic astrology.

Like the use of Latin in medieval Europe, the use of Akkadian in the Achaemenid inscriptions conveyed prestige in at least two senses. As the language of learning that was ancient, manifold and still productive, Akkadian connoted high civilization. As the language of the Assyrian and Babylonian kings who had conquered western Asia, and whose lands were now subject in turn to the Achaemenids, it connoted domination over the world beyond Iran.

The Achaemenid kings could have called on writers of the best Babylonian to convey this prestige, yet the Akkadian of their inscriptions is not quite the language of Mesopotamian royal inscriptions, nor of Mesopotamian literature and scholarship, nor even of Achaemenid Babylonian law and business. Compared with these, the Akkadian of the inscriptions has many peculiarities of form, syntax, vocabulary and style. Some of these features may reflect the difficulties of transposing texts that were conceived in Persian and perhaps transmitted through Aramaic, yet even the Cyrus Cylinder (cat. 6), a monolingual Babylonian text that was composed in Babylonia, on Babylonian models, presumably by Babylonians working to Cyrus's orders, contains grammatical anomalies. Like the Old Persian, the Akkadian of the Achaemenid inscriptions was evidently meant more for display than for communication.

EGYPTIAN

A few Achaemenid inscriptions also have versions in Egyptian. Usually, the three versions in the cuneiform scripts form a tight cluster, set off from the Egyptian. For example, among the stelae found near the modern Suez Canal, with inscriptions that commemorate Darius's construction of a canal between the Mediterranean and the Red Sea, is one with the trilingual cuneiform versions, a second, identical stele with a longer version in Egyptian, written in hieroglyphs, and a third with the trilingual text on one face and the Egyptian version on the other.

Other quadrilingual inscriptions have been found on objects made in Egypt, but not displayed or deposited there. Dishes of Egyptian granite found at Persepolis have rims decorated with the king's name and title in four languages, in the ranked order Old Persian–Elamite–Akkadian–Egyptian. Granite and alabaster jars of Egyptian form, some of them found at Persepolis, Susa and perhaps in Babylonia, have the king's name and title carved on their shoulders, with the Egyptian in a cartouche below (cat. 140). Most imposing is the monumental statue of Darius that stood at the gate of the palace complex at Susa and was made in Egypt, as its inscriptions state in four languages; the three in cuneiform are carved on one side of the robe, the Egyptian in an equivalent space on the other (cat. 88).

ARAMAIC

Conspicuous for its absence from the monumental inscriptions is Aramaic, even though it was the premier language of official communication between Achaemenid provinces, and also used alongside indigenous written languages for legal and administrative recording in many parts of the empire, including Egypt, Babylonia and Persia itself.

Aramaic is a northwest Semitic language, related to Hebrew and Phoenician, spoken in Syria and northern Mesopotamia since at least the end of the second millennium BC, and written from about 950 BC. The Aramaic alphabet of twenty-two characters was commonly written on perishable materials such as leather and papyrus, but it was also used for lapidary inscriptions both on monuments and on portable objects such as seals, weights and coins (cats 132, 212, 290, 296, 417). As spoken Aramaic dialects spread across western Asia, written Aramaic became a lingua franca in the Assyrian and Babylonian empires, and under the Achaemenids its use spread to the remotest corners of the empire, from Egypt and Anatolia to Central Asia. Even in documents from sites so widely separated, the grammar is consistent enough that their language is considered a single dialect, called Imperial Aramaic.

The single extant Aramaic version of an Achaemenid royal inscription was not displayed alongside the cuneiform versions. It is a fragmentary translation of the text on the cliff at Bisitun in Media. The surviving Aramaic version – what remains of an oversized papyrus scroll – includes parts of the narrative of the wars that Darius waged against his rivals in Iran. At the end the Aramaic departs from the Bisitun text, adding a version of part of the eulogy on Darius's tomb at Naqsh-i Rustam in Persia. This Aramaic text was far removed from the monuments not only in space, but also in time and purpose. It came from the edge of the empire, the island of Elephantine in southern Egypt, where a garrison of Judean troops manned a fortress, keeping their records and correspondence in Aramaic. The manuscript was written about a hundred years after the reign of Darius I. It was not displayed, but copied out by scribes as a literary text, an advanced exercise – part of the training of clerks – not only in the scribal art, but also in Achaemenid political ideology.

INSCRIPTIONS

Although some objects with Achaemenid inscriptions were carried to distant provinces (cats 140, 290), the great majority of the multilingual inscriptions were displayed or deposited in the central territories of the empire: at the palaces and royal tombs at Pasargadae, Persepolis and Naqsh-i Rustam in Persia; at Susa in Elam; at Babylon; and on the cliffs at Bisitun and Alvand in Media. Exceptional outliers are a trilingual inscription carved by Xerxes on a cliff at the citadel at Van in eastern Anatolia, and the Suez stelae of Darius I from Egypt.

First and foremost are the texts that Darius I had carved on the relief sculpture commemorating his rise to power on the cliff face at Bisitun (figs 2 and 6). The

first in Elamite only, and later with versions in Akkadian and Old Persian. Captions were added to identify the sculptures of Darius and his defeated enemies, connecting the images to the text. An addition, in Old Persian only, describes Darius's victories in Elam and Scythia during the first two years of his reign.

The Bisitun texts were, most scholars now believe, the oldest Achaemenid trilingual inscriptions, carved on the rock between 520 and 518 BC. The first part of the narrative resembles Herodotus's description of Darius's accession, but the continuation describes events that were unknown to the Classical historians. The hopes that this raised for constructing a new version of Persian history based on the Persians' own annals were disappointed, for this elegant composition proved to be the only one of the Achaemenid multilingual inscriptions that narrated the deeds of kings. Unlike the inscriptions of the Assyrian kings, which presented their empire as the accomplishment of warriors, the Achaemenid inscriptions presented theirs as part of a timeless order of the world. Their foremost topic was the king himself, created by the great god Ahuramazda to

6 Drawing of the rock carving at Bisitun. The epigraphs are written in Old Persian (Per.), Elamite (Sus.) and Babylonian (Bab). See also fig. 2. *From King and Thompson 1907, pl. XIII.*

relief shows Darius standing in triumph before his adversaries. The main text states his royal lineage, describes the events of his accession, narrates the defeat of his opponents in Babylonia, Elam and Iran, and exhorts future observers to believe his account and protect his monument. This composition was displayed

maintain this order, and their foremost purpose was to mark the presence of the king.

Most of the other trilingual texts are building inscriptions, connected with the palace complexes or with the royal tombs. Some were displayed on panels incorporated in the exterior ornamentation of monumental buildings (cats 63–5). Others were carved on massive stone tablets (cat. 5), often in several exemplars that were laid in foundations and perhaps sometimes also displayed in the buildings. One was put on gold and silver tablets deposited under the corners of the Apadana at Persepolis (cat. 2). Short texts on column bases and stone window frames or door frames state the king's name and title, and sometimes the name of the building (cats 8, 10–11). Still shorter texts accompanying relief sculptures at some of the royal tombs identify the figures as representatives of subject nations. Most of the inscriptions are in the names of Darius I and Xerxes, and a few in the names of Artaxerxes I, Darius II and Artaxerxes III. Short inscriptions in the name of Cyrus the Great were probably added to his palaces at Pasargadae under Darius (fig. 7). Others on silver vessels in the names of Darius's ancestors, if they are authentic Achaemenid texts at all, were written in the reigns of later Achaemenid kings.

The king's name and title identified stone or silver vessels that belonged to the royal households (cats 97, 103, 140) or that were royal gifts. His name and title were also put on cylinder seals used by high-ranking officials in the administration at the imperial courts or in provincial capitals, identifying their users both as the king's possessions and as his surrogates.

Longer texts are marked off into sections by the repetition of an introductory formula, 'the King declares'. Some sections are repeated among many inscriptions with little variation, though not always in the same order. One such stock section is a doxology devoted to the great god Ahuramazda, creator of heaven and earth, creator of man and of happiness for man, who made Darius (or Xerxes, etc.) king in the world, pre-eminent among rulers. Another is a statement of the king's name, royal epithets and descent in the Achaemenid line, of Persian and Iranian stock; another, an enumeration of subject lands and peoples; and another, a call for Ahuramazda's blessings on the king's works, his land and his household.

Some inscriptions consist of nothing more than combinations of such formulae, but others arrange them around passages with unique contents. Foundation documents from the palaces of Darius at Susa, for example, describe the many subject nations that produced, transported and crafted the building materials and ornaments, making the palace complex an embodiment of the empire (cat. 1). A text of Darius I displayed at Persepolis exhorts future rulers to protect the Persian people from war, want and wickedness. Inscriptions on Darius's tomb at Naqsh-i Rustam eulogize the king as a skilled warrior, a wise and temperate ruler, and a man superior to fear and anger; this eulogy was reproduced with few variants on a stone tablet in the name of Xerxes. Another text of Xerxes describes how Darius designated him to be his successor, and how he continued the work Darius began. Another describes Xerxes' proscription of religious practices that were not devoted to the worship of Ahuramazda. An inscription of Artaxerxes I, on column bases from the great columned hall at Susa, summarizes the building's history: constructed by Darius I, destroyed by fire in the time of Artaxerxes I and reconstructed by Artaxerxes II under the protection of the gods.

In their general tenor and purpose these texts do not depart from the already ancient tradition of Near Eastern royal inscriptions in which kings commended themselves and their works to posterity, but in their particular rhetoric, style and structure the Achaemenid inscriptions are independent of older imperial models. The

7 Pillar in Palace P at Pasargadae with inscriptions of Cyrus in Old Persian, Elamite and Babylonian. These inscriptions are thought to have been added in the reign of Darius.

complex narrative structure of Darius's apologia at Bisitun suggests that it arose from an indigenous literary tradition, though one that had never been fixed in monumental writing.

Where traditions of monumental royal inscriptions were already thousands of years old, as in Babylonia and Egypt, the Achaemenid rulers contributed little in indigenous forms. The exceptional Cyrus Cylinder (cat. 6) from Babylon is written on a barrel-shaped clay object of the kind long used for building inscriptions of Babylonian kings, meant to be deposited in the foundations of their constructions. The account of Cyrus's capture and restoration of Babylon is cast entirely in Babylonian terms, with none of the formulaic passages of the trilingual inscriptions. Its reference to a century-old inscription left by Ashurbanipal of Assyria places Cyrus in a Mesopotamian version of imperial history. Later Achaemenid kings, however, rarely took such pains to express themselves in the forms and styles of their subjects.

Many of the inscriptions are multilinguals in the narrowest sense, with closely corresponding versions. In other cases, the relationships among the versions varied. Thus, in a trilingual inscription of Xerxes on the façade of one of the grand stairways at Persepolis, displayed in three panels of equal size, the Akkadian version fills out the available space with phrases that are absent from the other versions. In the Suez stelae and on the statue of Darius I found at Susa (cat. 88) the three versions in cuneiform scripts are arranged symmetrically with the Egyptian version, occupying the same amount of space, and the Egyptian fills out the space with a longer text. At times, the different languages convey purposefully different nuances. Thus, the foundation inscriptions of Darius carved on an immense stone block in the south face of the terrace at Persepolis are actually four independent texts with related contents. The two Old Persian texts focus on the Persian people and their conquests, the Elamite text on the founding of the building complex where there had been none before, and the Akkadian on the vast extent of the nations who made the buildings – in effect, the Persian texts focus on the rulers, the Elamite text on the place, and the Akkadian text on the subjects.

Where the versions of the long Bisitun inscription differ, the Elamite and Old Persian almost always agree and the Akkadian departs from them. Some of the departures are words added for a Babylonian reader, as, for instance, when the other versions speak of 'Persia, Media and the other lands' and the Akkadian has 'Persia, Media, Babylonia and the other lands'. The Aramaic version regularly agrees with the Akkadian. The Akkadian and Aramaic, then, perhaps represent a

text edited for the subject lands beyond Iran, the Elamite and Old Persian, a text meant for the Iranian territories.

But for whom were such editorial nuances intended? People admitted to the palaces could at least see some inscriptions on the sides of buildings, and at the king's table they could see some on the gold bowls and stone plates. But other inscriptions were buried in the foundations of great buildings or carved high on cliffs, too distant to read. Even so, Darius could be sure that someone would eventually scale the cliffs or dig out the foundations, and so it seems that the texts were meant for posterity: as Darius says near the end of the Bisitun text, it was addressed to future kings. At least some of them were also meant for contemporaries, as Darius says elsewhere in the Bisitun text, calling on anyone who sees the monument to believe what he sees and to make it known to the people.

Darius tells of his own measures to make the inscription known in the Old Persian and Elamite versions, saying that he had the text sent out to all the people. One result was that the Aramaic version was still being copied after a hundred years. Another was a stone stele once displayed at Babylon, with a relief that reproduced part of the sculptured scene from Bisitun and an abridged edition of the Akkadian version of the Bisitun text. Judging by the end of the Aramaic fragment, the tomb inscription of Darius was also promulgated, and perhaps other Achaemenid inscriptions were as well. The Babylon stele shows that the texts were sent to provincial capitals, and the Aramaic manuscript that they reached even remote outposts far down the chain of imperial command.

In the forms that have come down to posterity, then, the trilingual inscriptions on stone tablets, column bases, glazed bricks and rock walls were meant not to communicate the great king's words but to mark the great king's presence. Yet other vehicles communicated the contents of some inscriptions among the great king's subjects in monolingual versions. They spread the rulers' conceptions of kingship and empire, but they did not impose the rulers' language. Although the dialects of the Persians and Medes left marks in the written languages of subject nations in the form of many loanwords, Achaemenid rule never spread Iranian languages in western Asia in the way that Hellenistic rule spread Ancient Greek or Roman rule spread Latin. Then as now, language was an important way to represent cultural identity. The identity that the Achaemenid inscriptions represent is one of many kinds and many tongues.

3

THE DECIPHERMENT
OF ACHAEMENID CUNEIFORM

Irving L. Finkel

INTRODUCTION

There is an unmistakable quality of romance about the decipherment of extinct writing. Messages from antiquity, the most remote of words and ideas, can survive for millennia to preserve a wealth of information, but when they remain undeciphered they merely tantalize and madden the modern would-be reader. The decipherer's record to date, however, is more than impressive; relatively few scripts from antiquity still defy interpretation, and many today can be read with facility. The intervening struggles have been arduous. Often there is only a small band of heroic decipherers, the odds are usually strongly pitched against them, and they do not always work in harmony, but compete for fame and glory as well as scholarship.[1]

The decipherment of ancient cuneiform writing is a classic case. The word 'cuneiform', which is commonly used today, deriving from the Latin *cuneus* ('wedge'), describes the characteristic wedge-shaped strokes in clay from which the individual signs were composed. The term seems first to have been applied by Thomas Hyde, musing in Oxford in 1700, although other writers in the eighteenth and nineteenth centuries favoured 'arrow' or 'cuneatic' writing. Cuneiform script on clay dominated the ancient Middle Eastern world for three millennia before its final disappearance, ultimately supplanted by alphabets, in the second century AD. Cuneiform writing became, more or less at one blow, extinct.

There was, in fact, more than one type. The oldest is that which ultimately evolved out of an elementary picture writing, well before 3000 BC, under level-headed administrative circumstances in southern Mesopotamia, at much the same time that experimental proto-Elamite script was in use in Iran. Mesopotamian cuneiform proper came to be used to write Sumerian and then Akkadian (Babylonian and Assyrian), as well as a cluster of other ancient Middle Eastern languages, such as Hittite in Anatolia, Hurrian in Syria, and Elamite in Iran. The Akkadian language,

pedantically dressed in cuneiform script, became the lingua franca for much of that world, and cuneiform writing and learning found a home and application in far-flung courts and contexts.

Classic Mesopotamian cuneiform writing is complex and opaque, and probably deliberately so. Essentially it is a 'syllabary', in which no consonant can stand alone, although there were individual signs for the four vowels A, E, I and U. In writing, consonants had always to be preceded or followed by a vowel, resulting in a full crop of primary signs such as UB or BA. There was, too, an abundance of more complex signs, such as NAM or BULUG. The principal factors that complicated Mesopotamian syllabic cuneiform are:

1. There was always more than one cuneiform sign available to write any given syllable – in the case of *ba*, for example, there are a good dozen possibilities.
2. Any given sign had more than one value – such as the sign UB standing for 'ub' and 'ár'.

This quality of polyvalence made the script difficult of access, involving a fluctuating working repertoire of many hundreds of signs, while the complexity of the texts that resulted was compounded by a liberal sprinkling of ideograms, determinatives and phonetic complements, and the fact that no gaps were left between the words.

Furthermore, throughout its long history Mesopotamian cuneiform was used to write both Sumerian and Akkadian, languages which were linguistically wholly unrelated to one another. Connections and interdependence between the two languages within the culture meant that it was always possible for a Babylonian or Assyrian scribe to write a word or words in Sumerian, leaving it to the reader to supply the translation where needed. The phenomenon occurs spasmodically in our own writing, with such commonplaces as '$' for 'dollar', but in cuneiform it is a regular feature that can produce problems of its own.

ACHAEMENID CUNEIFORM

The 'Old Persian' cuneiform script developed by the Achaemenids was an altogether different proposition. As discussed by Matthew Stolper (pp. 18–24), the script seems to have come into being during the reign of Darius I, while its application was limited to the royal inscriptions on stone or other durable materials of the Achaemenid kings. Old Persian cuneiform died out forever after the Macedonian conquest.

What needs to be stressed is that – despite the fact that individual Old Persian signs (with the single possible exception of 'L') bear no relation to individual Mesopotamian signs – Achaemenid cuneiform constituted a direct throwoff from Elamite or Mesopotamian cuneiform. The very nature of the script derived from writing on clay: inscriptions on stone were always secondary in Mesopotamia. The Old Persian lapidary script represented a concoction of fresh 'cuneiform-style' signs, used in a new (and immeasurably simpler) fashion.[2] It would be interesting to know what experiment and suggestion might have preceded the finalization of the finished script for court use.

Achaemenid cuneiform is sometimes referred to as an alphabet, although this is technically not quite accurate. There are forty-four independent signs, which may be subdivided as follows:

1. Thirty-six phonetic characters, including the three vowel signs A, I and U. Certain characters write a consonant independent of the following vowel, such as P or S; others write consonants whose shape changes with the following vowel, such as da[(a)], t[(a-i)] or g[(u)].
2. Seven ideograms, including KING, LAND or the name of AHURAMAZDA.
3. A word divider.

In addition, there was a set of Mesopotamian-style numerals.

THE DECIPHERMENT
OF ACHAEMENID CUNEIFORM

The decipherment of Achaemenid cuneiform was a wonderful achievement, both in itself, and in its broader consequences, for the long-awaited breakthrough with Old Persian led directly to the unlocking of the parent Mesopotamian, i.e. Babylonian cuneiform, and subsequently to other scripts. In a linear sense the decipherment has made available to modern scholarship the whole panoply of ancient Near Eastern history and thought that is familiar today.

There are parallels between the decipherment of hieroglyphic and cuneiform. In both cases the spelling of proper names, or rather royal personal names, initiated the crucial breakthrough by providing the first clue as to sign and sound equivalents. In both cases the underlying language survived in developed form – Coptic for Egyptian, Avestan for Old Persian – which led in time to the mastery of grammar, syntax and vocabulary that is required for accurate translation. Then there is the tangled question of retrospective credit. That the ambitious Jean-François Champollion was the true decipherer of ancient Egyptian is commonly known, despite the highly significant early progress in penetrating hieroglyphic writing made by Thomas Young.[3] Sir Henry Creswicke Rawlinson, however, who scooped up most of the credit for deciphering cuneiform in general, is hardly a household name today, and in fact there was a procession of gifted individuals whose labours led to the decipherment of Old Persian who never achieved lasting fame at all.

Dramatis personae

In an effort to offset this injustice, the following acknowledges the individual contributors to the decipherment of Old Persian. Their specific chief contributions, arranged in chronological order, fall into three stages:

Stage 1

Old Persian is involved; the correct direction of the script is identified; three different kinds of writing are distinguished and one underlying text.

1620: Don Garcia dated the inscriptions from Takht-i Jamshid to Darius Hystaspes, and concluded that the site represented Persepolis and that the inscriptions were in Old Persian.

1621: Pietro della Valle established that inscriptions must be read from left to right.

1762: J.J. Barthélemey established that one type of Persepolis script was similar to the script on baked bricks already known from Babylon.

1777: Thomas Herbert suggested intriguingly that the script consisted of 'words or syllables'.

1778: Carsten Niebuhr provided excellent copies of many inscriptions from Persepolis, which underpinned all subsequent decipherment attempts. He observed that there were three kinds of script probably representing three languages. Of these, Niebuhr I was the simplest, composed of an 'alphabet of 42 letters' (some later abandoned), including the word-divider sign.

1798: Friederich Münter was certain that the inscriptions were Achaemenid. He proposed that Niebuhr I was alphabetic, Niebuhr II (later known to be Elamite) syllabic and Niebuhr III (later recognized as Babylonian) ideographic or hieroglyphic. He also proposed that the contents in the three languages were the same. With Old Persian (Niebuhr I) he hunted for vowels by frequency and correctly identified *a* (or *e*) and the consonant *b*; he also identified the word-divider and thought of the title 'king of kings'.

1798: Oluf Gerhard Tychsen listed twenty-four phonetic or alphabetic values, of which *a*, *u*, *d* and *s* are somehow roughly correct. He also noted repeated sequences and apparently identified the word-divider; however, he incorrectly dated inscriptions to the Parthian period.

In addition, the Orientalists A.H. Anquetil-Duperron and A.I. Sylvestre de Sacy had provided what was to be crucial input from non-cuneiform Persian sources. The former published the Zend (post-Avestan spelling) form, Goshtasp, of the dynastic name Hystaspes in 1771, while the latter, deciphering Pahlevi inscriptions from Naqsh-i Rustam in 1793, drew attention to the royal formula 'King RN [royal name], king of kings' in titulary that went back to Sasanian times.

Stage 2
Genuine primary decipherment is achieved and correct values established for a significant number of characters.

1802–3: Georg Friederich Grotefend was the most important decipherer of Old Persian cuneiform. Building on the insights of the scholars who preceded him, Grotefend arrived at the correct path, which was characterized by straightforward logic and simplicity. He concentrated on two particular passages from Persepolis that might have been specially carved for his purpose. The first was a doorway label attached to a palace sculpture of Xerxes, the second a similar label for Darius.

Text A (Xerxes), the ten-word inscription which finally proved to read:

> 'Xerxes, the great king, king of kings, son of Darius, the king, an Achaemenian.'

Text B (Darius), the fourteen-word inscription which finally proved to read:

> 'Darius, the great king, king of kings, king of countries, son of Hystaspes, an Achaemenian, who built this palace.'

Grotefend's procedure worked as follows:

Step 1: Document the overlapping sign sequences that appear in common between the two inscriptions.
Step 2: Attempt plausible meanings for the sign groups on the basis of reconstructed Old Persian names and words, and produce sign/sound equations.

Overlaps:

1. The seven-letter, A word 6 = B word 1. Since royal names were certainly involved, it seemed likely that the ruler at the beginning of A would be named as son of the ruler whose name also occurs at the beginning of B. This fitted admirably if the names were respectively Xerxes and Darius, and would mean that A referred to Xerxes, son of Darius, and B to Darius, son of Hystaspes. Grotefend guessed that each inscription began with a royal name, and reckoned on the basis of the Zend vocabulary published by Anquetil-Duperron and other sources that the reconstructed forms of the two names should be something like *Darheush* for Darius and *Khshhershe* for Xerxes. Shared signs between the names soon showed that he was on the right track, and he produced the following equations, shown here in Grotefend's original form, and the modern readings used today:

Grotefend:	d	a	r	h	e	u	sh
(Modern:	da	a	ra	ya	va	u	sha)

Grotefend:	kh	sh	h	e	r	sh	e
(Modern:	xa	sha	ya	a	ra	sha	a)

27

Similarly, Grotefend calculated that the name of Hystaspes, the father of Darius, should be something like *Gu/os(h)tasp*, and found something like it in B word 8:

𐎥 𐎥 𐎴 𐎫 𐎫 𐎹 𐎶

Grotefend:	g	o	sh	t	a	s	p
(Modern:	vi	i	sha	ta	a	sa	pa)

2. The identical seven-character sequence, A words 2 and 4 = B words 2, 4 and 6 also occurred with what had to be different grammatical case endings in A words 5 and 7, and B 5. The assumption that this sequence centred around the word 'king' made excellent sense. Thus A had to be understood as: '... the ... king, king of kings ... of the king ...' Judging by the Zend vocabulary the Old Persian word for 'king' would be something like *khscheïô*. The next step was to apply and supplement the values already established from the royal names:

𐎴 𐎴 𐎫 𐎹 𐎹 𐎥 𐎹

Grotefend:	kh	sh	e	h	i	o	h
(Modern:	xa	sha	a	ya	tha	i	ya

Grotefend's initial decipherment thus identified correctly, in addition to the already known *a* and *b*, the letters *sh*, *t*, *s*, *p*, *t*, *r*, *u*, *kh*, and the royal names and titles, and grasped the drift of the inscriptions involved. Later he identified *f* and *k*, and so, by 1802, twelve Old Persian values (more than a third of the whole system) had been identified. His later papers of the four that he produced were, however, less reliable.

1822: A.J. Saint-Martin was mostly anti-Grotefend, and erroneous, but he did identify the letter *v*, as well as *y* (properly *i*).

1823: Rasmus Rask greatly clarified consonantal use. He was the first to read the name 'Achaemenian' and identify the letters *m* and *n*. He wrote informedly about the language of the Old Persian texts.

1833–5: Eugene Burnouf also brought much-needed linguistic knowledge to the decipherment. He identified the names of certain Persian satrapies in a different Persepolis inscription earlier misunderstood by Grotefend, adding the correct identification of the letters *k* and *z*.

1836: Christian Lassen revised Grotefend's identifications on the basis of grammatical investigation of the underlying Persian words, which allowed the understanding of the peculiarities of the vowel usage exhibited by the signs, a point not truly advanced until Hincks in 1846.

This programme of research and painstaking letter identification took the decipherment virtually as far as was possible on the basis of the available material. Decipherers of Old Persian were still restricted to the short, usually trilingual inscriptions from Persepolis, supplemented by a few similar inscriptions from Mount Alvand (Ganj Nameh) and other places. Full decipherment was only to be accomplished with the help of more extensive textual material.

Stage 3

True decipherment was achieved, and the nature of the script clearly understood.

1835–46: Henry Creswicke Rawlinson, stationed in Persia in 1835, commenced the great work of copying the huge inscription at Bisitun that had been bequeathed to posterity by the stonemasons of Darius I. The romance of decipherment has no greater relevance than in Rawlinson's own account of this achievement,[5] which involved courage, fortitude, determination and very considerable endurance, given the inaccessible mountainous location of the precious testimony. He was undoubtedly ambitious, and while claiming to have matched Grotefend's basic identifications in his own right without sight of his publications he was wont to play down the insights and contributions made by Edward Hincks in the race to conquer the cuneiform conundra. Labouring over many years he succeeded in publishing Darius's text of 414 lines, which he was able to achieve through deep understanding of Persian and Sanskrit, bolstered by a sound knowledge of the relevant Classical sources. Later he made copies of the even less accessible Babylonian and Elamite versions of the Old Persian text at Bisitun, but claims that he played a lead role in the decipherment of either of these two languages are now regarded as unfounded.

1846–66: Edward Hincks, a busy Irish clergyman, made major contributions to the decipherment of all three of the languages at Bisitun in a series of monographs, and of all the decipherers is probably the one who has been least well served by history. He turned initially to cuneiform in the hope that it would facilitate his enquiries into Egyptian hieroglyphic, in which field he was likewise an important contributor. He was the first to establish for good the semi-syllabic (rather than truly consonantal) nature of the Old Persian signs which Rawlinson had long considered to be truly alphabetic, and it is now clear that much of Hincks's Old Persian work was made available without his knowledge to Rawlinson, who profited from it.[6]

CUNEIFORM CONSEQUENCES

In conclusion, Pallis's view of the achievement can be quoted:

> The foundations for a possible decipherment of the texts were thus laid by the discovery of the direction of the script, the three different kinds of writing, one of which was alphabetical and in the Old Persian language, while all three kinds of writing gave the same text. But from this to the final interpretation and reading of the Old Persian inscriptions a

period extending from 1798 to 1846 was to elapse, and it may be truly said that for the correct reading of each of the 33 letters the intense study of more than one investigator was often required.[7]

But for the existence of such inscriptions as the Achaemenid trilinguals from Persepolis – in which Babylonian and Elamite translations were appended to an original in Old Persian – Babylonian cuneiform, like Elamite, would probably have forever defied decipherment. The process by which these entirely different cuneiform languages were subsequently unlocked, in which Rawlinson and Hincks played crucial roles, is a triumph in its own right, since the range of difficulties that remained to be encountered were for long formidable.

1 For a broad view of the history of decipherment see Pope 1975, as well as more recently Daniels and Bright 1996: 139–88; Parkinson 1999.

2 Something similar had happened before at Ugarit, where thirty independent cuneiform signs had been developed to write the first attested consonantal alphabet; see, for example, Pardee 2004: 288–93.

3 See Parkinson 1999 for a detailed consideration of the decipherment of Egyptian hieroglyphs, and the respective contributions of Young and Champollion.

4 The information summarized here draws principally on Pallis 1954: 94–123, to which reference can be made for further details and full bibliographical sources. Portraits of many of the decipherers are to be found in Budge 1925.

5 An accessible account of Rawlinson's Bisitun adventures and deciphering pursuits is given in Adkins 2003.

6 See Larsen 1994: 178–88; Daniels 1996: 146–7.

7 Pallis 1954: 95–6, an opinion more in key with reality than the following more recent languid appraisal: 'Compared to that of Egyptian hieroglyphics, the story of the decipherment of cuneiform writing ... was a rather trivial affair. Recognised as phonetic or alphabetic signs from almost to the beginning, no break, no rupture, no *coupure epistémologique* seems to have been needed for the task to be accomplished' (Harbsmeier 1992: 56).

4

THE ARCHAEOLOGY
OF THE ACHAEMENID PERIOD

John Curtis

INTRODUCTION

As we have seen, the Achaemenid Empire covered a vast area, from Pakistan in the east to Egypt in the west and from the Aral Sea in the north to the Indian Ocean in the south. As it was clearly impossible to administer this huge tract of land directly from the Achaemenid heartland in Iran, the empire was divided into provinces and each put under the control of a local governor or satrap. In this way, there was a certain degree of standardization, at least from a fiscal point of view. But did this uniformity extend to arts and crafts? In other words, can any homogeneity be detected in the material culture record? On one level, there are certain types of building and classes of artefact that can be found throughout the empire, often decorated in a distinctive way. This sort of decoration is sometimes labelled 'court style', the presumption being that it constitutes an official art style. In terms of architecture we might refer to the distinctive columned buildings known as *apadanas*, which although few and far between are found in various parts of the empire. Also, the use of monumental masonry is sometimes regarded as being indicative of the Persian period, for example in Lebanon. In terms of iconography, items decorated with images of people in 'Median' or 'Persian' dress can be readily recognized as belonging to the Achaemenid period. There are some classes of artefact that are instantly identifiable, such as the *akinakes* (short sword) with its characteristic scabbard. Jewellery with polychrome inlay is one of the hallmarks of this period, as are *phialai* (carinated bowls) often in gold or silver. Then we can see from the presents brought by the various delegations on the reliefs at Persepolis that there were some items that were concurrently in use in various parts of the empire, such as animal-headed bracelets. Nearly all these things, however, are luxury items, or artefacts that would be associated with the ruling classes. Amongst artefacts of a humbler nature, it is much more difficult to find type fossils, although there are some: for example, faience pendants of Egyptian type are widely distributed. But these are exceptional – most everyday artefacts do not belong to types that are distributed throughout the length and breadth of the empire. Even pottery of Achaemenid date is notoriously difficult to recognize. With regard, then, to the uniformity of material culture in the Achaemenid Empire the picture is mixed, both with types of object and with different areas. In some central parts of the empire there is strong Achaemenid influence, but in other areas there seems to be a continuation of local traditions. It is this diversity that we shall consider in this review of the archaeology of the Achaemenid Empire.

8 Plan of Pasargadae showing Palaces P and S, the two pavilions and the formal gardens intersected by stone water channels.

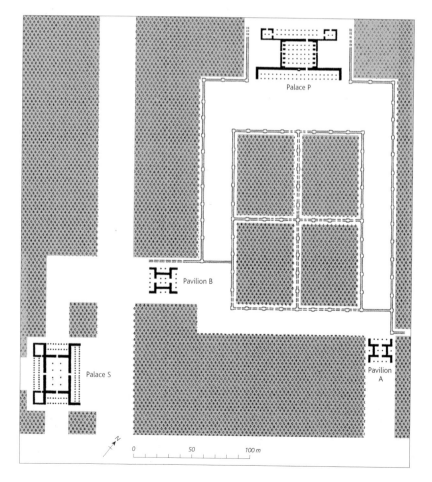

Palace P

Pavilion B

Palace S

Pavilion A

N

0   50   100 m

9 The ruins of Palace S at Pasargadae.

10 Stone relief in Gate R at Pasargadae showing a winged genie wearing an Egyptian-style crown. There were once inscriptions above the figure in Old Persian, Elamite and Babylonian recording 'I, Cyrus, the king, an Achaemenian'.

11 Palace P at Pasargadae. The stonemasons have combined black and white stone to create a pleasing bichrome effect.

PERSIA, ELAM AND MEDIA
PERSIA

Any review of the archaeology of the Achaemenid Empire should logically start in the Persian heartland, in Fars. There are a number of monumental sites here, of which the earliest is the capital city founded by Cyrus at Pasargadae,[1] some 40 km northeast of Persepolis. Here there are various buildings strung out across the Dasht-i Morghab (Plain of the Water Bird). The surviving buildings are of stone as opposed to the traditional materials of mudbrick and wood, and to help in making the transition Cyrus may have brought in stonemasons from the newly conquered territories of Ionia and Lydia. As well as Asia Minor, the building programme at Pasargadae shows influence from other regions, such as Assyria and Egypt, illustrating the eclectic nature of Achaemenid art and architecture.

Access to the central part of the site in ancient times would have been through a gate (Gate R) which was

12 A stone-lined water channel at Pasargadae. Such channels divided the royal gardens into four parts (*chahar bagh*), a plan which later became characteristic of Persian gardens.

13 The ruins of Persepolis as seen from the mountain (Kuh-i Rahmat, Mountain of Mercy) to the east of the terrace. The Hall of 100 Columns is in the centre of the picture with the Apadana behind it.

originally flanked by winged bulls of Assyrian type. They no longer survive, but a stone relief on one of the door-jambs that can still be seen shows a four-winged genie wearing an Egyptian crown (fig. 10). A trilingual inscription at the top of this relief (now missing) recorded in Old Persian, Elamite and Babylonian: 'I, Cyrus, the king, an Achaemenian'. Like other inscriptions at Pasargadae it was probably added in the reign of Darius after the Old Persian script had been introduced. There are two palaces at Pasargadae set in the midst of an extensive garden (figs 8–9, 11), as well as two small pavilions. This royal park was irrigated by a system of stone-lined water channels that can still be seen (fig. 12). Not only is this the first example of the gardens for which Persia later became famous, but it may be a fore-runner of the formal Persian garden that is divided into four parts (*chahar bagh*). The two palaces (S and P) both have rectangular columned halls, in one case with four surrounding porticoes and in the other with two. Stone *antae* (corner pillars), of which only a few survive, bear trilingual inscriptions giving the name of Cyrus.

Other major buildings at Pasargadae include the Zendan-i Suleiman (prison of Solomon), an enigmatic stone tower with blind windows, and the Tall-i Takht, a

14 Plan of the principal buildings on the terrace at Persepolis.

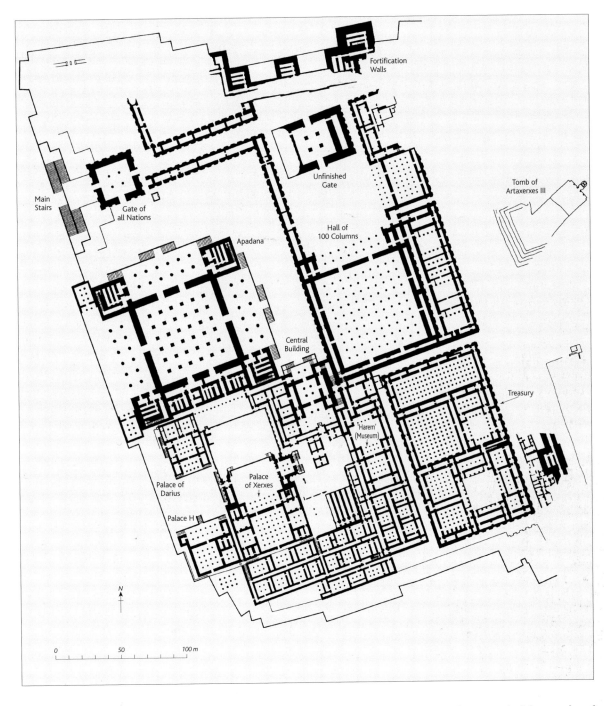

gigantic stone platform probably for a palace that was never built. The most impressive monument on the site, however, is undoubtedly the Tomb of Cyrus (fig. 1). This tomb has a gabled roof and stands on a stepped platform, all built from massive blocks of stone.

Amongst the small finds from Pasargadae, the most remarkable was a hoard of jewellery hidden in a pottery jar and buried under one of the pavilions. In the hoard were more than 1,000 items, including two gold ibex-headed bracelets, three pairs of elaborate gold earrings, a silver spoon, necklaces and a gold button with cloisonné decoration. These pieces of jewellery date from the fifth

and fourth centuries BC, and are wonderful examples of the art of the Achaemenid jeweller. Unfortunately, some of the other small finds from Pasargadae are not so securely dated to the Achaemenid period, particularly the pottery, much of which seems to date from the early Hellenistic period. This situation has come about because Pasargadae was continuously occupied until the end of the Achaemenid period and beyond, and there was never a single moment of destruction that would have trapped objects and pottery in a layer of ash and debris.

To the southwest of Pasargadae is Persepolis, one of the most spectacular sites in the ancient world, and arguably

15 Part of the monumental double staircase (southern flight) leading up to the terrace at Persepolis.

16 The 'Gate of All Nations' at Persepolis with pairs of winged human-headed bulls on either side and four columns between. Many travellers have left graffiti on the stonework here, including Henry Morton Stanley of the *New York Herald* in 1870.

17 The Hall of 100 Columns at Persepolis. The doorways are decorated with stone reliefs and the columns in the main hall would have had double-bull capitals.

the most important Achaemenid centre (fig. 13). It was founded by Darius probably in about 515 BC. The site is in the Marvdasht plain, 47 km northeast of Shiraz. The buildings are arranged on a raised terrace measuring about 455 x 300 m (fig. 14). This is about the same length as the acropolis at Athens, but four to five times as wide. On the east side the terrace is bounded by the Kuh-i Rahmat (Mountain of Mercy). Building probably continued for much of the Achaemenid period, but the most active builders seem to have been Darius, Xerxes, Artaxerxes I and Artaxerxes III. In 330 BC, in an act of drunken vandalism, Alexander set fire to Persepolis and destroyed most of the buildings. Some parts of the city stood proud above the debris, but much of it was hidden until revealed by excavations in the twentieth century.[2]

Access to the Persepolis terrace was by a double staircase (fig. 15), after which the visitor would have passed through the Gate of All Nations (fig. 16), consisting of two pairs of colossal human-headed winged bulls facing in opposite directions with four columns between them. After passing by the 'Fortification Walls' the Unfinished Gate is reached. This was again intended to be flanked by bulls. Many of the buildings on the Persepolis terrace have columned halls and columned porticoes (the so-called *apadana* plan).[3] These include the Hall of 100 Columns (fig. 17), the 'Harem', the Central Building, the Palace of Xerxes, Palace H, the Palace of Darius (fig. 18) and the Apadana (audience hall; fig. 19). Often the doorjambs bear carved decoration, as in the Hall of 100 Columns, the Central Building, the Palaces of Xerxes and Darius, and the 'Harem'. This decoration takes the form of the king or 'Persian hero figure' fighting a bull, a lion, or a griffin; the king with the crown price or attendants; attendants on their own; or subject peoples supporting the enthroned king under a canopy (fig. 27). Some of the palaces are raised on platforms and have staircases with carved decoration on the walls and parapets. Such decoration can be found on the Palaces of Darius and Xerxes, the Central Building, Palace H and the Apadana. The motifs include figures climbing staircases and bearing food, drink and live animals; Persian guards; Persian and Median nobles; sphinxes; and lions attacking bulls. The finest and most spectacular friezes, however, are on the north and east façades of the Apadana. The two sides are mirror images of each other, and show files of Persian and Median nobles, and twenty-three delegations from all around the empire bringing presents to the great king (fig. 21). Originally there were panels showing the king sitting on a throne in the centre of each façade, but for an unknown reason these were removed in antiquity and replaced by panels showing a lion attacking a bull.

Many of the objects found in the destruction level at

18 The south side of the Palace of Darius at Persepolis showing files of guards and the lion and bull combat scene.

19 The north side of the Apadana at Persepolis, decorated with processions of Persian and Median nobles and delegations bringing presents to the king. The east side of the Apadana (now protected by a roof, seen in the background) is a mirror image of the north side.

Persepolis come from the Treasury, which was a repository of vast wealth.

On the slopes of Kuh-i Rahmat to the east of the terrace are three tombs cut into vertical rock faces. They are thought to belong to Artaxerxes II, Artaxerxes III and Darius III. The tomb façades are cross-shaped with a blank panel at the bottom and a building façade in the centre with columns surmounted by double bull protomes. These support a roof represented by beams and a row of denticulation. An opening in the middle of the central section gives access to the tomb. In the top panel, two rows of tributaries support a platform or throne on which the king stands in front of a fire altar with Ahuramazda above. There are four more tombs of this kind that are rather better known than those at Persepolis at nearby Naqsh-i Rustam (fig. 22). These belong to Darius I, Xerxes, Artaxerxes I and probably Darius II. The tomb of Darius I is the only one that bears an inscription. Also at Naqsh-i Rustam is a curious structure known as the Kaba-i Zardusht. This is a stone tower with blind windows and small recessed niches, comparable to the Zendan-i Suleiman at Pasargadae. Its purpose is obscure.

was the great city of Susa, which had been continuously occupied from prehistoric times and already by the Achaemenid period would have been a series of gigantic mounds alongside the River Shaur. Susa was well known to the Greek authors and was at the end of the royal road from Sardis (see map, p. 11 top). It is often considered to have been an important administrative capital, but in fact only a handful of cuneiform tablets have ever been found there. On the other hand, Susa features in the Treasury Tablets and the Fortification Tablets from Persepolis. Excavations at Susa were first undertaken by the British archaeologist W.K. Loftus in 1850–52,[7] and

20 Stone relief on the west jamb of the southern doorway of the main hall of the Central Building at Persepolis showing the king with attendants.

21 Stone relief showing King Xerxes and the crown prince with attendants. This relief was originally the centrepiece of the decoration on the north side of the Apadana, but was removed in antiquity and put into store in the Treasury. It is now in the National Museum in Tehran.

As recently as 1985, an archaeologist was able to write that there is 'little enough [archaeological data from sites within Iran] for the Achaemenid period ... outside the Imperial centres of Pasargadae, Persepolis and Susa'.[4] By and large this is still the case, although it is now recognized that there are many Achaemenid-period buildings in the Marvdasht plain, particularly in the vicinity of Persepolis, and considerable advances have been made in identifying Achaemenid pottery.[5] There are also newly discovered columned buildings at Farmeshgan, Fahlian and Borazjan, all in Fars province.[6]

ELAM

The major Achaemenid centre in Elam (southwest Iran)

then by French archaeologists from 1884 onwards.[8]

As far as is known, neither Cyrus nor Cambyses left their mark on Susa, but Darius embarked on an ambitious building programme there (fig. 23). This started in around 519 BC, probably before the building work at Persepolis. After major landscaping works had been undertaken, Darius chose the north part of the site for the construction of his palace, which spread over about 5 ha (fig. 24). In the famous Foundation Charter he describes how he brought materials and workmen from all parts of the Persian Empire to facilitate the building works. The palace really consists of two parts: an *apadana* in the Persian style on the north side and a vast mudbrick building arranged around four courtyards in the

23 Plan of Susa.

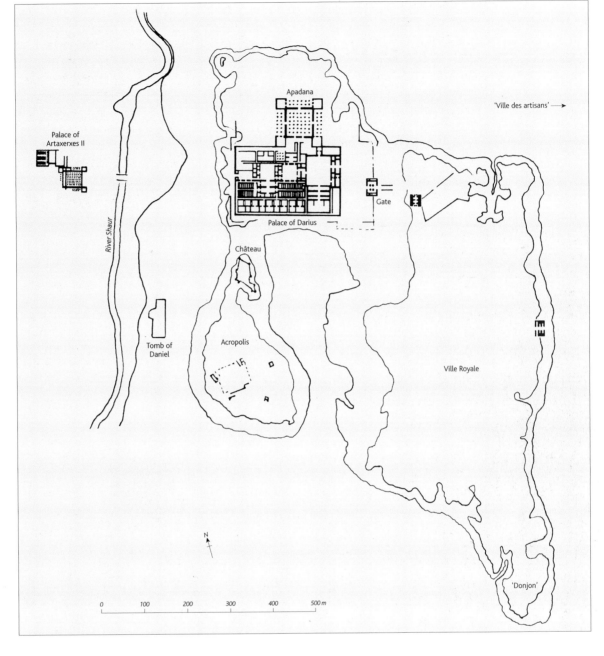

22 The Tomb of Xerxes at Naqsh-i Rustam. These tombs have façades decorated like an Achaemenid-period building, with columns and double-bull capitals. The king is shown at the top in an attitude of prayer, standing on a gigantic platform supported by figures of people from around the empire. See also figs 4 and 70.

Mesopotamian style on the south side. The *apadana* had a square central hall with thirty-six columns on square bases, surrounded on three sides by columned porticoes. Here there were bell-shaped column bases. All of the columns were surmounted by double-bull capitals (fig. 25). Four of the square column bases had trilingual cuneiform inscriptions recording that the palace (or perhaps just this part of it) was rebuilt by Artaxerxes II following a fire in the reign of his grandfather Artaxerxes I. The courtyards in the south part of the palace were decorated with friezes of glazed bricks.

Access to the palace was through a monumental gate, where the famous statue of Darius (cat. 88) was found. This was made in Egypt and brought to Susa in antiquity.

Elsewhere on the site is the so-called 'donjon' palace where Achaemenid architectural elements have been found, comprising stone reliefs showing figures at half life-size (cats 50, 199) – some of them climbing stairs – bell-shaped column bases and two square plinths. However, there is a suggestion that all these pieces had been reused in a later building. Also in this area was a well, in which was found a collection of Achaemenid-period ivories. On the third of the main mounds – the acropolis – two bronze bathtub coffins were found in a vaulted tomb. One coffin was empty, but the other contained a skeleton accompanied by a rich collection of jewellery, a silver bowl and two alabastrons (cats 278–9). In the north part of the same acropolis mound Loftus found many fragments

24 View of Susa showing in the foreground column bases from the Palace of Darius and in the background the castle built by French excavators in the nineteenth century.

25 A double-bull column capital from the Palace of Darius at Susa.

(enough to fill a wheelbarrow) of alabaster vases, some inscribed with the name of Xerxes in Old Persian, Elamite, Babylonian and Egyptian hieroglyphs (cats 141–5).

There are also Achaemenid remains on the large mound known as the 'Ville des artisans' to the east of the city centre, where houses belonging to the so-called 'village perse achéménide' were excavated by R. Ghirshman in the early 1950s.

On the other side of the River Shaur, to the west of the Palace of Darius, there is a palace of Artaxerxes II. Lastly, we should mention some building remains about 4 km north of the Palace of Darius, where the French excavator Dieulafoy believed that he had found an *ayadana* (house of gods) or a fire temple of the Achaemenid period. It seems likely, however, that the Achaemenid bell-shaped column bases found here had been reused in a later building.

This brief survey clearly shows that the extent of Achaemenid occupation at Susa was limited compared with Persepolis. This is borne out by the distribution of Achaemenid-period pottery on the site, which apparently has been found in only one area of the 'Ville Royale' and is very rare elsewhere.[9] This suggests that Susa had a small population in the Achaemenid period, at least when the king and his court were not there. This also seems to be the case for the Susiana plain, where settlements of this date are said to be infrequent.

MEDIA

The greatest Achaemenid monument in Media is undoubtedly the rock carving of Darius at Bisitun, 149 km west of Hamadan.[10] This is high on a cliff overlooking the Great Khorasan Road, the ancient highway that links Baghdad with Kermanshah, Hamadan and Tehran. The mountain itself was regarded as sacred (Diodorus II.2), and at its foot there are a number of springs feeding a pool and a small stream. The sculpture was carved in 520–519 BC to commemorate the suppression of a rebellion by Darius at the start of his reign. It shows Darius with his left foot on the prostrate body of the rebel leader Gaumata (the false Smerdis). In front of him are nine rebels roped together at the neck who are identified in epithets written in cuneiform as coming from various parts of the empire. Last in line is a Scythian with a pointed hat. Above the rebels is the godlike figure in a winged disc, either Ahuramazda or the figure of the dead king or the divine glory (*khvarnah* or *farr*). Accompanying the rock carving are long inscriptions all written in cuneiform but in three different languages: Old Persian, Elamite and Babylonian. All three versions contain more or less the same text describing how Gaumata seized the throne pretending to be Bardiya (Smerdis), the murdered brother of Cambyses. He was defeated and killed by Darius, who went on to put down various rebellions in different parts of the empire. The inscriptions end with thanks to Ahuramazda. The trilingual inscriptions at Bisitun were instrumental in the decipherment of cuneiform in the mid-nineteenth century.

There is another rock carving of Darius at Ganj Nameh, 12 km southwest of Hamadan. Here, on the slopes of Mount Alvand at the head of a picturesque valley, Darius cut on the rock face a rectangular panel

lenistic period at the earliest and no Achaemenid-period building has yet been found. However, a number of nineteenth-century travellers reported seeing column bases (some of Achaemenid type) and column drums at various locations within Hamadan. Also, there are six column bases or fragments with inscriptions of Artaxerxes II (404–359 BC) that apparently come from Hamadan, but of these only one was recovered during an official excavation, and even that was from a secondary context.[11] Nevertheless, there is clearly enough evidence to show that Artaxerxes II built or perhaps even restored a palace or palaces at Hamadan, but we

26 Excavations in progress at Hamadan in October 1995. The excavations were directed by M.R. Sarraf on behalf of the Iranian Cultural Heritage Organisation. The remains of Median and Achaemenid Hamadan have yet to be found.

with inscriptions in three languages (Old Persian, Elamite and Babylonian) praising Ahuramazda and glorifying himself. Nearby is a similar panel dating from the time of Xerxes and glorifying that king.

At Hamadan itself traces of the Achaemenid kings are more elusive (fig. 26). According to the Greek authors the Achaemenid kings had a summer capital at Hamadan (Ecbatana), and there was a treasury there. Herodotus marvels at the size and wealth of the city. However, this has not yet been borne out by archaeology. Many Achaemenid-style objects (including cats 97, 430) are said to come from Hamadan, but generally the information about provenance cannot be corroborated. Iranian excavations on the Ecbatana mound that have been in progress since 1983 have uncovered a huge mudbrick building, but it seems to date from the Hel-

do not know their exact location. From such a building might have come the fragment of a bull protome capital found during roadworks in 1962.

Elsewhere in Media, the small site of Tepe Nush-i Jan is primarily a religious centre that was abandoned at the end of the Median period, though some impoverished secondary occupation may have continued into Achaemenid times.

BABYLONIA

According to Herodotus (*History* III.92), in the Persian period Babylon was actually the most heavily taxed province, presumably reflecting the agricultural wealth of the area and its potential to produce large amounts of grain. There was inevitably some decline from the glorious days of the Babylonian Empire, and there is evidence of steep inflation during this time, but tablet archives from places such as Sippar, Nippur and Babylon show that commercial life continued to flourish, and some dynastic families such as the Murashu family in Nippur and the Egibi family in Babylon prospered. There were also developments in scientific subjects such as astronomy.[12]

A new palace was built at Babylon, probably by Artax-

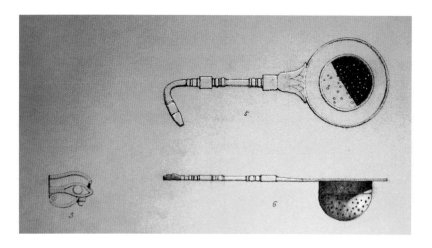

27 Achaemenid-period objects found at Nimrud by W.K. Loftus in 1854–5. See cat. 133. *Drawings by William Boutcher (British Museum Original Drawings I, pl. XXXI).*

erxes II (previously attributed to Darius I).[13] It is Persian in style with a central columned hall, and a pillared portico flanked by square towers. The stone column bases are either bell-shaped or consist of a simple torus. The external walls were decorated with panels of glazed bricks showing Persian guardsmen. Near to this palace, but not in it, was found a 'badly mutilated' column capital in the form of two back-to-back bull protomes. Also testifying to the interest that the Persian kings took in Babylon are two basalt fragments inscribed with the Babylonian version of the Bisitun inscription, perhaps originally accompanied by a relief of Darius.[14] A silversmith's hoard found at Babylon, containing scrap silver, coins, a silver amphora handle in the form of a winged bull (cat. 129) and fragments of an Achaemenid-style silver bowl, testify to the survival of arts and crafts.[15] Elsewhere in Babylonia evidence for monumental Persian-style buildings comes from Abu Chulfat, Hatab, about 40 km southeast of Nippur, where bell-shaped column bases have been found.[16]

At other sites in Babylonia buildings continued to be erected in the traditional Mesopotamian style and there are many graves. Apart from Babylon itself, sites with Achaemenid occupation include Kish, Nippur, Ur, Uruk, Isin, Tell ed-Der and Borsippa.[17] The graves, usually beneath the floors of houses, often include artefacts that are diagnostic of this period, such as earrings with clusters of granules, terracotta horse and rider figurines, and Egyptian-style 'eye-of-Horus' amulets. Many of the burials were in bathtub-shaped terracotta coffins. One such coffin from Ur contained a collection of almost 200 clay seal-

ings, including examples in both Persian and Greek style.[18] The large number of sealings here recalls the statement of Herodotus that every Babylonian had his own seal (*History* I.95). Characteristic of the Achaemenid period in southern Mesopotamia are bowls of very thin, high-quality pottery known as 'eggshell ware'.[19]

ASSYRIA

In contrast to Babylonia, Assyria was a backwater during the Achaemenid period, with most of the former Assyrian cities abandoned or only sparsely occupied.[20] Xenophon, who passed through Assyria with 10,000 Greek mercenaries in 401 BC, describes Nineveh (Mespila) as abandoned and lying in ruins and Nimrud (Larissa) as a deserted city with the exception of some local people who had taken refuge in the ziggurat (*Anabasis* III.4.7–11). Admittedly there are difficulties with identifying Achaemenid pottery in Assyria, but the extent of Achaemenid-period occupation, at least on the major sites, does seem to have been quite limited. At the same time agriculture may have prospered.

At Nineveh there is practically no evidence for Achaemenid occupation. At Nimrud traces of Achaemenid occupation have been found in the Burnt Palace and Nabu Temple complex, the Southwest Palace, the Town Wall houses and possibly the Central Palace, but it does not amount to much (fig. 27). The material includes some pottery vessels, some 'eye-of-Horus' amulets, some bronze kohl sticks and a bronze strainer with a calf's head at the end of the handle (cat. 133). The paraphernalia from a glassmakers' workshop is possibly of this date. At Khorsabad a silver disc-shaped earring and two silver bracelets with animal-headed terminals are all that can be confidently ascribed to the Achaemenid period, while at Assur there are only a few graves of this date. Both Achaemenid and Classical sources suggest that Erbil may have been an important centre at this time, but unfortunately the lack of excavation there means that this is not confirmed by archaeology.

Turning to the smaller sites in Assyria, there was a small fortified palace in the Achaemenid period at Tell ed-Daim to the northeast of Kirkuk. From this palace come bronze wall-plaques, horse harness, kohl tubes, pottery vessels and pottery 'scoops' that can be compared with two silver examples in the British Museum (cats 136–7). It remains to mention a few sites in the Eski Mosul Dam Salvage Project where Achaemenid remains have been found, such as at Kharabeh Shattani (some pottery forms) and Tell Jigan (a grave).

In many respects the identification of Achaemenid sites in the Jazira – that part of north Syria between the Tigris and Euphrates rivers – is as problematic as it is in

28 The Phoenician temple enclosure at Amrit in Syria. The shrine in the centre is known as al-Ma'bid ('the temple').

Assyria, with which area it seems to have been lumped together for administrative reasons in the Achaemenid period. Slowly, however, progress is being made, and a number of small sites are recognized as having been occupied in the Persian period.[21]

BEYOND THE RIVER

The areas to the west of the River Euphrates (western Syria, Lebanon, Israel, Jordan and Cyprus) were included in Herodotus's fifth satrapy (*History* III.91), which was known in biblical sources (for example, Ezra 5: 21) as 'Beyond the River'.

SYRIA

In Syria there are some important cemeteries of the Persian period, particularly at Deve Hüyük to the west of Carchemish on the River Euphrates, and at Neirab, 10 km southeast of Aleppo.[22] The graves at Deve Hüyük in

29 Double-bull capital found on the College site at Sidon in Lebanon around 1880, suggesting that there was once a Persian-style *apadana* in Sidon.

particular contained a wide range of weapons, horse harness, jewellery, toilet equipment, pottery vessels, bronze bowls and figurines. Many of these objects are of characteristic Persian-period type, and together they give a very good impression of the material culture of this period. Monumental buildings of this period, however, are scarce. An exception is the religious compound dedicated to the Phoenician gods Melqart and Eshmun at the coastal site of Amrit (Marathos), 8 km south of Tartus. The architectural details of the central shrine show some Egyptian influence (fig. 28). In addition to this temple (*al-ma'bid*), there are two funerary towers (*meghazil*), one of which has lions carved in Persian style around the base. The presence of monumental buildings on the Syrian coast rather than inland is probably a reflection of Achaemenid priorities, as the Persian rulers were anxious to have good relations with the coastal cities of Phoenicia, on whose navies they were dependent for the invasion of Egypt and the war against Greece.

LEBANON

In Lebanon the most important centre during the Achaemenid period was probably the harbour city of Sidon, which had its own mint and was the seat of a dynasty of local kings. One of these, Tennes, led a revolt against Artaxerxes III in 351 BC that was put down with great severity. Within the modern city of Sidon there are now few traces of the Achaemenid period, but in the nineteenth century a double-bull capital in white stone was found during building work (fig. 29). It is apparently

30 The temple of Eshmun near Sidon in Lebanon. The use of massive stone blocks is characteristic of the Persian period in this region.

31 Phoenician stone sarcophagus from Sidon, fifth to fourth centuries BC. *British Museum ANE 125097, acquired in 1862.*

testimony to the existence of an *apadana*-style building in Sidon. A short distance to the north of the modern city is the sanctuary dedicated to Eshmun, the Phoenician god of healing.[23] The temple here was built on a platform of massive stone blocks considered in this region to be typical of the Persian period (fig. 30). It was constructed in the late sixth century BC by the king Eshmunazar II, who was buried in a black stone sarcophagus (now in the Louvre) in the cemetery at Magharat Abloun to the southeast of Sidon. Here were found a number of sarcophagi with lids, which have at one end a human face in relief and at the other end a raised ledge (fig. 38). Such coffins, including that of Eshmunazar, are inspired by Egyptian anthropoid sarcophagi, but become typical for the fifth to fourth centuries BC at Sidon.[24] They are generally made from white stone.

Of the other burial grounds in the vicinity of Sidon, the most notable is at Helaliyeh in the northeastern suburbs, which was discovered in 1887 and excavated by Hamdy Bey, the Director of the Imperial Museum in Constantinople. As well as anthropoid sarcophagi of the Persian

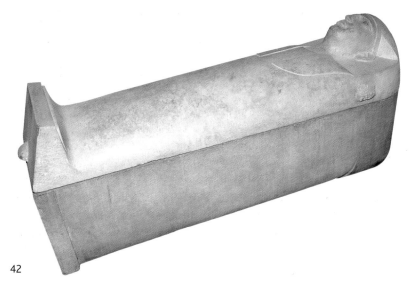

period this necropolis contained elaborately decorated rectangular stone coffins of Hellenistic date, including the famous Alexander sarcophagus that is now in the Archaeological Museum in Istanbul. The sarcophagus is that of an unknown local ruler, but is named after Alexander because he figures prominently in the carved decoration, which shows scenes of hunting and warfare.

Apart from Eshmun, there is another monumental construction of this period at Byblos. This is a fortified structure built from stone blocks known as the 'Persian castle'. Elsewhere in Lebanon the Persian period is best represented in the rich cemetery at Kamid el-Loz, where many graves of Achaemenid date have been excavated.

Evidence for the Persian period, particularly in the form of the distinctive two-handled jars or amphorae with carinated shoulders, was also found in the rescue excavations at Beirut[25] and at other sites in the Lebanon such as Sarepta.[26]

ISRAEL AND JORDAN

In Israel and Transjordan the Persian period used to be regarded as a dark age when there was little evidence of occupation, but an increasing number of sites, particularly in Israel, are now recognized as having been occupied during that time.[27] The process of identification has been helped by the association of local material with dated coins, seals, imported Attic pottery, Egyptian imports and occasional Aramaic inscriptions. It is now clear that many settlements were continuously occupied from Iron Age II to the Persian period and sometimes even into Hellenistic times. Local pottery types continue from Iron Age II, but amongst the forms that are characteristic of the Persian period are amphorae with carinated shoulders, sausage jars and triangular jar rims. Objects that are distinctive of this period include cuboid stone incense-burners, terracotta horse and rider figurines, and carinated bowls both in metal and pottery. Artefacts in distinctive 'Persian' style that might be found throughout the empire are rare but they are occasionally found.[28] Even though there are hints of some major projects, such as the rebuilding of the temple in Jerusalem that is supposed to have happened following the return of the Jews from exile in Babylon (Ezra I: 1–4), there is little evidence of monumental building activity. In fact, much of the evidence for the Persian period comes from cemeteries such as at Tell Fara and 'Atlit in Israel, and Tell es-Saidiyeh in Jordan. One particularly rich tomb at Tell Fara contained a bed and a stool partly of bronze and some silver plate.[29]

CYPRUS

Cyprus was occupied by the Persians in about 525 BC and remained under Persian control, albeit somewhat loosely, until the invasion of Alexander in 333 BC. Local kingdoms continued to exist, and there is evidence of Greek, Phoenician and Persian influence.[30] The extent of Persian influence has often been downplayed, but it is particularly marked in some of the statuary where the Persian-style beards are unmistakable.

THE ARABIAN PENINSULA

We know from Herodotus (*History* III.9) that the Arabians presented to the Persian king 1,000 talents (nearly 25 tons) of frankincense every year, implying that frankincense was being collected on a large scale in Yemen at this time. However, we know nothing about how the industry was organized or the routes by which the frankincense was exported, and there is very little evidence for Achaemenid presence in the Arabian peninsula at this time apart from some sporadic finds.[31]

The Achaemenid period in Bahrain is represented by, amongst other things, a silversmith's hoard of scrap metal, and a coffin burial with a bronze situla, bowl, strainer and ladle.[32]

EGYPT   NEAL SPENCER

The short reign of Pharaoh Psamtek III was brought to an end by the invading forces of Cambyses' army in 525 BC, heralding a century of Persian rule over all Egypt (often referred to as the 27th dynasty).[33] Later Egyptian tradition, and Herodotus who visited Egypt in the fifth century BC, depict Cambyses as epitomizing amoral rule. This is particularly emphasized in the *Demotic Chronicle*,[34] a lengthy papyrus in which the foreign rulers are contrasted with some of the idealized Egyptian pharaohs of the fourth century BC. Cambyses is portrayed as hindering the continuing function of temples; in contrast, Darius I is credited with the compilation of Egyptian laws and publication of them in several languages. However, consideration of contemporary Egyptian sources and the results of recent excavations demand a more balanced view of this first Persian period.

A Persian satrap, usually part of the royal family, was installed to oversee Egypt, along with an uncertain number of other Persian officials. Aramaic was the language of the new Persian administration,[35] but many legal documents, such as those recording marriages or loan agreements, continued to be produced in demotic (cat. 315), the cursive script used to write the Egyptian language. These were dated in the traditional fashion, by reference to the regnal year of the ruler; in essence the Persian kings were treated as Egyptian pharaohs in these documents. Persians who settled in Egypt may have become quickly Egyptianized, and thus are difficult to identify in the archaeological record.[36]

Much of the minutiae of government must have remained in the hands of Egyptian officials.[37] The hieroglyphic texts on the statue of Udjahorresnet, now in the Vatican, outline his career, rising from commander of the royal navy in the reigns of the Egyptian pharaohs Amasis and Psamtek III to that of chief physician under Cambyses and Darius I.[38] The biographical text includes the claim that Udjahorresnet composed a traditional Egyptian throne name for Cambyses, *Mesiture* ('offspring of [the sun-god] Ra'), and succesfully petitioned him to improve the temples at the dynastic capital Sais, and help remove foreigners (troops?) dwelling within it. Cambyses then ordered the provision of 'offerings to Neith-the-Great ... and to the great gods of Sais, as it had been before. His majesty commanded [to perform] all their festivals and all their processions, as had been done before.'

Later in his career Udjahorresnet spent time at the court of Darius I, who subsequently sent him back to Egypt to restore further parts of the temple at Sais. There are several allusions to the Persian invasion in his biographical text, typically oblique, as the 'very great turmoil when it happened in the whole land'. Udjahorresnet's text clearly testifies to Cambyses' interest in supporting the temples, at least later in his reign, and presumably for well-founded political reasons. Similar motives must have led to him allowing traditional ceremonies associated with the burial of the unique and divine Apis bull to take place at Memphis (cat. 267 attests to the cult of the Buchis bull at Armant in southern Egypt in the reign of Darius III).

In addition to supporting the work at Sais, the majority of the temple of Amun of Hibis, in el-Kharga oasis west of the Nile valley, was built in the reign of Darius I in a wholly Egyptian style.[39] Darius I is depicted as an Egyptian pharaoh, performing offering rites before the gods of the temple. Other remnants of architectural activity in his reign are known from Qasr el-Ghueita in the same oasis, from the temple at el-Kab in the southern Nile Valley and in the greywacke quarries at Wadi Hammammat in the Eastern Desert. A wooden shrine bearing painted depictions of the king wearing the double crown of northern and southern Egypt was found at Tuna el-Gebel.[40] No traces have been found of Egyptian-style temple building under subsequent Persian kings. Darius I is also credited with completing the canal linking the Nile and Red Sea through the Wadi Tumilat.

Few towns of the first millennium BC have been excavated in Egypt, but Persian occupation levels have been found at Tell el-Muqdam in the central Delta[41] and at the oasis town of Ayn Manawir. The latter was founded during the fifth century BC: recent excavations have uncovered a temple to Osiris, parts of the village and a series of *qanats*, an irrigation system that may have been introduced from Iran.[42] At the southern frontier town of Elephantine, houses of this period have been excavated, along with a Jewish temple. Aramaic papyri from the same site reveal the presence of Ionians, Phoenicians, Carians and Greeks living in the town, and a dispute between Egyptian priests and the Jewish temple.[43] Text archives from Thebes and Ayn Manawir underscore how life continued much as before.[44]

A series of anti-Persian rebellions are known to have taken place in the fifth century BC, and Amyrtaeus succeeded in ousting Persian forces in 404 BC. Nonetheless, Egypt would not be free from the military threat of Persia in the six decades of independence which followed. An extensive temple-building programme was undertaken by the last Egyptian pharaohs (the 30th dynasty), with particular emphasis placed on the expansion of sacred space, an ideological response to the threat from Persia, to complement the realities of the military defences. Persian forces attempted to enter Egypt in 385–382, 373, 359 and 351–350 BC. Nonetheless, in the short reign of Djedhor an ill-fated campaign into Palestine, with the help of an Athenian general, was directed against Persian forces,[45] attesting to some degree of military ambition on the part of the Egyptian pharaohs. Defences and fortifications of the fifth and fourth centuries BC have been discovered in the northeastern Delta, usually massive mudbrick structures with fortifying bastions on their outer face, enclosing a series of smaller buildings.[46]

Egypt's armies were defeated in 343 BC, when Artaxerxes III reached Memphis after advancing up the Pelusiac branch of the Nile. This second period of Persian domination of Egypt lasted just over a decade (343–332 BC) and is difficult to identify in the archaeological record. There is no evidence of temple-building in the Egyptian style during this second occupation, and the early Ptolemaic 'Satrap Stela' presents a critical view of Xerxes' approach to Egyptian temples.[47] The biographical texts from the tomb of a high priest in Middle Egypt, Petosiris, provide oblique references to troubles during this occupation: '... while the ruler of the foreign lands [the Persian king] was protector of Egypt and nothing was in its former place since fighting started in Egypt. The south being in turmoil, the north in revolt, the people walked with [heads turned back]. All temples were without their servants, the priests fled, not knowing what was happening.'[48]

Further north, the biographical text of another member of the priesthood reveals an underlying dislike of the Persian forces, as Djedhor describes the preparation of sacred falcon burials, in a place 'hidden from the foreigners'.[49] Both texts were composed for religious contexts, whether tomb or temple, and cannot be treated as unbiased accounts.

Persian involvement in Egypt ended with the arrival of Alexander the Great in 332 BC. The Egyptian priest Samtutefnakht recorded, upon a stela now in Naples, his participation in the battles between Persian armies and those of Alexander. Addressing his local town god, Heryshef, he states 'you protected me in the combat of the Greeks, when you repulsed those of Asia [i.e. the Persians]. They killed a million at my sides, and no-one raised his arm against me.'[50]

ANATOLIA

When Cyrus came to the throne in 550 BC he already had effective control of eastern Turkey as far as the River Halys, following the stand-off between the Medes and the Lydians when their battle of 585 BC was interrupted by a solar eclipse. In this part of Turkey, partly within the satrapy of Armenia, there is an inscription of Xerxes high up on the citadel rock at Van,[51] and there is a columned building apparently of the Achaemenid period at Altintepe near Erzincan. It is perhaps from this site that the collection of silver plate bequeathed by A.W. Franks to the British Museum comes (cats 160–9).[52] Then in 547 BC Croesus of Lydia crossed the River Halys to attack the Achaemenid Persians and was roundly defeated. Within a short time most of western Turkey, including the east Greek settlements in Ionia and the peoples of Anatolian stock living in Lydia, Lycia, Caria and Cappodocia, came under the control of Cyrus. Craftsmen, particularly stonemasons from Ionia and Lydia, were used in building projects in Iran. The formerly powerful and wealthy state of Lydia, credited with inventing coinage, was to become a province of the Persian Empire for the next two centuries. The capital of Lydia remained at Sardis, which was a terminal of the road stretching from Susa to Asia Minor.[53]

Testifying to the extraordinary wealth of Lydia in the Achaemenid period and the diverse range of influences in Lydian art is the collection known as the 'Lydian hoard'.[54] This is material from at least four tumuli (burial mounds) in the Uşak-Güre region about 80 km east of Sardis, and from a tomb (Harta) about 60 km north of Sardis. Much of this material was illicitly excavated and taken out of the country, but it was returned to Turkey in 1993.

The contents of these tombs show a combination of Anatolian, Greek and Persian influences, with the last being particularly marked. Many of the vessels in particular belong to types that were current throughout the Persian Empire or have iconographic details that are distinctively Persian. Amongst the vessels in the tombs are silver *oinochoai* (wine-jugs), some very similar to the gold example from the Oxus Treasure (cat. 125); bronze tre-foil-mouthed jugs; silver pitchers; silver ladles, some with handles ending in calf's heads (cf. cats 134–5); silver *phialai* with gold and silver appliqués showing Persian-style figures and back-to-back bull protomes (cf. cat. 111); hemispherical silver bowls that recall a gold bowl in the Oxus Treasure (cat. 99); a silver strainer-vessel (cf. cat. 132); silver goblets; and a silver scoop (cf. cats 136–7). Other items that may be identified as Per-

32 Partial reconstruction in the British Museum of the Nereid Monument from Xanthos in Asia Minor. This tomb for Arbinas, ruler of Xanthos *c.* 390–370 BC, is in the form of a Greek temple, but there is evidence of Persian influence.

sian in type include silver incense-burners like the examples shown on Achaemenid seals and in reliefs; alabastrons in stone and silver (cf. cats 140, 278–9); a jasper plate (cf. examples from Persepolis); and seal rings and pendants with typical Achaemenid designs. Some of the jewellery is clearly Greek in style, but distinctively Persian is a pair of gold bracelets with terminals standing proud like the Oxus Treasure bracelets (cat. 153), but in this case with lion protomes. Owing more to local and Greek influences are the marble *klinai* (couches), on which the bodies of the deceased were laid, and the wall-paintings in the tombs.

One of the most important Achaemenid centres in Asia Minor was at Daskyleion, Turkey, which was the capital of a satrapy at least from the time of Xerxes. In

excavations here in 1954 more than 400 clay *bullae* were found – seal impressions on clay that had been used to seal documents, probably written on papyrus.[55] They were perhaps from the archive of the satrap. A few of the seal impressions have inscriptions of Xerxes or Artaxerxes, and some of the seals are in the Achaemenid court style. Some of these impressions would have been made with pyramidal stamp seals, often of blue chalcedony, that are characteristic of the western satrapies of the Persian Empire and particularly Lydia.[56] The majority, however, are in the so-called 'Graeco-Persian' style, a term coined for the mainly scaraboid seals to reflect the fact that they are influenced by both Greek and Persian artistic traditions. Such seals survive in large numbers, often unprovenanced. There are also some funerary stelae from Daskyleion, one of them inscribed in Aramaic, which again are called 'Graeco-Persian'. They show interesting scenes of daily life during this period.[57]

In 546–545 BC Lycia in the southwest corner of Asia Minor was invaded by the Persians under their general Harpagos, and except for a period in the fifth century BC when the Lycians paid tribute to Athens they remained under Persian control until the conquests of Alexander in about 333 BC. They even provided naval assistance (as did neighbouring Caria) for the Persian invasion of Greece in 480 BC. The Lycians spoke an Anatolian language that is not yet properly understood and used an alphabet that was partly borrowed from Greek. During the period of Persian domination Lycia was ruled by local dynasts who were buried in monumental tombs. These were raised high off the ground by platforms or pillars that recall tombs in Iran such as that of Cyrus at Pasargadae, but as there are no Lycian tombs earlier than the time of Cyrus it is not clear whether the influence flowed from east to west or vice versa. Many of the Lycian tombs exhibit a mixture of native Lycian, Greek and Persian influences, which has led to them being sometimes referred to as Irano-Lycian monuments.[58]

The earliest of the Lycian tombs are known as pillar tombs. In these the tomb chamber is supported on a stone pillar. An example of such a monument is the Harpy Tomb now in the British Museum, which was built around 480 BC and named after the four bird-like women that are shown on it. Some scholars have seen Persian influence in the stone carvings that decorated the outside of the tomb chamber, particularly the scene showing a ruler seated on a throne holding a flower in one hand and a long staff in the other, which can be compared with the 'audience relief' of the great king at Persepolis.

Perhaps the best-known of the Xanthos tombs is the temple tomb known as the Nereid Monument that has

33 Partial reconstruction in the British Museum of the Tomb of Payava from Xanthos, built about 360 BC. Much of the sculptural decoration on the tomb is Greek, but there are Persian elements including a representation of a satrap (provincial governor) in Persian dress.

been partially reconstructed in the British Museum (fig. 32). This is the tomb of Arbinas, ruler of Xanthos about 390–370 BC. The tomb is built in the form of a Greek temple, and the figures of Nereids (daughters of the sea-god Nereus) between the columns, the column capitals and some of the reliefs are purely Greek in inspiration. On the other hand, Arbinas himself is shown on one of the friezes like a Persian ruler: he reclines on a couch, holding a bowl in one hand and a rhyton terminating in a winged griffin in the other.

There is also Persian influence in the Tomb of Payava, who was probably a local ruler of Xanthos (fig. 33). It was constructed in about 360 BC, and has been partly rebuilt in the British Museum. It is a tall, rectangular tomb, with a barrel-vaulted roof (probably a Lycian element) and sculptured decoration on four sides. In one of these scenes there is a figure in Persian dress seated on a throne, probably the satrap Autophradates. Most of the other sculptured decoration on the tomb is Greek in style, showing the mixture of eastern and western influences that prevailed in Xanthos at this time.

34 Wall painting in a tomb at Karaburun, near Antalya, showing a Lycian noble of the Achaemenid period reclining on a banqueting couch.

Evidence of the affluent lifestyle enjoyed by Lycian nobles in the Persian period is provided by wall-paintings in some of the tombs, for example at Karaburun near Antalya (fig. 34). Here a Lycian grandee, wearing Persian jewellery such as lion-headed bracelets, reclines on a banqueting couch. His servants wear Persian costume.[59]

The funerary monuments of Lycia also influenced the

form of tombs elsewhere in Asia Minor such as the Mausoleum at Halikarnassos (Bodrum) in Caria which was one of the Seven Wonders of the World. This was a tomb for Mausolus who died around 353 BC. It consists of a high platform (recalling Lycian tombs) surmounted by a columned building with a pyramid-shaped roof, on top of which was a stone model of chariot and horses. The statues and friezes which decorated the monument were predominantly Ionian Greek in style, but fragments from the Mausoleum that are now in the British Museum include a colossal statue of a figure in Persian dress on horseback.

From Halikarnassos, and now in the British Museum, there is also an alabastron with an inscription of Xerxes in cuneiform and hieroglyphic (cat. 140), and a silver *phiale* with a lotus flower design.

THRACE

Ancient Thrace is the area stretching from the River Danube in the north to the Aegean Sea in the south, and bounded on the east by the Black Sea. It was occupied by Thracian-speaking tribes. From the second half of the seventh century BC onwards the Greeks established settlements along the Black Sea coast and on the Aegean coast. The Persian presence in this area was relatively short-lived. In 512 BC they crossed over into Europe in order to wage war against the Scythians who lived to the north of the Black Sea, and later in the reign of Darius and in that of Xerxes they used southern Thrace as a platform for their campaigns against Greece. Persian military strongholds were established at Doriscus and Aenus on the Aegean Sea. After their defeat in 476 BC they withdrew to the Asiatic mainland.

Before the Persian incursions into Thrace there is little evidence for the fine silverworking tradition found in the hoards dating from this time onwards. Outstanding is the Rogozen Treasure, from northern Bulgaria just south of the Danube, probably buried in the mid-fourth century BC, that contained 165 silver vessels, some of them gilded, weighing 20 kg.[60] Other important collections come from graves at Duvanli and Vratsa, and from hoards found in Borovo and Lukovit, all in central and northern Bulgaria. The Achaemenid Persian influence in some of these silver vessels has been much discussed and, at least superficially, it is undeniable. We might point to silver *phialai* of classic Persian shape ranging from plain *omphalos* bowls to fluted examples, to bowls with lotus and bud pattern, and to an elaborate silver bowl from Rogozen decorated with opposing pairs of horned and winged lions (fig. 35). Then, there is an amphora from Duvanli with handles in the form of winged lions with ibex horns; a rhyton ending in a bull protome from Borovo; and a jug from Rogozen with embossed decoration showing a lion

35 Silver bowl of Achaemenid shape from Rogozen in northern Bulgaria decorated with opposing pairs of horned and winged lions. *Bulgarian National Museum of History, Sofia.*

36 Elaborate gold earring or pendant showing Persian influence from Akhalgori, Georgia. *Georgian State Museum, Tbilisi.*

jumping on the back of a stag and biting its neck. There is clearly some Persian influence here, and a few of the pieces may actually have been made in Achaemenid centres particularly in Asia Minor, but we should not underestimate the extent of Greek influence or indeed the contribution of local Thracian silver-smiths. Ancient Thrace was a melting-pot of different cultures, and this is reflected in the silver vessels. There is also clearly Scythian influence in some of the sheet metal decoration.

THE CAUCASUS

The extent to which the Achaemenid kings exercised control over Transcaucasia (the republics of Armenia, Georgia and Azerbaijan) has been disputed in the past. Armenia, at least, was part of a satrapy and we know that some of the former Urartian sites continued to be occupied in the Achaemenid period. These include Arinberd (Erebuni on the outskirts of Erevan) and Armavir (Argishtihinili) as well as Van Kale in eastern Turkey.[61] According to Herodotus, however, Colchis (western Georgia) was not part of a satrapy as such and the Colchians are listed with those peoples who rendered gifts instead of paying tribute:

> Gifts were also required of the Colchians and their
> neighbours as far as the Caucasus mountains (which is as far
> as the Persian rule reaches, the country north of the
> Caucasus paying no regard to the Persians); these were
> rendered every four years and are still so rendered, namely,
> an hundred boys and as many maidens.

(*History* III.97, Loeb translation by A.D. Godley)

The assertion by Herodotus that Persian rule extended as far as the Caucasus mountains has in the past been disputed, particularly by Soviet scholars, but recent archaeological discoveries have tended to confirm the Achaemenid presence there.

Thus, bell-shaped column bases of Persepolis type, attesting to the presence of Achaemenid official buildings, perhaps even audience halls for local governors, have been found at Gimbuti in Iberia (eastern Georgia), at Qaracamirli and Sari Tepe in Azerbaijan, and at Beniamin in Armenia.[62] There is also at Samadro in Iberia a tower-like building resembling the enigmatic structures at Pasargadae and Naqsh-i Rustam.[63] The associated pottery at some of these sites includes *phialai* of the distinctive Persian type, thought to be reproductions in pottery of metal prototypes. There is also from central and eastern Georgia painted pottery that is comparable to the 'Triangle Ware' of northwest Iran.[64]

Colchis was an area of legendary wealth, as reflected in the story of Jason and the Argonauts who travelled there in search of the Golden Fleece, and this reputation is amply borne out by the contents of the rich graves and hoards of the fifth to fourth centuries BC. These include the graves at Vani, Sairkhe and Pichvnari in western Georgia, and the Kazbeg Treasure and the Akhalgori Tomb of the late fourth century BC in Iberia (fig. 36). Amongst the large quantities of gold and silver plate and the jewellery there is much that shows the influence of Achaemenid Persia, particularly some of the elaborate rhytons and *phialai*. There is also Greek influence, however, which is only to be expected considering that Greeks were settling on the east coast of the Black Sea from the seventh century BC onwards. Of course, the contents of many graves of this period were much more modest. Thus, a grave found near Erevan contained two bronze pendants, an iron spearhead and a carinated bronze bowl (cats 282–5).

CENTRAL ASIA

It is often not appreciated that the Achaemenid Empire included a vast part of Central Asia to the east of the Caspian Sea, and that Cyrus himself was eventually killed campaigning against 'pointed-hat Scythians' probably to the northeast of the Aral Sea. In antiquity these regions, corresponding to the provinces of Parthia, Chorasmia, Aria, Bactria, Sogdiana and Scythia, were inhabited by Iranian tribes.

Probably the best-known hoard of gold and silver objects of the Achaemenid period derives from Central Asia. This is the Oxus Treasure that apparently comes from ancient

37 Map showing the location of Takht-i Kuwad and Takht-i Sangin on the north bank of the River Oxus.

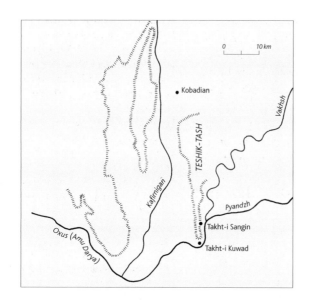

38 Decorated felt saddle blanket with stepped edging in Achaemenid style from barrow 5 at Pazyryk in southern Siberia. *State Hermitage, St Petersburg.*

Bactria.[65] It consists of about 180 objects in gold and silver that are now in the British Museum. Amongst them are chariot models (cats 399–400), a gold scabbard showing a lion hunt (cat. 431), jewellery including two large gold armlets with griffin terminals (cat. 153), statuettes (cats 258–62), figures of animals, vessels (cats 98–100, 105), clothing ornaments (cats 183–9) and about fifty gold plaques, mostly with designs of human figures (cats 213–57). These plaques are clearly votive, and they and the other objects in the treasure have the appearance of material that was dedicated to a temple perhaps over a period of several centuries. Originally associated with the treasure were about 1,500 coins covering a span of about 300 years down to the early second century BC. If the coins really do belong with the treasure, they might then indicate that it was buried around 200 BC. The treasure was apparently found on the north bank of the River Oxus between about 1876 and 1880. It was allegedly scattered about in the sands of the river, and it has traditionally been associated with a site named Takht-i Kuwad, now in Tadjikistan. There has been much speculation over the years about whether the Oxus Treasure can be considered as a homogeneous collection and even whether it is all genuine. Claims that pieces are faked, however, are not well founded, and scientific examination, art historical analysis and the emergence of new parallels all point to its authenticity. The question of provenance is more problematic, but Takht-i Kuwad remains a possibility. Until recently it was an important ferry-station and there is an ancient site here about a quarter of which has now been washed away by the river.

Some 5 km to the north of Takht-i Kuwad, however, is the important site of Takht-i Sangin, where Russian excavations between 1976 and 1991 uncovered a temple on a citadel set within an enclosure of about 75 ha (fig. 37).[66] The central columned hall of the temple was surrounded by storerooms containing more than 5,000 objects dating from between the sixth century BC and the third century AD. The temple was apparently built right at the end of the Achaemenid period or a little later, but some of the objects derive from the Achaemenid period. Outstanding amongst them is an ivory scabbard carved with the figure of a lion. The discovery of this temple has led to suggestions that the Oxus Treasure originally came from Takht-i Sangin, but this remains unproven. It is true that there are three gold votive plaques from Takht-i Sangin, but they are of a different character to those in the Oxus Treasure and there are also other difficulties with this hypothesis.

Other hoards from Central Asia include Mir Zakah in Afghanistan, where coins, jewellery and precious objects were deposited in a shrine, and the fourth-century BC Chaman-i Hazuri hoard from Kabul with a mixture of Achaemenid and other coins. Both contained bent-bar coins thought to be equal to two Achaemenid *sigloi*.[67]

It is clear that sites such as Merv, Samarkand (Afrasiab), Kandahar, Balkh – where Artaxerxes III is supposed to have established a temple of Anahita – and Gonur, the capital of Margiana,[68] were important in the Achaemenid period, but as yet relatively little is known about them. This has led one commentator to claim that 'the material traces of the Persian presence in Central Asia are slender'.[69] Nevertheless, recent excavations at smaller sites in Uzbekistan, Turkmenistan and Tadjikistan are casting light on the Achaemenid period in Central Asia. In particular, there is a palace with columns and column capitals in Achaemenid style at Kalal Gir in Chorasmia (Uzbekistan).[70]

On the frontier of the Achaemenid empire, in southeast Kazakhstan 50 km east of Almaty, is the burial mound (*kurgan*) at Issyk where an important Scythian (Saka) chieftain was buried.[71] His costume is paralleled on the gold plaques in the Oxus Treasure, and amongst the grave goods there is further evidence of Achaemenid connections, particularly in the way the animals are depicted.

Beyond the borders of the Achaemenid Empire are the frozen tombs discovered at Pazyryk in the Altai district of southern Siberia. Two of the barrows (2 and 5) contained objects showing evidence of Achaemenid connections (fig. 38), particularly the pile carpet decorated with figures of horsemen and animals, and the felt wallhanging showing an enthroned figure and a horseman.[72] The explanation for these links is not obvious, but they could be attributed to long-distance trade connections or even a shared cultural heritage between the peoples of this area and the Achaemenid Persians.

Other scattered finds in northern regions, including silver *phialai* and rhytons of Achaemenid type,[73] almost certainly *are* evidence of trade contacts.

EASTERN IRAN AND NORTHWEST INDIA

In eastern Iran, in Sistan, beyond the central deserts, the largest site is Dahan-i Ghulaman, probably an Achaemenid provincial capital, excavated by an Italian mission in 1962–6.[74] The plans of seven large buildings have been recovered, one of them apparently religious in character but probably not a fire temple as sometimes suggested. Further east were the Achaemenid provinces of Arachosia, Sattagydia, Gandara and India (Hindush), corresponding to parts of modern Afghanistan and Pakistan.[75] Indians are shown on the Apadana reliefs (delegation XVIII) wearing only a skirt (a *dhoti*) and bringing a donkey, axes and pannier-bags with pottery jars. Herodotus says (*History* III.94) that the Indians paid a greater tribute than any other province, namely 360 talents of gold dust, but in spite of this apparent wealth, Achaemenid settlements in this area remain elusive. The great sites of Charsada and Taxila were occupied at this time, but we know little about them. More information is likely to be obtained from sites such as Akra in the Bannu district of Pakistan, currently being excavated by a joint Pakistani–British expedition.[76]

1 Stronach 1978.

2 Schmidt 1953; Schmidt 1957; Sami 1970.

3 See below, p. 50.

4 Moorey 1985: 21.

5 Sumner 1986.

6 For a recent survey of Achaemenid-period sites in Iran see Boucharlat 2005.

7 Curtis 1993.

8 Amiet 1988.

9 Boucharlat 1997: 64.

10 King and Thompson 1907; Schmitt 1991.

11 Knapton, Sarraf and Curtis 2001.

12 Walker 1997.

13 Haerinck 1997.

14 Seidl 1976.

15 Reade 1986.

16 Haerinck 1997: pl. 6.

17 Moorey 1980a: 131; Kuhrt 1990.

18 Collon 1996.

19 Fleming 1989.

20 Curtis 2005.

21 Lyonnet 2005.

22 Moorey 1980.

23 Stucky 1998; Stucky and Mathys 2000.

24 Jidejian 2000.

25 Jabak-Hteit 2003.

26 Bettles 2003.

27 Stern 1982; Stern 2001; Bienkowski 2001.

28 One might point to a bronze caryatid censer with a woman wearing a Persian-style dress, and a bronze bowl with a floral design from a tomb at Umm Udhaina in Amman (Bienkowski 1991: figs 114–15).

29 Stern 1982: figs 92, 236, 241.

30 Karageorghis 2001: 199–200.

31 These include two silver bowls of characteristic Persian shape from a grave at Samad al Shan in Oman (Yule 2001: pl. 555b–c); and a stone slab in the Yemen National Museum with a figure in the Persian style shown holding a flower in one hand and an incense-burner in the other (Costa 1978: no. 32).

32 Moorey 1980b: 131.

33 For general summaries of this period, with further bibliography, see Lloyd 1983; Mysliwiec 2000: 135–59; Burkard 1995; Briant 1988.

34 Johnson 1983.

35 One papyrus records the taxation of trading ships entering and leaving Egypt during the fifth century BC: Briant and Descat 1998.

36 Note the Egyptian-style funerary stela, attesting to the marriage of Artam, a Persian, with an Egyptian woman, Tanofrether: Mathieson *et al.* 1995.

37 For example, the position of 'overseer of works in Upper and Lower Egypt' continued under Persian rule: Burchardt 1911: 69–71.

38 Lichtheim 1980: 36–41; the discovery of his tomb, and a discussion of this official's role, is covered in Bareš 1999.

39 Winlock 1941; Davies 1953.

40 Mysliwiec 2000: 144–6, pls 5–6.

41 Redmount and Friedman 1997: 57–8.

42 See Wuttmann *et al.* 1998.

43 Porten 1996.

44 Pestman 1994.

45 Will 1960.

46 Valbelle and Defernez 1995.

47 Lloyd 1982: 175–6.

48 Lichtheim 1980: 45–54.

49 Sherman 1981: 82–102.

50 Lichtheim 1980: 41–4.

51 Kent 1953: no. XV.

52 Summers 1993.

53 On the route of the Persian royal road through Anatolia, see French 1998.

54 Özgen and Öztürk 1996.

55 Kaptan 2001.

56 Boardman 1970.

57 Akurgal 1966; Lemaire 2001.

58 Özgen and Öztürk 1996: 47.

59 Ibid.

60 Fol *et al.* 1986.

61 Summers 1993: 86.

62 For a brief survey see Curtis and Kruszynski 2002: 5–6.

63 Knauss 2001: 130.

64 F. Knauss, lecture on 'Ancient Persia and the Caucasus' at the British Museum, 13 July 2004.

65 Dalton 1964; Curtis 2003.

66 Litvinsky and Pichikiyan 2000.

67 Bivar 1988: 195–7.

68 Sarianidi 2002: 75.

69 Francfort 1988: 179.

70 Francfort 1988: 179–81.

71 Akishev 1978.

72 Rudenko 1970: fig. 145, pls 154, 174–5.

73 Moorey 1980a: 140–41.

74 Gnoli 1993.

75 For a general survey of the Achaemenid period in northwest India see Chattopadhyaya 1974.

76 Khan *et al.* 2000.

5

THE PALACE

John Curtis and Shahrokh Razmjou

THE TRADITION AND ORIGINS OF COLUMNED HALLS

Columned halls are a distinctive feature of the architecture of the Achaemenid period, built throughout the period and in different parts of the empire. They were characterized by having a central-columned hall (a 'hypostyle' hall), four corner towers and usually three-columned porticoes. The corner towers had an internal staircase to access the upper floor. Sometimes the buildings were raised on terraces and approached by monumental staircases. It is common to refer to all buildings of this type as *apadanas*, but this is not technically correct. In Old Persian inscriptions three different words are used for the term 'palace'. They are *apadana*, *hadish* and *tachara*, and the differences between them are not entirely clear. While *apadana* is the word that is generally most familiar to archaeologists and art historians, it is in fact found in only four Old Persian inscriptions, one from the reign of Darius II (424–405 BC) and three from the reign of his successor Artaxerxes II (405–359 BC).[1] It has been suggested that the term *apadana* was reserved only for the grandest buildings, perhaps those that had stone (rather than wooden) columns on top of the column bases. However that may be, we will use *apadana* here to refer loosely to columned buildings of the type described.

Apart from the two palaces at Pasargadae, many of the buildings on the Persepolis terrace conform to the basic *apadana* plan. To these should be added the remains of the unfinished palace at Dasht-i Gohar, between Persepolis and Naqsh-i Rustam, that was probably constructed for Cambyses.[2] In addition to the palace at Borazjan near the Persian Gulf, there are a number of similar buildings in Fars province. At Susa is the Palace of Darius and outside the city walls on the other side of the River Shaur is the smaller palace of Artaxerxes II. In eastern Iran there are columned buildings at Dahan-i Ghulaman. We know there was an *apadana* palace in Hamadan but its precise location remains unknown. Outside Iran various finds, sometimes made by chance,

attest to the presence of Achaemenid-period columned halls in Babylon, in Sidon, at Gumbati in Georgia, at Sari Tepe and Qaracamirli Koyi in Azerbaijan, and at Benjamin in Armenia. There are also columned halls of Achaemenid date at erstwhile Urartian centres such as Arinberd and Armavir, but they are not *apadana*-style constructions.

The origin of these columned halls that are typical of the Achaemenid period has been much debated. It seems certain that they should be traced back to the columned halls that have been excavated in northwest Iran at Hasanlu, dating from the Iron Age IV period (*c.* 1000–800 BC).[3] The columned hall found at Muweilah in Sharjah, United Arab Emirates, which apparently dates from before 800 BC, is very unlikely to have provided the inspiration for the columned halls of Fars, even though it is just on the other side of the Persian Gulf, but probably derives from the same tradition.[4]

In Iran itself a number of columned halls may be noted in the Iron Age III period. Although they are not *apadana*-type structures, they provide evidence of a tradition of columned halls that continued from Hasanlu down to the Achaemenid period. At Ziwiyeh in Iranian Kurdistan a columned hall was discovered during recent Iranian excavations,[5] and columned halls have been found at each of the three sites that are believed to be Median, namely Baba Jan, Godin Tepe and Nush-i Jan.

AN ANALYSIS OF ARCHITECTURAL ELEMENTS

Although in all *apadana* buildings extensive use was made of stone, the walls themselves were made of mudbrick that has not usually survived or has been removed by archaeologists. We know there were windows at the lower level as the stone window frames sometimes survive, but the existence of high-level windows is still debated. Probably, though, the palaces had high-level windows that could be accessed by a balcony. The lower-level windows had double shutters as indicated by a bolt-hole in the centre of the frame. The floors of the palaces were sometimes made of red-polished lime plaster, or they were paved with bricks or stone. Such floors were probably then covered with fine carpets. The roofs were held up by columns which supported gigantic cedar beams. These are thought to have been imported from the Lebanon. Above the cedar beams would have been further timbers and matting, and the roof would have been sealed with mud plaster in the traditional ancient Near Eastern method. The edge of the roof of the Apadana at Persepolis probably had a crenellated parapet.

The column bases are all of stone. The earliest type of column base is a square plinth with two steps, above

Plate 14.

Column bases of South Palace

Ruins of Susa.

H.A.C.

39 Stone column bases found during the excavations at Susa by W.K. Loftus in 1850–52. These column bases were found in the southern part of the 'Ville Royale' mound (see fig. 23) where they had probably been reused. *Drawing by H.A. Churchill.*

which is a cushion-shaped torus, which may be an element in its own right or part of the base of the column itself. Such column bases are found at Pasargadae, where the torus is either plain (in Palace S) or has horizontal fluting (in Palace P), and at Persepolis (cat. 7). The stepped bases with torus are also shown on the tomb façades at Naqsh-i Rustam and Persepolis, and occur in the palace at Borazjan. This stepped base continued in use throughout the empire. There is an example from Hamadan inscribed with the name of Artaxerxes II.[6]

The second type of column base is bell-shaped. This is not known at Pasargadae, but is common at Persepolis and Susa (fig. 39). Sometimes square column bases and bell-shaped column bases are combined in the same building, as in the Palace of Darius at Susa, and in the Apadana at Persepolis. In both cases the column bases in the central hall are square plinths and those in the colonnades are bell-shaped.[7] At Susa both types rested on great slabs of stone that are approximately square. There are different types of bell-shaped base but they all

have some form of floral or leaf decoration on the sides. There is sometimes a torus on the top of the base. Some of the bell-shaped bases are massive; for example, cat. 9 from the Hall of 100 Columns at Persepolis weighs about 4 tons. The column bases supported wooden or, more commonly, stone columns. The stone shafts were normally fluted and up to 20 m high. The stone columns were polished and partly painted, while the wooden columns had a plaster coating and were painted with designs in blue, white, red and black.

The column capitals, at least at Persepolis, are very elaborate (fig. 40). At the bottom of the capital is a circle of pendant leaves, above which is a palm capital; then a shaft with volute decoration and finally the figural part of the capital, which consists of human or animal forms back-to-back. There are four different types of column capital at Persepolis, featuring bull protomes, lions, griffins (known as 'homa birds') and human-headed bulls (figs 41–4). The protomes are arranged back-to-back with a saddle between them to carry the gigantic cedar beams that supported the roof. The capitals were originally painted, as shown by surviving paint on the tongues of the lion capitals from the Apadana at Persepolis. These capitals vary greatly in size.

A number of the *apadana* buildings have stone panels

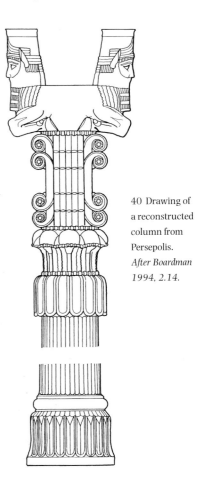

40 Drawing of a reconstructed column from Persepolis. *After Boardman 1994, 2.14.*

41 Double-bull column capital, probably from one of the porticoes of the Apadana at Persepolis.

42 Column capital in the form of griffins (locally known as 'homa birds') probably from the Unfinished Gate at Persepolis.

attendants. In the centre of each façade was originally the enthroned king, but these panels were at some stage removed and replaced. Other buildings at Persepolis with staircase reliefs are the Central Building, the Palace of Xerxes, Palaces G and H, and the Palace of Darius. They all show processions of nobles in Median and Persian dress, and figures in Median and Persian dress climbing stairs and carrying food, drink and live animals. Similar reliefs are also known at Susa, from the Shaur Palace. All these reliefs are thought to have been originally painted. The most elaborate doorway reliefs are in the Hall of 100 Columns at Persepolis, where the four doorways in the north and south walls show rows of subject peoples supporting the enthroned king while Ahuramazda hovers above (cat. 38). The smaller doorways in the side walls show the king or at least the Persian royal hero figure in single combat with monsters and bulls. These reliefs inside doorjambs were painted and decorated with attached ornaments such as golden bracelets and sheet gold crowns. Other doorway reliefs can be found in the so-called Harem, the Central Building, the Palace of Xerxes and the Palace of Darius. In addition to the motifs described, there are representations of the king and attendants, and in the Palace of Darius the king and the crown prince.

with carved decoration in low relief. These stone reliefs may either have lined doorways or, when the *apadana* building was raised on a terrace, decorated the sides of the staircases and parapets that led to the terrace. In this way they are different from Assyrian palace reliefs which decorated the inside walls of rooms of state. The best known examples of stone relief decoration from the Achaemenid Empire are on the Apadana at Persepolis. Here, the north and east sides of the building have double staircases with an elaborate series of reliefs that are mirror images of each other. On both the northern and eastern façades the sculptures show on one side twenty-three delegations from all around the Persian Empire bringing presents and tribute, and on the other side files of Median and Persian nobles, guards and

Michael Roaf has shown that the masons who undertook the work in the Apadana were probably organized in teams, and that the work of individual teams is demarcated by masons' marks.[8] A double diamond shape is particularly common. We know the names of a few people engaged in the masonry work at Persepolis, but only because they are listed in the Elamite texts recording payments. Their names are not recorded because of their achievements. This is in keeping with the earlier tradi-

tions of Assyria where the artists are similarly anonymous. In contrast to Greece, it does not seem to have been the practice in the ancient Near East to acknowledge the brilliance of individual artists even if it was recognized.

As well as sculpted stone wall reliefs, the Persians made use of glazed brick decoration in their palaces. This was a particular feature at Susa, where courtyards in the south part of the palace were decorated with friezes of glazed bricks showing files of guardsmen, lions and a pair of sphinxes. In addition, glazed-brick panels showing figures in Median and Persian dress bearing food and animals decorated some of the stairways. At Persepolis glazed-brick decoration with floral and geometric designs is known from the outside façades of the towers of the Apadana.[9] Before the Achaemenid period, glazed brick decoration is well known both from Assyria (for example at Nimrud and Khorsabad) and from Babylonia, where the most famous monument in glazed bricks was the Ishtar Gate at Babylon. There is also occasional glazed-brick decoration at sites in Iran such as Bukkan in Kurdistan. However, the glazed bricks of the Achaemenid period are different from these earlier examples in that they are not glazed mudbricks with straw temper but instead made of coarse quartz faience. Also the glazes are by this period retained between black cloisons (partitions). In one respect they are similar to the earlier bricks, however, in that all have fitters' marks, albeit of different kinds, painted on the top. These marks, whose identification still remains largely enigmatic, were intended to show the builders the order of the bricks within the complete panels.

Within Persian palaces many of the entrances were closed by massive double doors of wood, which were decorated with horizontal strips made from bronze or pre-cious metal. They sometimes bore friezes of mythical beasts such as winged bulls or winged lions (cats 84–5). The doors themselves were fixed to poles that turned on large sunken pivot-stones, above which were stone slabs decorated with floral designs (cat. 86). The tradition of decorating wooden doors with strips of bronze is particularly well attested at Balawat in Assyria.

Following traditional Elamite, Babylonian and Assyrian practice the Persian kings buried foundation deposits under newly constructed buildings. The best-known deposits of this type were found at Persepolis under the four corners of the Apadana. Here there were stone boxes each containing a gold and a silver tablet with a trilingual cuneiform inscription of Darius giving his name and titles, and asking for the protection of Ahuramazda (cats 2–3). Metal plaques of this kind were also found in the palace of the Assyrian king Sargon at Khorsabad, but more common in Assyria and Babylonia were barrel-shaped clay cylinders inscribed in cuneiform. Belonging to this tradition is the so-called Cyrus Cylinder (cat. 6) that was inscribed and buried at Babylon on the orders of Cyrus after he had captured Babylon in 539 BC.

THE ORIGINS OF ACHAEMENID ARCHITECTURAL DECORATION

There is no doubt that columned halls of the type discussed above (apadanas) are Iranian in inspiration, but some foreign influences can certainly be seen in the construction of these palaces. This is reflected in the famous inscription of Darius in which he describes the construction of his palace at Susa.[10] He tells us that the work was undertaken by craftsmen from various places. Thus the stonemasons were Ionians and Sardians, the goldsmiths were Medes and Egyptians, the carpenters were Sardians and Egyptians, the men who 'adorned the wall' were Medes and Egyptians, and the builders of the brickwork (perhaps the glazed brick panels?) were Babylonians. The materials also came from around the empire, from places as diverse as Gandara, Bactria and Egypt. Interestingly, the stone itself came from a nearby Elamite village. The involvement of foreign craftsmen is therefore indisputable, and their contribution can most easily be observed in the stoneworking techniques. Before the reign of Cyrus there was no tradition of constructing large stone buildings, therefore to do so Cyrus had to seek help from abroad; it was forthcoming from Lydia and Ionia in Asia Minor. The involvement of Ionian and Lydian stonemasons, especially in the early period at Pasargadae, is thought to be indicated by a number of elements: for example, by the use of claw-toothed picks and chisels; by a particular way of creating tight joints between stone blocks and column drums (anathyrosis);

43 Part of a lion-headed column capital from the main hall of the Apadana at Persepolis.

44 Double-bull column capital from the Palace of Darius at Susa. Found during the excavations by W.K. Loftus in 1850–52. *Drawing by H.A. Churchill.*

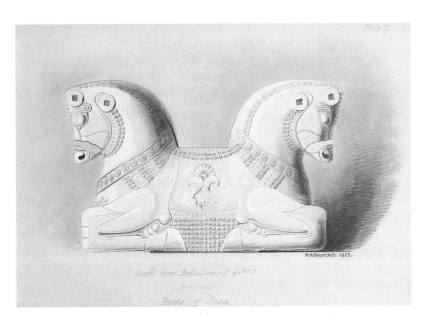

by the use of metal dovetail clamps to hold the stone blocks together; by the 'drafted margins' on the stone blocks of the Tall-i Takht; and by the column bases with horizontally fluted tori in Palace P. Lydian influence has also been detected in the Tomb of Cyrus (fig. 1). There is no previous tradition in Iran for this type of tomb, which has led scholars to suggest that the design comes from Asia Minor, but although such tombs are certainly known in that area they do not actually predate the Tomb of Cyrus. It is suggested that specific features indicating foreign influence include the double molding that is convex above and concave below (*cyma reversa*), and the denticulation under the cornice molding.

At Persepolis Classical archaeologists have been quick to assert Greek influence and Greek planning, but neither stands up to scrutiny. It is true that there are a few Greek inscriptions in a quarry near Persepolis, but these might be post-Achaemenid, and there are isolated graffiti in Greek style at Persepolis. It is also often noted that the zigzag hem found on Persian dress from the time of Darius is Greek in origin, and there is an argument that the plasticity of the Persepolis sculptures owes something to Greek influence. However, none of this amounts to substantial Greek influence.

In fact, the main influence at Persepolis and earlier at Pasargadae is Assyrian. The concept of stone relief decoration on a large scale clearly comes from Assyria, even though in Assyria the reliefs decorate rooms of state inside palaces and the subject matter is largely different. While Assyrian reliefs mostly show military campaigns and scenes of hunting, Achaemenid reliefs focus on courtly processions, the bringing of gifts, and preparations for ceremonies. There are, however, some points of contact, such as scenes of the king sitting in state, a hero figure in single combat with a monster, and various kinds of hybrid creatures. The Assyrian influence is particularly clear in the colossal human-headed winged bulls in the Gate of All Nations at Persepolis, but there are perceptible differences between the Persepolitan bulls and their Assyrian counterparts. More closely following Assyrian originals are the doorway reliefs in the two palaces at Pasargadae. Only the bottom parts survive, but Assyrian-style figures such as the lion-demon, the bull-man and a figure wearing a fish-cloak can be clearly recognized.

An Egyptian influence can also be detected in Achaemenid art, testifying to its eclectic nature. For example, in a doorway relief at Pasargadae the winged figure wears an Egyptian crown, and in some of the buildings at Persepolis there is Egyptian-style feather decoration above the windows and doorways.

In spite of the various foreign influences that can be identified, however, the end product is distinctively Persian.

THE FUNCTION OF PALACES

There is still some debate about how palaces were used. On the whole, suggestions for function are based more on the character of the relief decoration and less on the finds. But it is problematic to base identifications on the iconography as palaces and their function developed during the Achaemenid period and through the reigns of different kings. However, there seems to be general agreement that the great columned halls (*apadanas*) were designed and built for receiving processions and for general gatherings. The reliefs on the Apadana at Persepolis show delegations from twenty-three countries under Persian control bringing gifts to a meeting that was also attended by nobles or important officials. The Apadana could hold up to 10,000 guests at ground level alone, not including other levels in the building. Some palaces such as the Hall of 100 Columns were used for a similar purpose but for receiving different types of guest. This palace was perhaps a meeting place for military officials after it was completed in the time of Artaxerxes I.[11] The Central Building was on a smaller scale and was used as a meeting place for Persian and Median nobles, as well as princes. This can be seen from the reliefs on the sides of the northern staircase of the palace and the benches included in the design of the two porticoes.

In addition to palaces that were used for official meetings, there are others such as the Palace of Darius (*tachara*) and the Palace of Xerxes (*hadish*) at Persepolis that have traditionally been interpreted as residences of the Persian kings. This is mainly based on an assumption that the figures in the reliefs ascending the stairs are servants providing food and live animals for a banquet. However, they could also be regarded as priests bringing offerings for a ritual ceremony. In this case, the palaces would have been sacred places where such ritual ceremonies could be performed and it is unlikely that they were residential palaces in daily use.

Another palace with the same plan and characteristics as the *tachara* palace is the Harem. This was so called because of some small compartments in the south part, its location and comparisons with nineteenth-century Ottoman architecture. However, such comparisons have no academic value and should be disregarded.

The palace gates were a mixture of gate and palace, and their function was to provide indirect access to the royal area, and also to divide and direct the guests and visitors towards the other palaces. The Gate of all Nations at Persepolis could also have been used as a waiting hall: the benches inside provided seating for more than one hundred visitors.

The Treasury was a depository of valuable objects, but it did not have a financial function. The Persepolis

Tablets mention a treasury that was a focus for accounts, payments and financial activities, but its location is not clear. The building that is nowadays known as the Treasury on account of the finds made there had another purpose (see below). The function of some minor palaces is still not clear, but they could have been supplementary buildings related to the neighbouring major palaces.

FINDS FROM THE PALACES

The palaces originally contained a huge amount of valuable material in the form of objects, ornaments, decorations and luxury furniture. Most of these were looted and taken away by the Macedonians or destroyed, and the remnants were found as broken fragments scattered on the floors and buried under the debris of the burnt roofs and collapsed walls. Classical historians have testified to this wealth of artefacts. Diodorus mentions that the vaults of the palaces at Persepolis were packed full of gold and silver, and that thousands of animals were required to carry it away (Diodorus, XVIII.70.5–71.2). The Persian kings were also given lavish presents, such as the golden plane tree and golden vine that were supposed to have been presented to Darius by Pythius of Lydia.[12] In addition to the Macedonian looting, however, major buildings that were still visible attracted treasure-hunters, or were cleared out by later kings and rulers. The upshot is that there are not many finds from the major buildings.

Objects found include freestanding statues of animals, close to life-size, that guarded entrances to some of the palaces.[13] These statues include seated dogs on a leash (cat. 90), lions, ibexes and bulls, most of them found headless. Fragments of small statues have also been discovered, notably the lapis lazuli head of a young Persian prince that was found in the Hall of 32 Columns (cat. 87) and the fragment of a hand holding a lion made of reddish stone.[14] Other fragments of small statues from the Persepolis palaces represent animals, men, deities or a mixture of these. These small statues probably stood inside false window frames or on pedestals. There are also remains of burnt textiles that might have been curtains or drapes (tapestries). The many pins and nails that have been recovered are evidence for numerous missing attachments. Fragments of thin gold leaf used for gilding furniture and artefacts have also commonly been found in the palaces.[15] A bronze group in the shape of two galloping horses – probably a harness fitting or a fragment of an Archaic Greek bronze *krater* rim – was found in the portico of the Hall of 100 Columns (cat. 446).

The best finds, however, come from the Treasury. Broken fragments of objects were scattered on the floor, while some other items fell from above after the collapse of the second floor of the building. Most of the objects were probably stored on wooden shelves that were burnt in the fire of 330 BC. In addition to valuable objects made from gold, lapis lazuli and ivory, gems, fine cloths, inlays and jewellery, there were also fragments of pottery, clay and stone. The Treasury Tablets that were stored in a room on the second floor belong to a period from late in the reign of Darius I to early in the reign of Artaxerxes I. They were kept there for about a century to the end of the Achaemenid period and record payments to the artisans who worked at Persepolis. Another set of objects includes pestles, mortars and plates made of green chert that were used in ritual ceremonies (cats 211–12). Some have inscriptions indicating that they were not reused. A bronze pedestal in the shape of three roaring lions was also found in the Treasury (cat. 96). These lions originally surrounded a pole in the centre that is now broken. Stone vessels from different periods were also deposited here, including one bearing the name of the Assyrian king Ashurbanipal (cat. 117). A number of eye stones include examples with the name of the Babylonian king, Nebuchadnezzar II.[16] Some of the objects bear names of pharaohs of the 26th dynasty of Egypt (cat. 92). Another find was the headless statue of a seated woman, probably made in Greece or Asia Minor (cat. 441).

The Treasury contained a mixture of valuable objects and items that were kept because of their historical and cultural value and identity. These objects were from different periods, different places and different cultures. Sacred objects that had been used once in a ritual ceremony were also stored there. All these objects suggest that one function of the Treasury at Persepolis may have been as a museum or a royal archive.

1 Stronach 1985: 433–4
2 Stronach 2001: fig. 3.
3 Stronach 2001: 97.
4 Stronach 2001: fig. 2; Magee 2001.
5 Motamedi 1995–6: pl. on p. 353.
6 Knapton *et al.* 2001: figs 1a–b.
7 Curtis 1993: fig. 2; Stronach 1985: fig. 1.
8 Roaf 1983.
9 Schmidt 1953: figs 35A–B.
10 Kent 1953: DSf.
11 Krefter 1971: 59–61.
12 Briant 2002: 235–6.
13 Schmidt 1953: 73, 240, fig. 46A–B; Schmidt 1957: 69–70, pls 36–7.
14 Schmidt 1957: pl. 35/1.
15 Briant 2002: 236.
16 Schmidt 1957: 56–8, pl. 25/2.

FOUNDATION DEPOSITS

1

1 Large clay tablet with foundation inscription of Darius I (522–486 BC)

This inscription was written in Old Persian. It describes the construction of Darius's palace at Susa, and how he brought workmen and materials from different parts of the empire. The translation is reconstructed from various surviving versions of the Darius foundation inscription:

Saith Darius the King: Ahuramazda, the greatest of the gods – he created me; he made me king; he bestowed upon me this kingdom, great, possessed of good horses, possessed of good men.

By the favor of Ahuramazda my father Hystaspes and Arsames my grandfather – these both were living when Ahuramazda made me king in this earth. Unto

Ahuramazda thus was the desire: he chose me as [his] man in all the earth; he made me king in all the earth.

I worshipped Ahuramazda. Ahuramazda bore me aid. What was by me commanded to do, that he made successful for me. What I did, all by the favor of Ahuramazda I did.

This palace which I built at Susa, from afar its ornamentation was brought. Downward the earth was dug, until I reached rock in the earth. When the excavation had been made, then rubble was packed down, some 40 cubits in depth, another [part] 20 cubits in depth. On that rubble the palace was constructed.

And that the earth was dug downward, and that the rubble was packed down, and that the sun-dried brick was molded, the Babylonian people – it did [these tasks].

The cedar timber, this – a mountain by name Lebanon – from there was brought. The Assyrian people, it brought it to Babylon; from Babylon the Carians and the Ionians brought it to Susa. The *yaka*-timber was brought from Gandara and from Carmania.

The gold was brought from Sardis and from Bactria, which here was wrought. The precious stone lapis lazuli and carnelian which was wrought here, this was brought from Sogdiana. The precious stone turquoise, this was brought from Chorasmia, which was wrought here.

The silver and the ebony were brought from Egypt. The ornamentation with which the wall was adorned, that from Ionia was brought. The ivory which was wrought here, was brought from Ethiopia and from Sind and from Arachosia.

The stone columns which were here wrought, a village by name Abiradu, in Elam – from there were brought. The stone-cutters who wrought the stone, those were Ionians and Sardians.

The goldsmiths who wrought the gold, those were Medes and Egyptians. The men who wrought the wood, those were Sardians and Egyptians. The men who wrought the baked brick, those were Babylonians. The men who adorned the wall, those were Medes and Egyptians.

Saith Darius the King: At Susa a very excellent [work] was ordered, a very excellent [work] was [brought to completion]. Me may Ahuramazda protect, and Hystaspes my father, and my country.

Susa, Palace of Darius, uncovered *in situ* buried under a threshold in the southern area of the palace

Excavations of J. de Morgan and R. de Mecquenem, 1911

H 22.5 cm, W 26.5 cm, Th 2.5 cm

Louvre, Sb 2789

Scheil 1929: nos 1, 3–34, pls VIII–IX; Kent 1953: DSf; Harper, Aruz and Tallon 1992: 271–2, no. 190

2

2 Silver foundation plaque of Darius I

Foundation boxes containing plaques of gold and silver, each with the same text written in Old Persian, Elamite and Babylonian, were discovered by Ernst Herzfeld in the southeastern and northeastern corners of the main hall of the Apadana at Persepolis. The text reads:

> Darius the Great King, King of Kings, King of countries, son of Hystaspes, an Achaemenian.

> Saith Darius the King: This is the kingdom which I hold, from the Scythians who are beyond Sogdiana, thence unto Ethiopia; from Sind, thence unto Sardis – which Ahuramazda the greatest of the gods bestowed upon me. Me may Ahuramazda protect, and my royal house.

Persepolis, Apadana
H 32.5 cm, W 33 cm, Th 0.2 cm
Tehran, 4116
Schmidt 1953: 70 and 79, figs 42 a–b, 43;
 Kent 1953: DPh; Schmitt 2000: DPh

3 Stone box

Used for the original deposit of a pair of gold and silver foundation plaques.

Persepolis, Apadana
H 15 cm, W 45 cm
Tehran, 25
Schmidt 1953: 79, fig. 43b

3

4, silver coins, obv.

4, silver coins, rev.

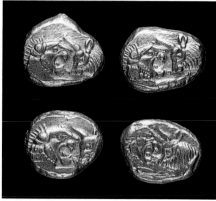

4, gold Croeseids

4 Coin hoard from the Apadana foundation deposit

The coins found in the excavations of the Apadana at Persepolis potentially shed important light on both the history of Greek coinage and the ideology and symbolism of the early Achaemenid Empire. Crucial to both, however, is an appreciation of the date of the deposit. The coins contained fall into two broad categories: gold coins of the type produced by the Achaemenid administration in Sardis (cf. cat. 316), and silver coins of Greek and Cypriot cities. The broad range of dates that can be established from historical and archaeological sources for the foundation of the Apadana at Persepolis provides an important date before which these coins must have been produced. In turn, the choice of coins has suggested to a number of scholars an attempt to chart the boundaries of the empire in the reign of Darius. Given the marginal part that coinage played in much of the empire, however, the use of coinage in this symbolic way must be questioned. It may rather be the case that the coins were deposited, much as they must have been used in Iran at this period, as items of bullion, rather than as geographically significant artefacts.

Four gold and three silver coins were found beneath the southeast foundation deposit:

One silver, uncertain Cypriot mint,
  c. 520–500 BC (Tehran, 33)
One silver, Paphos?, *c.* 520–500 BC (Tehran, 42)
One silver, Lapethus?, *c.* 520–500 BC
  (Tehran, 38)
Four late gold Croeseids, *c.* 520–500 BC
  (Tehran, 8)

Persepolis, Apadana
Tehran, 8, 33, 38, 42
Schmidt 1957: 110, 113–14, pl. 84; Kagan 1994; Meadows 2003

5 Large stone slab with the *Daiva* text of Xerxes

This slab is one of eight examples that were found together in a room in the Garrison Quarters. They were intended as foundation inscriptions, but were never used as such. Five of the slabs are inscribed in Old Persian, two in Babylonian and one in Elamite. This example is in Old Persian. In the inscription Xerxes lists the countries of which he was king, and says that in one of them false gods (*daivas*) were worshipped. He replaced them with the worship of Ahuramazda and Arta ('order', 'truth').

Saith Xerxes the King: when that I became king, there is among these countries which are inscribed above [one which] was in commotion. Afterwards Ahuramazda bore me aid; by the favour of Ahuramazda I smote that country and put it down in its place.

And among these countries there was [a place] where previously false gods were

5

worshipped. Afterwards, by the favour of
Ahuramazda, I destroyed that sanctuary
of the demons, and I made proclamation,
'The demons shall not be worshipped!'
Where previously the demons were
worshipped, there I worshipped
Ahuramazda and Arta reverently.

Persepolis, Room 16, Treasury Fortification
H 53 cm, W 52 cm, Th 10 cm
Tehran, 16
Kent 1953: XPh; Schmidt 1953: fig. 87D–E; Schmidt
   1957: 52–3, pl. 21a; Seipel 2000: 112

6 Cyrus Cylinder

The Cyrus Cylinder was found in 1879 in the
course of Hormuzd Rassam's excavations at
Babylon. A small fragment of the cylinder,
detached at the time of excavation, came into
the collection of Yale University (NBC 2504)
and was rejoined in 1971. The cylindrical form
is typical of royal inscriptions of the Neo-
Babylonian period, and the text shows that the
cylinder was written to be buried in the foundations of the city wall of Babylon. It was deposited there after the capture of the city by Cyrus in
539 BC, and presumably written on his orders.

The text, written in Babylonian script and
language, records that Nabonidus, the last
King of Babylon (555–539 BC), had perverted
the cults of the Babylonian gods, including
Marduk, the city-god of Babylon, and had
imposed labour-service on its free population,
who complained to the gods. The gods
responded by deserting Babylon, but Marduk
looked around for a champion to restore the old
ways. He chose Cyrus, King of Anshan (Persia),
and declared him king of the world. First Cyrus
expanded his kingship over the tribes of Iran
(described as Gutians and Ummanmanda),
ruling them justly. Then Marduk ordered Cyrus
to march on Babylon, which he entered without a fight. Nabonidus was delivered into his
hands and the people of Babylon joyfully
accepted the kingship of Cyrus.

From this point on, the document is written
as if Cyrus himself is speaking: 'I, Cyrus, king
of the world ...'. He presents himself as a worshipper of Marduk who strove for peace in
Babylon and abolished the labour-service of its
population. The people of neighbouring countries brought tribute to Babylon, and Cyrus
claims to have restored their temples and
religious cults, and to have returned their
previously deported gods and people.

The text ends with a note of additional food
offerings in the temples of Babylon and an
account of the rebuilding of Imgur-Enlil, the
city wall of Babylon, during the course of which
an earlier building inscription of Ashurbanipal,
King of Assyria (668–627 BC), was found.

The whole document is written from a
purely Babylonian point of view in traditional
Babylonian terms, and it has been suggested
that its author took the Ashurbanipal inscription as his literary model. There is no acknowledgement that Cyrus himself worshipped the
Iranian god Ahuramazda. He is the tool of
Marduk, just as in the biblical book of Ezra he
is presented as the servant of the god of Israel
who is instructed to rebuild the temple in
Jerusalem and allow the Jews deported by
Nebuchadnezzar II to return home.[1]

Because of its references to just and peaceful
rule, and to the restoration of deported peoples
and their gods the cylinder has in recent years
been referred to in some quarters as a kind of
'charter of human rights'. Such a concept
would have been quite alien to Cyrus's contemporaries, and indeed the cylinder says
nothing of human rights; but the return of the
Jews and of other deported peoples was a
significant reversal of the policies of earlier
Assyrian and Babylonian kings.

Found in March 1879 at Amran, Babylon, during
   the excavations of H. Rassam, and acquired in 1880
L 22.86 cm
British Museum, ANE 90920
Pritchard 1950: 315–16; Walker 1972; Berger 1975

1 Ezra I.2, 7, III.7, V.13, VI.3; see also 2 Chronicles
   XXXVI.22, 23.

COLUMNS

7

7 Small limestone column base

Circular torus on a square double-stepped plinth.

Persepolis
H 46 cm, W 68 cm, Diam 67.5 cm
Persepolis Museum, 3500

8 Small bell-shaped column base

This column base, made of grey limestone with fluted sides, contains a trilingual inscription of Xerxes I (486–465 BC) in Old Persian, Elamite and Babylonian: 'Xerxes, the king, says: by the grace of Ahuramazda, this residence [*hadish*], Darius, the king, has built, he who was my father.'

Susa, Acropolis (not *in situ*, but probably from
   the Palace of Darius)
Excavations of J. de Morgan, 1898
H 39 cm, Diam 55 cm
Louvre, Sb 131
De Morgan 1900: 90, fig. 131; Kent 1953: XSa

9 Massive bell-shaped column base

Made of dark grey stone with carved floral decoration on the sides. From the reign of Xerxes or Artaxerxes I.

Persepolis, Hall of 100 Columns
Obtained from Persepolis by the Oriental Institute
   Expedition, University of Chicago, and transferred
   to the British Museum in 1974
H 98.5 cm, Diam 151 cm (base), Diam 96 cm (top)
British Museum, ANE 136209

8

10 Fragment of torus from a column base in dark grey stone

With the right-hand side of a six-line Elamite inscription and the left-hand side of a five-line Babylonian inscription of Artaxerxes II (404–359 BC). The complete inscription, which would have been recorded in Old Persian, Babylonian and Elamite, would have read:

Saith Artaxerxes the Great King, King of Kings, King of Countries, King in this earth, son of Darius the King, of Darius [who was] son of Artaxerxes the king, of Artaxerxes [who was] son of Xerxes the King, of Xerxes who was son of Darius the King, of Darius who was son of Hystaspes, an Achaemenian. By the favour of Ahuramazda, Anahita and Mithra, this palace [*apadana*] I built. May Ahuramazda, Anahita and Mithra protect me from all evil, and that which I have built may they not shatter or harm.

Hamadan
Found before 1885
H 7 cm, W 12.5 cm, L 51 cm
British Museum, ANE 90854
Knapton, Sarraf and Curtis 2001: 102, fig. 2a;
    Kent 1953: A²Ha

11 Fragment of torus from a column base in dark grey stone

With the right-hand side of a five-line Babylonian inscription and the left-hand side of a seven-line Old Persian inscription of Artaxerxes II (404–359 BC). The complete inscription would have been the same as that in cat. 10.

Hamadan
Found before 1885
H 10 cm, W 16.5 cm, L 51 cm
British Museum, ANE 90855
Knapton, Sarraf and Curtis 2001: 102–4, fig. 2a;
    Kent 1953: A²Ha

9

10

11

61

12 Part of massive stone column capital

In the form of a human-headed bull protome. The human figure has a long beard and wears a horned cap, a mark of divinity.

Persepolis, southern porch of Central Building
H 175 cm, W 80 cm, L 80 cm
Tehran, 2011
Sami 1970: fig. on p. 173

12

13

13 Fragment of massive column capital

In polished dark grey stone, showing part of a human-headed bull protome, preserving one bull's leg and the beard from a human head.

Persepolis
H 43 cm, W 30 cm, L 37 cm
Persepolis Museum, 1544

14

14 Fragment of a human head from a column capital

Made in black polished stone.

Persepolis
H 53 cm, W 44 cm, Th 48 cm
Persepolis Museum, 1535
Sami 1955: fig. between 26 and 27

15 Massive stone lion's paw from a column capital

Column capitals such as this, showing the foreparts of two lions back to back, occur only in the Apadana.

Persepolis, Apadana
H 36 cm, W 53 cm
Tehran, 2014

15

16 Reconstructed column

The capital is in the form of two bull protomes
back to back. Beneath them is elaborate volute
decoration surmounting a palm capital supported by pendant leaf mouldings. The
column base is bell-shaped with carved floral
decoration. The fluted column shaft would
originally have been much taller. This is an
example of one of the small columns from
Persepolis.

Persepolis, southern portico of Apadana
H 3.7 m, W 1.9 m (capital), Diam 76 cm (base)
Tehran, 397

18

18 Gold finger-ring

This ring has a slender rounded hoop and
pointed oval bezel engraved with a pair of bull
protomes joined back to back.

Oxus Treasure
Bequeathed in 1897 by A.W. Franks
Diam 2.15 cm (hoop), 1.7 cm (bezel), Wt 6.5 g
British Museum, ANE 124007
Dalton 1964: no. 106

17

17 Terracotta architectural ornament

Ornaments such as this example, in the form
of the foreparts of a bull with folded legs, may
have been influenced by the column capitals
showing double bull protomes. Possibly post-
Achaemenid (second century BC).

Susa, southern part of Ville Royale
Excavations of J. de Mecquenem, 1935
H 22 cm, W 17 cm
Louvre, Sb 3080
De Mecquenem 1943: 63–4, fig. 52

19 Stamp seal

The foreparts of three bulls on this discoid
white chalcedony seal rotate towards the right
around concentric circles. In the field are a
lozenge and a crescent. For a similar seal, cf.
cat. 293.

Old acquisition, no information about provenance
H 1.2 cm, Diam 2.5 cm (base)
British Museum, ANE 127400

19

16

PERSEPOLIS RELIEFS

20 Plaster casts of stone reliefs

These were taken from the bottom register on the west wing of the north side of the Apadana at Persepolis.

The north and east sides of the Apadana have decorative schemes that are basically mirror images of each other, although there are some important differences in minor details. On each face, twenty-three delegations from around the Persian Empire are shown bringing presents for the king. The delegations are depicted in three registers walking towards the central staircase, while on the opposite side there are nobles in Persian and Median dress, and guards also facing the central staircase. Each of the delegations is led by an usher in Median or Persian dress, and the individual delegations are separated by cypress trees. These reliefs were originally brightly painted. The reliefs on the north face of the Apadana have been partially exposed for many centuries, and in some cases are now badly weathered, while those on the east face were uncovered by the Chicago expedition in the 1930s and are now in a much better state of preservation. In 1892, when the Weld-Blundell expedition made these casts, only the reliefs on the north face were accessible. Those in the bottom register are in better condition than those in the higher registers, which is presumably why they were chosen for casting (see overleaf for detailed description).

H 1.21 m, L 15.26 m

Harcourt-Smith 1931: no. 4; 1932: pls 3–4, 5a;
　Schmidt 1953: pls 32A, 35A, 38A, 41A, 44A, 61

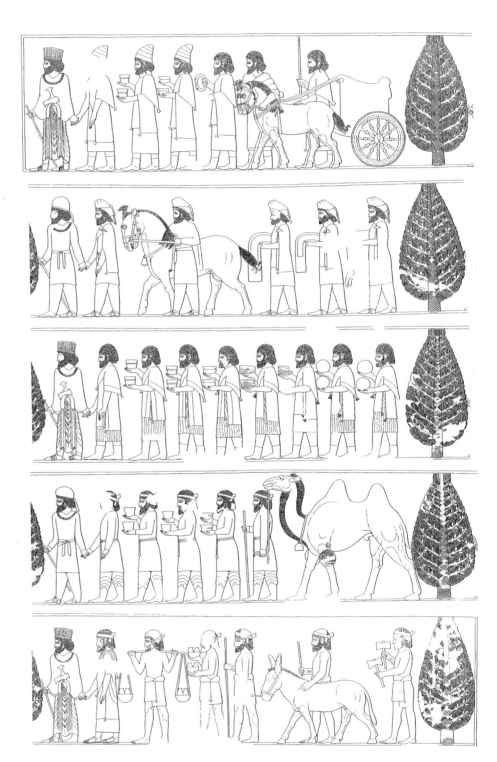

Below is the north side of the Apadana at Persepolis showing the twenty-three tribute delegations bringing presents to the king. Pieces from the upper register were removed by early travellers to Persepolis and are now distributed in museums around the world.

On this series of casts five different delegations are shown. They are, from left to right:

Delegation VI. Lydians, led by an usher in Persian dress. They wear cloaks and beehive-shaped hats, and bring bowls, bracelets and a chariot pulled by two small horses.

Delegation IX. Cappadocians, led by an usher in Median dress. They wear trouser-suits and cloaks fastened at the shoulder with Phrygian fibulae and ridged hats with tied ear-pieces. They bring a horse and folded costumes.

Delegation XII. Ionians, led by an usher in Persian dress. They are bare-headed, wear cloaks with a fringe at the bottom, and bring bowls, lengths of cloth and balls of wool.

Delegation XV. Probably Parthians, or Bactrians, led by an usher in Median dress. They wear headbands and belted tunics over pleated trousers tucked into high boots, and bring bowls and a two-humped Bactrian camel.

Delegation XVIII. Indians, led by an usher in Persian dress. Except for the leader they are bare-footed and wear only a skirt (*dhoti*) and a hairband, and bring a donkey, axes and jars carried by hand and in panier-bags.

21

21 Fragment of stone corner block with relief decoration

The relief shows a bearded figure in Persian dress wearing a headdress, facing left and holding a staff in his left hand with the right hand folded over his left wrist.

Persepolis, Apadana, north façade of northwest staircase (cf. Schmidt 1953: pl. 25B–C)

Obtained at Persepolis in 1811 and presented by the 5th Earl of Aberdeen in 1861

H 58 cm, W 23.5 cm, Th 14 cm

British Museum, ANE 118864

Barnett 1957: no. 20, pl. XXI, no. 3; Mitchell 2000: pl. XXIa

22

23

22 Fragment of stone relief showing a bearded figure in Persian dress

The figure, facing right, is wearing a torc, twisted headband and circular earrings, with a short sword (*akinakes*) in his belt.

Persepolis, Apadana, east wing of north staircase. Probably the top part of the figure introducing the royal chariots (see Schmidt 1953: pl. 57; cf. pl. 52)

Obtained at Persepolis in 1811 and presented by the 5th Earl of Aberdeen in 1861

H 51 cm, W 24.5 cm

British Museum, ANE 118848

Barnett 1957: no. 5, pl. XV/2; Mitchell 2000: 52, pl. XXIIa

23 Stone relief showing two grooms

The figures are depicted in Median dress, facing right, and carrying saddlecloths and whips.

Persepolis, north side of Apadana, east wing

Obtained at Persepolis in 1811 and presented by Sir Gore Ouseley in 1825

H 32 cm, W 75 cm

British Museum, ANE 118839

Ouseley 1821: pl. XLVI; Barnett 1957: no. 1, pls XV/1, XVIII/2; Curtis 2000: 51, fig. 53; Mitchell 2000: pl. XXIIe

24 Fragment of stone relief showing the leg of a stool

Decorated with flanges, a lion's paw and a floral moulding. This is possibly being carried on the back of the royal groom (cat. 23) and is perhaps a mounting stool. Such stools would have been made of wood with elaborate bronze fittings.

Persepolis, Apadana, east wing of north staircase (see Schmidt 1953: pl. 58; cf. Schmidt 1953: pls 51–2)

Possibly obtained at Persepolis in 1811 and presented by the Royal Institution in 1870

H 30.5 cm, W 7.6 cm

British Museum, ANE 118847

Barnett 1957: no. 2, pl. XVIII/2; Mitchell 2000: 53

24

25

25 Fragment of stone relief showing a charioteer

The figure is standing in a chariot box, the front part of which is preserved. It has rosettes around the edge. There is a quiver on the front of the box and another (only the top of which is visible) mounted on the side. The charioteer holds a stick, and reins that pass over the backs of two horses and run through a terret that is set on the yoke. There is a fan-shaped yoke ornament above the terret and a tassel hangs down from the yoke.

The heads of the horses are preserved on a fragment that is now in the Miho Museum in

Japan. This fragment was found with the main piece at Persepolis in 1811, but was apparently given to Sir Gore Ouseley and became part of his collection. It passed to his son Sir Frederick Ouseley who founded a school called St Michael's College in Tenbury, England. After the school closed down in 1985 the relief was sold at auction and was eventually purchased by the Miho Museum. A cast of this piece is shown in the exhibition. It would originally have been part of a scene that showed a procession of Persian guards, followed by an usher and four grooms carrying whips, saddle cloths and a stool, then an usher with three horses and grooms, and finally another usher

with two royal chariots each pulled by two horses.

Persepolis, Apadana, top register of east wing of north staircase

Obtained at Persepolis in 1811 by the Hon. Robert Gordon, a member of Sir Gore Ouseley's mission to Persia, and given to his brother the 4th Earl of Aberdeen, who presented it to the British Museum in 1817

H 56 cm, W 88 cm

British Museum, ANE 118843

Ouseley 1821: pl. XLV; Barnett 1957: no. 7, pls 15/3; 18/1; Curtis 1998; Mitchell 2000; Curtis 2000: 51, fig. 52

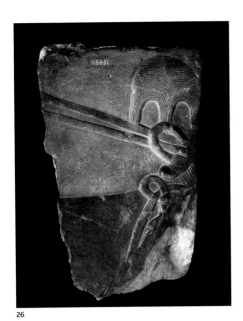

26

27

26 Fragment of stone relief showing part of a horse and chariot

On this fragment can be seen part of a draught horse, two reins and part of the yoke, harness and yoke ornament of a chariot facing right. The yoke ornament is decorated with a hair-like pattern. There are traces of red pigment on the right edge.

Persepolis, Apadana, top register of east wing
  of north staircase
Obtained at Persepolis in 1811 and presented
  by the 5th Earl of Aberdeen in 1861
H 17.5 cm, W 18 cm, Th 10 cm
British Museum, ANE 118851
Barnett 1957: no. 8; Mitchell 2000; Ambers and
  Simpson 2005: 6–7

27 Fragment of cornerstone relief with two figures (one on each face)

On one face can be seen a guard in Persian dress, facing left. On the other is a figure in Persian dress, facing right, holding a staff in his right hand, with his left hand placed over his right forearm.

Persepolis, Apadana, possibly from northwest
  staircase
Obtained at Persepolis in 1811 and presented
  by the 4th Earl of Aberdeen in 1818
H 58 cm, W 33 cm, Th 21.50 cm
British Museum, ANE 118844
Barnett 1957: no. 21, pl. XX/2; Mitchell 2000:
  pl. XXId

28 Fragment of stone relief showing the top part of a guard in Persian dress

The guard is armed with a spear and bow, and carries a bowcase. He is facing left and ascending a staircase, and above him is a border of rosettes.

Persepolis, north side of Apadana, south side
  of northwest staircase
Obtained at Persepolis in 1811 and presented
  by the 4th Earl of Aberdeen in 1818
H 58 cm, W 42 cm
British Museum, ANE 118845
Barnett 1957: no. 4, pl. XX/4; Mitchell 2000:
  pl. XXIb; Curtis 2000: 50, fig. 51

28

71

29

29 Fragment of stone relief showing a guard in Persian dress

The guard is facing left and holding a spear in both hands, with a bow over his left shoulder and a quiver on his back.

Persepolis, Apadana, probably from north
   or northwest flight of north staircase
   (cf. Schmidt 1953: pl. 55/6)
Obtained at Persepolis in 1811 and presented
   by the 5th Earl of Aberdeen in 1861
H 35 cm, W 26 cm, Th 14 cm
British Museum, ANE 118866
Ouseley 1821: pl. XLV; Barnett 1957: no. 10,
   pl. XIX/1; Mitchell 2000: pl. XXIIb

30 Fragment of stone relief showing a guard in Persian dress

The guard is facing right with a *dipylon*, or figure-of-eight shield, on his left side and a spear in his right hand.

Persepolis, Apadana, north staircase
   (see Schmidt 1953, pl. 53)
Obtained at Persepolis in 1811 and presented
   by Sir Gore Ouseley in 1825
H 90 cm, W 60 cm
British Museum, ANE 118837
Ouseley 1821: pl. XLVI; Barnett 1957: no. 13,
   pl. XX/3; Mitchell 2000: pl. XXIId

31 Fragment of stone relief showing the head of a bearded Persian

The head is incomplete, but is wearing a head-dress and facing left.

Persepolis, Apadana, probably from south face
   of inner or outer flight of north staircase
   (cf. Schmidt 1953: pl. 86)
Purchased from Messrs Rollin & Feuardent, Paris,
   in 1895
H 13 cm, W 12 cm
British Museum, ANE 92253
Barnett 1957: no. 11; Mitchell 2000: 53

31

30

32 Fragment of stone relief showing two guards in Persian dress

Both guards are facing right and hold a spear.

Persepolis, Apadana. Compare east staircase,
  western façade of northern parapet of inner
  landing, Apadana (Schmidt 1953: 82–3,
  pl. 26A–B)
H 70 cm, W 50 cm
Louvre, AO 14051
Contenau 1934: 99–103; 1947: 2264, fig. 1287

33 Stone relief showing a file of four so-called Susian guards

The figures are facing right and armed with
spears.

Persepolis, north side of Apadana, upper register
  of east wing
Obtained at Persepolis in 1811 and presented
  by Sir Gore Ouseley in 1825
H 60 cm, L 107 cm
British Museum, ANE 118838
Ouseley 1821: pl. XLVI; Barnett 1957: no. 3,
  pls XV/2, XVII/2; Curtis 2000: 50, fig. 50; Mitchell
  2000: pl. 22c

32

33

34

35 Fragment of stone relief showing a bearded man

The man is facing left and wears a belted tunic and pendant earrings. He holds a staff in his right hand and leads on a rope a camel of which only the nose survives.

Persepolis, north staircase of Apadana, probably part of delegation XIII (Bactrians) (cf. Schmidt 1953: pl. 39)
Purchased from Messrs Rollin & Feuardent, Paris, in 1894
H 44 cm, W 34 cm, Th 14 cm
British Museum, ANE 118869
Barnett 1957: no. 9, pl. XVI/5; Mitchell 2000: 53

34 Fragment of stone relief showing a figure carrying an elephant tusk

The figure, facing left, has tightly curled hair; behind him is the nose of an animal that is being led on a rope. It can be deduced from the well-preserved east side of the Apadana (which is a mirror image of the north side from which this fragment comes) that this piece belongs to a scene showing delegation XXIII bringing presents to the king. The delegation consists of three people from Ethiopia (Kush). The first is led by the hand by a Median noble, the second carries a covered jar and the third (as on this fragment) carries an elephant tusk and leads an animal that has been variously identified as an okapi, a giraffe or a 'gnu'.

Persepolis, Apadana, west wing of north staircase
H 27.3 cm, W 36.8 cm, Th 18 cm
Tehran, 2005
Sami 1955: fig. between 20 and 21; Seipel 2000: no. 111

35

36

36 Fragment of stone relief showing a bearded man

The man wears a belted tunic and is facing left, on a staircase and leading a tributary represented by the front part of his bearded face. There is a fragment of a tree on the left side of the relief.

Persepolis, north staircase of Apadana, part of
  delegation XIX (possibly Thracians or Skudrians)
  (see Schmidt 1953, pl. 45a)
Obtained at Persepolis in 1811 and presented
  by the 5th Earl of Aberdeen in 1861
H 28 cm, W 37.3 cm
British Museum, ANE 118857
Ouseley 1821: pl. XLV; Barnett 1957: no. 15,
  pl. XVI/1; Mitchell 2000: pl. XXe

37 Stone panel with part of a trilingual inscription concerning Ahuramazda

The inscription on these pieces is in Old Persian. Part of a cypress tree in relief is preserved on the right of the slab.

Persepolis, Apadana, north side of right stairwell
  column
Obtained at Persepolis in 1811 and presented
  by Sir Gore Ouseley in 1825
Max. H 35 cm, W 61 cm and 80 cm
British Museum, ANE 118840 and 118841
Ouseley 1821: pl. XLVI; Kent 1953: XPb;
  Mitchell 2000: 49–52; Schmitt 2000: XPb

37

38 Plaster cast of stone relief decoration

Taken from the east jamb of the eastern doorway in the southern wall of the Hall of 100 Columns at Persepolis (illustrated opposite). The decoration shows a king, probably Xerxes, sitting on a throne, and holding a staff and flower. An attendant holding a fly-whisk stands behind the throne. Above the king is a canopy (baldaqin) richly decorated with files of bulls (above) and lions (below), and representations of the winged disc. Above the canopy, and at the top of the relief, is Ahuramazda in a winged disc. He holds a lotus flower in his left hand. The king's throne is supported on a gigantic platform (*takht*) in the form of an elaborate stool with lion's paws. The stool incorporates fourteen supporting figures with arms upraised arranged in three rows. All the figures are different and represent peoples from around the Persian Empire. There is uncertainty about the identity of some figures, but the following seems most likely:[1]

TOP ROW: Elamite, Armenian, Lydian, Assyrian

MIDDLE ROW: Egyptian, Ionian (?), Gandaran, Sagartian (?), Sogdian

BOTTOM ROW: Skudrian, Scythian, Arab, Libyan, Scythian

Cast made by the Weld-Blundell expedition
  to Persepolis in 1892
H 7.69 m, W 2.87 m
Harcourt-Smith 1931: no. 1 and plate; 1932: no. 1,
  pls 1–2; Schmidt 1953: pls 107, 110; Walser 1966:
  fig. 6; Curtis 2000: pl. 59

1 Based on Roaf 1983: 130.

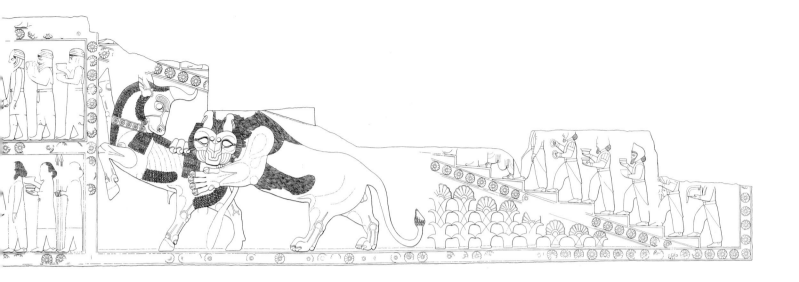

39 Plaster casts of the stone reliefs on the western façade of the west staircase of the Palace of Darius (*tachara*) at Persepolis (opposite)

The reliefs were probably added in the reign of Artaxerxes III (359–338 BC) and show on the left and right figures ascending staircases (see details overleaf). On either side of the central panel are scenes of a lion clinging onto the back of a bull and biting into its hindquarters. This is one of the most powerful images in Achaemenid art, but its exact significance is unknown. Around the edges of the façade is a palm-tree decoration.

The figures climbing the staircase on the left side are amost entirely missing, but we can see they had bare feet and long dresses. The first six figures on the right side are wearing trouser-suits, and pointed hats or helmets that cover the ears and are tied under the chin. Their tunics have bands of decoration on the upper part and on the sleeves. They bear gifts that include bracelets and bowls. In front of them are traces of figures wearing Persian dress. In the central panel are depicted groups of people bringing gifts. Those on the left (facing right) are led by a figure in Median dress wearing a trouser-suit and domed hat, and those on the right (facing left) are led by figures in Persian dress.

The group at the top left wear belted dresses, hairbands, boots and laces. They bring bowls and an animal skin, and can be compared with delegation VIII (Assyrians) on the Apadana.

The group at the bottom left wear trouser-suits, and helmets that cover the ears and are tied under the chin. They have elaborately decorated trousers and tunics with bands of decoration on the sleeves. They bring bracelets with animal terminals and a folded costume. There is no exact parallel on the Apadana reliefs, but their costumes have some similarities with those worn by the figures climbing the staircase on this façade, in particular the bands of decoration on the sleeves. This feature is also found on a gold plaque in the Oxus Treasure (cat. 213).

The group at the top right wear trousers tucked into high boots, belted tunics and turbans. They bring an amphora and bowls. Their costume is similar to that of delegation VII (Drangians) on the Apadana.

The group at the bottom right are bareheaded and wear trousers and belted tunics. They bring bowls and spears.

In the centre is a panel of inscription in Old Persian cuneiform as follows:

A great god is Ahuramazda, who created this earth, who created yonder sky, who created man, who created happiness for man, who made me Artaxerxes king, one king of many, one lord of many.

I am the son [of] Artaxerxes the King, [of] Artaxerxes [who was] the son [of] Darius the king, [of] Darius [who was] the son [of] Artaxerxes the king, [of] Artaxerxes [who was] the son [of] Xerxes the king, [of] Xerxes [who was] the son [of] Darius the king, [of] Darius [who was] the son of Hystaspes by name, of Hystaspes [who was] the son [of] Arsames by name, an Achaemenian.

Saith Artaxerxes the King: This stone staircase was built by me in my time.

Saith Artaxerxes the King: Me may Ahuramazda and the god Mithras protect, and this country, and what was built by me. (Kent 1953: A3Pa)

Casts made by the Weld-Blundell expedition to Persepolis in 1892
Max. H 2.18 m, L 13.41 m
Harcourt-Smith 1931: no. 2 and plate; 1932: pls 6, 7b; Schmidt 1953: pls 152–5; Calmeyer 1980: pl. I; Schmitt 2000: A³Pa

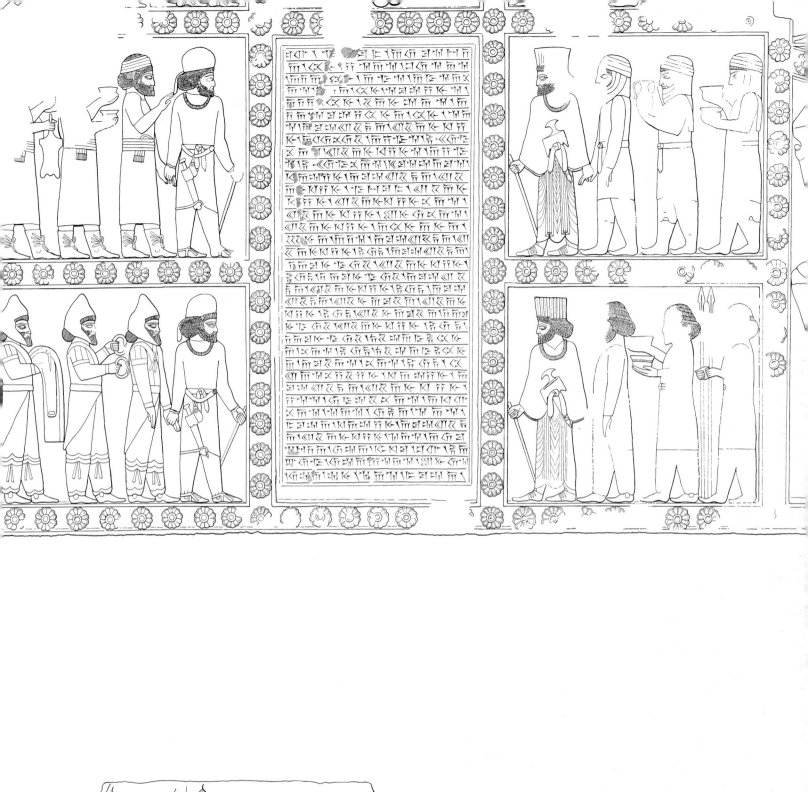

40 Stone relief showing a figure in 'Median' dress

The figure is ascending stairs to the right, carrying a covered goblet and wearing a short sword (*akinakes*).

Persepolis, Palace of Darius, probably from north
  wing of west staircase
Reign of Artaxerxes III
Purchased from Messrs Rollin & Feuardent, Paris,
  in 1894
H 75 cm, W 40 cm, Th 13 cm
British Museum, ANE 118868
Barnett 1957: no. 17, pl. 21/1; Curtis 2000: 53,
  fig. 57

41 Cast of relief showing the royal hero in combat with a monster

The composite monster facing to the left has the foreparts of a lion, the horns of a bull, the crest, wings and hindlegs of an eagle, and a scorpion's tail. The Persian royal hero, facing to the right, grasps the monster by its horn and plunges a short sword or dagger into its belly.

Persepolis, Palace of Darius, north jamb, southern
  doorway, west wall of main hall
Cast made by the Weld-Blundell expedition
  to Persepolis in 1892
H 2.54 m, W 1.39 m
Harcourt-Smith 1931: no. 8; Schmidt 1953: pl. 145B

42 Cast of relief showing the royal hero in combat with a monster

The composite monster is similar to cat. 41 above, but facing to the right; the Persian royal hero is facing to the left.

Persepolis, 'Harem' of Xerxes, north jamb, eastern
  doorway of main hall
Cast made by the Weld-Blundell expedition
  to Persepolis in 1892
H 2.54 m, W 1.39 m
Harcourt-Smith 1931: no. 10; Harcourt-Smith
  1932: pl. 11; Schmidt 1953: pl. 196A

43 Fragment of stone relief showing the head of a Median noble

The nobleman is facing to the right, and wearing a dome-shaped headdress and circular earring.

Persepolis, north staircase of Tripylon
Possibly reign of Artaxerxes I (cf. Schmidt
  1953: 107–11, pl. 72A–C)
H 22.2 cm, W 24 cm
Louvre, AO 17278
Contenau 1947: 2265, fig. 1288

43

44 Stone relief showing gift-bearers with a vase

Persepolis, probably from Palace of Artaxerxes I
H 36 cm, W 44 cm, Th 52 cm (60 cm along
  broken face)
Persepolis Museum, 553

44

45 Stone relief showing possibly a Sogdian gift-bearer carrying a jar

Persepolis, probably from Palace of Artaxerxes I
H 48 cm, W 35 cm, Th 12.0 cm
Persepolis Museum, 806

46 Stone relief showing a winged sphinx

The creature has a bearded male head and wears a horned headdress. There is a border of rosettes at top and bottom, and a stylized palm tree to the left. Originally this sphinx would have been one of a pair flanking a winged-disc figure of Ahuramazda. There are traces of green pigment on the earring.

Persepolis, originally set up on a façade of Palace G, constructed by Artaxerxes III; later transferred to north staircase of Palace H
Uncovered by Colonel John Kinneir MacDonald in 1826 and removed from the site by Dr John McNeill in 1828. Presented by the National Art Collections Fund in 1938
H 82.1 cm, W 75 cm, Th 9 cm
British Museum, ANE 129381
Barnett 1957: no. 22, pl. XXI/4; Curtis 2000: 53, fig. 55; Ambers and Simpson 2005: 9–11

47 Stone relief showing a priest or servant in Median dress

The figure, facing left, is carrying a goat and climbing a staircase.

Persepolis, precise location unknown but probably Palace G
Reign of Artaxerxes III
H 75 cm, W 38 cm, Th 13 cm
Louvre, AO 14050
Contenau 1934: 99–103; 1947: 2260, fig. 1282

47

48

48 Fragment of stone relief showing a figure facing left

The figure wears a Median belted tunic and domed hat, and carries a short sword and scabbard (*akinakes*). There is a border of rosettes above.

Persepolis, possibly from Palace G or west staircase
  of Apadana
Reign of Artaxerxes III
H 72 cm, W 31 cm, Th 9 cm
Tehran, 2006
Seipel 2000: no. 110

49 Fragment of stone relief showing a guardsman

The figure is facing right and holds a spear; his face is largely obliterated.

Persepolis, old collection
H 16.30 cm, W 27 cm
British Museum, ANE 134385
Mitchell 2000: 54

49

SUSA RELIEF

50

50 Fragmentary stone relief showing a priest or servant in Persian dress and wearing a turban

The figure is mounting a staircase and holding a covered vessel in both hands. He is following a partly preserved figure wearing a Median trouser-suit.

Susa, from the so-called 'Donjon' area at southern
end of the Ville Royale. Possibly reused from the
Shaur palace (see Boucharlat 1997: 60–61)
H 45.5 cm, W 54.5 cm, Th 16 cm
Louvre, Sb 8835
Cf. de Mecquenem 1934: 222–6, fig. 71; Harper,
Aruz and Tallon 1992: 217, 236–7

GLAZED BRICKS FROM SUSA

51 Panel made up of polychrome glazed bricks showing a guard

The guard is dressed in a richly decorated Persian costume with a bow, quiver and spear, facing right. Originally this figure would have been part of a procession of similar guards, perhaps the 'Immortals' who formed the king's personal bodyguard. The bricks are made of 'faience' in brown, yellow, white, green and black.

Susa, reconstructed from bricks found by Dieulafoy, de Morgan and de Mecquenem in area around entrance of Palace of Darius, western part of 'cour est'

H 189 cm, W 70 cm

On permanent loan from the Musée du Louvre

British Museum, ANE 132525

Cf. Dieulafoy 1893: 280–92, figs 154–64, pls IV–VI; de Mecquenem 1947: 47–54; Harper, Aruz and Tallon 1992: 226–8, nos 155–6

Curtis 2000: 45, fig. 47

52

52 Panel made up of polychrome glazed bricks showing a guard

Panel similar to cat. 51 above.

Susa, old collection, reconstructed 1999–2000
H 194.6 cm, W 81 cm
Louvre, Sb 21965

53 Glazed brick

This almost complete polychrome brick shows part of a dress decorated with a 'fortress' pattern worn by an archer facing right. The fortresses set within the squares each have three towers.

Susa, from area around entrance of Palace of Darius,
    western part of 'cour est'
H 8.5 cm, W 33 cm, Th 12 cm
Louvre, Sb 21240
Cf. Dieulafoy 1893: 280–92, figs 154–64, pls IV–VI
De Mecquenem 1947: 47–54

53

NINE FRAGMENTS OF POLYCHROME GLAZED BRICK
FROM STAIRCASE PANELS AT SUSA (CATS 54–65)

Several of the staircases in the Palace of Darius had polychrome glazed-brick decoration showing alternating Persian and Median priests, or servants climbing staircases and carrying live animals or food. Some of the fragments here (cats 54–5, 57–9) come from a staircase showing figures mounting from the left; others (cats 60–62) come from a staircase showing figures mounting from the right. This glazed-brick decoration, in relief or on flat bricks, is very similar to the stone decoration from Artaxerxes' palace at Shaur, Susa (cf. Louvre, Sb 3781 and Louvre, Sb 8835), and from Persepolis. Below are drawings of reconstructed stairway panels from the Palace of Darius at Susa showing the possible original positions of the glazed brick fragments (after drawing by Audran Labrousse).

54 Fragment of a brick showing the head of a Persian priest or servant in relief

The figure, facing right, is wearing a white turban. Curls of hair are visible on the forehead, but he is apparently lacking a moustache and beard. He is probably a Persian priest or servant carrying provisions up a staircase, according to reliefs found at Susa and Persepolis showing similar figures.

Susa, from a staircase in the Palace of Darius
  decorated with figures moving to the right
Excavations of J. de Mecquenem
H 8 cm, W 13 cm, Th 7.5 cm
Louvre, Sb 18653
Harper, Aruz and Tallon 1992: 233–4, no. 161

55 Fragment of a brick showing an elaborately decorated costume

The costume was probably worn by a priest or servant in Persian dress mounting a staircase and carrying provisions.

Susa, from a staircase in the Palace of Darius
  decorated with figures moving to the right
H 8 cm, W 11 cm
Louvre, Sb 14419

56 Fragment of a brick showing part of an elaborately decorated costume

The costume is worn by a figure in Persian dress, possibly mounting a staircase. It has also been suggested that this brick could be part of a frieze showing a conquering king standing on an enemy, as at Bisitun (Canby 1979: 315–20, figs 1–3, pl. 50: 2).

Susa, possibly from a staircase in the Palace of
  Darius decorated with figures moving to the right
H 8 cm, W 15 cm
Louvre, Sb 14233

54

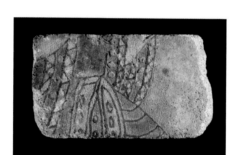

55

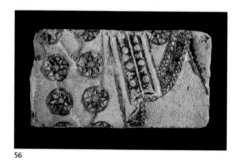

56

57

58

57 Fragment of a brick showing two feet

The figures are either moving to the right or ascending a staircase. The one in front wears a Median trouser-suit with highly decorated trousers and shoes fastened with ties; and the figure behind wears Persian dress leaving the ankles bare and shoes fastened with thongs and studs.

Susa, from a staircase in the Palace of Darius
  decorated with figures moving to the right
H 8.5 cm, W 11 cm, Th 12.5 cm
Louvre, Sb 14426

58 Fragment of a brick

This fragment shows a similar scene to that in cat. 57.

Susa, from a staircase in the Palace of Darius
  decorated with figures moving to the right
H 8.5 cm, W 15 cm, Th 8 cm
Louvre, Sb 14427
Harper, Aruz and Tallon 1992: 239, no. 168

59 Fragment of a brick with a representation of a hand

The hand probably belonged to a priest or servant, perhaps holding a vessel represented now only by a knob on the lid. The figure wears a bracelet.

Susa, from a staircase in the Palace of Darius
  decorated with figures moving to the right
H 4.7 cm, W 10.7 cm, Th 7.5 cm
Louvre, Sb 14232
Harper, Aruz and Tallon 1992: 235, no. 164

59

60

61

62

63

64

65

60 Fragment of a brick decorated in relief with the head of a kid or lamb

The animal, facing left, is probably being carried by a Median or Persian priest or servant.

Susa, from a staircase in the Palace of Darius
  decorated with figures moving to the left
H 8 cm, W 13.5 cm, Th 11 cm
Louvre, Sb 18652

61 Fragment of a brick decorated in relief with the forelegs of a kid or lamb

The animal, facing left, is being carried by a priest or servant. The figure, probably a Mede, is wearing a richly decorated costume with sleeves.

Susa, from a staircase in the Palace of Darius
  decorated with figures moving to the left
H 8 cm, W 15 cm, Th 13 cm
Louvre, Sb 14392
Harper, Aruz and Tallon 1992: 238–9, no. 167

62 Fragment of a brick showing a duck's head decorating an elaborate tray

The tray is probably being carried by a Persian or Median priest or servant moving to the left.

Susa, from a staircase in the Palace of Darius
  decorated with figures moving to the left
H 5 cm, W 7.5 cm, Th 5 cm
Louvre, Sb 18654

63 Glazed brick with part of foundation inscription of Darius in Old Persian

This glazed brick, together with cats 64 and 65, was part of a monumental inscription which made up the glazed decoration in the Palace of Darius at Susa. The inscription was written in three languages (Old Persian, Elamite and Babylonian) and contains a version of the foundation inscription of Darius (DSf; cf. cat. 1).

Susa, Apadana
Excavations of J. de Morgan

H *c.* 10 cm, L *c.* 35 cm, Th *c.* 15 cm
Louvre, Sb 3340
Chevalier 1997: no. 22: 194 and fig. 98

64 Glazed brick with part of foundation inscription of Darius in Elamite

Susa, Apadana
Excavations of J. de Morgan
H 8 cm, W 34 cm, Th 12 cm
Louvre, Sb 3341
Scheil 1929: 54–5; Chevalier 1997: no. 20: 194
  and fig. 96

65 Glazed brick with part of foundation inscription of Darius in Babylonian

Susa, Apadana
Excavations of J. de Morgan
H 8.5 cm, W 35 cm, Th 10.5 cm
Louvre, Sb 3342
Scheil 1929: 55–6; Chevalier 1997: no. 21: 194
  and fig. 97

SEALS SHOWING THE 'PERSIAN ROYAL HERO'

66 Stamp seal showing the royal hero in combat with a winged bull

On this conoid, grey chalcedony seal, the Persian royal hero, facing right, holds a sword in his lowered right hand and grasps a rearing winged bull by the throat.

Old acquisition, no information about provenance
H 2.5 cm, Diam 2 cm (base)
British Museum, ANE 89893

67 Stamp seal showing the royal hero in combat with lion-griffins

On this conoid, greyish-blue chalcedony seal, the Persian royal hero stands on addorsed, winged, pedestal sphinxes and grasps two lion-griffins by the throat.

Purchased in 1899 from Moss & Co.
H 2.8 cm, Diam 2.1–2.4 cm (base)
British Museum, ANE E 30755

68 Cylinder seal showing the royal hero in combat with lion-griffins

On this seal of banded grey and white agate the Persian royal hero, facing left, grasps two rampant winged lion-griffins by the throat.

Acquired from G. Eastwood in 1885
H 2.2 cm, Diam 1.15 cm
British Museum, ANE 89549
Merrillees 2005: no. 48

69 Stamp seal showing the royal hero in combat with lion-griffins and lions

This conoid seal is made of banded white, grey and brown artificially dyed sardonyx. Depicted is the Persian royal hero standing on two confronted pedestal lion-griffins and grasping two inverted lions by their hindlegs.

Old acquisition, no information about provenance
H 3.1 cm, Diam 2.5 cm (base)
British Museum, ANE 89891
Pope 1938: IV, pl. 124L

71

70 Cylinder seal showing the royal hero grasping two lions by the mane

The stylized tree at the end of the scene is of Babylonian type. An Aramaic inscription gives the name of the owner: *bl'tn*, perhaps 'Bel has given'. The seal is made of orange-brown jasper.

Ex Spencer-Churchill Collection. A previous owner, the Revd H.O. Reichardt, wrote in 1883 that it was said to have come from northern Lebanon
H 2.7 cm, Diam 1.4 cm
British Museum, ANE 134761
Merrillees 2005: no. 50

71 Cylinder seal showing a double contest scene

A Persian royal hero below a winged disc grasps two lions, each by a hindleg; a second Persian royal hero holds a short sword in his right hand and the horn of a winged human-headed bull in his left. Made of blue chalcedony with gold caps decorated by granulation.

Said to come from Rudbar, Gilan
H 3.3 cm, Diam 1.3 cm
Tehran, 5941

72 Cylinder seal showing a double contest scene

A figure in a draped, fringed garment holds a whip at his side, places one foot on the leg of a fleeing bull and grasps it by the horn. The Persian royal hero holds a short sword at his side and grasps an inverted lion by the hindleg. There is a base-line beneath the scene and a double line above. The engraving is unusual and resembles that of some archaic Greek gems. The seal is made of grey-brown chalcedony.

Borsippa
Ex Rich Collection; purchased from Mary Rich in 1825
H 4.9 cm, Diam 2.25 cm
British Museum, ANE 89337
Pope 1938: 1V, pl. 124B; Merillees 2005: no. 30

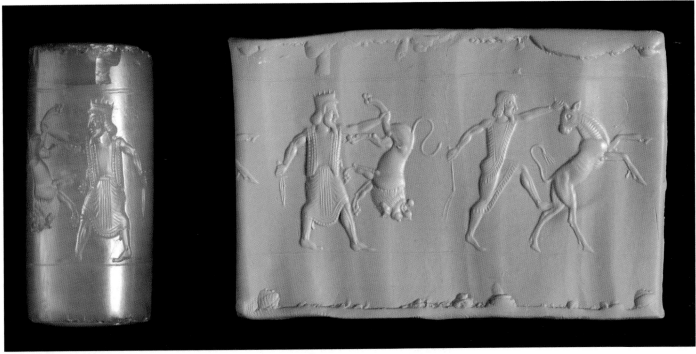

72

73 Cylinder seal showing the royal hero in combat with bulls

The Persian royal hero stands on addorsed winged and crowned pedestal sphinxes, on which stand rampant bulls that turn back to look at the hero who grasps each of them by a horn.

Marina D. Giovino has pointed out that the symbols at the end of the scene are Egyptian hieroglyphs for the name Ahmose. This could be Ahmose, son of Pharaoh Ahmose II (570–526 BC) of the 26th Dynasty. Below is a small seated archer facing left, with a feathered headdress and a quiver on his back; this motif dates back to the time of Tutankhamun. The stone – banded brown and white artificially dyed sardonyx – was carefully chosen so that the banding frames the scene.

Acquired from J. Bonomi in 1835
H 3.15 cm, Diam 1.0 cm
British Museum, ANE 89585
Merrillees 2005: no. 56

74 Cylinder seal showing hero in combat with a lion

The Persian hero aims an arrow at a rampant lioness; she suckles a cub that stands on its hindlegs on another reclining cub. A Bes figure stands at the side with a horned animal slung across his shoulders. Made of blue chalcedony.

Ex Southesk Collection; purchased with the
    assistance of the National Art Collections Fund
    in 1945
H 2.4 cm, Diam 1.2 cm
British Museum, ANE 129571
Boardman 2000: 161, fig. 5:12; Merrillees 2005:
    no. 60

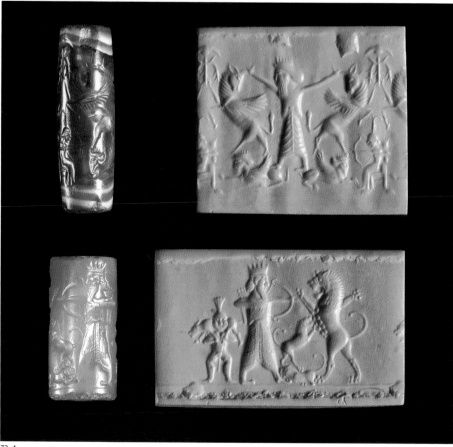

73–4

75 Clay impression of cylinder seal showing two royal heroes

The royal heroes with their hounds stand back to back, hunting lions with bow and spear below a winged disc.

From a grave of the Persian period at Ur
Excavations of C.L. Woolley, 1931–2 (U.18124)
H 5.4 cm, W 3.8 cm
British Museum, ANE 1932-10-8, 192
Legrain 1951: no. 759; Stern 1982: 212; Collon
    1996: 68, pl. 12, fig. 2; Boardman 2000: 157,
    fig. 5.4, a

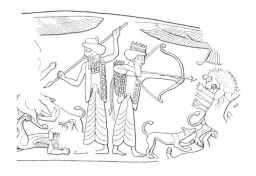

75

ARCHITECTURAL ELEMENTS

76 Square faience tile with polychrome glazed decoration

The decoration is in green, white, brown and yellow, and shows a sixteen-petalled rosette set between two bands of interlocking triangles. The sides of the tile are also glazed but plain. Such tiles are thought to have decorated the sides of staircases. Similar tiles were found in the area to the south of the Apadana at Susa.

Susa

H 36.5 cm, W 34 cm, Th 8.8 cm

Louvre, Sb 3337

Dieulafoy 1893: 297–301, figs 173–7, pls VIII–X; de Mecquenem 1947: 78–9, figs 47, 1–2; Harper, Aruz and Tallon 1992: 231–2, no. 159

76

77 Square plaque in 'Egyptian blue' decorated with a bird of prey

The bird is holding discs in its talons and has another disc on top of its head. There is a border of recessed triangles which originally contained red, white and green inlays. Illustrated alongside the plaque is a computer-aided reconstruction by Shahrokh Razmjou showing its original colours.

Persepolis, found in the Hall of 32 Columns in 1948

H 12.3 cm, W 12.3 cm

Tehran, 2436

Sami 1970: fig. on p. 100

77

78

78 Part of a lapis-lazuli disc showing a winged bull in relief

The bull is shown within a border of rosettes. There were possibly two opposed bulls originally. This was perhaps an architectural decoration.

Provenance unknown
H 12 cm, W 14 cm, Th 1.4 cm
Reza Abbasi, 31
Hakemi 1977; Seipel 2000: no. 122

79

79 Square slab in grey limestone with relief decoration showing a rosette

The twelve-petalled rosette is set within a border of embossed circles. Several examples of such slabs were found by the Oriental Institute Expedition, but none in their original positions (Schmidt 1953: 93, fig. 37E, 192, 262; Schmidt 1957: 75, fig. 12).

Herzfeld believed that they were positioned under the pivot-stones of doors, but this seems improbable. A more likely suggestion is that they decorated the sides of staircases or a pavement.

Persepolis
H 34.5 cm, W 33.5 cm, Th 7 cm
Persepolis Museum, 321

80

80 Glazed brick merlon decorated with an arrowhead design

The design, in white on a green background, is both a decorative motif and a representation of a functional arrow-slit. Such merlons were placed above the friezes of glazed-brick decoration at Susa.

Susa, Palace of Darius
H 30 cm, W 25 cm, Th 8 cm
Louvre, AOD 496
Dieulafoy 1893: 274–89, 304, fig. 160, pls IV, XIII/7

81 Bottle-shaped baluster from an elaborate staircase

A series of balusters would have supported a hand-rail or coping. Made from 'Egyptian blue'.

Susa, Palace of Darius
Excavations of J. de Morgan
H 20.2 cm, Diam 5 cm
Louvre, Sb 2792
De Mecquenem 1943: 40–41

81–2

82 Bottle-shaped baluster

This example is similar to cat. 81 above but is made of faience.

Susa, Palace of Darius
Excavations of J. de Morgan
H 21 cm, Diam 6 cm
Louvre, Sb 2793
De Mecquenem 1943: 40–41

83 Wall peg in 'Egyptian blue' with inscription

The trilingual inscription, highlighted by white paste, is in Old Persian on the upper line, and Elamite and Babylonian on the lower line. It reads 'Peg of lapis lazuli [sic] made in the house of Darius the King'.

Persepolis, north part of 'Harem' of Xerxes,
   floor of Room 8
H 8.5 cm, Diam 11.4 cm
Tehran, 2405
Kent 1953: DPi; Schmidt 1957: 50, fig. 4; 2000: DPi

83

GATES

84 Piece of gold gate-band with embossed and chased decoration

This shows a file of winged bulls between borders with decoration of embossed circles.

Persepolis, found in southeast part of Apadana in
    1941
H 12 cm, L 31 cm, Wt 274 g
Tehran, 173
Sami 1970: fig. on p. 162

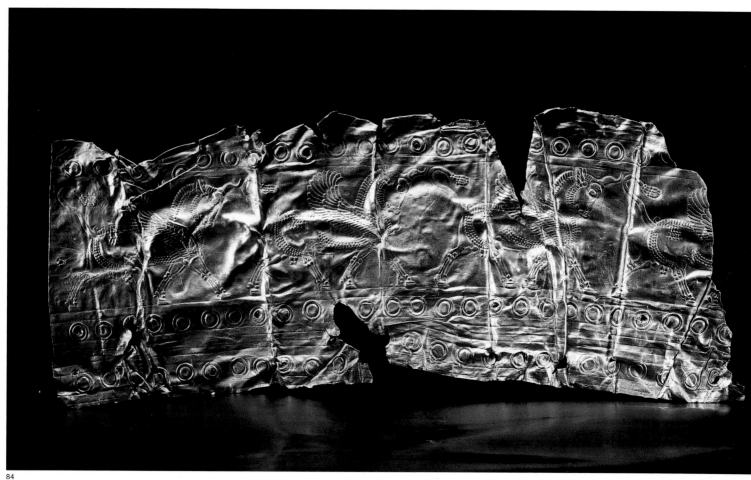

84

85

85 Part of bronze gate-band with embossed and chased decoration

This shows a file of winged lions, with eagle talons on their front legs, set between perforated borders at top and bottom. It is in two pieces.

Said to be from Hamadan
H 20.4 cm, L 77.7 cm
Tehran, 1392

86 Cap for a gate pivot-stone

In grey limestone, engraved with a floral design in low relief.

Persepolis
38.5 cm x 33.3 cm, max. Th 8 cm
Persepolis Museum, 315
Cf. Sami 1955: fig. between 52 and 53

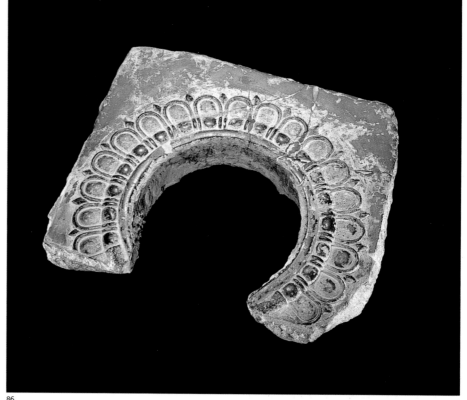

86

STATUES

87

87 Lapis-lazuli head of a statue

Head of a young beardless man wearing a castellated crown. The statue may have been made entirely of lapis lazuli or from different materials. The eye-sockets are now empty but would have been inlaid with different material.

Persepolis, found in the Hall of 32 Columns in 1946
H 6.6 cm, W 6 cm
Tehran, 1294-7719
Sami 1970: 96, no. 6, and fig. opposite

88 Statue of Darius

The statue is set on a rectangular base; the head and upper body are now missing. This magnificent piece is the finest statue in the round to have survived from the Achaemenid period. The king wears a Persian dress with a dagger stuck into his belt. The pleats of the robe are inscribed, on the right in cuneiform in the three official languages of the empire – Old Persian (DSab), Elamite and Babylonian – and on the left in Egyptian hieroglyphs. These inscriptions give the titles of the king and record that the statue was made in Egypt on the orders of Darius, probably to be set up in a temple at Heliopolis. Although the king wears a Persian costume, the pillar at the back and the decoration on the base are Egyptian in style. On the front and back of the base is a representation of Hapi, the Egyptian god of the Nile, and on the two long sides the peoples of the empire are represented by twenty-four cartouche fortresses, each with the name in hieroglyphs and a representation of

them above. The people shown are Persian, Mede, Elamite, Arian, Parthian, Bactrian, Sogdian, Arachosian, Drangian, Sattagydian, Chorasmian, Sakan, Babylonian, Armenian, Lydian, Cappadocian, Skudrian, Assyrian, Arabian, Egyptian, Libyan, Nubian, Makan and Indian. The statue is of grey granite that chemical analysis has indicated comes from the Wadi Hammamat in eastern Egypt. It was made in Egypt and later brought to Susa possibly in the reign of Xerxes. Below is a reconstruction drawing by Shahrokh Razmjou showing the original form of the statue. There are traces of brownish reddish paint on the folds of the dress.

Susa, found against one of the doorjambs in the monumental gate to the east of the Palace of Darius
Excavations of Jean Parrot, 1972
Total H 2.66 m; base 104 x 64 cm, H 51 cm
Tehran, 4112
Roaf 1974; Boucharlat 1997: 57–9; Jaffar-Mohammadi and Chevalier 2001: 80–81; Razmjou 2002a; 2002b

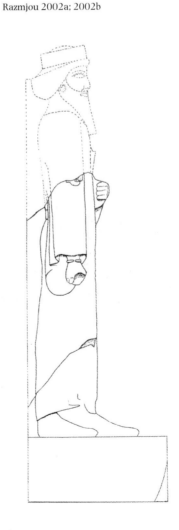

88

89 Fragment, possibly of a royal head from a monumental statue

It has been suggested that this dark grey limestone fragment, preserving the mouth and parts of the nose and beard, is from a second statue of Darius I, possibly a twin to cat. 88.

Susa, Apadana mound
Excavated by J. de Mecquenem
H 27 cm, W 28 cm
Louvre, Sb 6734
Scheil 1929: 57, pl. 13; Root 1979: 110ff.; Luschey 1983; Harper, Aruz and Tallon 1992: 219–21, no. 153

89

90 Polished black limestone statue of a large mastiff seated on a base

The head is mostly reconstructed.

Persepolis, found in vestibule of southeast tower, Apadana
H 100 cm, W 39 cm (base), L 68 cm (base)
Tehran, 340
Schmidt 1953: 73, 240, fig. 46B; 1957: 69–70, pl. 36A–B

90

FURNITURE

91 Bronze furniture foot

This consists of a floral moulding surmounted by a lion's paw, which supports a rosette flanked by volutes. Thrones with furniture legs of this type are represented on reliefs at Persepolis (cats 24, 38).

Provenance unknown
H 20 cm, W 11.5 cm
Louvre, AO 2787
Herzfeld 1941: fig. 364, top centre; Jamzadeh 1996: fig. 7

92 Bronze bull's head with hieroglyphic inscription

This bronze fitting terminating in a bull's head was undoubtedly made in Egypt, probably during the period of the 26th Dynasty (664–525 BC). It was perhaps brought to Iran following the incorporation of Egypt into the Persian Empire. The inscription in Egyptian hieroglyphs beneath the bull's head is a dedication to a god by Wah-ib-re (the throne-name of the Egyptian king Psamtek I, 664–610 BC). The bull's eyes are inlaid and there are sockets for inlaid horns that would probably have been of a different material. At the back and bottom the fitting is hollow and there are indications that it was fixed to a larger object, probably made of wood or ivory. It may have come from the side of an elaborate piece of furniture such as a throne or a chair.

Persepolis, found near the Apadana in 1942
H 18.4 cm, L 21.4 cm
Tehran, 2338
Korostovtsev 1947; Seipel 2000: no. 130

93 Wooden furniture leg showing the head and front legs of a lion

Originally painted, this was probably from a footstool. It apparently comes from Egypt and probably dates from the 27th Dynasty (525–404 BC) when Egypt came under Persian control. The style of the lion's head is unmistakeably Persian.

Probably from Egypt
Collected by M. Daniel Fouquet, 1850–1914, a
  Cairo-based doctor. Purchased at Christie's in 1996
H 23 cm, W 7 cm, Th 10 cm
British Museum, ANE 1996-9-28, 1
Curtis 2000: fig. 66; Simpson 1996

91

92

93

94 Bronze furniture foot in the form of a lion's paw

The paw is surmounted by a rosette flanked by two volutes. Similar bronze furniture feet are now in the Israel Museum, all from thrones of the type depicted on the Persepolis reliefs.

Provenance unknown
Bequeathed by Sir Robert Mond in 1939
H 12.5 cm, W 8.5 cm
British Museum, ANE 136050
Tadmor 1974: pl. 6A–C

94

95 Foreparts of lion in lapis lazuli

The head, shoulders and one paw are preserved. This may have come from an elaborate piece of furniture or have formed part of a stand for a vessel or basin. In the mouth there are holes for inlaid teeth which may have been of ivory or another material.

Fragments of a similar lion in lapis lazuli are now in the Persepolis Museum and the Oriental Institute, Chicago.

Persepolis, found in one of the passages of the underground rooms to the east of the Palace of Xerxes in 1951
H 15.5 cm, W c. 11 cm, L 17.5 cm
Tehran, 1188
Sami 1970: 96, no. 7, fig. on p. 140

95

96

96 Massive bronze stand consisting of three conjoined lions

The lions, heads turned to the side, are joined to each other at rump and shoulder, and there is a large circular socket in the space between them for a pole or tube. The precise function of this stand is unknown, but it may have supported an incense-burner, an offering stand or a standard. An elaborate incense-burner of the Neo-Elamite period (probably sixth century BC), found in a tomb at Arjan near Behbehan, also has lions incorporated in the base, although here they are standing on their hindlegs and combined with other figures (Seipel 2000: no. 50). Boardman identifies this stand as being Assyrian (in which case it could be booty from an Assyrian palace); but nothing comparable has been found in Assyria or is shown on the Assyrian reliefs, and the style of the prowling lions with their heads turned and the tear-shaped folds on the sides of their faces is more Persian than Assyrian.

Persepolis, Treasury, close to north wall of Room 38
H 28 cm, L 39 cm
Tehran, 19
Schmidt 1953: 182, fig. 80F; 1957: 69, pls 33–4;
    Seipel 2000: no. 120; Boardman 2000: fig. 4.6

6

THE ROYAL TABLE

St John Simpson

And those pitiless Persian hosts! They compelled us to drink sweet wine, wine without water, from gold and glass cups.
(Aristophanes, *The Acharnians* 72–3)

Classical Greek descriptions imply that gold and silver were commonly used by the Persian court and its aristocracy, and that wine was synonymous with the Persian banquet, only served in clay vessels when the great king wished to insult an individual.[1] After the Greek victory at Plataea in 479 BC, the camp of the Persian general Mardonius was sacked:

> Treasure there was in plenty – tents full of gold and silver furniture; couches overlaid with the same precious metals; bowls, goblets, and cups, all made of gold; and wagons loaded with sacks full of gold and silver basins ... It is said that Xerxes on his retreat from Greece left his tent with Mardonius. When Pausanias saw it, with its embroidered hangings and gorgeous decorations in silver and gold, he summoned Mardonius' bakers and cooks and told them to prepare a meal of the same sort as they were accustomed to prepare for their former master. The order was obeyed and when Pausanias saw gold and silver couches all beautifully draped, and gold and silver tables, and everything prepared for the feast with great magnificence, he could hardly believe his eyes for the good things set before them.

> (Herodotus, *History* IX.80)

The court of Cyrus was said to travel with 'water, ready boiled for use, and stored in flagons of silver', and 'many were the gold and silver drinking cups' said to have been salvaged from the Persian fleet wrecked off Magnesia (Herodotus, *History* I.188; VII.190). Drinking cups (*ekpomata*), personal adornments and certain types of furniture, including 'couches with silver legs', feature as symbols of oriental luxury in Xenophon's *Cyropaedia* (V.2.7) and *Anabasis* (IV.2.27, 4.21).[2] On entering Persepolis, Alexander's army is said to have found that 'the wealth of this city eclipsed everything in the past. Into it the barbarians had packed the riches of all Persia: mounds of gold and silver, huge quantities of clothing,

and furniture which was not functional but ostentatiously ornate' (Quintus Curtius Rufus, *The History of Alexander* V.6.3). The systematic destruction of Persepolis during Alexander's sack in May 330 BC is illustrated by the removal of even the gold appliqués on the sculptures, and much of this costly metal rapidly found its way into the melting pot.

The recycling of metals was (and is) normal practice, and the stripping of an imperial treasury provided unimaginable revenue opportunities for the conqueror, yet it illustrates the biggest problem facing a reconstruction of the royal table. The Persian king was said to have presented one individual with 'one hundred large *phialai* of silver and silver mixing bowls' and 'twenty gold *phialai* set with jewels', which may refer to the cloisonné work typical of Achaemenid goldsmiths (Athenaeus, *Deipnosophistae* II.48f.). Similar levels of luxury at the Sasanian, Abbasid and Fatimid courts are described by medieval Islamic authors, yet practically nothing of this quality survives from any of these periods.[3] From this bleak position we must use the evidence of surviving objects – especially from hoards and graves – Attic imitations and contemporary depictions, particularly from Persepolis, to reconstruct cautiously what tableware was used at the Persian court and beyond (fig. 45).[4] The context in which such objects are said to have been used at the uppermost levels of society is occasionally illustrated by contemporary and later Classical observers, all foreign but some at least partly sympathetic. Finally, a large number of unprovenanced objects, typically made of gold or silver, but occasionally of lapis lazuli, bronze or other materials, have also emerged in Iran since the 1940s; however, these should be treated with extreme caution as many are fake and their apparent stylistic connections with Neo-Elamite, Median or other tableware traditions may be deeply misleading.[5]

Vessels are carried by as many as twelve of the twenty-three delegations shown on the Apadana reliefs at Persepolis. Among these are amphorae with plain or flut-

45 Achaemenid luxury tablewares in the British Museum.

ed bodies and opposing plain or zoomorphic handles, one of which sometimes doubles as a short open spout. These are shown being carried proudly by members of delegations I (Medes), III (Armenians) and VI (Lydians) (fig. 46).[6] Silver and gilt-silver versions of these vessels survive, either complete or as isolated handles or spouts, for instance from Duvanli (Thrace), and in the Oxus Treasure and a hoard at Babylon (cats 127–9); the bodies of complete examples are decorated with vertical fluting, guilloche, palmettes, lotus flowers and overlapping white lotus leaves. These are an Achaemenid invention, probably inspired by earlier Iranian forms of zoomorphic spout and epitomized by some types of Iron Age pottery.

Pairs of horizontally fluted or plain beakers are shown being carried by members of delegations XII (Ionians) and XV (Parthians?); plain versions are also carried by delegations I (Medes), IV (Arians?), VI (Lydians) and VII (Drangians) (fig. 47).[7] Attendants depicted on other staircase reliefs at Persepolis, as well as on a glazed brick

staircase at Susa, carry stemmed bowls covered with plain hemispherical lids or bowls, bowls with rolled-over rims (or possibly flat lids) and pairs of plain hemispherical bowls, sometimes covered with boat-shaped lids.[8] Pairs of plain bowls with rolled-over rims and plain hemispherical bowls (*mastoi*) are carried by delegation XIII (Bactrians?); small alabastrons are carried nested in baskets by delegation XVIII (Indians?),[9] and another type of lidded vessel is shown being carried by a member of delegation XXIII (Nubians).[10] Finally, pairs of plain or horizontally fluted shouldered bowls (*phialai*) are depicted on the Apadana being carried by delegations V (Babylonians), VI (Lydians), VIII (Assyrians), XII (Ionians) and XV (Parthians?).[11] Variations exist in the form, size and weight of these bowls, and three examples, with weights ranging from 214 to 634 g, were said to have been found near Erzincan in eastern Turkey (cats 106–8). Their general shape is derived from an earlier Late Assyrian tradition, and depictions on a fifth-century Lycian tomb-painting at Karaburun indicate that they

46 Metal drinking bowls and spouted amphorae carried by delegation VI (Lydians) on the east side of the Apadana at Persepolis.

47 Metal drinking bowls and beakers carried by delegation XV (Parthians or Bactrians) on the east side of the Apadana at Persepolis.

were balanced in one hand, with the fingertips supporting the sides and bottom:

> For these cup-bearers to kings perform their business very cleverly; they pour in the wine without spilling it, and give the cup, holding it on three fingers, and presenting it in such a manner as to put it most conveniently into the hand of the person who is to drink ... For these cup-bearers to kings, when they give the cup, dip a little out with a smaller cup, which they pour into their left hand and swallow; so that, in case they mix poison in the cup, it may be of no profit to them.
>
> (*Cyropaedia* I.3.8–9)[12]

The allusion to dipping out a small quantity probably refers to the use of a dipper ladle which the Karaburun mural shows to have been suspended from the little finger. A number of silver and bronze ladles survive with plain or faceted handles, typically ending in a ring handle usually decorated with an animal's head or a pair of addorsed animals (cats 134–5).[13] The drinking bowls themselves were probably made and used as part of a standardized banqueting service. Graves excavated from the Levant to the Persian Gulf illustrate how single plain or occasionally decorated bronze and (less commonly) silver examples were often interred together with a ladle and strainer (cats 132–3).[14] There has been little research into the capacities of these drinking wares, but measurements of and experiments with Achaemenid silver within the British Museum suggest that they were only filled as far as the carinated shoulder – above which the vessel becomes unbalanced when held in one hand – and therefore originally held up to just over a litre. However, this was not the only means of drinking. Xenophon refers to encountering villagers in eastern Turkey who are said to have drunk

> barley-wine in large bowls. Floating on the top of this drink were the barley-grains and in it were straws, some larger and others smaller, without joints; and when one was thirsty, he had to take these straws into his mouth and suck. It was an extremely strong drink unless one diluted it with water, and extremely good when one was used to it.
>
> (*Anabasis* IV.5)

The purpose of the straws was to avoid drinking the coarse elements in the drink; depictions and excavated metal filters originally fitted on to the straws confirm this to have been a popular form of drinking throughout the Levant, Mesopotamia and the Persian Gulf as early as the third millennium BC.[15] The alternative was to sieve the liquid as it was poured, and this became a popular method from the Late Assyrian period onwards (cats 132–3).[16] The employment of royal servants whose task this was is suggested by Athenaeus's reference to 'wine filterers' in Darius III's household (*Letter of Parmenion* XIII.608a).

Shallow lobed bowls are a particularly distinctive type of Achaemenid tableware, but oddly are not depicted at Persepolis (cats 102, 104; fig. 48).[17] Four complete silver examples said to have been acquired at Hamadan in

48 Detail from the so-called Darius Vase (Naples 3253) showing a Persian holding three stacked *phialai*. From *Furtwängler 1906, pl. 88*.

about 1932, with a combined weight of 600 sigloi at 5.44 g, are inscribed: 'Artaxerxes the great king, king of kings, king of countries, son of Xerxes the king [who was] son of Darius the king; in whose royal house this saucer [*or* wine-drinking vessel] was made' (cat. 103).[18] The *rhyton*, or 'pourer', is another quintessential Persian form of vessel which is nevertheless also absent from depictions at Persepolis. It typically consists of a conical or trumpet-like horn, usually hammered from relatively thin sheet metal and inserted, sometimes at right angles, into a proportionately much smaller cast or hammered animal-headed protome, with a pouring hole or spout typically in the muzzle or chest.[19] A second type of rhyton was simply in the form of an animal head but an added spout crucially differentiates this from animal-head buckets and cups (protomes), which continued in use (and inspired Athenian potters to make versions in

clay). Most surviving rhytons are silver, although gold (mostly dubious) and bronze versions are also known. Faience (cat. 122) and pottery rhytons also survive.[20] An exceptional (albeit fragmentary and highly weathered) glass rhyton excavated at Persepolis has a protome in the form of a bull, with a lion pouncing on the back of its neck (cat. 121). This classic example of official imagery proves the impact of 'court style' or 'international Achaemenid style' on workshop production and recalls the stylized realism of the silver amphora handles. As with the most elaborate metalwork, the ears and horns of the bull on this rhyton were separately attached from another material, and additional inlay was set within a rectangular strip on the neck (although these are now missing). The vessel lacks a pouring spout, presumably because of the risk of drilling a hole through the finished piece.

A gilt-silver rhyton with horizontally fluted horn and separately cast griffin protome was acquired as part of the 'Erzincan' group and holds a litre and a half (cat. 119). Banquet scenes on Persian-period and later monuments in southwest Turkey illustrate that rhytons were used together with shouldered drinking bowls, rather than being held aloft and used to jet their contents directly into the mouth as is generally assumed to have been Persian practice (cat. 123).[21]

Other tablewares include hemispherical cups, either plain gold or silver decorated with gold cut-outs, and holding between about 300 and 400 ml (cats 99, 111); cylindrical plain bronze beakers; shallow silver or gold bowls decorated with petals radiating from a central rosette; twin-spouted amphorae (cat. 126); and gold jugs with zoomorphic handles (cat. 125). The exact functions of some other metalwares are less clear, but a plain shallow gold bowl in the Oxus Treasure (cat. 98) and a large silver plate with a straight rim and a diameter of 30 cm from the 'Erzincan' group were presumably intended for serving (cat. 109). However, not all vessels were used as tablewares. Straight-sided horizontally fluted metal buckets with swinging handles were probably used to contain perfumed water as they are carried by towel-bearing attendants on the Persepolis sculptures.[22] Small pear-shaped bottles with flanged rims shown carried by other royal attendants closely resemble polished calcite alabastrons found at Persepolis, Babylon (with manufacturing waste) and other sites, and originally contained perfume.[23] Lidded *pyxides* were also used as small containers (cat. 151). Three shallow silver scoops are attested from Erzincan and Ikiztepe (cats 136–7), and resemble two grey stone examples found at Persepolis (cats 138–9). These have been plausibly interpreted as incense ladles, but whether these should be regarded as ritual paraphernalia rather than tablewares depends on whether incense was considered integral to the banquet. The handled beaker with a floral or pomegranate-knobbed lid shown on one of the Oxus Treasure plaques (cat. 227) might be a form of ritual vessel; a plain tall goblet with a flaring neck is depicted on another such plaque (cat. 228).

Most Achaemenid metalwares were made by hammering or raising sheet metal, adding decoration in repoussé, outlining the details by chasing, and finishing with a burnish which sometimes leaves a slightly fluted surface. Such vessels characteristically have centering marks which are probably related to the marking out of the designs. In the case of lobed bowls, punches with tear-shaped ends were sometimes used to create lobes of precisely the same shape and size, and an actual punch of this type was found at Ikiztepe. A smaller number of other vessels and protomes appear to have been cast, probably in clay moulds.[24] These were standard metal-working techniques and doubtless employed to a greater or lesser extent by workshops throughout the empire. Sheet metal cut-outs and overlays were occasionally applied to the exterior of small shallow bowls and drinking cups as alternatives to repoussé or gilding, and created a bichrome effect (cats 101, 111).[25] These may be the product of an Anatolian atelier; a large proportion of surviving Achaemenid silverwares have been found in Turkey which appears to have played a particularly important role in the creation of iconic 'Persian' wares.[26]

'Every year the king sends rich gifts to the man who can show the largest number' of sons (Herodotus, *History* I.136). According to the *Cyropaedia* (I.3.7; VIII.2.3–4, 6, 8; 3.3, 33; 4.24, 27; 5.29), gold drinking vessels were one category of royal gift; others included bracelets, torques, robes, horses with gold-studded bridles, oxen and dishes from the royal table.[27] This form of payment in kind offers one explanation for the circulation of Achaemenid metal plate and other 'luxury' items to the extremities of the Persian Empire and beyond.[28] Silverwares were also particularly valued for their high metal content and used as currency in financial transactions, either through the weight of the complete vessel or through subdivision by cutting off pieces as 'small change'.[29] Hoards of Achaemenid silver, either as complete vessels or a mixture of complete vessels, coins, ingots and vessel fragments – so-called *hacksilber* – are attested from a number of sites.[30] Those vessels and sigloi which have been analysed confirm many to have been made to a high fineness of 97–9 per cent and to contain small traces of gold and lead, although this is typical of most ancient silver and is not specifically characteristic of Achaemenid production.[31] The quantity of metal sheet used for a particular vessel was calculated as units of coin, either Persian darics for the gold or sigloi for the silver, the respective weight of which were 8.25–8.46 g and about 5.20–5.49 g (replaced in the first half of the fifth century BC by the slightly heavier standard of about 5.40–5.67 g).[32] There is evidence for the punch-marking of some silver plate, perhaps as a form of quality control, and Greek and Aramaic personal ownership marks or monograms were occasionally scratched on the undersides (cats 102–3).[33] These provide context for Xenophon's statement that 'If they possess a great number of cups, they are proud of possessing them' (*Cyropaedia* VIII.8.18).

Other luxury tablewares were made from colourless or naturally tinged light-greenish glass. Forms include bent-horn rhytons, with zoomorphic protomes and plain or horizontally fluted upper portions, bottles, beakers, chalices, and shallow and shouldered bowls, either plain or decorated on the exterior with lobes or petals (cats 113–14).[34] These shapes and surface treatments mostly imitate Achaemenid metalware, yet the attempted decolourization of some also implies conscious imitation of the properties of rock crystal. The glassworkers thus adapted their medium to suit two different decorative concepts rather than simply creating artificial copies of one category. Although there is no evidence for the relative values of glass or rock crystal at this period, finds excavated in the (looted) Treasury at Persepolis and earlier (unrobbed) Assyrian royal tombs at Nimrud suggest that rock crystal was a luxury material and was scarcer than glass.[35] The imitation of this material is part of a long Near Eastern glassworking tradition, as antimony oxide was used as a decolourizing agent from as early as the eighth century BC.[36] The place (or more likely places) of production of the Achaemenid glasswares is uncertain and in any case may have employed the use of imported glass chunks or ingots.[37] The comparative rarity of these glass vessels (fragments from as few as nine recognizable forms were found in the Persepolis Treasury) and their excavated findspots imply that they were luxury wares; glass did not become common until the advent of mass-produced blown glass from the first century AD onwards. These vessels were instead made by casting, followed by grinding and polishing; the interiors of the closed forms appear to have been hollowed with a bow-drill.

Ground, drilled and polished coloured stone vessels were also popular and a great variety of inscribed and uninscribed examples were found in the Treasury at Persepolis (cats 115, 146–9). These included shallow serving trays (some originally with snug metal lids), palettes, shallow and footed bowls, bowls decorated with one or more reversed ducks' heads (a tray of this type is shown being carried by servants on reliefs from Susa),[38] plates, and a granite or meta-gabbro chalice inscribed 'Palace of Ashurbanipal' and representing old Assyrian booty (cat. 117). The vessels were made of rock crystal, porphyry, jasper, serpentine, basalt, granite, hematite, slate, chlorite, calcite, banded marble, limestone, gypsum and an unidentified grey-and-white speckled stone. The sources of these stones are uncertain, but the jasper may be from southwest Turkey, as evidence for a workshop was found at Sardis and a finished plate of the same material was found at Ikiztepe.[39] Veined greenstone was also used for mortars and shallow plates (cats 211–12), and alabastrons and footed bowls were made from Egyptian calcite (cats 140–45). The scarcity of lapis may reflect the difficulty of obtaining sufficiently large pieces and its effective imitation in Egyptian blue and glass.[40]

49 Servant or priest carrying plain hemispherical bowls shown on the southern staircase of the Palace of Darius at Persepolis.

Not everyone could afford tablewares of metal, glass or stone, and far away from the court, potters strove to copy or reinterpret the same shapes in clay. Horizontal fluting was a popular Achaemenid metalworking technique and, together with several metalware forms, was imitated in black gloss by Athenian potters.[41] Lobed bowls and spouted amphorae were imitated in burnished greyware, the dark surfaces of which perhaps recalled the appearance of naturally tarnished silver (cat. 116). In other cases potters used red burnished slip to emulate the visual effect of gold; one particularly fine burnished pottery *phiale* was decorated with low ribs radiating out from the base.[42] Similar imitation is reflected even in conservative parts of the Persian Empire such as Edom in southern Jordan, where painted wares continued to be made in the earlier Edomite tradition but copying the forms of Achaemenid *phialai*.[43] The ubiquity of local ceramic versions of these shouldered bowls implies widespread aspi-

ration to the metropolitan tastes of the Persian elite, and a change in the style if not the quantity of wine consumption.

Other forms are presently unknown in metal and some may represent potters' responses to local consumer needs: for instance, the rounded bodies and pinched spouts of upright-spouted Achaemenid pottery jars from northwest Iran are features typical of working with clay rather than copying vessels made of other materials. The development of local traditions is also evident in the Egyptian manufacture of faience rhytons, or the Babylonian production of eggshell-thin pottery bowls.[44] The perfect balance of these bowls was achieved by leaving the base slightly thicker than the lower walls, and thus maintaining the natural resting position of a rounded bowl; they are well balanced when held with one hand but are unsuitable for consuming liquids. They were thrown from the hump on a fast wheel using a fine, possibly levigated, non-tempered clay which was pared down at a leather-hard stage in order to enhance the thinness of the walls. Their light weight is as much a reflection of the fineness of the clay as it is the thinness of the vessel walls: a certain degree of variation in technique which may suggest the work of different individuals or workshops.

Cultural revolutions do not necessarily accompany dynastic change, and the end of the Achaemenid Empire was no exception. The strength of tradition of the manufacture and use of Achaemenid tablewares ensured that they continued into the Hellenistic and even early Parthian periods. A scene in the late fourth-century (Ptolemaic) tomb of Petosiris at Hermopolis Magna shows Egyptian craftsmen making Achaemenid-style rhytons with horse, horned lion and goat protomes, cups, ladles and a bier decorated with lion-griffins, in addition to a Greek-style *turibulum* (incense-burner) decorated with horses.[45] There are also strong indications of continuity within Iran, as several regional traditions of painted pottery – Ardabil Painted Ware, Classic and Western Triangle Ware, Festoon Ware – survive from the late Achaemenid period until the third or early second centuries BC.[46] The shapes of these vessels imply functions of pouring and serving: the deliberate zoning of painted decoration on the upper interior rim of the shouldered bowls supports evidence suggested above that they were only part-filled. By contrast, shallow plates were typically decorated with a single bold motif in the centre, which implies that it only became visible when the vessel was emptied or displayed.

Any attempt to discuss the range and function of Persian tablewares should finally try to take stock of what was actually being consumed. The huge variety of available food and drink is implicit within the size of the Persian Empire and its complex blend of personal statuses, ethnicity, local traditions, resources and growing seasons. Typological classifications of vessels do not prove what may have been consumed within them, nor is there proof that particular types of vessel were exclusively used for certain foods, drinks or occasions. Organic residue analysis has yet to be applied to any tablewares of this period and interpreting the altered chemistry of ancient decayed residues contains further pitfalls for the unwary. We should therefore conclude by returning to the written sources for some authentic flavours. Some of these are captured by the Greek authors. Herodotus famously stated:

> Of all the days in the year, the one which they celebrate most is their birthday. It is customary to have the board furnished on that day with an ampler supply than common. The richer Persians cause an ox, a horse, a camel, and an ass to be baked whole and so served up to them: the poorer classes use instead the smaller kinds of cattle. They eat little solid food but abundance of dessert, which is set on table a few dishes at a time; this it is which makes them say that 'the Greeks, when they eat, leave off hungry, having nothing worth mention served up to them after the meats; whereas, if they had more put before them, they would not stop eating'. They are very fond of wine, and drink it in large quantities.

(*History* I.133)

This suggests that Persian banquets were typically composed of multiple courses served on a large number (hence variety of types) of dishes. Xenophon reiterates this with his claim: 'Of meats cooked for their tables, whatever were invented in former times, not one is discontinued; but they are always contriving new dishes, as well as sauces, for they have cooks to find out varieties in both' (*Cyropaedia* VIII.8.16). 'Cooks who specialize in dairy dishes' are mentioned by Athenaeus (*Letter of Parmenion* XIII.608a). Xenophon returned to this theme by stating that 'The Persian king has vintners scouring every land to find some drink that will tickle his palate; an army of cooks contrives dishes for his delight' (*Agesilaus* IX.3), and Cyrus was said to have employed a host of 'bakers, cooks, cup-bearers, bathers, men who set dishes on the table and remove them' (*Cyropaedia* VIII.8.20; cf. also VIII.2.6) (fig. 49). According to Heracleides of Cumae (quoted by Athenaeus), 'All who attend upon the Persian kings when they dine first bathe themselves and then serve in white clothes, and spend nearly half the day on preparations for the dinner' (*Deipnosophistae* IV.145b). Unsurprisingly, hierarchy was emphasized by complicated seating patterns at formal banquets (*Cyropaedia* VIII.4.3–5, 6.11), and another writer stated:

> Of those who are invited to eat with the king, some dine outdoors, in full sight of anyone who wishes to look on; others dine indoors in the king's company. Yet even these do not eat in his presence, for there are two rooms opposite each other, in one of which the king has his meal, in the other the invited guests.

(Heracleides, cited by Athenaeus, *Deipnosophistae* IV.145b.e.f)

The ultimate status of the Persian banquet is underlined by its attempted reconstruction by Pausanias after the Greek victory at Plataea (Herodotus, *History* IX.80).

Elaborate etiquette, conspicuous consumption and intensity of labour in the preparation of food are hallmarks of courtly cuisine, although these were interpreted by the Greeks as a sign of decadence, just as the Arabs later mocked Sasanian cookery.[47] One later account purports to list the ingredients for the great king's dinner, which included 'sweet grape jelly, candied turnips and radishes prepared with salt, candied capers with salt, from which delicious stuffings are made', terebinth oil, 'Ethiopian cumin' and Median saffron (Polyaenus, *Strategemata* IV.3.32).[48] Some of these suggest traditional highland Iranian products, notably the saffron and the terebinth (from pistachio nuts), whereas others hint at gourmet dishes and imported luxury spices. Fruit and nuts are also classic ingredients of later Persian cookery, and references to the planting of quince and pear trees in a cuneiform text from Persepolis add substance to Classical allusions to the consumption of dates, pomegranates, figs, apples, raisins and almonds.[49]

The only Classical account to actually specify how the king ate claimed that 'Ochus [Artaxerxes III] stretched out his hands; with his right hand he took up one of the knives laid out on the table and with the other he picked up the largest piece of bread, put some meat on it, cut it up, and ate greedily' (Aelian, *Varia Historia* II.17). Thus flat bread may have been commonly used as a form of edible 'trencher' plate as well as a convenient scoop, but knives used at the table cannot be distinguished typologically from those used for other purposes (nor is it likely that such a distinction was made in antiquity). Silver duck-headed spoons are attested from Pasargadae and Ikiztepe,[50] although forks only came to be used in Iran during the Sasanian period.

Xenophon's experiences in 401/400 BC capture another side of wining and dining in Persia. In Babylonia they drank 'date wine' and 'a sour drink made the same by boiling'. In eastern Turkey they quaffed 'old wines with a fine bouquet' and either used 'a reed [to] suck the [barley] wine into one's mouth' or drank from 'the bowl ... sucking it like an ox' (*Anabasis* I.5; II.3; IV.4–5). The Persians may indeed have been 'very fond of wine' (Herodotus, *History* I.133), but the choice of red or white, and grape, date or barley ensured that this was not simply an early case of Shiraz.

1 Ctesias *ap*. Ath. XI.464a.

2 Tuplin 1990.

3 Al-Qaddumi 1996; note that the necklace worn by the griffin on the protome of the gilt silver rhyton from Erzincan was originally set with a semi-precious stone (cat. 119) and the lobes on costly metal *phialai* could have been set with stones.

4 Schmidt 1957: 81–95, pls 47–70; Amandry 1959; Miller 1993; 1997; Calmeyer 1993.

5 Muscarella 1977; 1980; cf. also Henkelmann 2003.

6 Schmidt 1953: pls 27, 29, 32.

7 Schmidt 1953: pls 27, 30, 32–3, 41; cf. Miller 1993, 126–7, taf. 29–30; Venedikov and Gerassimov 1975: 360, pl. 151.

8 Schmidt 1953: pls 85–6, 132–5, 155–6, 163–5, 168–71; Harper, Aruz and Tallon 1992: 224–5, fig. 51 (minus the stemmed bowls).

9 Schmidt 1953: 94, pls 39, 44. The same bowls are also represented on other staircases; cf. Schmidt 1953: pl. 85.

10 Schmidt 1953: pl. 49; Schmidt (1957: 95) speculates that these may have held gold dust.

11 Schmidt 1953: pls 31–2, 34, 38, 41; cf. Özgen and Öztürk *et al*. 1996: 94–6, 98–101, nos 42–4, 46–9.

12 On the typology and depictions cf. Luschey 1939; Mellink 1971: 252–4, pls 55–6; 1972: 265–6, pls 58–9; details also reproduced in colour by Özgen and Öztürk *et al*. 1996: 47.

13 Stern 1982: 146–7; Özgen and Öztürk *et al*. 1996: 83–6, nos 24–31.

14 Cf., for example, Moorey 1980a: 183–7; 1980b: 28–38, and refs; Stern 1982: 144–7; Özgen and Öztürk *et al*. 1996: 170–72, nos 122–4.

15 Moorey 1980a; 1980b: 42, fig. 7, no. 130.

16 Moorey 1980a; cf. Özgen and Öztürk *et al*. 1996: 109, no. 64.

17 Examples include Amandry 1959; Dalton 1964: 8–9, 44, pls VIII, XXIII, nos 18, 180; Moorey 1980b, 35–6, fig. 6, nos 92–9; Stern 1982: 144–6; Muscarella 1988: 218–19, nos 326–7; Gunter and Jett 1992: 66–8; Özgen and Öztürk *et al*. 1996: 87–93, 97, nos 33–41, 45; Lordkipanidze 2001: 154–7, 166–71.

18 Curtis, Cowell and Walker 1995; Gunter and Cool Root 1998; cf. Vickers 1996: 55.

19 Hoffmann 1961; Ghirshman 1962; Moorey 1985: 33–4; Gunter 1988; Shefton 1998: 643–55; Ebbinghaus 1999; 2000.

20 Faience: for example, Hoffman 1958; pottery: Moorey 1980b: 26–7, fig. 5, nos 66–8.

21 Ebbinghaus 2000; cf. Shefton 1998: 648, n. 91.

22 An Achaemenid development of a popular earlier type; an undecorated bronze version was excavated at Persepolis in 1892.

23 Sami 1970: 98, 173; Schmidt 1957: pls 148–50, 183–4; cf. Moorey 1980b, 47–8, and refs; Stern 1982: 49–50; Özgen and Öztürk *et al*. 1996: 131, no. 86; Harper, Aruz and Tallon 1992: 242–3, 252, no. 180. Note, however, that decorated silver versions are also attested (Özgen and Öztürk *et al*. 1996: 121–3, nos 75–7).

24 Punch: Özgen and Öztürk *et al*. 1996: 61, 229, no. 219; clay moulds: Moorey 1980b: 30 cites an unpublished example found in Iraq.

25 Moorey 1988b; cf. Moorey 1980b: 37, fig. 6, no. 111; Miller 1993: 143, taf. 18,3; Özgen and Öztürk *et al*. 1996: 87.

26 Melikian-Chirvani 1993.

27 Sancisi-Weerdenburg 1989; Tuplin 1990: 25; Briant 1989; 2002: 200, citing Athenaeus, *Deipnosophistae* IV.144a, XII.529d, 539d, 545d.

28 For example, Miller 1997: 125–33; Zournatzi 2000.

29 Zournatzi 2000.

30 Akhalgori in Georgia (Smirnov 1934), 'Erzincan' in eastern Turkey (Dalton 1964: 42–5, nos 178–86; cf. Amandry 1956: 12, fig. 1), Babylon (Reade 1986).

31 Curtis, Cowell and Walker 1995; Gunter and Jett 1992; Hughes 1984; 1986; Vickers and Gill 1994: 49, n. 137; Zournatzi 2000. No equivalent data are published for the gold vessels although darics were made of 23.25 carat gold.

32 Vickers 1991; 1996: 55; 2002; Vickers and Gill 1994: 46–52.

33 Gunter and Cool Root 1998: 13–15; Özgen and Öztürk *et al*. 1996: 33, 93–4, 98, 103–106, nos 40–42, 46, 54, 56, 59–60; Shefton 1993: 203.

34 For examples, cf. Fossing 1937; Schmidt 1957: 91–3, pls 66–7; von Saldern 1959; 1963; Barag 1968; 1985: 68–9; Oliver 1970; Vickers 1972; Stern 1997: fig. 5; Seipel 2000, 206–207.

35 Vickers 1996; Hussein and Suleiman 1999: 243, 390, pls 38, 175.

36 Von Saldern 1959; Stern 1997: 194. However, the Achaemenid pieces are not perfectly colourless and typically have a light greenish tinge.

37 A red glass ingot is reported from Persepolis (Barag 1985: 59, n. 159). In addition to those workshops believed to have been situated within Iran (or at least a core portion of the Persian Empire), Triantafyllidis (2003) argues that four related workshop traditions centred on Rhodes, Gordion and Ephesus, Macedonia and the Euxine Pontus were responsible for making a range of imitative glass types between the late sixth and early third centuries BC.

38 Jaffar-Mohammadi and Chevalier 2001: 118, no. 16.

39 Özgen and Öztürk *et al*. 1996: 130, no. 85; evidence was also found for the working of rock crystal at Sardis: McLauchlin 1989.

40 Lapis was regularly used during this period for seals, pendants and jewellery inlay (for example, Schmidt 1957: 56; Stronach 1978: 170, pls 152c–d; Harper, Aruz and Tallon 1992: 245–7, nos 171–3), but the literature also includes modern fakes carved from lazulite and other objects of Egyptian blue which have been misidentified.

41 Miller 1993.

42 For dark burnished skeuomorphs of Achaemenid metalwares: Stronach 1978: 184, 242–3, fig. 106: 11; Mamédova n.d.: no. 17; red slipped skeuomorphs: Dusinberre 1999; Gunter 2000: 32, 55, no. 32.

43 Hart 1995: 57–8, 210–11, fig. 6.8.

44 Fleming 1989.

45 Boardman 2000: 186.

46 Haerinck 1978; Kroll 2003: 285.

47 Sancisi-Werdenburg 1995; Simpson 2003.

48 Briant 2000: 286–92; cf. Amigues 2003.

49 Briant 2000: 291–2 for refs.

50 Stronach 1978: 169, 202–3: fig. 86: 5, pls 150b–151; Özgen and Öztürk *et al*. 1996: 112–13, nos 67–8.

BOWLS AND CUPS

97

97 Gold bowl

Carinated gold bowl with embossed fluted and floral decoration, and a cuneiform inscription around the neck. The inscription is written in Old Persian, Babylonian and Elamite, and records 'Xerxes the king'.

Said to be from Hamadan
H 11.6 cm, Diam 20.5 cm, Wt 1407 g
Tehran, 7985
Illustrated London News, 21 July 1956, pl. on p. 107;
    Sept Mille Ans 1961: no. 666, pl. LVIII; Ghirshman
    1964: fig. 309; Seipel 2000: illustration 8

97, base

98

100 Shallow gold bowl

With embossed decoration showing winged lions standing on their hindlegs, almond-shaped lobes and a central omphalos.

Oxus Treasure
Bequeathed in 1897 by A.W. Franks
H 2.33 cm, Diam 12.1 cm, Wt 73.5 g
British Museum, ANE 123919
Dalton 1964: no. 18, pl. VIII

99

100

98 Shallow plain gold bowl

The bowl is much dented and has a low central omphalos.

Oxus Treasure
Bequeathed in 1897 by A.W. Franks
H 5.5 cm, Diam 16.3 cm, Wt 326.6 g
British Museum, ANE 123922
Dalton 1964: no. 21, fig. 44 on p. 9

99 Plain hemispherical gold bowl

According to Barbara Ambruster (see p. 124), this bowl was cast by the lost wax technique. The wax model was manufactured using a lathe, as with the jug, cat. 125. This bowl has a central point indicative of the use of a lathe.

Oxus Treasure
Bequeathed in 1897 by A.W. Franks
H 6.7 cm, Diam 9.9 cm, Wt 306.5 g
British Museum, ANE 123921
Dalton 1964: no. 20, pl. III

101 Shallow silver bowl

Between the lobes on the underside of the bowl are applied silver cut-outs showing rampant winged lions with the head and feather crown of the Egyptian dwarf-god Bes.

Purchased in 1971 (on deposit in the British
    Museum since 14 July 1970)
H 3.3 cm, Diam 17.2 cm, Wt 300.9 g
British Museum, ANE 135571
Moorey 1988: pl. IVa; Collon 1995: fig. 148;
    Abdi 1999: fig. 8/1; Curtis 2000: fig. 61; cf. Özgen
    and Öztürk *et al.* 1996: pl. 88, no. 34

102 Silver bowl

With embossed omphalos and decoration showing lobes and petals.

Said to be from Mazanderan, northern Iran
Formerly in the collection of Thomas L. Jacks of
    the Anglo-Iranian Oil Company, and then in the
    Ernest Brummer Collection until 1964. Purchased
    in 1998 with contributions from the National
    Art Collections Fund, the British Museum Friends
    and the Friends of the Ancient Near East
H 4 cm, Diam 30.7 cm, Wt 952 g
British Museum, ANE 1998-1-17, 1
Catalogue of the Ernest Brummer Collection, Sotheby's,
    16 November 1964, no. 165 with pl.; Simpson 1998

103 Silver bowl

With an embossed decoration showing a stylized lotus-flower design. There is an inscription of Artaxerxes I (465–424 BC) in Old Persian cuneiform around the inner rim:

> Artaxerxes, the great king, king of kings,
> king of countries, son of Xerxes the king,
> of Xerxes [who was] son of Darius the king,
> the Achaemenian, in whose house this
> silver drinking cup was made.

This bowl is one of four similar examples that were found before 1935. Others are in the Metropolitan Museum of Art, New York, the Freer Gallery, Washington, and the Reza Abbasi Collection in Tehran. The authenticity of the text has sometimes been questioned because of the inclusion of the words 'bātugaza' for wine-cup and 's-i-y-m-m' for silver, which are not otherwise attested in Old Persian inscriptions.

Provenance unknown
Purchased in 1994 with contributions from the
    National Art Collections Fund and the British
    Museum Friends
H 4.7 cm, Diam 29 cm, Wt 803 g
British Museum, ANE 1994-1-27, 1
Herzfeld 1935; Kent 1953: A[I]; Curtis, Cowell and
    Walker 1995; Curtis 2000: fig. 62; Sims-Williams
    2001; Vickers 2002

101

102

104

104 Silver bowl

With an embossed decoration showing a stylized lotus-flower design.

Said to have been found near Erzincan, now
  in eastern Turkey
Bequeathed in 1897 by A.W. Franks
H 4.55 cm, Diam 25.8 cm, Wt 541.3 g
British Museum, ANE 124082
Dalton 1964: no. 180, pl. XXIII; Curtis, Cowell
  and Walker 1995: pl. XXVIIIa–b

105 Shallow silver bowl

With embossed decoration on the underside
showing a central rosette and radiating petals.

Oxus Treasure
Bequeathed in 1897 by A.W. Franks
H 2.53 cm, Diam 14.5 cm, Wt 247 g
British Museum, ANE 123920
Dalton 1964: no. 19, pl. V

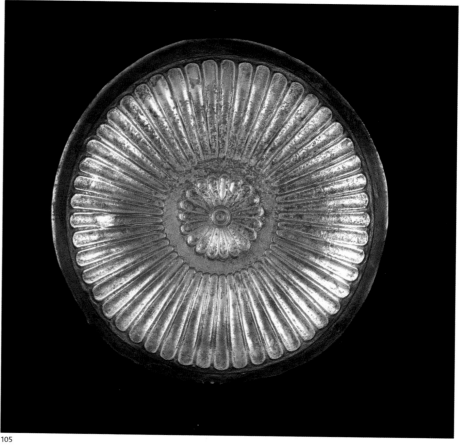

105

106 (centre), 107 (left), 108 (right)

106 Deep silver bowl

With a central shoulder, rounded bottom and flared rim.

Said to have been found near Erzincan, now in eastern Turkey
Bequeathed in 1897 by A.W. Franks
H 11 cm, Diam 17.4 cm, Wt 423.7 g
British Museum, ANE 123256
Dalton 1964: no. 184

107 Deep silver bowl

Similar to cat. 106 above.

Said to have been found near Erzincan, now in eastern Turkey
Bequeathed in 1897 by A.W. Franks
H 12.7 cm, Diam 21.1 cm, Wt 634.8 g
British Museum, ANE 123258
Dalton 1964: no. 182, fig. 72 on p. 75

108 Deep silver bowl

Similar to cat. 106 above.

Said to have been found near Erzincan, now in eastern Turkey
Bequeathed in 1897 by A.W. Franks
H 12.2 cm, Diam 21.2 cm, Wt 214.1 g
British Museum, ANE 123255
Dalton 1964: no. 183

109 Shallow silver bowl

Plain, with a flat narrow border.

Said to have been found near Erzincan, now in eastern Turkey
Bequeathed in 1897 by A.W. Franks
H 2.5 cm, Diam 30 cm, Wt 610 g
British Museum, ANE 123259
Dalton 1964: no. 181

110 Large bronze bowl

Of similar shape to cat. 106.

Susa, no known provenance
H 26.3 cm, Diam 41.4 cm
Louvre, Sb 13757

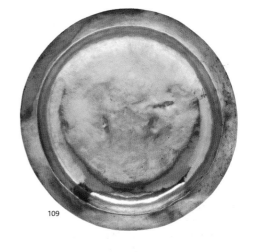

109

110

111 Hemispherical silver bowl

Decorated on the outside with applied sheet gold cut-outs showing battlements at the top and two rows of figures, possibly a king, below, separated by a band of rosettes. Each figure wears a crown and Persian dress, and has a bow and a quiver on his back. There is a comparable bowl in the Lydian Treasure (Özgen and Öztürk *et al.* 1996: no. 33).

Provenance unknown
Purchased in 1966, formerly in the Spencer-
    Churchill Collection
H 6.9 cm, Diam 10.3 cm, Wt 188 g
British Museum, ANE 134740
Catalogue of Exhibition of Persian Art 1931: Gallery I,
    case 10, no. F; Barnett and Curtis 1973: pl. LIVa;
    Moorey 1988b: 233–4, pl. I; Curtis 2000: fig. 63

112 Bronze bowl

With high sides, and embossed and chased decoration showing two pairs of winged lions back to back separated by rosettes.

Said to come from Hamadan
H *c.* 12 cm, Diam *c.* 18 cm
Tehran, 1394-7819

111

112

113

114 Glass dish

Cast in greenish colourless glass, decorated with petals in relief on the lower part in Achaemenid style. This is one of the few examples of glass bowls of this shape that have been found outside the Persian Empire.

Said to come from Cumae, near Naples
Donated by the executors of Felix Slade in 1870.
  Previously in the collection of Dr Eugene Piot
H 3.9 cm, Diam 17.4 cm
British Museum, GR 1870.6-6.7
Harden 1981: 1266

113 Glass bowl

With flared rim of typical Achaemenid shape and flower decoration in low relief on the underside.

Provenance unknown
H 9.4 cm, Diam 19.7 cm
Museum of Glass and Ceramics, Tehran, no. 2-A
Seipel 2000: no. 119

114

115 Shallow bowl

Slightly carinated with a flat base. In polished black-and-white veined stone.

Persepolis (L182)
H 2.8 cm, Diam 12.4 cm
Tehran, 514

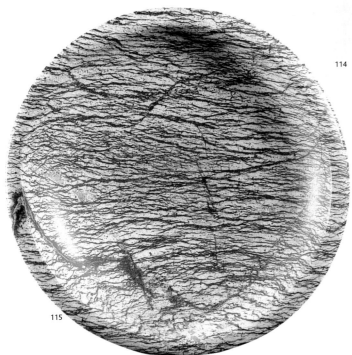

115

119

116 Shallow bowl

In grey pottery with flared rim and applied gadroons, probably in imitation of a metal prototype.

Pasargadae, found in 1962 (PAS 62 276)
H 5.8 cm, Diam 11.5 cm
British Museum, ANE 135953
Stronach 1978: fig. 106/11

117 Bowl

Of polished speckled black-and-white stone, originally with four handles in the form of lions. Bands of precious metal may also have been pinned to the exterior. An inscription in Assyrian cuneiform mentioning Ashurbanipal, King of Assyria (668–627 BC), is incised on the exterior: 'Palace of Ashurbanipal, great king, [mighty king, king] of the world, king of Assyria'. This bowl may have been brought to Iran following the sack of the Assyrian cities in 612 BC.

Persepolis, fragments found in Hall 41 and Corridor
  31 of the Treasury (PT4 368; PT5 156, 244)
H 9.2 cm, Diam 23 cm
Tehran, 2590
Schmidt 1957: pl. 49/1a–d; Calmeyer 1994

116

117

RHYTONS

118 Gold rhyton

Gold horn-shaped rhyton terminating in the foreparts of a winged lion. There is a frieze of lotus and bud decoration just beneath the rim.

Said to be from Hamadan
H 21.3 cm, W 18 cm, Diam 12.5 cm, Wt 1897 g
Tehran, 1321
Illustrated London News, 21 July 1956, pl. on p. 107; Sept Mille Ans 1961: no. 664, pl. LVII; Ghirshman 1964: fig. 290; Muscarella 2000: 53, no. 7; Seipel 2000: no. 113

118

120 Silver horn-shaped rhyton

This rhyton has a gold bull protome with its forelegs folded beneath it.

Said to be from Marash, Syria
Purchased in Aleppo in 1923 by C.L. Woolley
H 22.5 cm, Diam 16.1 cm (rim)
British Museum, ANE 116411
Woolley 1923: 69–72, pl. 68

119 Silver horn-shaped rhyton with partial gilding

This rhyton has a protome in the form of a horned winged griffin with lions' paws. It has a fluted body and the rim is decorated with floral designs. There is a pouring hole in the chest of the animal protome.

Said to have been found near Erzincan, now
  in eastern Turkey
Bequeathed in 1897 by A.W. Franks
H 23 cm, Diam 14.5 cm (rim), Wt 891 g
British Museum, ANE 124081
Dalton 1964: no. 178, pl. XXII; Curtis 2000: fig. 60

121 Glass horn-shaped rhyton

The protome is in the form of a bull with its front legs folded beneath it, with sockets for separate ears and horns. It is being attacked by a lion which has jumped onto its back and is about to bite its neck. The two animals have been manufactured separately and then joined together. The middle part of the rhyton has been restored.

Persepolis
From the excavations of A. Sami
H 19.5 cm, max. Diam 10 cm
Tehran, 1421
Ghirshman 1962: fig. 26

122 Rhyton fragment

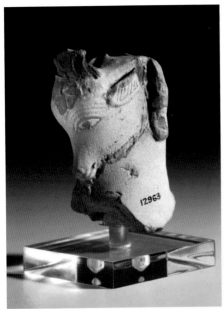

Terminal from a faience rhyton, with traces of green glaze, in the form of a bull's head.

Said to be from Tell el-Yahudiya, Egypt
Purchased from the Revd John Greville Chester
  in 1871
H 9.2 cm, W 4.83 cm, Th 5.81 cm
British Museum, AES 12963

122

123 Frieze from the Nereid Monument at Xanthos

This frieze shows the local ruler Arbinas (*c.* 390–370 BC) reclining on a couch, holding a bowl in one hand and a rhyton terminating in a winged griffin in the other.

Excavated by Sir Charles Fellows and acquired
  in 1848
L 115.6 cm
British Museum, GR 1848.10-20.97
Smith 1900: II, no. 903; Shahbazi 1975: 96–8,
  pl. LXIX; Chilas and Demargne 1989: 207–8,
  pl. 133; Ebbinghaus 2000

123

124

124 Clay counter-impression from a gem

The impression shows a fluted jug and rhyton with winged sphinx protome similar to that shown on the Nereid Monument (cat. 123).

From Ur, found in a coffin of the Persian period
Excavations of C.L. Woolley, 1931–2 (U.18124)
British Museum, ANE 1932-10-8, 226
Collon 1996: 74, pl. 20, fig. 10g

JUGS AND JARS

125 Gold jug

With fluted body, flared rim and handle terminating at the top in a lion's head.

Oxus Treasure
Bequeathed in 1897 by A.W. Franks
H 13 cm, rim Diam 8.65 cm, Wt 368.5 g
British Museum, ANE 123918
Dalton 1964: no. 17, pl. VII; Curtis 2000: fig. 72

Technical report by Barbara Ambruster

This jar with animal-shaped handle is cast in the lost wax technique and reveals a high standard of craftsmanship. The wax model was fashioned by using rotary motion. At the bottom of this gold vessel a central point indicates where it was fixed on the turning spindle of a lathe. For manufacturing this hollow object, a clay core was first worked on the axes of the lathe, using cutting tools such as scrapers, chisels or other kinds of blade. Then after drying the clay core, a thin layer of wax was applied and worked on the lathe. The jug's outer shape with parallel ribs reflects this way of preparing a perfectly cylindrical wax model using a rotating spindle. The inner surface still bears traces of the rough metal surface of the cast. The bottom is smooth and polished but the turning point of the lathe can still be seen.

After the body of the jug has been cast by the lost wax method, the separately cast handle with polygonal section and a lion's head was attached. The lion's head was fixed by soldering, and the lower part was riveted. The handle was cast by the lost wax technique and details of the decoration were then executed with chasing tools.

126 Silver amphora

With two handles and vertical fluting on the lower part of the body. There are two pouring spouts at the base.

Provenance unknown
H 24.3 cm, Diam 13.7 cm, Wt 912 g
Tehran, 1387
Sept Mille Ans 1961: no. 683, pl. LVI; Seipel 2000: no. 115

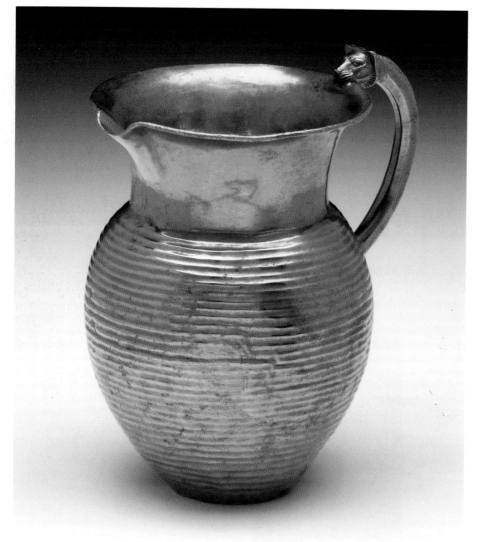

126

125

AMPHORA HANDLES

127 Gilded silver handle of a vase in the form of a leaping ibex

The hindlegs are attached to a flat plate with incurving sides decorated with an engraved palmette. The forelegs are flexed and rest against a curved bar originally attached to the rim of a vessel. The body of the figure is hollow and there is a rectangular aperture on the underside.

Oxus Treasure
Bequeathed in 1897 by A.W. Franks
L 21 cm, Wt 481 g
British Museum, ANE 123911
Dalton 1964: no. 10, pl. V

128 Gilded silver and bronze amphora handle in the form of a leaping winged ibex

This handle combines elements of Persian and Greek style. The hind feet rest on the head of a satyr at the handle attachment. It forms a pair with an ibex handle in Berlin (8180).

Tyzskiewicz Collection, acquired in 1898
H 26.5 cm, L 15 cm
Louvre, AO 2748
Amandry 1959: pls 26/2, 27/2–3, 28/4; Abdi
 1999: fig. 8/3; Boardman 2000: 188, fig. 5.70a–b

129 Silver amphora handle in the form of a winged bull

The bull's head is turned backwards and the body is hollow.

From a hoard of silver found at Babylon, Iraq
Excavations of Hormuzd Rassam, 1882
H 13.1 cm, Wt 200.5 g
British Museum, ANE 120450
Robinson 1950: pl. XXIII; Reade 1986: 80, no. 24,
 pl. II

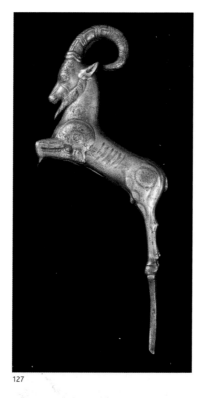

127

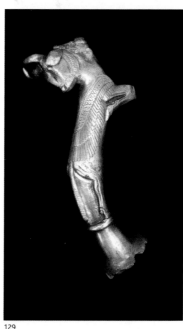

129

128

STRAINERS

130 Glazed pottery jar

With globular ridged body, made in cream-coloured clay.

Persepolis
H 19.6 cm, Diam 10.7 cm
Tehran, 2070

131 Polychrome glazed jar

The jar has petal decoration around the shoulder, and a tall neck and flat rim.

Persepolis
H 12.5 cm
Tehran, 2071

132 Silver strainer

The handle terminates in a calf's head with a lotus flower design where it meets the bowl of the strainer. Two Aramaic letters are engraved on the handle.

Purchased by C.L. Woolley in Beirut and acquired in 1925
L 25.3 cm, max. Diam 9.2 cm
British Museum, ANE 117840
Moorey 1980b: 186–7, pl. Ib

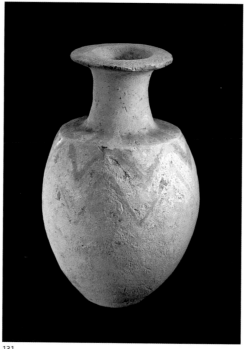

131

132

130

LADLES

133 Bronze strainer

With a calf-head terminal on a handle with bead-and-reel decoration. There is a lotus flower engraved on the junction with the bowl.

Found in the Southwest Palace, Nimrud, Iraq
Excavations of W.K. Loftus, 1854–5
L 21.5 cm, max. Diam 9.7 cm
British Museum, ANE 118462
Moorey 1980b: 186, pl. Ia; Curtis (ed.) 1997: pl. 4

134 Silver ladle

With a calf-head terminal on a loop handle set at a right-angle to the bowl.

Purchased in Aleppo by C.L. Woolley and acquired in 1923
L 22 cm, Diam 5.3 cm (bowl), Wt 87 g
British Museum, ANE 116410
Moorey 1980b: 187, pl. IIa

135 Silver ladle

With a calf-head terminal on a loop handle and beaded stem.

Provenance unknown, acquired in 1958
L 20.5 cm, Diam 5.8 cm (bowl), Wt 100.5 g
British Museum, ANE 118014
Moorey 1980b: 187, pl. IIb

133

134 (right), 135 (left)

SCOOPS

It is sometimes suggested that these scoops were used for shovelling incense, in which case they might have been used in religious ceremonies. Apart from the examples listed below, there are scoops from the Achaemenid-period site of Tell ed-Daim in northern Iraq (al-Tekriti 1960: pl. 5/17–18), and there is a silver example in the Lydian Treasure (Özgen and Öztürk *et al.* 1996: no. 70).

136 Silver scoop

Rectangular scoop with low vertically corrugated sides, rounded at one end and squared-off at the other. It is open at the square end and the base of the closed end has a rounded depression. Possibly used as a scoop for incense.

Said to have been found near Erzincan, now
  in eastern Turkey
Bequeathed in 1897 by A.W. Franks
L 25.3 cm, max. W 5.95 cm, Wt 215.1 g
British Museum, ANE 123263
Dalton 1964: no. 185, pl. XXIII

137 Silver scoop

As cat. 136 above.

Said to have been found near Erzincan, now
  in eastern Turkey
Bequeathed in 1897 by A.W. Franks
L 23.5 cm, max. W 6.5 cm, Wt 226.5 g
British Museum, ANE 123264
Dalton 1964: p. 45, no. 186

138 Scoop

In grey stone, of same shape as the silver examples above. The base of the closed end has a triangular depression.

South Persepolis, found in Hall 5, complex B
Excavations of A. Tadjvidi (70/IV/70)
H 3.4 cm, max. W 8.9 cm, L 23.6 cm
Tehran, 4182
Tajvidi 1976: 114–16, pl. 64

139 Scoop

In grey stone, of same shape as cats 136–7.

South Persepolis, found in Hall 5, complex B
Excavations of A. Tadjvidi (70/IV/1)
H 2.45 cm, max. W 7 cm, L 23.0 cm
Tehran, 4183
Tajvidi 1976: 114–16, pl. 63

136–7

138

139

ALABASTRONS

140 Calcite alabastron

With cuneiform inscriptions in Old Persian, Elamite and Babylonian, and Egyptian hieroglyphs of Xerxes I (485–465 BC), reading 'Xerxes great king'. This vessel, restored from fragments, has a pair of lug handles on the shoulders and a flat, ledge-shaped rim.

Found at Halikarnassos by Sir Charles Thomas
  Newton
Acquired in 1857
H 28.5 cm, max. W 17.5 cm
British Museum, ANE 132114
Newton 1863: vol. 1, 91, vol. 2, fig. 667; Weissbach
  1911: 118–19

140

141 Calcite alabastron fragment

With a ledge-shaped rim and a lug handle below the shoulder; the base is missing. It is inscribed with a trilingual inscription in Old Persian, Elamite and Babylonian cuneiform of Xerxes I (485–465 BC), reading 'Xerxes great king'.

Susa, found in the northern part of the citadel
  mound by W.K. Loftus
Acquired in 1853
H 15.8 cm, W 10.65 cm
British Museum, ANE 91459
Curtis 1993: no. 78, pl. 19a

142 Calcite alabastron fragment

With part of a trilingual inscription in Old Persian, Elamite and Babylonian cuneiform of Xerxes I (485–465 BC), reading 'Xerxes great king'.

Susa, found in the northern part of the citadel
  mound by W.K. Loftus
Acquired in 1853
H 9.1 cm, W 4.35 cm
British Museum, ANE 91453
Curtis 1993: no. 79, pl. 19a

141

143 Calcite alabastron fragment

With part of a trilingual inscription in Old Persian, Elamite and Babylonian cuneiform of Xerxes I (485–465 BC), reading 'Xerxes great king'.

Susa, found in the northern part of the citadel
  mound by W.K. Loftus
Acquired in 1853
H 9.1 cm, W 4.6 cm
British Museum, ANE 91454
Curtis 1993: no. 80, pl. 19a

144 Calcite alabastron fragment

With part of a trilingual inscription in Old Persian, Elamite and Babylonian cuneiform of Xerxes I (485–465 BC), reading 'Xerxes great king'.

Susa, found in the northern part of the citadel
  mound by W.K. Loftus
Acquired in 1853
H 7.1 cm, W 4.2 cm
British Museum, ANE 91455
Curtis 1993, no. 81, pl. 19a

145 Calcite alabastron fragment

Inscribed within a cartouche with the name of Xerxes I (485–465 BC) in Egyptian hieroglyphs, reading 'Xerxes great king'.

Susa, found in the northern part of the citadel
  mound by W.K. Loftus
Acquired in 1853
H 6.55 cm, W 2.45 cm
British Museum, ANE 91456
Curtis 1993: no. 82, pl. 19a

142–5

PLATES AND TRAYS

146 Plate of polished, red-veined white stone

Persepolis, possibly found at the northeastern corner
of the Treasury
H 5.5 cm, Diam 20 cm
Tehran, 2299
Possibly Schmidt 1957: pls 57/7, 59/3

147 Plate of polished dark speckled stone

Said to be from Qasr-i Abu Nasr
H 2.2 cm, Diam 21.1 cm
Tehran, 2512

146

147

148 Tray of grey stone

With concave sides and four handles terminating in ducks' heads, and a palmette between each pair of handles.

Persepolis, found in Hall 38 of the Treasury
H 2 cm, W 22 cm, L 36 cm
Tehran, 2199
Schmidt 1957: pls 53/2, 54/2

148

149 Tray of marverred red stone

With a single handle in the shape of a duck's head.

Persepolis, found in Hall 38 of the Treasury
H 6.5 cm, W 18.5 cm, L 40.7 cm
Tehran, 2335
Schmidt 1957: pls 53/5, 54/3

149

150

151 Silver pyxis

Round, with horizontally fluted sides, and a flat base and lid. The inside of the lid is decorated with incised figures of a man and woman.

Said to have been found near Erzincan, now
  in eastern Turkey
Bequeathed in 1897 by A.W. Franks
Diam 12.7 cm
British Museum, ANE 123265
Dalton 1964: 43–4, figs 19, 71, no. 179

150 Hollow gold fish

With a hole in the mouth and a loop for suspension above the left fin. Possibly a vessel for oil or perfume. Alternatively it may have been part of an elaborate group of pendants.

Oxus Treasure
L 24.2 cm, Wt 370 g
British Museum, ANE 123917
Dalton 1964: no. 16, pl. VI

151

7

JEWELLERY AND PERSONAL ORNAMENTS

John Curtis[1]

It is known that there was prosperity and great wealth during the Achaemenid period, particularly amongst court circles. This is attested by the ancient sources and to a lesser extent by archaeological discoveries. It is therefore surprising that more jewellery does not survive from this period.[2] The main collections from greater Iran are the hoard from a water jar found near one of the pavilions at Pasargadae, the jewellery accompanying the skeleton in a bronze coffin at Susa, and part of the Oxus Treasure. To this list should now be added the so-called 'Ardebil Treasure' in the Miho Museum in Japan, but like other recent examples of Achaemenid jewellery these pieces are entirely without provenance. Further afield, there are splendid examples of Achaemenid jewellery from Georgia and in the Lydian Treasure from western Turkey. There are also representations of jewellery in Achaemenid art, for example on the reliefs from Persepolis, on the glazed-brick panels from Susa, on the statue of Darius from Susa (cat. 88) and on the statue of Ptahhotep, treasurer of Egypt under Darius I, who is represented in Persian dress (fig. 50). This statue is now in the Brooklyn Museum.[3] In spite of the fact that the amount and range of Achaemenid jewellery are limited, the repertoire does include some magnificent examples. Thus Roger Moorey was able to write: 'Some of the most spectacular examples of this workmanship (the handiwork of the craftsmen employed by the Achaemenid kings and their courts) are to be found amongst the jewellery they produced'.[4]

Achaemenid jewellery is distinguished for the fine quality of the inlaid polychrome decoration that is characteristic of this period. In this tradition various items of jewellery were inlaid with pieces of stone, glass, faience (paste) and perhaps enamel, all of different colours. The inlays were fitted into cavities (cloisons) on the surface of the goldwork and held in place either by red-coloured cinnabar (native mercury sulphide, which occurs naturally in Iran) or by bitumen. The most popular inlay stones were turquoise, lapis lazuli and carnelian, while other stones used from time to time included onyx, rock crystal, agate, lazulite and mother-of-pearl. True cloisonné enamel (powdered glass fused in place rather than pieces of glass inlay cut to fit) is rare but occasionally attested. We know from the foundation inscription of Darius from Susa that some at least of the gold used in this period came from Bactria (northern Afghanistan) and the same inscription informs us that lapis lazuli and carnelian came from Sogdiana (to the east of the River Oxus) and turquoise from Chorasmia (to the east of the Caspian Sea). It used to be thought that the tradition of polychrome cloisonné jewellery was transmitted to Achaemenid Iran from Egypt, where there was a tradition of polychrome jewellery going back to the Middle Kingdom in the second millennium BC. This view was supported by the fact that according to Darius's foundation inscription, 'The goldsmiths who wrought the gold [i.e. in the palace], they were Medes and Egyptians ...'. The role of these goldsmiths in the building of the palace is not clear, but evidently they were master craftsmen who might also have been making jewellery. However, the four tombs of Assyrian queens discovered at Nimrud in 1989–90 contained many fine pieces of jewellery with polychrome inlay. This indicates that the technology was already present in the ancient Near East in the ninth to eighth centuries BC, and could easily have been passed from Assyria to Achaemenid Iran. In jewellery of the Achaemenid period polychrome decoration is found in bracelets and torcs, earrings, pectorals, beads and clothing ornaments.

BRACELETS AND TORCS

Bracelets, usually with animal-head terminals, were very popular during the Achaemenid period. In the glazed-brick panels from Susa both the archers and other figures wear bracelets (cats 51–2), and on the statue from Susa Darius wears bracelets decorated with calves' heads. Ptahhotep also wears bracelets. Particularly elaborate examples of surviving jewellery are the

50 Stone statue of Ptahhotep, treasurer of Egypt under Darius. He wears bracelets, a torc and a pectoral in the Persian style. *Brooklyn Museum 37.353.*

51 Bracelets with griffin terminals carried by delegation VI (Lydians) on the east side of the Apadana at Persepolis.

gold bracelets with ibex-head terminals from Pasargadae (cat. 152), which are decorated with filigree work and granulation. In the Oxus Treasure, terminals are in the form of lions' heads, lion-griffins' heads, rams' heads, goats' heads, ducks' heads, winged goats, bull protomes and dragons. These bracelets belong to a long-established Near Eastern tradition but new in this period is the extensive use of polychrome inlays. Many of the bracelets have cells or cloisons for inlay just behind the animals' heads, often in order to create some special effect such as the mane of a lion. The best-known examples of inlaid bracelets are the armlets from the Oxus Treasure (cat. 153). They have lion-griffin terminals and were originally inlaid with coloured stones, glass and faience. It is uncertain whether such armlets were ever actually worn, as the lion-griffins standing up proud of the hoop would have made them very impractical. Two other bracelets in the Oxus Treasure, those with winged goat terminals and those with bull protomes, may have been similarly difficult to wear, but not impossibly so like the Oxus armlets.

Xenophon tells us in the *Anabasis* that bracelets were among the gifts that were highly esteemed amongst the Persians (*Anabasis* I.2.27). He records that Cyrus the Younger gave Syennesis 'gifts which are regarded at court as tokens of honour – a horse with a gold-mounted bridle, a gold necklace and bracelets, a gold

dagger and a Persian robe'. The high regard in which bracelets were held is reflected by the fact that large animal-headed bracelets are shown being presented to the king by four of the delegations on the Apadana reliefs at Persepolis. These are delegations I (Medes), VI (Lydians), XI (pointed-hat Scythians) and XVII (Sogdians or Chorasmians). In one case (delegation VI) the terminals are in the form of winged griffins comparable with the Oxus Treasure bracelets (fig. 51).[5]

Less certainly identified as bracelets are those pieces where the hoop is coiled round two to three times in a spiral shape. Such pieces in the Oxus Treasure have lion's-head, goat's-head and ram's-head terminals (cats 154–9). They either have fine ribbed decoration on the hoop, or hoops of twisted metal. These pieces might originally have been torcs that were worn around the neck, as Dalton tells us that 'when found they were doubled up and twisted out of shape; and their present symmetrical form was given to them subsequent to their discovery'.[6] We know that torcs were worn in the Achaemenid period: there is the magnificent example with lion's-head terminals from Susa (cat. 270) and Darius III wears a torc with animal-head terminals on the Alexander Mosaic from Pompeii.[7] A particularly magnificent torc with terminals in the form of recumbent ibexes is shown on the statue of Ptahhotep.

EARRINGS

The most distinctive form of earring in the Achaemenid period was a flat, round shape that did not quite describe a full circle (penannular); a wedge-shaped opening was left in the top part, and across this opening was a hinged pin or holder for fixing it to the ear. This pin usually had holes at either end and was held in place by two small pegs. The simpler expressions of this earring type have a flat surface area, hollow in the centre, sometimes decorated around the edge with globules set on stalks, probably imitating flowers. There is a silver example from Babylon (cat. 179) and a gold example with a representation of the Egyptian dwarf-god Bes (cat. 177), who became a popular motif in the Achaemenid Empire. A splendid earring of this shape from the coffin burial at Susa (cat. 269) has cloisonné decoration on both sides in lapis lazuli and turquoise. The most elaborate examples of this earring type are from the hoard found near one of the pavilions at Pasargadae (cats 173–5). The forms are made from gold wire and combine exquisite filigree and granulation work. They all have pendants, either mounted in the body of the earring or suspended from it, or both. The overall effect of these earrings must have been dazzling, an effect enhanced by the tiny pendants. David Stronach has written: 'Regardless of their shape all such pendants were hung as loosely as possible, each shimmering and trembling at the slightest movement'.[8]

Earrings can be seen on the Persepolis reliefs and on the glazed-brick panels from Susa being worn by figures in both Persian and Median dress. Generally these earrings seem to be simple circular rings,[9] but occasionally they resemble the flat form we have been describing.[10] The human-headed bulls that flank gateways and appear on column capitals have lunate (crescentic) earrings that were a common type in Assyria and reflect the

52 Relief on the east jamb of the western doorway in the north wall of the main hall, Palace of Darius, Persepolis, showing the king with two attendants. The holes in the sculpture are for the attachment of gold bracelets and a gold crown. The inlaid beard may have been of lapis lazuli.

Assyrian origin of the man-headed bull.[11] Several of the delegations bringing gifts on the Apadana reliefs wear circular rings with drop-like pendants.[12]

Earrings were also part of the kingly appareil. Thus the Greek author Arrian, writing in the second century AD but quoting an earlier source, refers to 'earrings of stones set in gold' (presumably gold earrings with polychrome stone inlays) amongst the precious objects in the Tomb of Cyrus at Pasargadae.[13]

PECTORALS

The form was only introduced into the ancient Near East in the Achaemenid period. It was borrowed from Egypt, where earlier examples are known. A particularly fine pectoral is shown on the Egyptian statue of Ptahhotep in Persian costume now in the Brooklyn Museum. This is a rectangular example with a design showing a king, prob-

ably Darius, before two deities. Such pectorals are not yet known from the archaeological record proper, but a very fine unprovenanced pectoral pendant showing a battle scene is now in the Miho Museum in Japan. It has provision for polychrome inlays, and on the back is a crudely incised Greek inscription giving the weight.[14]

BEADS

The best evidence for beads in the Achaemenid period comes from the coffin burial at Susa, where at least five necklaces were found, some of them with multiple strands. The most elaborate gold beads are inlaid with turquoise and lapis lazuli, while others are decorated with granulation. The simple gold beads are barrel-shaped or melon-shaped. One of the necklaces was made up of fine pearls. In addition, a wide variety of stones was used, and in one of the necklaces Françoise Tallon has noted turquoise, lapis lazuli, carnelian, emerald (amazonite), agate, jasper, feldspar, flint, quartz, amethyst, haematite, marble and breccia.[15]

CLOTHING ORNAMENTS

There is a long tradition of decorating textiles and clothes with golden ornaments in the ancient Near East[16] and this clearly continued into the Achaemenid period. Herodotus tells us that the Immortals were richly adorned with gold (*History* VII.83). On the reliefs at Persepolis the robes of the Persian kings are in some cases richly decorated with motifs that include lions and patterned roundels (fig. 52).[17] The finest clothing ornaments to have survived are the pair of inlaid roundels or 'buttons' from the coffin at Susa (cat. 271) and a single example from Pasargadae.[18] All are typical examples of cloisonné jewellery with polychrome inlays. The roundel from Pasargadae is decorated like a flower and is inlaid with turquoise and white-and-grey faience.

Other clothing ornaments, sometimes called bracteates, are gold plaques that have loops or small rings fixed to the back so that they can be sewn onto cloth. Sometimes they have holes around the edge. There are a number of these bracteates in the Oxus Treasure, the most remarkable of which is a gold cut-out crowned figure in Persian dress holding a flower (cat. 189). The gold roundels in the Oxus Treasure (cats 183–8) have motifs that include a lion-griffin, an eagle, a crowned sphinx, a figure in a winged disc and the Egyptian dwarf-god Bes. An openwork roundel has a sphinx with a monstrous wing. From Persepolis is a miniature gold lion (cat. 190). Of unknown provenance, but sometimes ascribed to Hamadan for no good reason, are gold plaques in the form of striding lions and animal heads, and openwork roundels showing rampant lions back to back and a human bust within a crescent. All these forms except the animal heads occur amongst a group of fifty-three unprovenanced appliqués that are now in the Oriental Institute in Chicago.[19] There are more examples allegedly from Hamadan in the National Museum in Tehran.

TECHNOLOGICAL ASPECTS OF THE OXUS TREASURE BRACELETS (CAT. 153)
Barbara Regine Armbruster

The two Oxus bracelets have characteristics of sculpture. Both are constructed from several parts, which were executed individually and then joined. The three-dimensional design of figural representation was originally enriched by polychrome decoration, contrasting with the shine of the gold. Another element of the design is the relief work, which, depending on the reflection of the light, or its absence in shadowed parts, varies from light to dark, contrasting with the smooth undecorated hoop. A colourful effect was achieved by the incrustation of inorganic material.

53 (below left)
Tool marks from punches on an Oxus Treasure bracelet.

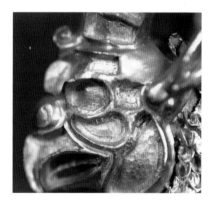

54 (above right)
A soldered sheet on an Oxus Treasure bracelet.

The animal-shaped terminals as well as the central part of the round-sectioned hoop are hollow. Several authors have suggested that the central part of the hoop was solid,[20] but a hole where one of bracelets has been damaged clearly shows its tubular section.

CASTING
Except for the wings and cloisons, the tubular hoop, head and horns, including the deep settings, were cast over a clay core in the lost wax process. The relief parts on the surface of the hoops as well as the griffins' extremities and details of the head were also modelled in wax. In some places traces of working in wax with tracers and scrapers are recognizable. Raw cast surfaces resulting from the casting process remain on the crest, which imitates pearled wire, on the neck and on unfinished edges.

A wax model with all the relief details was worked over a clay core and joined to wax channels. The whole was covered with tempered clay in several layers, interrupted by drying. The clay core was kept in place by being fixed to the clay mould with metal sticks. The dried clay mould was then heated in a furnace to melt out the wax. Gold melted in a crucible was poured into the hollow of the mould. After solidification of the metal the mould was destroyed and the casting channels cut off.

Finishing of the raw casts was carried out partly by plastic shaping techniques. The smooth surfaces of undecorated parts indicate that they were polished.

PLASTIC SHAPING
The cast metal surfaces of the bracelets and the elements of relief were reworked by plastic shaping techniques, such as chasing, and the use of punches, chisels and a hammer. Tool marks from punches are visible on the metal surfaces (fig. 53). This work was done from the outside, while the inside was filled by the clay core.

Hammering techniques were used in the production of the sheet metal strips and wires for the wings and additional cloisons. Pliers were used for bending the sheet strips into cloisons.

JOINING AND REPAIRS BY SOLDERING
Mounting and joining by soldering was used for the wings and several cloison clusters. Soldering was carried out using a gold alloy with a lower melting point than the base metal. The various elements were assembled, and small particles of solder applied and fused in the heat of a furnace.

The cast settings have very thin cast bottoms that were reworked with punches and often cracked. Several instances of damage can be detected. In one case such a hole was repaired by the addition of a small sheet fixed by soldering (fig. 54).

INCRUSTATION
Except for the wings, the hollows of the square and rounded settings were all prepared as negative forms in wax, cast and finished. In the case of the Oxus bracelets none of the recesses indicates their production by carving or chiselling in the metal, or deep chasing, as O.M. Dalton proposed.[21] The bracelets attest to three methods of manufacturing the combination of settings and subdivision cluster elements.

Some recesses were realized by subtractive carving in the wax model before casting. They were reworked after casting by means of plastic shaping. This is the case for the inlay compartments without any subdivision cells on the legs, horns and the front part of the head, as well as for the oblong sunk panel composed of several individual depressions representing the tail.

Other settings were cast as the previous ones, but then enriched with subdivision elements. These cloisons consist of thin sheet metal elements mounted by soldering. Thin strips bent in the shape of cells were soldered vertically onto a ground sheet with the outside shape of the desired inlay. This ensemble was then inlaid in the compartment and fixed by gold chips cut from the walls. With a sharp engraver or chiselling tool several deep incisions were made on the inner wall of the setting, creating a sharp spur. The spur was then bent in order to

55 (below left) A wing-shaped soldered sheet on an Oxus Treasure bracelet.

56 (above right) Spurs cut into the edge of a wing on an Oxus Treasure bracelet.

hold the fine inserted sheet. This second method was applied to the incrustations on the neck, the side and back of the head, the breast and the rectangular hollow at the back.

The third variety of setting is the one used exclusively for the wings. They were worked separately from the cast hoop, by fashioning a baseplate with a thick rectangular section wire that formed the rim of the setting. The wings were then fixed to the cast bracelet by soldering. The final work consisted of filling the large wing-shaped depression with small cell elements. As in the second method, fine gold strips were bent in the shape of feathers and a large quantity of these elements were attached by soldering them onto a wing-shaped sheet (fig. 55). The ensemble was finally fixed in the depression by means of spurs cut in the rim of the wing (fig. 56).

The inlay material had to be shaped according to the outline and height of the settings. O.M. Dalton mentions a lazulite (lapis lazuli?) fragment left in one compartment.[22]

WORKSHOP

These outstanding bracelets of complex shape reflect the sophisticated technical knowledge of the Achaemenid period. The goldsmiths were specialized professionals with a high level of skill in both artistic and aesthetic terms. Several fine metal-working techniques were combined and executed in a predetermined sequence of

steps. The bracelets represent one of the most difficult manufacturing achievements of the Oxus Treasure finds apart from the miniature chariot. The workshop which produced such elaborate gold jewellery must have been well equipped. Tool marks and surface textures, and the form and decoration of the objects under consideration indicate that the equipment included the following items: a furnace with bellows, a clay crucible, clay moulds and crucible tongs needed for melting and casting in lost wax. Grinding stones and abrasives were used for smoothing and polishing the cast surface. Reworking the cast settings and the relief decoration was done using punches, chisels and engravers. For the manufacture of sheet metal and square section wire, hammers and anvils of stone or metal were needed. Pliers were used for bending strips, sheets and wire. Dividing sheet metal into strips or other shapes was carried out by means of a hammer and chisel with a sharp cutting edge. Soldering was done in the furnace using a gold alloy with a lower melting temperature than the base metal. Measuring tools such as dividers and rulers served during the manufacturing process for dimensional accuracy.

1 This chapter was to have been written by Dr P.R.S. Moorey, but he was unable to complete it before his untimely death on 23 December 2004.

2 For Achaemenid jewellery see Amandry 1958, Rehm 1992 and Moorey 1998.

3 Moorey 1988: pls 58a–b.

4 Moorey 1998: 155.

5 Walser 1966: pl. 47 for the representation on the east side of the Apadana; on the north side of the Apadana, delegation VI is bringing animal-headed bracelets – see cat. 20.

6 Dalton 1964: 32

7 Roaf 1990: 215–16; Dalton 1964: fig. 13 on p. xxxi.

8 Stronach 1978: 169.

9 For example, Walser 1966, pl. 69.

10 For example, Rehm 1992: fig. 57.

11 For example, Rehm 1992: fig. 60.

12 For example, delegations XIII, XV; Walser 1966: pls 62, 65–6.

13 Arrian, *Anabasis of Alexander* VI.29.6.

14 Bernard and Inigaki 2000.

15 Harper, Aruz and Tallon 1992: 248.

16 Oppenheim 1949.

17 Kantor 1957: pls XI–XII.

18 Stronach 1978: pl. 157a–b.

19 Kantor 1957: pls III–VI.

20 For example, Dalton 1964: 32.

21 Dalton 1964: 33.

22 Dalton 1964: 34.

BRACELETS AND ARMLETS

152 Pair of gold bracelets with ibex-head terminals

The heads are cast and have separately applied ears and horns. The junctions between the spirally twisted wire hoop and the terminals are covered with sleeves, which have applied wire decoration (filigree) in spiral and plaited shapes.

Pasargadae, found in a pottery jar near Pavilion B
 together with cats 172–5
Diam 7.0 cm, Wt 42.8 g
Diam 6.5 cm, Wt 41.8 g
Tehran, 3183
Stronach 1978: 168. no. 1, fig. 85/4, pls 146–7

152, detail of ibex-head terminal

152

154 (right), 155 (left), 156 (centre)

153 Pair of gold bracelets or armlets with leaping lion-griffin terminals

The monsters have an eagle's head and wings, a lion's body and forepaws, and a goat's horns and back legs. There are cells or cloisons for polychrome inlays of stone, glass and faience on the heads, necks, wings and horns, and larger cavities for inlay on the bodies of the animals. A few of the smaller inlays survive. The hoops of these massive armlets have an in-swing opposite the terminals. The component parts of the armlets have been made separately.

Oxus Treasure

a) Bequeathed in 1897 by A.W. Franks
H 12.8 cm, W 11.57 cm, Wt 397.1 g
British Museum, ANE 124017
Dalton 1964: no. 116, pl. I; Curtis 2000: fig. 69

b) Purchased from Capt. F.C. Burton in 1884
H 12.4 cm, W 11.7 cm, Wt 395.5 g
Victoria & Albert Museum, 442-1884 (on long-term
  loan to the British Museum)

154 Spiral gold bracelet or torc with lion's-head terminals

The bracelet has two coils and a ribbed hoop. There are fine cavities for inlays, now missing, on the necks of the lions, perhaps to imitate manes, and larger cavities for further inlays behind these.

Oxus Treasure
Bequeathed in 1897 by A.W. Franks
Diam 10.35 cm, Wt 265.5 g
British Museum, ANE 124018
Dalton 1964: no. 117, fig. 65 on p. 34

155 Spiral gold bracelet or torc with lion's-head terminals

Similar to cat. 154 above, with two coils and a ribbed hoop, but with provision for larger inlays on the lions' necks.

Oxus Treasure
Bequeathed in 1897 by A.W. Franks
Diam 11.1 cm, Wt 242 g
British Museum, ANE 124019
Dalton 1964: no. 118, pl. XVII

156 Spiral gold bracelet or torc with lion's-head terminals

The bracelet has three coils. The ribbed hoop does not belong with the heads and is probably modern.

Oxus Treasure
Bequeathed in 1897 by A.W. Franks
Diam 6.4 cm, Wt 73 g
British Museum, ANE 124027
Dalton 1964: no. 125, not illustrated

153a (top), 153b (bottom)

157 Spiral gold bracelet or torc with ram's-head terminals

With three coils and a ribbed hoop. There are cavities for inlays, now missing, on the necks of the rams.

Oxus Treasure
Bequeathed in 1897 by A.W. Franks
Diam 8.55 cm, Wt 224.5 g
British Museum, ANE 124035
Dalton 1964: no. 132, pl. XX

158 Spiral gold bracelet or torc with goat's-head terminals

With three coils and a twisted hoop.

Oxus Treasure
Bequeathed in 1897 by A.W. Franks
Diam 8.1 cm, Wt 230.5 g
British Museum, ANE 124041
Dalton 1964: no. 138, pl. XVII

159 Spiral gold bracelet or torc with goat's-head terminals

Similar to cat. 158, with two coils and a twisted hoop.

Oxus Treasure
Bequeathed in 1897 by A.W. Franks
Diam 10.1 cm, Wt 240.5 g
British Museum, ANE 124042
Dalton 1964: no. 139, not illustrated

160 Penannular gold bracelet with lion's-head terminals

There are cavities for inlays, now missing, near the terminals. They were intended to show lions' manes. The hoop is ribbed.

Oxus Treasure
Bequeathed in 1897 by A.W. Franks
Diam 6.3 cm, Wt 29 g
British Museum, ANE 124021
Dalton 1964: no. 120, pl. XVIII

162 Penannular gold bracelet with lion's-head terminals

There are longitudinal channels on the terminals behind the lions' heads, perhaps to imitate manes. The hoop is ribbed.

Oxus Treasure
Bequeathed in 1897 by A.W. Franks
Diam 7.9 cm, Wt 40 g
British Museum, ANE 124025
Dalton 1964: no. 123, not illustrated

163 Penannular bracelet with gold lion-griffin terminals

As above, there are longitudinal channels on the terminals behind the lions' heads, perhaps to imitate manes. The terminals are set on a modern twisted silver wire hoop.

Oxus Treasure
Bequeathed in 1897 by A.W. Franks
Diam 6.55 cm, Wt 27.5 g
British Museum, ANE 124034
Dalton 1964: no. 131, pl. XVIII

164 Penannular gold bracelet with ram's-head terminals

The necks of the animals and their eyes have cavities for inlay, some of which still contain pieces of turquoise.

Oxus Treasure
Bequeathed in 1897 by A.W. Franks
Diam 7.25 cm, Wt 67 g
British Museum, ANE 124036
Dalton 1964: no. 133, fig. 67, pl. XIX

161 Penannular gold bracelet with lion's-head terminals

Gold wire has been wound around the necks of the lions. The hoop is ribbed.

Oxus Treasure
Bequeathed in 1897 by A.W. Franks
Diam 7.9 cm, Wt 48 g
British Museum, ANE 124026
Dalton 1964: no. 124, pl. XIX

165 Penannular gold bracelet with goat's-head terminals

Oxus Treasure
Bequeathed in 1897 by A.W. Franks
Diam 7.45 cm, Wt 89 g
British Museum, ANE 124043
Dalton 1964: no. 140, pl. XIX

157–8

159

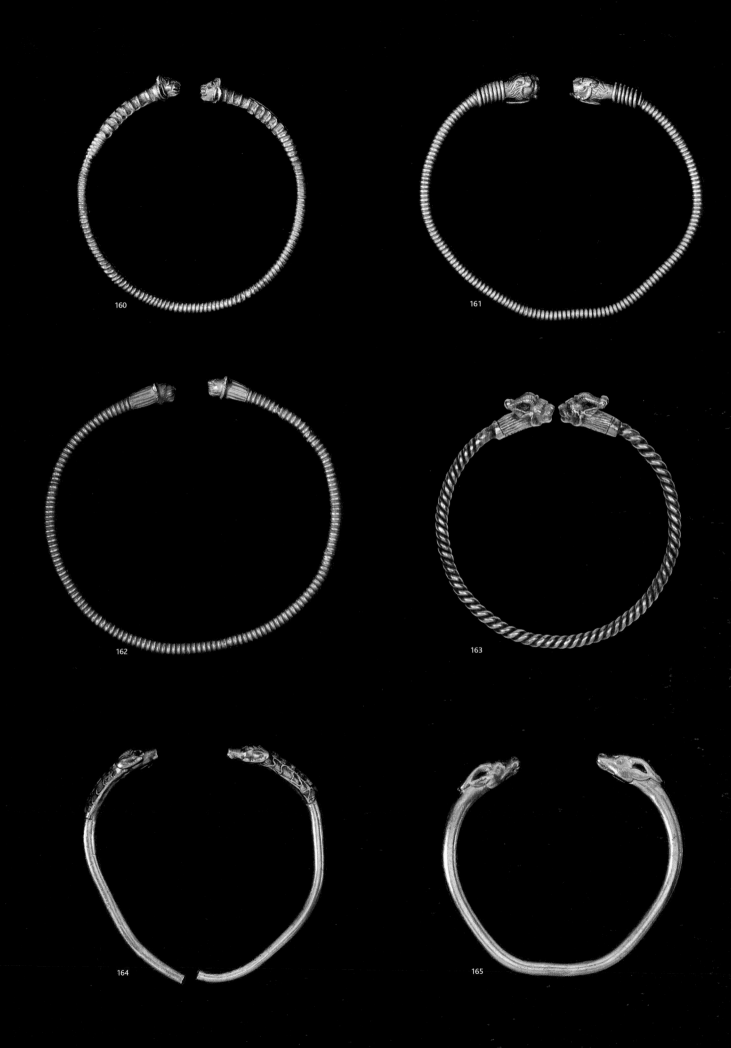

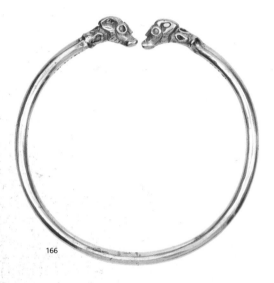

166

167

166 Penannular bracelet with gold goat's-head terminals

There are cavities for inlays that are now missing on the necks of the goats. The terminals are set on a modern plain silver hoop.

Oxus Treasure
Bequeathed in 1897 by A.W. Franks
Diam 6.8 cm, Wt 23 g
British Museum, ANE 124037
Dalton 1964: no. 134, pl. XVIII

167 Penannular bracelet with gold goat's-head terminals

The heads, necks and horns of the goats have cavities for inlays that are now missing. The terminals are set on a modern plain silver hoop.

Oxus Treasure
Bequeathed in 1897 by A.W. Franks
Diam 6.3 cm, Wt 32 g
British Museum, ANE 124038
Dalton 1964: no. 135, pl. XVIII

168 Penannular gold bracelet with terminals in the form of winged goats

The winged goats, with folded front legs, on this bracelet can be compared with the amphora handle cat. 127. The hoop is ribbed.

Oxus Treasure
Bequeathed in 1897 by A.W. Franks
Diam 8.3 cm, Wt 58.5 g
British Museum, ANE 124040
Dalton 1964: no. 137, pl. XX

169 Gold bracelet with terminals in the form of bull protomes

Partly restored. The protomes stand proud of the ribbed hoop.

Oxus Treasure
Bequeathed in 1897 by A.W. Franks
Diam 5.55 cm, Wt 27 g
British Museum, ANE 124044
Dalton 1964: no. 141, not illustrated

170 Penannular gold bracelet with duck's-head terminals

Oxus Treasure
Bequeathed in 1897 by A.W. Franks
Diam 7.5 cm, Wt 38.5 g
British Museum, ANE 124045
Dalton 1964: no. 142, pl. XIX

171 Pair of gold bracelets with terminals in the form of monstrous animal heads

The monsters have long snouts, rows of teeth, triangular-shaped eyes and long tails which interlock at the back of the hoop. The cast is solid. These bracelets can be associated either with art from the Caucasus or with the Scythian-style art of western Siberia.

Oxus Treasure
Bequeathed in 1897 by A.W. Franks
Diam of each 7.9 cm, Wts 140.5 and 138.8 g
British Museum, ANE 124047-8
Dalton 1964: nos 144–5, fig. 68, pl. XX; Curtis and Kruszynski 2002: nos 169–70, fig. 41, pl. 15

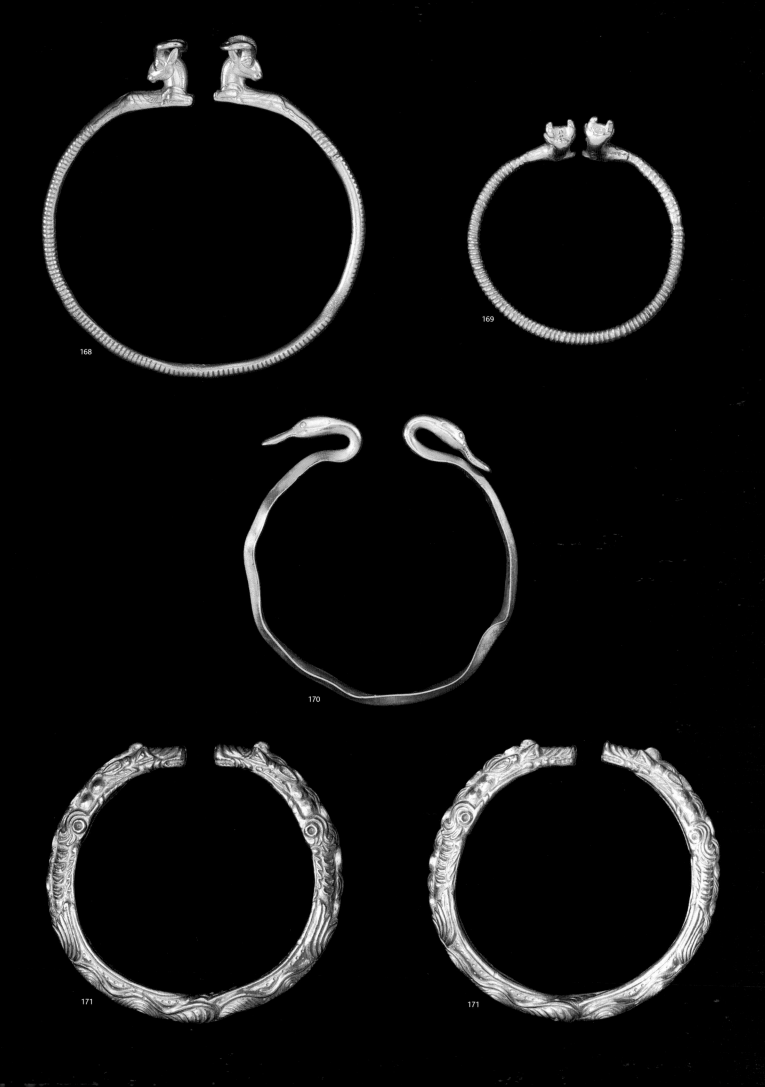

168

169

170

171

171

NECKLACES

172 Necklace with cast gold pendants

The pendants are in the form of a full-face head of Bes, a human head in profile with a flat hat or crown, an ibex head in profile, and a roaring lion head in profile.

Pasargadae, found in a pottery jar near Pavilion B together with cats 152, 173–5

H of pendants 0.9–1.3 cm

Tehran, 3193

Stronach 1978: 170–71, nos 13–16, pl. 154

EARRINGS

173 Pair of gold earrings

With circular openwork bodies consisting of a border of gold wire flowers around the outside and two rows of gold discs decorated with granulation in the centre. The middle of the earring is clear of ornament. In the top centre there is a bar from which three ball-shaped pendants are suspended. At the top of the earring is a hinged pin for attaching it to the ear.

Pasargadae, found in a pottery jar near Pavilion B together with cats 152, 172, 174–5

Diam 4.9 cm, max. Th 0.9 cm, Wt 19 g

Tehran, 3184

Stronach 1978: 169, no. 3, fig. 85/2, pl. 149

174 Pair of gold earrings

With circular wire mesh bodies. In the centre are three bars from which are suspended pendants in the form of pomegranates in the upper and middle rows, and circular discs in the bottom row. From the bottom of the earring hangs a lapis-lazuli pendant in a wire mesh cage adorned with gold granules. At the top of the earring is a hinged pin for attaching it to the ear.

Pasargadae, found in a pottery jar near Pavilion B together with cats 152, 172–3, 175

Diam of each example 5.1 cm, Th 0.9 cm, Wt 20 g

Tehran, 3185

Stronach 1978: 168–9, no. 2, fig. 85/1, pl. 148

172

173

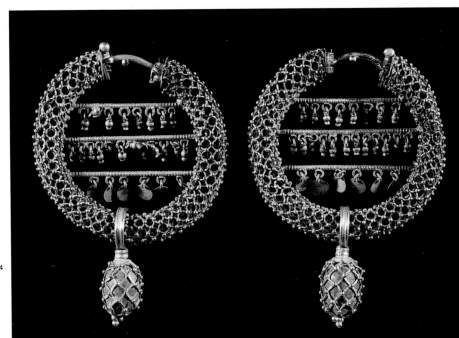

174

175

176

177

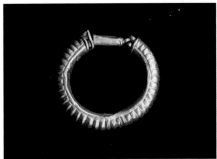

178

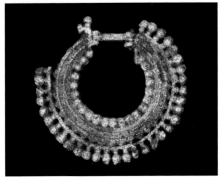

179

175 Pair of gold earrings

Made of gold wire supporting eight leaf or petal shapes that were inlaid with turquoise paste. There are clusters of granulation all around the edge of the earring, and at the bottom are three pendants in the form of leaves or petals that were also inlaid. The middle of the earring is clear of ornament. At the top of the earring there is a hinged pin for attaching it to the ear.

Pasargadae, found in a pottery jar near Pavilion B
together with cats 152, 172–4
Diam of each example 3.6 cm, H 4.4 cm, Wt 9.0 g
Tehran, 3186
Stronach 1978: 169, no. 4, fig. 85/3, pl. 150a

176 Penannular gold earring

In the form of a flower with petals around the edge. There are two bands of granulation on the central flat part. At the bottom is a bar with three small rings from which were suspended three further petals or cones; only one remains. There is a hinged holder at the top.

Said to be from Aleppo, Syria
Purchased from J.J. Naaman in 1912
Diam 2.1 cm, Wt 10.1 g
British Museum, ANE 1912-7-11, 1

177 Penannular gold earring

Flat with circular aperture at the top. Around the edge are globules set on stalks, perhaps in imitation of a flower. On the flat part of the earring there is embossed decoration showing the Egyptian dwarf-god Bes holding two ibexes by the horns, and above them two long-legged and long-necked birds, perhaps storks.

Said to be from Syria
Diam 5.5 cm, Th 0.5 cm
Louvre, AO 3171
Ghirshman 1964: pl. 323; Abdi 1999: fig. 6/5;
Abdi 2002b: fig. 12

178 Penannular gold earring

Hollow, with ribbed decoration around the outside. There is a hinged holder at the top.

Oxus Treasure
Bequeathed in 1897 by A.W. Franks
W 2.8 cm, Wt 2.5 g
British Museum, ANE 124059
Dalton 1964: no. 156, pl XXI

179 Penannular silver earring

Flat with a hollow centre. There are rows of globules around the inner and outer edges, those on the outside perhaps in imitation of a flower. There is a hinged holder at the top.

From a hoard of silver found at Babylon, Iraq
Excavations of Hormuzd Rassam, 1882
Diam 5.2 cm, Wt 16 g
British Museum, ANE 1882-12-20, 25
Robinson 1950: pl. XXIV, no. 25; Reade 1986:
80, no. 25, pl. IIIa

FINGER-RINGS

CLOTHING ORNAMENTS

180

181

180 Gold finger-ring

The ring has a plain hoop and flat oval bezel, with intaglio design showing a woman wearing a crown and a long dress. A plait of hair hangs down her back. She sits on a chair with a low back and holds a flower in one hand and a wreath in the other.

Oxus Treasure
Bequeathed in 1897 by A.W. Franks
L of bezel 2.25 cm, Wt 17.5 g
British Museum, ANE 124004
Dalton 1964: no. 103, fig. 52 on p. 26, pl. XVI

181 Gold finger-ring

The ring has a plain flat hoop and flat circular bezel, with a cross composed of lozenges. The cavities on the bezel were originally inlaid.

Oxus Treasure
Bequeathed in 1897 by A.W. Franks
Diam of bezel 2.44 cm, Wt 8.5 g
British Museum, ANE 124013
Dalton 1964: no. 112, fig. 61 on p. 30

182

182 Gold finger-ring

This example has a large circular bezel decorated in relief with the coiled figure of a lion. On the bezel are cavities for inlays that are now missing. The twisting and distorting of animals into impossible circular shapes is a characteristic feature of Scythian art, whose influence may be detected here.

Oxus Treasure
Bequeathed in 1897 by A.W. Franks
Diam of bezel 2.65 cm, Wt 11 g
British Museum, ANE 124012
Dalton 1964: no. 111, fig. 60 on p. 30; Curtis and
  Kruszynski 2002: no. 171, fig. 41, pl. 15

183 Circular gold plaque

With embossed decoration showing a lion-griffin seated to the right looking back over its shoulder. The plaque has a ribbed border and there are four hoops on the back for attachment.

Oxus Treasure
Bequeathed in 1897 by A.W. Franks
Diam 4.75 cm, Wt 5 g
British Museum, ANE 123929
Dalton 1964: no. 28, pl. XII

184 Circular gold plaque

With embossed decoration showing the head of the Egyptian dwarf-god Bes. There is a guilloche pattern border in which are four holes for attaching the plaque.

Oxus Treasure
Bequeathed in 1897 by A.W. Franks
Diam 4.35 cm, Wt 4.5 g
British Museum, ANE 123933
Dalton 1964: no. 32, pl. XII

185 Circular gold plaque

With embossed decoration showing a bird of prey with outstretched wings and legs, and a disc above the head. There is a ribbed border. A thick gold wire is soldered as an attachment loop on the reverse.

Oxus Treasure
Bequeathed in 1897 by A.W. Franks
Diam 4.8 cm, Wt 5.5 g
British Museum, ANE 123934
Dalton 1964: no. 33, pl. XII

186 Circular gold plaque

With openwork design showing a sphinx with a wing ending in a head of a bird of prey. The sphinx has her head turned backwards to contemplate the monster. The plaque has a ribbed border. There is no obvious means of attachment.

Oxus Treasure
Bequeathed in 1897 by A.W. Franks
Diam 5 cm, Wt 4 g
British Museum, ANE 123927
Dalton 1964: no. 26, pl. XII

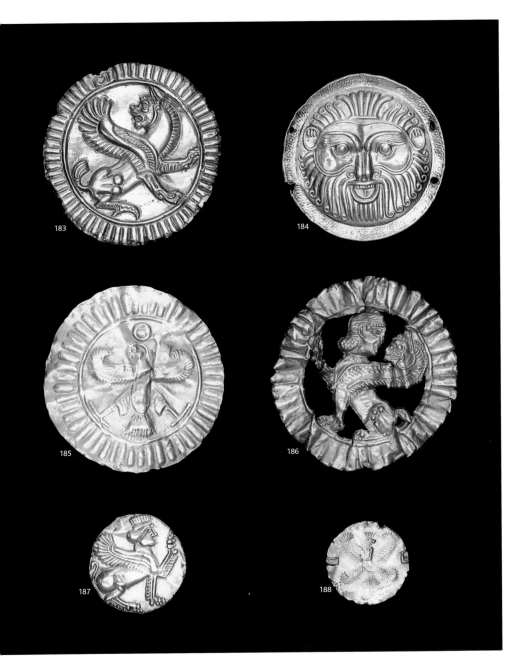

189

189 Gold cut-out plaque

Showing a figure of a beardless man (sometimes identified as a female) wearing a crown and a Persian costume. He holds a flower in his left hand and has his right hand upraised.

Oxus Treasure
Bequeathed in 1897 by A.W. Franks
H 6.15 cm, W 2.05 cm, Wt 4 g
British Museum, ANE 123939
Dalton 1964: no. 38, pl. XIII

190 Miniature gold lion striding to the right

Persepolis, found in Room 77 of the Treasury
 (PT6 694)
H 0.75 cm, L 1 cm
Tehran, 2351
Schmidt 1957: 77, fig. 14B; cf. Miller 1997: 42,
 figs 7–8

190

187 Circular gold plaque

With embossed decoration showing a crowned sphinx seated to the right with her left foreleg raised.

Oxus Treasure
Bequeathed in 1897 by A.W. Franks
Diam 2.6 cm, Wt 1 g
British Museum, ANE 123928
Dalton 1964: no. 27, pl. XXI

188 Circular gold plaque

With embossed decoration showing the bust of a bearded figure with Persian crown in a winged disc. Contrary to the usual representations (for example, cats 38, 203), this has four wings curled at the tips in addition to the tail-feathers.

Oxus Treasure
Bequeathed in 1897 by A.W. Franks
Diam 2.2 cm, Wt 0.5 g
British Museum, ANE 123936
Dalton 1964: no. 35, pl. XXI; Abdi 1999: fig. 6/3

191 Gold cut-out plaque

Showing a striding lion with cavities on its body for polychrome inlays that are now missing. There are rings behind the head and feet for attachment.

Ex Coutoulakis Collection. Purchased in 1956
L 3.1 cm, W 2.5 cm
British Museum, ANE 132108
Barnett 1960: 29, pl. VII; cf. Miller 1997: 42, figs 7–8

191–2

192 Gold roundel

With open-work design showing two rampant lions with tails crossed and heads turned back to face each other.

Ex Coutoulakis Collection. Purchased in 1956
Diam 4.3 cm
British Museum, ANE 132111
Barnett 1960: 29, pl. VII

193 Five gold animal-head attachments

Each has three rings on the reverse for fastening.

Ex Coutoulakis Collection. Purchased in 1956
L 2.2 cm, W 1.75 cm
British Museum, ANE 132103-7
Barnett 1960: 29, pl. VII

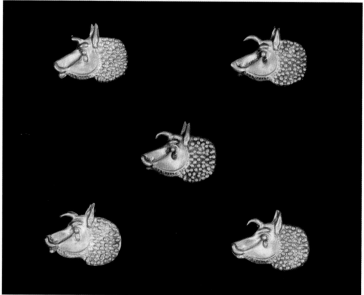

193

194 Gold plaque in the form of a lion-griffin, with the body of an ibex and a leaf-shaped tail

There are cavities for inlay on the flank and shoulder. At the back of the plaque are two long prongs for attachment. Its most likely purpose was as a hair or cap ornament. Scythian influence is evident in the folded legs of the beast. A torc from barrow 2 at Pazyryk in Siberia has mounted on it composite figures that bear some resemblance to this plaque (Rudenko 1970: fig. 50 on p. 107).

Oxus Treasure
Bequeathed in 1897 by A.W. Franks
L 6.15 cm, Wt 44.3 g
British Museum, ANE 123924
Dalton 1964: no. 23, fig. 46, pl. I; Curtis and Kruszynski 2002: no. 172, fig. 42, pl. 16

194

KOHL BOTTLES

These bottles contained kohl which was used as eye make-up; it was usually applied with a metal rod.

195 Bronze kohl bottle

In the form of a woman with large pierced ears and hands clasped under her breasts.

Provenance unknown
Purchased in 1958
H 7.28 cm, W 2.5 cm
British Museum, ANE 132353
Barnett 1963–4: pl. XXXIa–c; Culican 1975: 105, fig. 5A

196 Bronze kohl bottle

In the form of a woman wearing a pleated dress and holding with both hands a circular object to her left breast.

Provenance unknown
Purchased in 1959
H 10 cm, W 2.5 cm
British Museum, ANE 132620
Barnett 1963–4: pl. XXXId; Culican 1975: 105, fig. 5B

195 (right), 196 (left)

197

197 Glass kohl bottle

Square-shaped bottle tapering to the base, with small knobs on the shoulders. The rod-formed body is of opaque black glass and there is thread decoration in yellow and white. Square kohl bottles of this characteristic type are widely distributed in the central part of the Achaemenid Empire and date from the sixth to the fourth centuries BC.

Provenance unknown
Purchased in 1969
H 6.6 cm, W 1.1 cm (top)
British Museum, ANE 135125
Barag 1985: no. 77, fig. 6, pl. 10

8

RELIGION AND BURIAL CUSTOMS

Shahrokh Razmjou

INTRODUCTION

Achaemenid religion is still a subject of discussion amongst scholars: although there are many documents and archaeological sources available for studying it, there are problems of definition and interpretation of the evidence. Central to the discussion is whether or not the Achaemenid kings were Zoroastrian. This is the religion named after the prophet Zarathustra, known by the Greeks as Zoroaster, who may have lived some time around the beginning of the first millennium BC. At that time the Iranians believed in a variety of gods; Zoroaster reformed their ancient religion and promoted the belief that there was one great god, Ahuramazda, supported by divine beings or immortal spirits known as *yazatas*. This is recorded in the holy book, the Avesta, the older part of which is a direct dialogue between Zoroaster and Ahuramazda. In Zoroastrianism fire is respected as a sacred element as in other ancient Iranian beliefs.

Apart from Zoroastrianism, in the Achaemenid period the Iranian religions known as Mithraism, Zurvanism and Mazda-worship are also attested. Mithraism was based on the sun god Mithra. His cult was later spread by Roman soldiers through Europe as far as England, and its traditions influenced Christianity. Zurvanism was named after Zurvan, the god of limitless time, who was thought to have given birth to Ahuramazda and to Ahriman, the personification of evil. Mazda-worship refers to the veneration of Ahuramazda, but not in association with the teachings of Zoroaster. At the same time local religions that existed in Iran before the arrival of the Achaemenid Persians continued to flourish. After their arrival from the north and their settlement near the Elamites, the Persians could have adopted Elamite religious beliefs, but their religion remained Iranian and in due course influenced the Elamites. At the same time, Elamite religion may have had some influence on Persian religion, but the Elamites did not influence Persian religion as much as it was inspired by Iranian elements. It is not clear whether the Achaemenid kings were Zoroastrians, or whether they followed a form of Mazda-worship independent of Zoroastrianism.

THE EARLY ACHAEMENID PERIOD

The situation is particularly unclear in the case of the early Achaemenid kings. In the inscriptions of Cyrus the Great there is no direct mention of his religion. However, the Greek texts report that he was accompanied by *magi* (Iranian priests), and Strabo records that he founded a temple at Zela in Asia Minor (Strabo XI.8.4). This was a great artificial mound encircled by a wall which people could walk up to and pray.[1] An open-air site, it was reminiscent of the sacred precinct in Pasargadae, and so might have been related to the Iranian tradition of worship in the open air. It was a temple of Anaïtis (Anahita, the Iranian goddess of waters), who according to Strabo was the goddess of Cyrus's fathers (XI.8.4–5). On the other hand, in the Cyrus Cylinder he speaks respectfully of the Babylonian god, Marduk; and in the Old Testament Cyrus is given the honorable title of 'Messiah' and is introduced as a person who was anointed by Yahweh (Isaiah 45:1, 4).

Likewise, we know practically nothing about the beliefs of Cyrus's son, Cambyses. We can say, though, that despite the testimony of the Greek historians it is clear from textual sources that he was favourable to the Egyptian cults. The first direct evidence for early Achaemenid religion comes, in fact, from the reign of Darius. When he states that he re-established and restored everything as before (DB I.63–4), this probably implies that the situation under Cyrus and Cambyses was similar to that in his own time.

THE PANTHEON

From the time of Darius onwards, the Achaemenid kings describe themselves in their royal inscriptions as worshippers of Ahuramazda, the Wise Lord (see, for example, DB V.16–17). The Achaemenid pantheon included other gods that were called *bagas*, but Ahuramazda had the highest position and was described by the Achaemenid kings as 'the great god' or 'the greatest of gods' (see, for example, DNa 1; DPd 1–2). Ahuramazda is probably represented in Achaemenid art by the winged disc with a human figure holding a ring or flower (cat. 38).[2] In his inscription at Bisitun Darius repeatedly says that Ahuramazda helped him and bestowed upon him the kingship. It is therefore very likely that in the reliefs the flying figure in front of Darius holding the ring of kingship and power is in fact Ahuramazda. Some scholars have argued that these representations are not of Ahuramazda himself but symbolic representations of the divine glory; in either case, the figure is related to the god Ahuramazda.

In their early inscriptions the Achaemenid kings speak of Ahuramazda and 'other gods of the royal family' without mentioning their names (DPd 23–4). Evidence for the names of these other deities can, however, be found in personal names and in other sources, principally the administrative texts known as the Persepolis Fortification Tablets. Mithra, the Iranian sun god, appears in some personal names such as Mitradata, who was chief of the Treasury in Babylon under Cyrus.[3] Mithra also appears in administrative ritual payments and receives rations as a god. Other gods in the Achaemenid pantheon included Arta (XPh 53–4), Anahita (goddess of waters), Spenta-Armaiti (the earth goddess),[4] Nariyosanga (the messenger god) (PF 1960; PF-NN 2362) and Turma (perhaps Zurvan, the god of limitless time). Some names of the months in the Achaemenid calendar also appear in ritual payment texts as gods (nappan) who received rations; some of these are still unidentifiable.[5] Xerxes included Arta in his royal inscription(s), and in the time of Artaxerxes II the names of Mithra, the sun god, and Anahita, the goddess of waters, appeared together in royal inscriptions after the name of Ahuramazda. Artaxerxes promoted Mithra and Anahita to positions alongside Ahuramazda. He also built temples for Anaïtis (Anahita) in Ecbatana and other cities, and installed statues of the goddess.[6] This was a departure from earlier practice and in conflict with Herodotus's statement that the Iranians never erected statues of gods (History I.131; Strabo XV.3.13). A seal shows a figure who might be Artaxerxes II praising a goddess in Persian dress standing on a lion, probably a representation of Anahita.[7]

One important sacred motif in Achaemenid art is the figure of a man standing in a crescent moon. Although still unidentified, this figure is surely a representation of a divine figure in the Achaemenid pantheon. He often appears together with the winged figure mentioned above and is frequently shown on seals and jewellery (e.g. cat. 413). A number of other sacred and mythological figures also appear in Achaemenid iconography, such as a man in Persian royal dress, lions, bulls, griffins, man-headed bulls, winged lions and composite creatures. Unfortu-nately these mythical beings cannot now be identified because of the lack of written sources, but their identity must have been very clear to visitors to Persepolis in the Achaemenid period. Foreign sacred motifs were also incorporated in Achaemenid iconography, such as Bes, the Egyptian god of happiness and the family. He might possibly have represented the Persian 'happiness' that was the fourth creation of Ahuramazda, but he more probably had a different meaning for the Persians than for the Egyptians.

RELIGIOUS IDEOLOGY

In their royal inscriptions the Achaemenid kings provide some evidence for their religious ideology. They state that they are 'worshippers of Ahuramazda' and that they are 'against the Lie'. In Achaemenid ideology the Lie was explained as the ultimate danger to the country of which future kings should be warned (DB IV.37–40). The Achaemenid kings also believed in a creation myth. Many Achaemenid inscriptions start with the formula 'A great god is Ahuramazda, who created this earth, who created yonder sky, who created man, who created happiness for man' (see, for example, DNa 1–8). It is clear from this that the Persians believed in different levels of creation. In their royal inscriptions the Achaemenid kings also speak about the law that was established by Ahuramazda, and life after death and the happiness and blessing for those who worship Ahuramazda in the afterlife: 'The man who has respect for that law, which Ahuramazda has established, and worships Ahuramazda and Arta reverent[ly], he both becomes happy while living, and becomes blessed when dead' (XPh: 46–56).

PRIESTS

The priests in Iranian religion were called *magi*, derived from the word *magu* ('priest'). Their role in the earlier Median period has been described as dream-interpreters and royal advisers (see, for example, Herodotus, *History* I.120). Their importance in the early Achaemenid period is demonstrated by the rebellion of Gaumata the Magus, as reported in the inscription of Darius at Bisitun and the Classical sources. He claimed to be Bardiya (Smerdis), the brother of Cambyses, and seized the throne. He was eventually killed by a group of seven nobles including Darius I, a member of the royal family. The sources describe Gaumata as a Median *magus* who was based in Median territory (DB I.36–7, 58–9). His rebellion therefore had a political aspect, perhaps aimed at restoring the Median monarchy (Herodotus, *History* III.65), but there were also religious overtones. As his earliest act Gaumata started to demolish temples, which were rebuilt in the same year by Darius (DB I.63–4).

There has been much discussion about the type of temples destroyed by Gaumata and his fellow *magi*.[8] According to the Fortification Texts there were many temples and sanctuaries in Persia itself that received payments from the government for Iranian, Elamite and even Babylonian gods. It is possible that the Median *magi* did not like this and targeted the Persian or even Elamite temples because they contained statues or belonged to foreign gods. Both Herodotus and Strabo mention the traditional religious differences between the Persians and the Median *magi*. They report that the Iranians had no temples or shrines and prayed in the open air or at the top of mountains (Herodotus, *History* I.131; Strabo XV.3.13). This type of worship is also shown in Achaemenid iconography, especially in the ritual scenes on the tomb façades of Persian kings after Darius. The destroyed temples were 're-established' by Darius and the situation was 'restored' to what it was in the past. Darius uses the word *ayadana* that seems to be a general term for 'temples' in Old Persian deriving from the word *yada* 'to worship'.[9] Other types of sacred places were known as *kušukum* or *hapidanuš*, both of which received offering rations (PF 352: 11; PF 329:7; PF 2009: 22; PF 2085: 13; PF-NN 2023).

In spite of their early political problems with the *magi*, the Persian kings kept them in their service at court and some of them had administrative positions. *Magi* are sometimes shown in the art of the Achaemenid period. A good example is a relief from Daskylion in Asia Minor that shows two Iranian priests, one apparently beardless, standing in front of a shrine with the heads of a sacrificed bull and a ram placed on an altar (fig. 57). They hold bundles (*barsoms*) in one hand with the other raised as a sign of prayer. Their noses and mouths are covered with the lower part of their turbans. It was a tradition for the *magi* to cover their mouths when they stood in front of the holy fire to save it from being polluted by their breath. The same tradition exists today among Zoroastrian priests who cover their mouths with a piece of cloth called a *padam*. The *barsom* is another indication that the priests are participating in a ritual ceremony. Some of the gold votive plaques in the Oxus Treasure that were perhaps presented to a temple also show priests. They wear a Median type of costume, some have a *padam* with headdress, and they also hold *barsoms*. Sometimes their dresses have bands of decoration and bird designs.

Another source of evidence for the *magi* is provided by seals and seal impressions. On some seals ritual ceremonies are shown in detail. Sometimes the priests have *barsoms* and headdresses, and stand with mouths covered in front of a fire altar (cat. 200). Sometimes they also hold

57 Drawing of a stone relief from Daskyleion in Turkey showing two priests in Median dress standing in front of an offering table supporting the heads of a ram and a bull.

a pitcher, perhaps containing oil to feed the fire (cat. 227). When the king is shown in front of a fire altar, a priest with headdress can be seen performing the ceremony on the opposite side (cat. 201). In the presence of the king, the priests wear a Persian-style dress and folded headdress, but in scenes without the king, the priests are dressed in Median-style costume. Representations of the same costumes can also be found at Persepolis and Susa. In the palace reliefs at Persepolis individuals dressed in this way are shown ascending the staircases of palaces, carrying food and animals (cats 40, 47): these figures were previously regarded as servants. A fragment of glazed brick from Susa shows a beardless person (a priest) in a white headdress (cat. 54). This is significant as the white colour was a sign for priests in Iranian religion. There is also another example of the same headdress in black, but this may possibly be an indication of a priest of lower rank. Some of the images on the glazed bricks show the richly decorated dresses (cat. 55). Being beardless was a tradition for Assyrian, Egyptian and Elamite priests in the ancient Near East, and it must have been the same for the higher rank of Persian priests. A fragmentary stone relief from Susa shows a beardless person wearing the same headdress with a *padam* on his chin (cat. 50), indicating that he was engaged in a ritual practice and was probably a priest. According to this evidence, therefore, the function of the palaces seems to have been ritual rather than residential.

The Fortification Texts mention different titles and designations for the *magi*, while the Elamite priests are simply called *šatin*. The *magi* have Iranian titles such as *haturmakša* (*Āzarvaxš*), *pirramasda* and the Elamite title *lan-lirira* used for *magi* who perform the *lan* ceremony.[10] Traditionally the *magi* were expected to go through seven priestly ranks.

The Achaemenid period provides a good example of collaboration between the different priests. The texts show that the Elamite *šatins* were sometimes responsible for the offerings to Iranian gods, and the Persian *magi* were sometimes in charge of payments for Elamite deities. There was also a type of religious collaboration, with Persian and Elamite gods being mentioned in texts together and receiving their offerings together. This is all the more remarkable in that the Persian and Elamite religions had different origins and were quite different from each other.

In some scenes priests are shown with a pestle and mortar, used for crushing a floral material to obtain a sacred liquid (cat. 200). In some seals a plate is also added to the pestle and mortar.[11] During excavations in the Treasury at Persepolis a collection of pestles, mortars and plates made of green stone was discovered, some of them with Aramaic inscriptions indicating that they belonged to a ritual ceremony (cats 211–12).[12]

After being inscribed, these pieces were given to the royal archive and kept there as sacred relics. They have been related to a ceremony of *haoma* crushing.[13] *Haoma* was a god and a plant that only the *magi* knew how to prepare. The liquid of the crushed plant was mixed with milk and had health-giving properties; it also bestowed supernatural power and immortality.[14]

KINGS

As well as the *magi*, the kings also performed ritual ceremonies. They presided over ritual performances in the open air that mainly happened at night-time under a crescent moon. This scene is represented on the façades of the royal tombs and on seals. Such ceremonies were possibly performed at the plinths of the sacred precinct at Pasargadae.[15]

RELIGIOUS CEREMONIES

Some of the different ceremonies performed during the Achaemenid period are named in the payment texts. The most frequent one seems to have been the *lan* ceremony. There are no details in the texts about it, but we know that it was performed by both Persians and Elamites. It usually involved offerings of food and drink, such as small cattle, grain, barley, flour, figs, dates, wine and beer.[16] In some texts it is mentioned that the workmen (*kurtash*) consumed the rations being offered (cf. texts PF 336, PF 337 and some unpublished texts), suggesting that the offerings were distributed amongst the people after the ceremony.

A room has recently been identified at Persepolis that was probably used for performing sacrifices.[17] When this room was added to the Tachara Palace, the name of the palace was changed to *Hadiš*, reflecting the fact that Xerxes was now making sacrifices here to Ahuramazda.[18] In Asia Minor the sacrificial ceremony was performed with a bull and a ram, as can be seen at Daskyleion and Xanthos.

According to texts, some ritual ceremonies were performed in a formal walled garden known as a 'paradise' (*pairidaēza*).[19] Such heavenly gardens had an important role in Achaemenid ideology and religion, and were established by Persian kings everywhere in their territory, albeit with different functions.

The Fortification Tablets also record payments for offerings to mountains and rivers, which were sacred to the Achaemenids. Classical sources report that the Persians offered sacrifices to heaven on the highest peaks of mountains.[20] From the time of Darius the tombs of the Achaemenid kings were situated on mountainsides, and the famous inscription and relief of Darius at Bisitun is on the top of a mountain called *Bagastana*, or the 'place of gods'. In the Fortification Tablets rivers are sometimes mentioned by name (PF-NN 339, 379, PF 339, PF-NN 2259, 2183, 2200, PF 1955). Water also received payments, but it is not clear whether the payments were intended for water in general or for a specific river or lake (PF-NN 1064). It seems that the sacred places known as *hapidanuš* can be related to water or a water resource.[21]

RELIGIOUS TOLERANCE

Because their empire encompassed a variety of peoples with different religions, the Persian kings adopted a policy of religious tolerance throughout their domain. They not only allowed subjects to follow their own religious beliefs and perform their own ritual ceremonies freely, but they also provided financial aid for building or rebuilding temples dedicated to foreign gods and religions.[22] Cyrus initiated this policy by returning the treasures of the Jews to them and giving official permission for the rebuilding of the Temple of Solomon. In Babylon he ordered that the Babylonian temples should be rebuilt.[23] The Persepolis Fortification Tablets show that even at the heart of the empire, in Persia itself, there were Elamite sacred places and that Elamite gods received regular rations together with Iranian gods. The Achaemenids clearly believed in religious co-existence.

But there were two limits to this policy of religious tolerance. One was that the religion of the royal family should not be disturbed, as is evident in the story of Gaumata the Magus. In a similar vein Xerxes, who worshipped Ahuramazda, demolished *daivadanas* ('temples of demons'), as he calls them in his so-called *Daiva* inscription (cat. 5), in a country that he refuses to name and 'where previously the demons were worshipped'. Secondly, nobody was allowed to disturb rituals or sacred places anywhere in the empire that were under the protection of the Achaemenid government. An example of this is the warning given by Darius the Great to his satrap in Asia Minor about receiving tax from the 'gardener-priests of Apollo'.[24] The Graeco-Persian wars started for the same reason: when the Athenians crossed the sea, and sacked and burned the city of Sardis with its Lydian sanctuaries, Xerxes felt obliged to capture Athens and burn the temple on the Acropolis in return.[25] We know also that the Jews of Elephantine who expected religious protection complained to the Persian satrap about the destruction of their temple by Egyptian priests.[26]

According to textual evidence, during the Achaemenid period the *magi* travelled to other countries of the empire, settled there and started scholarly interactions with other priests and religions. Because of such interaction, those religions changed and developed. Strabo, for example, reports the presence of the *magi* in Cappadocia in large numbers (Strabo XV.3.15). Egypt also had Iranian *magi*, and from the time of Cyrus Babylon became another major centre for them. In Babylon they not only performed rituals, but they were also involved with astronomy, astrology, medicine and chemistry. The mixture of *magi* knowledge and wisdom with Babylonian skill and expertise had many positive results, including the completion and establishment of the Zodiac in the Achaemenid period.[27] Indeed, the words magic and magician ultimately derive from their name and their skills.[28] In Christianity the three wise men who went to honour the infant Jesus have also been known as the 'Magi'.

PERSIAN RELIGION AFTER THE ACHAEMENIDS

Iranian religions suffered greatly from the invasion of Alexander, but although he destroyed the first Persian Empire, these religions managed to survive. In Zoroastrian tradition Alexander is called the *gojastak*, 'the accursed', and is accused of beheading priests, destroying temples and burning the original manuscript of the holy book, the Avesta, that was kept in a place called *Dez-Nepešt*, meaning the Castle of Inscriptions or Fortress of Archives.[29] After this, Zoroastrian priests memorized the texts and passed them from generation to generation until they were collected and written down again under the Parthian king Vologases I.[30] Although the Sasanian kings who revived the Persian Empire saw themselves as the inheritors and successors of the Achaemenid kings, their religion exhibited a number of differences. Nevertheless, the influence from the Achaemenid period remained strong.

BURIAL CUSTOMS

Textual evidence for burial traditions in the Achaemenid period is limited to the Classical sources, and from them it is clear that there were different traditions. Herodotus refers to different burial rites for the *magi*, who were mainly Median priests, and for the Persians:

> But there are other matters concerning the dead which are
> secretly and obscurely told – how the dead bodies of Persians
> are not buried before they have been mangled by bird or dog.
> That this is the way of the Magians I know for a certainty; for
> they do not conceal the practice. But this is certain, that before
> the Persians bury the body in earth they embalm it in wax.

(*History* I.140)

The same difference was later noted by Strabo: 'They [the Persians] smear the bodies of the dead with wax before they bury them, though they do not bury the Magi but leave their bodies to be eaten by birds' (Strabo XV.3.20). Strabo records a similar custom at Taxila, now in Pakistan: 'Aristobolus mentions some novel and unusual customs at Taxila: ... the dead are thrown out to be devoured by vultures' (Strabo XV.1.62). Later in the Sasanian period,

Zoroastrian priests also followed this tradition. According to ancient Iranian belief, water, soil, air and fire are the four sacred elements and should not be polluted by corpses.[31] Therefore dead bodies were exposed on high towers called Towers of Silence and the bones stripped clean by birds. Afterwards the bones were collected and put in ossuaries or chambers carved in the rock known as *astōdān* ('the place of bones').[32] This may have been an original tradition of the *magi* even before the Achaemenid period.

There is no doubt, however, that the majority of people did not follow this tradition because there are not many ossuaries or other evidence to testify to such a practice.[33] On the contrary, there are many burials indicating that burial was a common practice. But both ideologies did believe in the sacred nature of fire, which as the symbol of the light of the great god should not be polluted by dead bodies. Further evidence for this is found in an epigram about a Persian slave called Euphrates who talks to his master. In this piece he says:

> Do not burn me, Philonymos, and do not pollute fire by
> contact with me. I am a Persian, of Persian parentage,
> master, and the pollution of fire is more grievous to us than
> death. Bury me in the earth, but do not sprinkle my body
> with lustral water, for I also revere streams.[34]

The Achaemenid kings followed another burial tradition. There is no evidence from the period before Cyrus, but Xenophon – who had a close connection with a prince of the Persian royal family, Cyrus the Younger – reports that Cyrus the Great gave the following instructions for his burial to the Persian nobles and his sons:

> Now as to my body, when I am dead, my sons, lay it away
> neither in gold nor in silver nor in anything else, but commit
> it to the *earth* as soon as may be. For what is more blessed
> than to be united with earth, which brings forth and
> nourishes all things beautiful and all things good?

(Xenophon, *Cyropaedia* VIII.7.25–6)

When Cyrus asks for a burial without gold and silver he probably means without a coffin made of those materials, as burial in the earth within coffins was a tradition amongst the Persians. It is also possible that his concern with burial in the earth could be a mark of respect for Spenta-Armaiti, the goddess of earth who is also named in the Fortification Tablets.[35]

There is another reference to burial in the case of Smerdis (Bardiya), when Prexaspes tells Cambyses that he *buried* Smerdis with his own hands (Herodotus, *History* III.62). According to Herodotus (*History* VII.24), Mardonius was also buried.

In spite of his alleged instructions, in due course Cyrus was buried in a monumental free-standing tomb, which still stands at Pasargadae. It is a rectangular structure with a gabled roof that stands on the top of a stepped platform.[36] There is a small entrance to the tomb that was originally closed by two stone doors. According to the 'Alexander historians', the tomb was disturbed at the time of Alexander's invasion. Both Arrian and Strabo say that the body of Cyrus was inside a golden coffin (Arrian VI.29.5–6; Strabo XV.3.7). Arrian describes it as follows:

> In the chamber lay a golden sarcophagus, in which Cyrus's body had been buried; a couch stood by its side with feet of wrought gold; a Babylonian tapestry served as a coverlet and purple rugs as a carpet. There was placed on it a sleeved mantle and other garments of Babylonian workmanship. According to Aristobulus, Median trousers and robes dyed blue lay there, some dark, some of other varying shades, with necklaces, scimitars and earrings of stones set in gold, and a table stood there. It was between the table and the couch that the sarcophagus containing Cyrus's body was placed.
>
> (Arrian VI.29.5–6)

According to Arrian (Alexander VI.29.8) and Plutarch, there was a Persian inscription on the tomb which in style is reminiscent of the Achaemenid royal inscriptions:

> O man, whosoever thou art and whenceoever thou comest, for I know that thou wilt come, I am Cyrus, and I won for the Persians their empire. Do not, therefore, begrudge me this little earth which covers my body.
>
> (Plutarch LXIX)

The Tomb of Cyrus is a unique structure of its type, though there is a close parallel at Sardis in Asia Minor. There is also another example of a stepped tomb at Bozpar, known as Gour-i Dokhtar ('the tomb of the daughter').[37] Although it seems to be a primitive version of Cyrus's tomb, it could actually be a later structure. There seems to be another tomb of this type known as Takht-i Gohar (also known as Takht-i Rustam) midway between Persepolis and Naqsh-i Rustam.[38] It is a similar structure to the Tomb of Cyrus but was left unfinished. It was perhaps prepared for Cambyses,[39] but due to his untimely death on his way back from Egypt the tomb was never finished. Artachaees, a member of the Achaemenid dynasty, may also have had a tomb: when he died, Xerxes ordered that he should be buried in a tomb and the whole army poured libations on it (Herodotus, History VII.117).

Although Cambyses is reported to have died on his way back to Iran, there is a tablet that gives evidence of his burial in Persia. It is a report of rations paid to the keepers of his tomb, and refers to the *šumar* of Cambyses and lady Upanduš, perhaps his queen, in *Narezzaš* (Neiriz) in Fars Province.[40] The word *šumar* that appears in the Persepolis Fortification Tablets is used to mean 'tomb' and 'burial', mainly those of the nobles and royal family.[41] The tablet

states that the keepers of the tomb are receiving small cattle, perhaps as the offering for a ritual or perhaps as their own ration. Another text from Persepolis has a similar report, but this time it refers to the *šumar* of Hystaspes, father of Darius the Great at Persepolis.[42] If the text refers to Persepolis itself, and not the surrounding area, it indicates that the site was used for royal burials many years before the time of Artaxerxes II who was buried there. This tomb has not yet been found.

In contrast to Cyrus, Darius designed a different type of tomb for himself that was cut into a mountain at Naqsh-i Rustam. The façade of the tomb is in the shape of a huge cross. On the upper part, Darius is shown in front of the winged figure, a fire altar and a crescent moon, on a throne supported by the people of the empire. The central part of the façade is designed to replicate the southern façade of the Tachara Palace at Persepolis.[43] The only difference is the lack of windows, which were clearly not necessary. The same façade was repeatedly used up to the end of the Achaemenid period by other Persian kings. Four of these cross-shaped tombs were carved high in the cliff face at Naqsh-i Rustam and had no access, while two were carved on the mountainside above Persepolis and were accessible. Ctesias talks of how Darius's tomb was cut into the rock and tells a story about how some relatives of Darius who went to see his tomb fell from the rock (*Persica* XV).

Beyond the entrance to Darius's tomb is a chamber with three smaller vaulted chambers, each containing three graves. The interior plan of each royal tomb is slightly different, and the number of graves, or burial cists, inside the vaulted chambers varies. These graves are carved out of the stone and each grave had a stone lid. In each tomb, cists were prepared for the king and his closest family members.[44] Each grave was made larger than life-size so it could have contained a body complete with tiara or royal crown. But more probably the bodies were placed in golden coffins and then lowered into the burial cists.[45] The tombs seem also to have been robbed at the time of Alexander's invasion, because it is clear from the account of Diodorus that he was aware of the internal shape of the sealed royal tombs:

> At the eastern side of the terrace at a distance of four plethora is the so-called royal hill in which were the graves of the kings. This was a smooth rock hollowed out into many chambers in which were the sepulchres of the dead kings. These have no other access but receive the sarcophagi of the dead which are lifted by certain mechanical hoists.
>
> (Diodorus XVII.71)

As the tombs must definitely have contained treasure, they would have been too much of a temptation for the Macedonian invaders. The tombs are now empty and all that remained for modern archaeologists of the once glorious funerary equipment inside the tombs was a plain bronze fastening, found on the floor inside the tomb of Artaxerxes III at Persepolis.[46] These tombs cannot be considered as *astōdāns*. They are in fact rock-cut tombs for the burial of bodies and had the effect of preserving the bodies inside a mountain and keeping them away from contaminating the sacred elements.[47]

In other places where there were no mountains out of which to make rock-cut tombs, such as Susa, the dead were buried in coffins. A good example of this type of burial is a royal coffin that was found at Susa by Jacques de Morgan.[48] This was an undisturbed coffin made of bronze in the shape of a bath-tub. The form of this coffin is a development of the pre-Achaemenid Arjan coffin that contained the body of a king called Kidin-Hutran, son of Kurlush, from the late Neo-Elamite period.[49] Another Iranian parallel is an Iron Age coffin from Ziwiyeh.[50] Parallel coffins have also been found in Assyria,[51] from where the tradition certainly derives. In later excavations at Susa four fragments of anthropoid coffins were also found, closely parallel to anthropoid sarcophagi from Sidon[52] and from Cyprus. This type of sarcophagus may have been restricted to royal or noble burials. At Ur in Mesopotamia Leonard Woolley found many terracotta coffins of bath-tub shape dating from the Persian period.[53]

In western Asia Minor two types of tombs were constructed: rock-cut tombs and free-standing monuments. Both have similar features to the Achaemenid tombs in Iran.[54] There is also an *astōdān* with an inscription that records the owner as Artimas, son of Arziphius – the satrap of Cyrus the Younger in Lycia.[55] The sarcophagus of a Persian satrap was found at Sidon, dated to the fifth century BC.[56] Inside the sarcophagus was a skeleton with gold beads and a gold plaque.[57] This is another example of Persian nobility buried in a sarcophagus. It is clear, therefore, that each part of the empire followed its own traditions for burying the dead.

In conclusion, the Achaemenids believed in burying their dead, but they attempted to insulate the body from the natural elements. Thus they made their burials in the mountains and rocks, or they protected their graves by using stone slabs and other materials; they also used coffins to keep soil away from the body. They do not appear to have followed the *magi* tradition of exposing bodies. In the case of royal burials, bodies were covered with wax, put into metal coffins and buried in stone monuments or mountains. The burials also contained offerings and personal effects.[58]

1 Boyce 1979: 60.
2 For a brief background of this figure see Boyce 1982: 96.
3 Dandamaev and Lukonin 1989: 328.
4 Razmjou 2001: 7–15.
5 Razmjou 2004: 15–34.
6 Fried 2004: 131.
7 Moorey 1988a: no. 48.
8 For example, see Dandamaev and Lukonin 1989: 350.
9 Kent 1953: 169; Boyce 1982, 88–9.
10 Razmjou 2004: 107–8.
11 Boardman 2000: pl. 5.31.
12 Schmidt 1957: 53–6.
13 Bowman 1970: 6ff.
14 Hinnels 1985: 33; Boyce 1975: 157ff.
15 Stronach 1978: 141.
16 Razmjou 2004: 104–5.
17 Razmjou 2003.
18 Briant 2002: 551.
19 Brandenstein and Mayrhofer 1964: 137.
20 Herodotus, *History* I.131; Strabo XV.3.13.
21 Hinz and Koch 1987: 619.
22 Dandamaev and Lukonin 1969: 348–9.
23 For the Cyrus Cylinder see Berger 1975: 407–10; British Museum tablet: 38217; a brick inscription British Museum 1923-11-10,221/118362.
24 Fried 2004: 109.
25 Herodotus, *History* V.99–106; also Briant 2002: 148.
26 Cowley 1923: no. 30.
27 Britton and Walker 1996: 48–9; Sachs and Hunger 1988: 54–5: no. 463.
28 The Oxford Dictionary 1998: 185, under 'magic'.
29 Shaki 1996: 348.
30 Kellens 1989: 35.
31 Shahbazi 1987: 851.
32 Ibid.
33 Grenet 1990: 559–60; L'vov-Basirov 2001: 107.
34 Benveniste 1929: 38; for original source see Stadtmueller 1899: 62, 105.
35 Razmjou 2001: 7–15.
36 Stronach 1978: 36, 107–10.
37 Stronach 1978: 300–302.
38 Stronach 1978: 302–4, figs a, b.
39 Herzfeld 1941: 214.
40 Henkelman 2003: 110–11.
41 Henkelman 2003: 102.
42 Henkelman 2003: 103–4.
43 Schmidt 1970: 81.
44 Schmidt 1970: 88.
45 Ibid.
46 Schmidt 1970: 106; Schmidt 1957: pl. 45/19.
47 Boyce 1982: 112.
48 De Morgan 1905: 29–58.
49 Potts 1999: 303.
50 Godard 1950: 13–18.
51 Curtis 1983.
52 Excavated by Mehdi Rahbar (unpublished), personal communication.
53 Woolley 1962: 67–87.
54 L'vov-Basirov 2001: 101.
55 Shahbazi 1987: 851–2.
56 Kleeman 1958.
57 Jidejian 1971: 131ff.
58 L'vov-Basirov 2001: 104.

REPRESENTATIONS OF PRIESTS

198 Fragment of stone relief showing the upper part of a figure

The figures wears Median dress and a cap that covers his ears and chin. He has a beard and moustache. He is facing to the left and holds in his hands a bowl with a rounded lid. This fragment belongs with those series of reliefs that show figures climbing staircases, bearing food, drink and live animals. They are either priests bringing offerings for a religious ceremony or servants bringing provisions for a banquet.

Persepolis, either from the south stairs of the
    Palace of Darius, or the east or west stairs
    of the Palace of Xerxes
Obtained at Persepolis in 1811 and presented
    by the 5th Earl of Aberdeen in 1861
H 30 cm, W 30 cm
British Museum, ANE 118855
Ouseley 1821: pl. XLV; Barnett 1957: no. 18,
    pl. XIX/2; Mitchell 2000: 50, 52, pl. XXc

198

199 Fragment of stone relief showing the head of a figure

The figure wears a Persian-style turban and faces to the left. This fragment presumably belongs to a series showing priests or servants mounting a staircase and carrying offerings or food. Compare the glazed brick fragments cats 54–5, 57–62.

Susa
Found by R. de Mecquenem with cat. 50 during
    his excavations in the 'Donjon' area in 1928–32,
    where they had been reused as paving stones in
    a post-Achaemenid house. The original location
    of the palace from which these pieces came is
    uncertain (see Boucharlat 1997: 60–61)
H 8.6 cm, W 13.0 cm
Louvre, Sb 3781
Cf. de Mecquenem 1947: 84, fig. 53/10, pl. VI/5;
    Amiet 1988: fig. 82 on p. 132

199

SEALS WITH RELIGIOUS SCENES

200 Cylinder seal showing two figures in Median dress

The figures are facing each other on either side of a flaming altar. The figure on the left holds a pestle and mortar, and that on the right holds the *barsom* in his right hand and raises his left. Above is a yoke-shaped symbol. The chalcedony (?) seal has been damaged by heating.

Provenance unknown
Purchased from George Eastwood in 1865
H 2.65 cm, Diam 1.1 cm
British Museum, ANE 89528
Merrillees 2005: no. 75

201 Stamp seal showing two figures in Persian dress

The figures stand facing each other beneath a winged disc. Between them is a flaming altar. Both figures hold a short stick or flower in their left hand and raise their right hand. The seal, in grey chalcedony, is tabloid in shape with rounded corners.

Said to be from Babylonia
Purchased from Prof. E. Herzfeld in 1936
H 2.6 cm, W 2.5 cm, Th 1.3 cm
British Museum, ANE 128849

202 Cylinder seal showing the Persian royal hero

The royal hero (headdress damaged by a chip) aims an arrow at a rampant, winged lion-griffin that raises its forepaws. Between the figures is a winged disc (chipped) above an oval formed by the crescent moon, in which is the bust of a crowned bearded figure in a decorated Persian robe. He faces the royal hero and holds a flower in his left hand, with the other hand raised. The seal is made of pale grey chalcedony.

Provenance unknown
Acquired from H.O. Cureton in 1849, who
    purchased it at the sale of the J.R. Steuart
    Collection at Sotheby's
H 2.2 cm, Diam 1.2 cm
British Museum, ANE 89422
Layard 1853: 607; Merrillees 2005: no. 59

203 Cylinder seal showing two bearded figures

Two four-winged bull-men raise their arms to support a pair of wings from which rises the bust of a bearded figure facing right with one hand raised. Below is an oval formed by the crescent moon in which is the bust of a bearded figure also facing right and with a raised hand. Both wear fillets or hats and Persian robes. The seal is made of streaked grey-blue chalcedony.

Acquired by A.H. Layard in Mesopotamia between
    1845 and 1851
H 2.6 cm, Diam 1.15 cm (base)
British Museum, ANE 89852 (N/1065)
Layard 1853: 607–8; Merrillees 2005: no. 73

204 Stamp seal showing two bulls

The bulls pace towards each other. Above them is a crescent in which is a bust with a headdress, now chipped, facing left with hand raised. The seal, of greyish-blue chalcedony, is conoid in shape.

Provenance unknown
Purchased from Prof. E. Herzfeld in 1936
H 3.0 cm, 2.1 cm x 2.5 cm (base)
British Museum, ANE 128851

205 Cylinder seal showing the Egyptian dwarf-god Bes and the Persian royal hero

Two scenes, on a continuous base-line, are divided by a lotus bud and a lotus flower. The Egyptian dwarf-god Bes embraces two deer, and stands on two crowned and winged pedestal sphinxes that recline facing each other. The Persian royal hero stands facing right, holding a flower in his left hand and raising his right hand towards a figure in a winged disc who is also holding a flower. Below the winged disc sit two winged lion-griffins, facing each other and each raising a paw; between them is a lotus flower. The seal is made of grey-blue chalcedony.

Said to be from Hillah, near Babylon
Purchased from Sir Keith Jackson, 4th Light
    Dragoons, via John Doubleday, in 1843
H 3.8 cm, Diam 2.1 cm
British Museum, ANE 89352
Pope 1938: IV, pl. 123B; Abdi 1999: fig. 1/6;
    Boardman 2000: 162, fig. 5/18; Abdi 2002b:
    fig. 9; Merrillees 2005: no. 55

206 Stamp seal showing the Egyptian dwarf-god Bes

Bes stands below a winged disc and extends his hands towards two inverted lions. The seal, made of pale blue chalcedony, is conoid in shape.

Provenance unknown
Acquired in 1926
H 3.25 cm, Diam 2.5 cm (base)
British Museum, ANE 91895
Pope 1938: IV, pl. 124R

207 Cylinder seal showing a falcon and ibex

The falcon stands facing an incense-burner, and the winged ibex leaps towards the right. It is tempting to see these as a cryptographic writing of a personal name – perhaps that of Udjahorresne, an Egyptian official during the reigns of Cambyses II (530–522 BC) and Darius I (522–486 BC). Both ends of the seal are decorated with a row of Egyptian hieroglyphs, the *udjat* eye symbol of the god Horus. The seal is made of grey-blue chalcedony.

Said to have come from Kermanshah, Iran
Purchased from Prof. E. Herzfeld in 1936
H 2.6 cm, Diam 2.0 cm
British Museum, ANE 128865
Merrillees 2005: no. 86

200

201

202

203

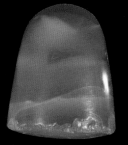

204

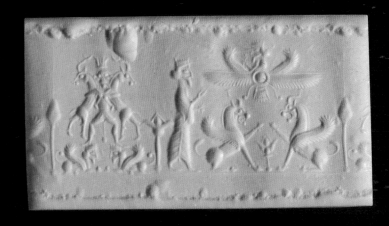

205

206

207

208 Cylinder seal showing a priest and the Persian royal hero

The seal, banded very dark brown and white, probably artificially dyed, is cut in two styles. On the left a Babylonian priest stands before an incense-burner and an altar supporting the symbols of the god Marduk. On the right, on a decorated dais, stands the Persian royal hero who grasps two rampant lions by the throat. The seal, made of eyed sardonyx, belongs to the very end of the sixth or the first years of the fifth century BC when both Babylonian and Achaemenid seals were in use.

Acquired by A.H. Layard in Mesopotamia between 1845 and 1851
H 3.7 cm, Diam 1.55 cm
British Museum, ANE 89324 (N 1069)
Layard 1853: 607; Pope 1938: IV, pl. 123C; Merrillees 2005: no. 31

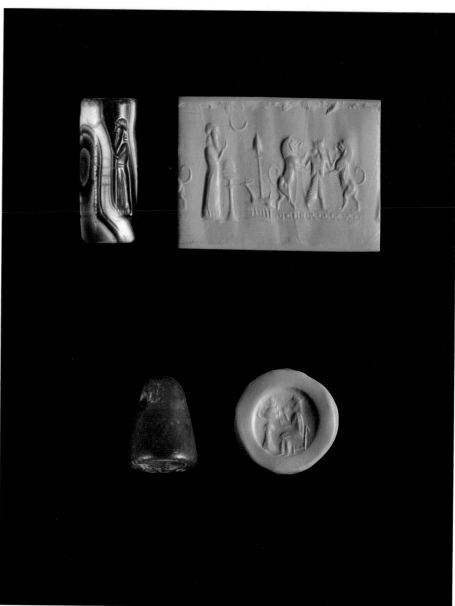

209 Stamp seal showing a figure in Median dress

The figure sits in a chair facing left. He holds a lotus flower in his left hand and raises an object, probably a cup, in his right hand. Before him is an incense-burner. The seal is conoid and in a greyish-brown stone.

Provenance unknown
Acquired before 1920
H 2.45 cm, Diam 1.8 cm (base)
British Museum, ANE 115523

208–9

210

210 Gold finger-ring with oval bezel

The ring is engraved in intaglio with a robed female figure seated facing right on a chair. She wears a headdress with five spikes and holds a lotus flower in her raised right hand; a bird perches on her left hand. Fifth to fourth centuries BC.

Oxus Treasure
Bequeathed in 1897 by A.W. Franks
Diam 1.9 cm (hoop), 2.04 x 1.54 cm (bezel), Wt 17.5 g
British Museum, ANE 124005
Dalton 1964: 27–8, no. 104, pl. 16, fig. 53; Pope 1938: IV, pl. 124W

PESTLES AND MORTARS

211 Stone pestle and mortar of banded light green chert

The pestle has an Aramaic inscription on the flat end of the handle, reading 'In the ritual [of the fortress], 1 *Gyt* [beside] Mazda-farnah [?] [the *segan* used] this [?] pestle [in year] 1'. It can probably be dated to the first year of Artaxerxes I (464/3 BC).

Persepolis, found in Room 38 of the Treasury
Pestle L 22.3 cm, Diam 4.8 cm (head);
   mortar H 17.3 cm, Diam 15.5 cm
Tehran, 2322 (pestle); 2323 (mortar)
Bowman 1970: no. 54, pl. 15 (pestle)

211, mortar

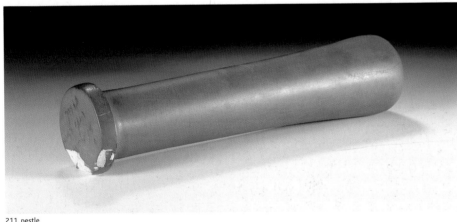

211, pestle

212 Stone bowl of banded green chert with an Aramaic inscription on the base

Such bowls are believed to have been used in a religious ceremony (see p. 152). The text, written in ink, records the participants in the ceremony and its date, and reads 'In the [*haoma*-] crushing ceremony of the fortress, beside Aratat-vahuš the *segan*, 1 [Arta]ma used this large plate worth 9 [shekel?] coins beside Baga-pata the treasurer who is in Arachosia. '*škr* of year 13[?]'. It is probably from the reign of Artaxerxes I (possibly 452/1 BC).

Persepolis, found east of the Hall of 100 Columns
   (Room 38) in 1949
H 4 cm, Diam 19.8 cm (rim), Diam 9.3 cm (base)
Tehran, 2974
Sami 1970: 98–9, pl. on p. 105; Bowman 1970:
   no. 43, pl. 11

212

VOTIVE PLAQUES FROM THE OXUS TREASURE

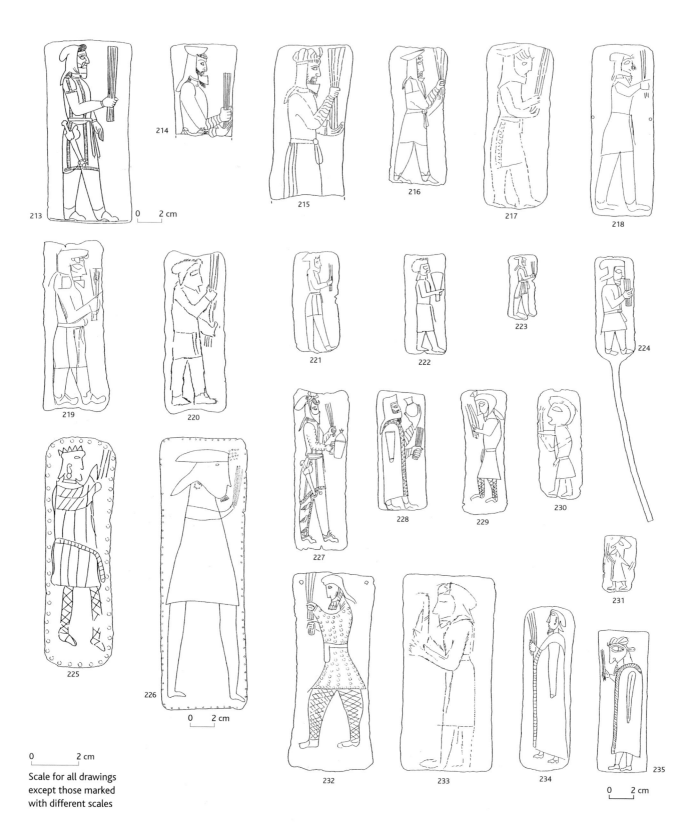

0   2 cm

Scale for all drawings
except those marked
with different scales

The Oxus Treasure contains fifty-one rectangular plaques in sheet gold whose purpose is generally assumed to be votive. All have representations of human figures except for three plaques with animals and one that is plain. Most of the plaques show men wearing Median or Persian dress, and generally carrying *barsoms* or flowers. It is possible that the figures carrying *barsoms* might be priests, or the *barsoms* might be indications of piety. In either case, it is likely that all the plaques were dedicated to a temple. These objects were bequeathed to the British Museum by A.W. Franks in 1897.

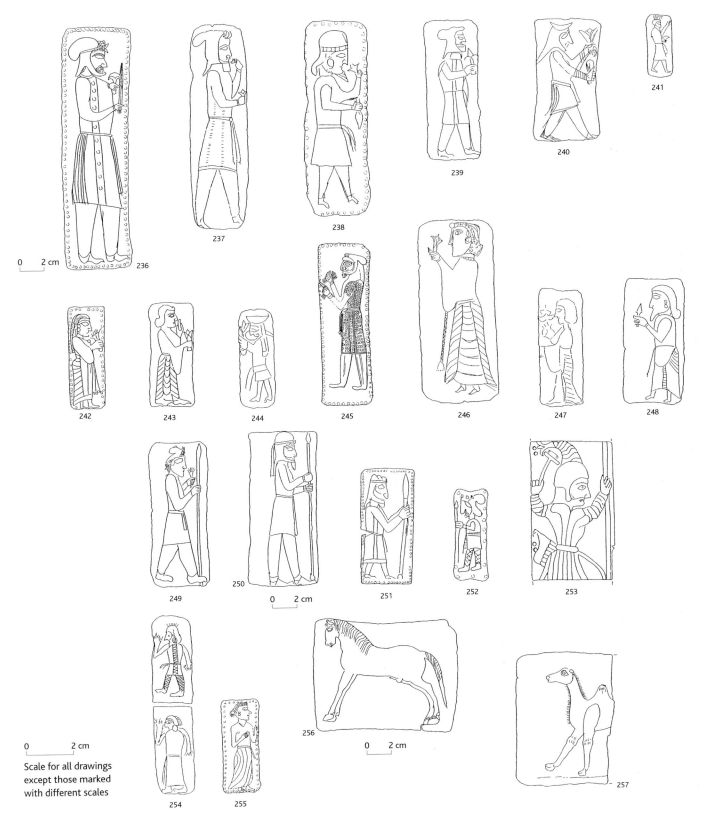

213

214

215

216

217

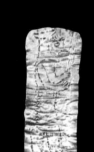

218

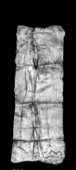

219

220

221

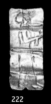

222

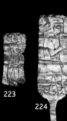

223

224

225

226

227

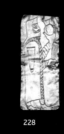

228

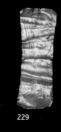

229

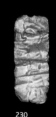

230

231

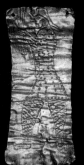

232

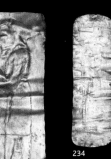

233

234

235

236

237

238

239

240

241

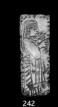

242

243

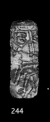

244

245

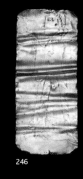

246

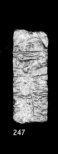

247

248

249

250

251

252

253

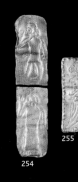

254

255

256

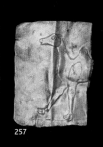

257

213–57 Rectangular plaques in sheet gold

213

Plaque with embossed and chased decoration showing a male figure facing right, wearing a belted tunic, trousers and a soft cap with neck-guard. His chin is covered. He wears an *akinakes* and carries a *barsom* in his right hand. His tunic is decorated with bands of embroidery or applied material. Two such bands run vertically down the length of the tunic, and there are further bands at the wrist and forming an inverted T-shape on the upper arm. Similarly decorated costumes are worn by tribute peoples coming from the north or northeast on the western façade of the Palace of Darius at Persepolis; an actual example of such a costume was found in the Issyk kurgan.

H 15.1 cm, W 7.5 cm, Wt 82.73 g
Analysis: Au 93%, Ag 2.3%, Cu 5.1 %, Pb <0.09%, PGE inclusions <5
British Museum, ANE 123949
Dalton 1964: no. 48; Curtis *et al.* 2003: fig. 2/1

214

Top half of a plaque with chased decoration showing the upper part of a male figure facing right. He wears a belted tunic and a soft cap with neck-guard and chin covering. His tunic has folds or decoration on the sleeves. He holds a *barsom* in his right hand and supports the base of it with his left hand.

H 7.8 cm, W 5.8 cm, Wt 21.06 g
Analysis: Au 94%, Ag 5.8%, Cu 0.6%, Pb <0.07%, PGE inclusions <5
British Museum, ANE 123951
Dalton 1964: no. 50; Curtis *et al.* 2003: fig. 3/13

215

The bottom part of this plaque has broken away. It has chased decoration showing a male figure facing right, wearing a belted tunic and soft cap with neck-guard and chin covering. His tunic has folds or decoration on the right-hand sleeve. He holds a *barsom* in his right hand and supports the base of it with his left hand.

H 6.3 cm, W 3.4 cm, Wt 6.54 g
Analysis: Au 90%, Ag 4.9%; Cu 5.4%; Pb 0.14%; PGE inclusions >20
British Museum, ANE 123953
Dalton 1964: no. 52; Curtis *et al.* 2003: fig. 3/17

216

Plaque with chased decoration showing a male figure facing right, wearing a belted tunic and trousers, and a soft cap with neck-guard and chin covering. His tunic has folds or decoration on the right-hand sleeve. He holds a *barsom* in his right hand. The left hand and arm is not shown.

H 5.75 cm, W 2.5 cm, Wt 2.27 g
Analysis: Au 85%; Ag 8.7%; Cu 6.1%; Pb 0.16%; PGE inclusions 1
British Museum, ANE 123952
Dalton 1964: no. 51; Curtis *et al.* 2003: fig. 3/14

217

Plaque with crudely chased decoration showing a male figure facing right, wearing a belted tunic and trousers, and a soft cap with neck-guard and chin covering. His tunic has a vertical band of decoration on the skirt. He holds a *barsom* apparently in his left hand and supports the base of it with his right hand.

H 6.85 cm, W 2.9 cm, Wt 4.34 g
Analysis: none
British Museum, ANE 123956
Dalton 1964: no. 55; Curtis *et al.* 2003: fig. 3/15

218

Plaque with crudely chased decoration showing a male figure facing right, wearing a belted tunic and trousers, and a soft cap with neck-guard and chin covering. He holds a *barsom* in his right hand. The left hand is not shown. There are two holes or raised dots on either side of the plaque.

H 7.1 cm, W 2.7 cm, Wt 3.82 g
Analysis: Au 89%; Ag 8.6%; Cu 2.2%; Pb 0.12%; PGE inclusions 1
British Museum, ANE 123954
Dalton 1964: no. 53; Curtis *et al.* 2003: fig. 2/2

219

Plaque with crudely chased decoration showing a male figure facing right, wearing a belted tunic and trousers, and a soft cap with neck-guard and chin covering. He holds a *barsom* in his right hand. The left hand is not shown.

H 7.15 cm, W 2.85 cm, Wt 4.15 g
Analysis: none
British Museum, ANE 123955
Dalton 1964: no. 54; Curtis *et al.* 2003: fig. 2/3

220

Plaque with crudely chased decoration showing a male figure facing right, wearing a belted tunic and trousers, and a soft cap with neck-guard. He holds a *barsom* in his right hand and apparently grasps it near the bottom with his left hand.

H 6.8 cm, W 2.7 cm, Wt 4.67 g
Analysis: Au 93%; Ag 3.6%; Cu 3.7%; Pb 0.12%; PGE inclusions 1
British Museum, ANE 123957
Dalton 1964: no. 56; Curtis *et al.* 2003: fig. 2/4

221

Plaque with chased decoration showing a male figure facing right, wearing a belted tunic and trousers, and a soft cap with neck-guard and chin covering. He holds a *barsom* in his right hand. The left hand is not shown.

H 4.25 cm, W 2.05 cm, Wt 3.37 g
Analysis: Au 92%; Ag 5.7%; Cu 2.7%; Pb <0.09%; PGE inclusions 1
British Museum, ANE 123960
Dalton 1964: no. 59; Curtis *et al.* 2003: fig. 2/5

222

Plaque with crudely chased decoration showing a male figure facing right, wearing a belted tunic and trousers, and a soft cap with neck-guard. He holds what is apparently a fan-shaped *barsom* in his right hand. The left hand is not shown.

H 4.2 cm, W 1.8 cm, Wt 1.68 g
Analysis: none
British Museum, ANE 123958
Dalton 1964: no. 57; Curtis *et al.* 2003: fig. 2/6

223

Plaque with chased decoration showing a male figure facing right, wearing a belted tunic and trousers, and a soft cap with neck-guard and chin covering. He holds a *barsom* in his right hand. The left hand is not shown.

H 2.75 cm, W 1.25 cm, Wt 0.65 g
Analysis: none
British Museum, ANE 123981
Dalton 1964: no. 58; Curtis *et al.* 2003: fig. 2/7

224

Plaque with long tail and chased decoration showing a male figure facing right, wearing a belted tunic and trousers, and a soft cap with neck-guard and chin covering. He holds a *barsom* in his right hand. The left hand is not shown.

H 11.1 cm, W 1.7 cm, Wt 2.92 g
Analysis: none
British Museum, ANE 123961
Dalton 1964: no. 60; Curtis *et al.* 2003: fig. 2/8

225

Plaque with crudely chased decoration showing a male figure facing right, wearing a belted tunic and trousers, and a soft cap with neck-guard and chin covering. His tunic has hatched decoration on the sleeves and there is cross-hatched decoration on his trousers. He wears a crown (?) on his head and possibly has an earring. He holds a *barsom* in his two raised hands. There are embossed dots all around the edge of the plaque.

H 9.65 cm, W 3.0 cm, Wt 6.16 g
Analysis: none
British Museum, ANE 123986
Dalton 1964: no. 85; Curtis *et al.* 2003: fig. 3/19

226

Plaque with very crudely chased decoration showing a male figure facing right, wearing a tunic and trousers, and a soft cap with neck-guard. The figure possibly has a beard and wears an earring. He holds a *barsom* in his right hand. The left hand is not shown. There are small embossed dots all around the edge of the plaque.

H 22.7 cm, W 7.5 cm, Wt 85.2 g
Analysis: Au 91%; Ag 4.8%; Cu 4.1%; Pb <0.08%;
  PGE inclusions <5
British Museum, ANE 123966
Dalton 1964: no. 65; Curtis *et al.* 2003: fig. 3/16

227

Plaque with chased decoration showing a male figure facing right, wearing a belted tunic and trousers, and a soft cap with neck-guard and chin- and mouth-covering. There is possibly a lock of hair on his forehead. He wears an *akinakes* on his hip, suspended from a sword-belt. There are two vertical strips of decoration, either embroidery or applied material, on his tunic (cf. cat. 213), and the outside of his trousers is decorated with representations of birds. He holds a *barsom* in his left hand and a jug with a lid in his right hand.

H 6.7 cm, W 2.4 cm, Wt 3.30 g
Analysis: Au 94%; Ag 2.2%; Cu 3.6%; Pb <0.24%;
  PGE inclusions >20
British Museum, ANE 123971
Dalton 1964: no. 70; Curtis *et al.* 2003: fig. 4/24

228

Plaque with chased decoration showing a male figure facing right, wearing a *kandys* (overcoat) and a soft cap with neck-guard and chin- and mouth-covering. His coat has a strip of decoration running its full length. He holds a *barsom* in his left hand and a jar in his right hand.

H 5.0 cm, W 2.1 cm, Wt 3.17 g
Analysis: Au 91%; Ag 7.3%; Cu 1.3%; Pb 0.05%;
  PGE inclusions 0
British Museum, ANE 123970
Dalton 1964: no. 69; Curtis *et al.* 2003: fig. 4/23

229

Plaque with crudely chased decoration showing a male figure facing left, wearing a belted tunic and trousers, and a soft cap with neck-guard and apparently a chin- and mouth-covering. His trousers have cross-hatched decoration. He holds a *barsom* in his left hand. The right hand is not shown.

H 5.2 cm, W 2.0 cm, Wt 2.01 g
Analysis: none
British Museum, ANE 123963
Dalton 1964: no. 62; Curtis *et al.* 2003: fig. 3/18

230

Plaque with very crudely chased decoration showing a male figure facing left, wearing a belted tunic and trousers, and a soft cap with neck-guard. He holds a *barsom* in his right hand and supports the base of it with his left hand.

H 4.6 cm, W 1.85 cm, Wt 2.01 g
Analysis: Au 79%; Ag 12.0%; Cu 8.3%; Pb <0.09%;
  PGE inclusions 5–10
British Museum, ANE 123964
Dalton 1964: no. 53; Curtis *et al.* 2003: fig. 2/10

231

Very small plaque with crudely chased decoration apparently showing a male figure facing left, probably wearing a belted tunic and trousers, and a soft cap with neck-guard and chin-covering. He holds a *barsom* in his right hand and an unidentifiable object in his left hand.

H 2.4 cm, W 1.4 cm, Wt 0.58 g
Analysis: none
British Museum, ANE 123973
Dalton 1964: no. 72; Curtis *et al.* 2003: fig. 2/11

232

Plaque with chased decoration showing a male figure facing left, wearing a belted tunic and trousers, and a soft cap with neck-guard and possibly chin-covering; there are, however, also indications that the figure has a beard. His tunic is decorated with small circles and his trousers have cross-hatched decoration. He holds a *barsom* in his left hand and grasps it towards the bottom with his left hand. There are two holes or raised dots on the upper corners of the plaque.

H 8.35 cm, W 3.7 cm, Wt 5.70 g
Analysis: Au 82%; Ag 16.0%; Cu 2.6%; Pb <0.07%;
  PGE inclusions 1
British Museum, ANE 123962
Dalton 1964: no. 61; Curtis *et al.* 2003: fig. 3/20

233

Plaque with crude and faintly chased decoration showing a male figure facing left, wearing a belted tunic and trousers, and a soft cap with neck-guard and chin-covering. He apparently holds a *barsom* in both hands.

H 8.2 cm, W 4.0 cm, Wt 16.65 g
Analysis: Au 88%; Ag 3.9%; Cu 7.6%; Pb 0.05%;
  PGE inclusions <5
British Museum, ANE 123965
Dalton 1964: no. 64; Curtis *et al.* 2003: fig. 2/9

234

Plaque with chased decoration showing a male figure facing left, wearing an overcoat (*kandys*) and a soft cap with neck-guard and chin-covering. He apparently has a beard. His coat has a strip of hatched decoration all down the front. He holds a *barsom* in his left (?) hand. The right hand is not shown.

H 6.85 cm, W 2.15 cm, Wt 2.59 g
Analysis: none
British Museum, ANE 123977
Dalton 1964: no. 76; Curtis *et al.* 2003: fig. 4/21

235

Plaque with chased decoration showing a male figure facing left, wearing an overcoat (*kandys*) and probably a soft cap with neck-guard and chin-covering (only roughly represented). He seems to have a beard. His coat has a strip of hatched decoration down the front and over the shoulder. He holds a *barsom* in his right (?) hand. The left hand is not shown.

H 11.8 cm, W 4.3 cm, Wt 42.7 g
Analysis: Au 94%; Ag 5.2%; Cu 0.6%; Pb 0.14%;
  PGE inclusions 5–10
British Museum, ANE 123969
Dalton 1964: no. 68; Curtis *et al.* 2003: fig. 4/22

236

Plaque with chased decoration showing a male figure facing right, wearing a belted tunic and trousers, and a soft cap with neck-guard and chin-covering. He is bearded and hair is shown on his forehead. His tunic has a vertical band of decoration with incised circles extending from the neckline to the bottom of the skirt. He holds what is possibly a *barsom* (though it has a pointed top) in his right hand and a flower in his left hand.

H 20.0 cm, W 5.9 cm, Wt 38.09 g
Analysis: Au 84%; Ag 12%; Cu 4.1%; Pb <0.19%;
  PGE inclusions >20
British Museum, ANE 123950
Dalton 1964: no. 49; Curtis *et al.* 2003: fig. 4/25

237

Plaque with chased decoration showing a male figure facing right, wearing a belted tunic and trousers, and a soft cap with neck-guard and chin-covering. Hair is shown on his forehead. He holds a flower in his right hand and what may be another flower in his left hand.

H 8.5 cm, W 2.5 cm, Wt 4.92 g
Analysis: Au 91%; Ag 4.9%; Cu 4.3%; Pb <0.07%;
  PGE inclusions 1
British Museum, ANE 123978
Dalton 1964: no. 77; Curtis *et al.* 2003: fig. 4/26

238

Plaque with crudely chased decoration showing a male figure facing right, wearing a belted tunic and trousers and a soft cap with neck-guard. There is a decorative band around his cap and he seems to have a pointed beard. He holds a flower in his left hand and an unidentifiable arrow-shaped object in his right hand. There are raised dots all around the edge of the plaque.

H 8.1 cm, W 2.75 cm, Wt 5.89 g
Analysis: Au 86%; Ag 10%; Cu 3.7%; Pb 0.18%;
  PGE inclusions <5
British Museum, ANE 123984
Dalton 1964: no. 83; Curtis *et al.* 2003: fig. 4/30

239

Plaque with crudely chased decoration showing a male figure facing right, wearing a belted tunic and trousers, and a soft cap with neck-guard and chin-covering. His tunic has a vertical band of decoration extending from the neckline to the bottom of the skirt. He holds a flower in his right hand. The left hand is not shown.

H 5.8 cm, W 2.35 cm, Wt 3.63 g
Analysis: Au 95%; Ag 2.4%; Cu 2.1%; Pb <0.05%;
  PGE inclusions >20
British Museum, ANE 123980
Dalton 1964: no. 79; Curtis *et al.* 2003: fig. 4/27

240

Plaque with crudely chased decoration showing a male figure facing right, wearing a belted tunic and trousers, and a soft cap with neck-guard and chin-covering. He holds a flower in his left hand and an unidentifiable object in his right hand.

H 5.05 cm, W 2.85 cm, Wt 3.70 g
Analysis: Au 90%; Ag 10%; Cu 0.4%; Pb <0.09%;
  PGE inclusions 0
British Museum, ANE 123979
Dalton 1964: no. 78; Curtis *et al.* 2003: fig. 4/31

241

Small plaque with crudely chased decoration showing a male figure facing right, wearing a belted tunic and trousers. He wears a crown (?) on his head. He holds what is apparently a flower in his right hand and his left hand is upraised.

H 2.65 cm, W 1.1 cm, Wt 1.36 g
Analysis: Au 94%; Ag 1.8%; Cu 4%; Pb <0.06%;
  PGE inclusions 0
British Museum, ANE 123959
Dalton 1964: no. 80; Curtis *et al.* 2003: fig. 4/28

242

Plaque with chased decoration showing a female figure facing right, wearing a long Persian dress with hanging sleeve. She has long hair draped over her shoulders and seems to be wearing earrings. She holds a flower in her right hand. The left hand is not shown. There are raised dots all around the edge of the plaque.

H 4.25 cm, W 1.55 cm, Wt 1.49 g
Analysis: Au 92%; Ag 6%; Cu 2.4%; Pb <0.07%;
  PGE inclusions 0
British Museum, ANE 123994
Dalton 1964: no. 93; Curtis *et al.* 2003: fig. 5/32

243

Plaque with crudely chased decoration showing a female figure facing right, wearing a long Persian dress with hanging sleeve. She holds a flower in her right hand and an unidentifiable object in her left hand.

H 4.35 cm, W 1.9 cm, Wt 2.40 g
Analysis: Au 90%; Ag 5.2%; Cu 4%; Pb 0.07%;
  PGE inclusions <5
British Museum, ANE 123990
Dalton 1964: no. 89; Curtis *et al.* 2003: fig. 5/33b

244

Plaque with crudely chased decoration showing a male figure facing left, wearing a belted tunic and trousers and a soft cap with neck-guard and possibly chin-covering. He holds a flower in his left hand. The right hand is not shown.

H 4.1 cm, W 1.55 cm, Wt 0.97 g
Analysis: none
British Museum, ANE 123982
Dalton 1964: no. 81; Curtis *et al.* 2003: fig. 4/29

245

Plaque with chased decoration showing a male figure facing left, wearing a belted tunic and trousers, and a soft cap with neck-guard and chin- and mouth-covering. His tunic is decorated with two vertical strips and a large number of small circles. He holds flowers or a bundle of grasses in each hand.

H 6.8 cm, W 2.25 cm, Wt 4.28 g
Analysis: none
British Museum, ANE 123972
Dalton 1964: no. 71; Curtis *et al.* 2003: fig. 2/12

246

Plaque with chased decoration showing a female figure facing left, wearing a long Persian dress with hanging sleeve. She wears a necklace and a jewel or brooch on her forehead, and a tassel hangs down in front of her skirt. She holds a flower in her left hand. The right hand is not shown.

H 7.65 cm, W 3.35 cm, Wt 7.45 g

Analysis: Au 90%; Ag 4.6%; Cu 5.5%; Pb <0.11%; PGE inclusions 0

British Museum, ANE 123991

Dalton 1964: no. 90; Curtis *et al.* 2003: fig. 5/34

247

Plaque with crudely chased decoration showing a female (?) figure facing left, wearing a long Persian dress with hanging sleeve. She holds a flower in her left (?) hand. It is not clear whether the other hand is depicted.

H 4.95 cm, W 1.9 cm, Wt 2.46 g

Analysis: none

British Museum, ANE 123992

Dalton 1964: no. 91; Curtis *et al.* 2003: fig. 5/35

248

Plaque with crudely chased decoration showing a male figure facing left, wearing a long Persian dress. He has a pointed beard and wears an earring. He holds an arrow-shaped object that may be a flower in his left hand. The right hand is not shown.

H 5.25 cm, W 2.65 cm, Wt 4.54 g

Analysis: Au 93%; Ag 4.3%; Cu 2.8%; Pb <0.06%; PGE inclusions 1

British Museum, ANE 123993

Dalton 1964: no. 92; Curtis *et al.* 2003: fig. 5/36

249

Plaque with crudely chased decoration showing a male figure facing right wearing a belted tunic and trousers, and a soft cap. There are indications of hair on his forehead and at the back of his neck. He holds a flower in his left hand and a spear in his right hand.

H 6.05 cm, W 2.55 cm, Wt 3.11 g

Analysis: Au 92%; Ag 4.7%; Cu 3.7%; Pb <0.07%; PGE inclusions 1

British Museum, ANE 123975

Dalton 1964: no. 74; Curtis *et al.* 2003: fig. 5/37

250

Plaque with chased decoration showing a male figure facing right, wearing a belted tunic and trousers, and a soft cap with neck-guard and chin-covering. He holds a spear with a ball at the end in both hands.

H 13.0 cm, W 6.0 cm, Wt 42.83 g

Analysis: Au 90%; Ag 6.1%; Cu 3.8%; Pb 0.12%; PGE inclusions 5–10

British Museum, ANE 123974

Dalton 1964: no. 73; Curtis *et al.* 2003: fig. 5/38

251

Plaque with chased decoration showing a male figure facing right, wearing a belted tunic and trousers, and a soft cap with neck-guard and chin-covering. His tunic has a vertical decorative stripe in the centre. He holds a spear with a ball at the end in both hands. There are raised dots all around the edge of the plaque.

H 4.85 cm, W 2.3 cm, Wt 2.85 g

Analysis: Au 97%; Ag 0.9%; Cu 2.3%; Pb <0.09%; PGE inclusions 1

British Museum, ANE 123976

Dalton 1964: no. 75; Curtis *et al.* 2003: fig. 5/39

252

Plaque with crudely chased decoration showing a male figure facing left, wearing a belted tunic and trousers, and a soft cap with neck-guard and chin-covering. His trousers have cross-hatched decoration and his tunic has a vertical band of decoration on the skirt. He holds a spear in his left hand. The right hand is not shown. There are a few raised dots around the edge of the plaque.

H 3.85 cm, W 1.5 cm, Wt 0.97 g

Analysis: none

British Museum, ANE 123967 and 123968

Dalton 1964: nos 66, 67; Curtis *et al.* 2003: fig. 5/40

253

Plaque with chased decoration showing a male figure facing right, wearing a belted tunic, a soft cap with a high top, neck-guard and chin- and possibly mouth-covering. He wears a quiver and wields an axe in his right hand. His left hand is upraised, possibly grasping a spear.

H 5.8 cm, W 3.55 cm, Wt 8.42 g

Analysis: Au 92%; Ag 7.8%; Cu 0.3%; Pb <0.05%; PGE inclusions 0

British Museum, ANE 123985

Dalton 1964: no. 84; Curtis *et al.* 2003: fig. 5/41

254

Long, narrow plaque broken into two pieces with crudely chased designs. The top piece shows a male figure facing left, wearing a belted tunic and trousers, and a soft cap with neck-guard and chin-covering. His tunic has a vertical band of cross-hatched decoration from the neckline to the bottom of the skirt. His trousers also have cross-hatched decoration. He does not seem to be holding anything in his hands, one of which is raised with the other hanging loose. The lower piece shows a female (?) figure in a belted robe, apparently wearing an earring. One arm is raised and the other hanging loose.

ANE 123983 (top): H 3.7 cm, W 1.75 cm, Wt 4.0 g

ANE 123996 (bottom): H 3.65 cm, W 1.7 cm, Wt 3.89 g

Analysis of 123983: Au 98%; Ag 1.2%; Cu 0.3%; Pb 0.09%; PGE inclusions 1

British Museum, ANE 123983 and 123996

Dalton 1964: nos 82, 95; Curtis *et al.* 2003: fig. 6/44

255

Plaque with chased decoration showing a female figure facing right, wearing a top with V-shaped neckline and a long skirt. She wears an earring. Both hands are raised and seem to be empty. There are raised dots all around the edge of the plaque.

H 3.9 cm, W 1.65 cm, Wt 1.62 g

Analysis: Au 90%; Ag 6.5%; Cu 3.4%; Pb <0.10%; PGE inclusions >20

British Museum, ANE 123995

Dalton 1964: no. 94; Curtis *et al.* 2003: fig. 6/43

256

Plaque with chased decoration showing a horse facing left.

H 9.4 cm, W 12.5 cm, Wt 38.29 g

Analysis (i): Au 69%; Ag 30%; Cu 0.5%; Pb <0.05%; PGE inclusions 5–10

Analysis (ii): Au 70%; Ag 29%; Cu 0.4%; Pb <0.07%; PGE inclusions 1

British Museum, ANE 124000

Dalton 1964: no. 99; Curtis *et al.* 2003: fig. 6/48

257

Part of a plaque with chased decoration showing the foreparts of a camel.

H 5.6 cm, W 4.25 cm, Wt 10.4 g

Analysis: Au 89%; Ag 11%; Cu 0.4%; Pb <0.12%; PGE inclusions >20

British Museum, ANE 123999

Dalton 1964: no. 98; Curtis *et al.* 2003: fig. 6/50

VOTIVE STATUETTES FROM THE OXUS TREASURE

It was a common tradition in the ancient world to donate or deposit statues in a temple, usually to represent the supplicant in the eyes of the deity. The donor might be asking for a favour or giving thanks, or simply presenting something as a mark of respect. The objects or statues would often be valuable, perhaps made of gold or silver. Objects donated in recognition of a favour granted are known as *ex-voto*, i.e. given following a promise. Some of the statuettes in the Oxus Treasure were probably presented to a temple together with other items in the treasure, but we have no scientific information about this. Together with other items in the Oxus Treasure, these objects were bequeathed to the British Museum by A.W. Franks in 1897.

258 (right), 259 (left)

258 Gold figurine of a man

The figure wears a Median-style trouser-suit with an overcoat (*kandys*) over his shoulders. The sleeves of the coat are left empty. On his head the man wears a high-topped helmet (*bashlyk*) that covers the ears and chin. He holds a *barsom* in his right hand.

H 5.6 cm, Wt 37.5 g
British Museum, ANE 123902
Dalton 1964: no. 2, pl. XIII

259 Gold figurine of a man

Similar to cat. 258 above. The figures wears an embroidered overcoat. Dalton says of this piece that it 'is regarded as probably an imitation made at Rawalpindi' (Dalton 1964: 2), but apart from its similarity to cat. 258 the reasons for this statement are not clear.

H 5.3 cm, Wt 33.5 g
British Museum, ANE 123903
Dalton 1964: no. 2: a, pl. XIII

260 Silver statuette, partially gilded, of a bearded man

The man wears a pleated costume in Persian style and holds a barsom in his left hand. He wears a cap around the top of which is a band with incised crenellations, probably showing that he is a king.

H 14.8 cm, Wt 387 g
British Museum, ANE 123901
Dalton 1964: no.1, pl. II; Curtis 2000: fig. 74

261 Silver statuette of a naked youth wearing a tall headdress

The youth stands on a two-stepped plinth, and has clenched fists in which are vertical holes for the attachment of objects that he was once holding (now missing). A roll of hair is shown under the headdress and he has pierced ears. The tall cap is covered with gold foil. The nudity of this figure, the lack of beard and the roll of hair on the forehead are sometimes taken as an indication of Greek influence, but the headdress is not Greek in character. It is reminiscent of the domed hats worn by some of the Median nobles, officials, guards and attendants in Median dress on the Persepolis

reliefs (for example, Ghirshman 1964: pls 209, 232, 236) and is paralleled on chariot lynch-pins from Bin Tepe in Lydia (with cheek-pieces).

H 29.2 cm, Wt 1,852.2 g
British Museum, ANE 123905
Dalton 1964: no. 4, pl. II; Boardman 1988: no. 235; Curtis 2000: fig. 71

262 Gold head

From a statuette showing a beardless youth with short wavy hair and pierced ears. The head is hollow and may originally have been part of a composite statue made of different materials. The artistry of this piece is crude and it is difficult to assign it to a particular school of art.

H 11.3 cm, W 8.35 cm, Wt 399 g
British Museum, ANE 123906
Dalton 1964: no. 5, pl. III

262

260

261

171

AMULETS

263

263 Faience pendant representing the head of the Egyptian dwarf-god Bes

Bes is shown with a lion's face and ruff, protruding ears and a feather crown. The crown has a horizontal hole so that the pendant could be suspended, perhaps on a necklace. Bes became very popular in the Achaemenid period, and amulets representing him are well known. The exact significance of Bes is unclear, but he probably had a protective function and amulets were worn to ward off evil spirits. In Egypt he protected women in childbirth. He also appears in the formal iconography of the Achaemenid period, for example on the Oxus Treasure gold chariot (cat. 399).

Persepolis
H 7.3 cm, W 3.8 cm
Tehran, 1206/7631
Abdi 1999: fig. 5/21; Seipel 2000: no. 132;
  Abdi 2002b: fig. 2

264 Faience pendant in the form of an udjat-eye, or 'eye of Horus'

The pendant has a horizontal hole towards the top for suspension. According to Egyptian mythology the god Horus lost his eye in a struggle with the rival god Seth. It was retrieved and became a powerful protective amulet. Examples are often found in Egyptian coffins and in mummy-wrappings. Like amulets of Bes, eye-of-Horus pendants became common in the popular art of the Achaemenid period.

Persepolis
H 4.1 cm, W 6.5 cm
Tehran, 40/2040
Seipel 2000: no. 131

EGYPTIAN RELIGIOUS OBJECTS

265

265 Egyptian stone stela (*cippus*)

With engraved decoration and hieroglyphic inscriptions, broken off at the bottom. On the front is a winged sun-disc with serpents emerging from it, beneath which are nine seated deities in high relief. Below them is a head of Bes with engraved figures of gods and Egyptian symbols on either side of him. On the back are more engraved figures of Egyptian gods and symbols above the remains of a hieroglyphic inscription. There are further hieroglyphs around the edge.

The purpose of such stelae was to enlist the help of various gods to protect a person from evil creatures. They were set up in temples or private houses, and smaller versions were worn as amulets. It is unknown how this object came to be at Susa. It may have belonged to an Egyptian workman or merchant, or it may have been brought back from Egypt by a Persian as a curio.

Susa, probably found by R. de Mecquenem in 1930
  in the 'Donjon' area
H 9.1 cm, W 9.4 cm
Tehran, 2013/103
Abdi 1999: fig. 7/2; 2002a; 2002b: fig. 6

264

266

267

266 Wooden door

Inlaid with polychrome glass (fragments of which survive), from a small shrine (*naos*). Beneath a winged sun-disc, Darius I (521–486 BC) is depicted as pharaoh, offering to the jackal-headed god Anubis. The goddess Isis stands behind, shown wearing cow-horns. The hieroglyphic labels identify the three figures, with Darius written out in phonetic hieroglyphs within the oval cartouche – a motif traditionally reserved for Egyptian kings and queens. Illustrated alongside the door is a computer-aided reconstruction by Shahrokh Razmjou showing its original colours.

Provenance unknown
Acquired in 1891 from the collection of William
  Edkins (previously in the collections of Peter
  Rainier and the 4th Duke of Northumberland)
H 28 cm, W 23.5 cm
British Museum, AES 37496
Yoyotte 1972: pl. 19/A; Bianchi 1983: 32

267 Upper part of a painted round-topped sandstone stela

Beneath a winged sun-disc and heaven sign, Alexander of Macedon is depicted as pharaoh, offering wine to the sacred Buchis bull, supported on a plinth. Parts of six lines of hieroglyphic text are preserved, recording the death of the sacred bull in the fourth year of Alexander, and noting that it was alive during the reign of Darius (III), who controlled Egypt from 336 BC until the conquest of Alexander in 332 BC.

From Armant, Egypt
Donated by the Egypt Exploration Society in 1929
H 54 cm, W 45 cm
British Museum, AES 1697/1719
Mond and Myers 1934: vol. II, 3, 28, vol. III,
  pl. XXXVII

THE SUSA TOMB

On 6 February 1901 the French archaeologist Jacques de Morgan discovered a very rich grave on the Acropolis at Susa. The body was in a plain bronze coffin with a ledge-shaped rim. There were fallen bricks in the coffin indicating that it had probably been placed in a vaulted tomb. The skeleton was flat on its back and with it was a magnificent collection of jewellery, some with very fine polychrome decoration. There were a pair of gold bracelets, a pair of gold earrings, a gold torc, a pair of gold roundels and at least five necklaces. These included one that is not in the present exhibition, a three-strand necklace of fine pearls and gold spacer beads inlaid with coloured stones. In addition to the jewellery, a silver bowl and two alabaster jars were found. Two coins that were minted at Arad on the Syrian coast between 350–332 BC seem to show that the burial dates from the very end of the Achaemenid period. Because the bones were small and the teeth were worn, and there were no weapons in the coffin, de Morgan concluded that the burial was that of an elderly woman, but this remains uncertain, particularly as we know that men wore expensive jewellery in the Achaemenid period. Illustrated below is a watercolour by Jacques de Morgan showing the coffin burial as discovered at Susa in 1901 (Musée du Louvre).

268 Pair of gold bracelets with lion's-head terminals

The hoops have an inward curve opposite the terminals in the characteristic Achaemenid fashion. The lions' heads, their necks and the sections of bracelet behind the necks all have cavities for polychrome inlays. Those that survive are in turquoise, lapis lazuli and mother-of-pearl. The delicate inlays on the lions' necks are perhaps intended to represent the manes.

Susa Acropolis
Excavations of J. de Morgan, 1901
H 6.4 cm, W 7.7 cm; H 6.3 cm, W 7.9 cm
Louvre, Sb 2761 and 2762
Harper, Aruz and Tallon 1992: nos 172–3

269 Pair of gold earrings

The earrings are penannular in shape, with a hinged wire holder at the top. They have hollow centres, outlined by granulation, a flower-shaped outline and cavities for cloisonné inlay on both sides. The surviving inlays are in turquoise and lapis lazuli.

Susa Acropolis
Excavations of J. de Morgan, 1901
H 4.1 cm, W 4.4 cm
Louvre, Sb 2764 and 2765
Harper, Aruz and Tallon 1992: no. 178

270 Gold torc with lion's-head terminals and ribbed hoop

The torc is in two sections that fit together at the back of the neck and are held in place with a pin. There are cavities for polychrome inlays on the lions' heads, on their necks and on the sections of bracelet behind their necks. Turquoise, lapis-lazuli and mother-of-pearl inlays survive. The cells on the lions' necks are mounted on a thin gold plate that is separately attached to the torc, and are technically examples of cloisonné work. The cavities on the hoop that are introduced in the casting process are examples of *champlevé* work.

Susa Acropolis
Excavations of J. de Morgan, 1901
Diam 20.2 cm
Louvre, Sb 2760
Harper, Aruz and Tallon 1992: no. 171

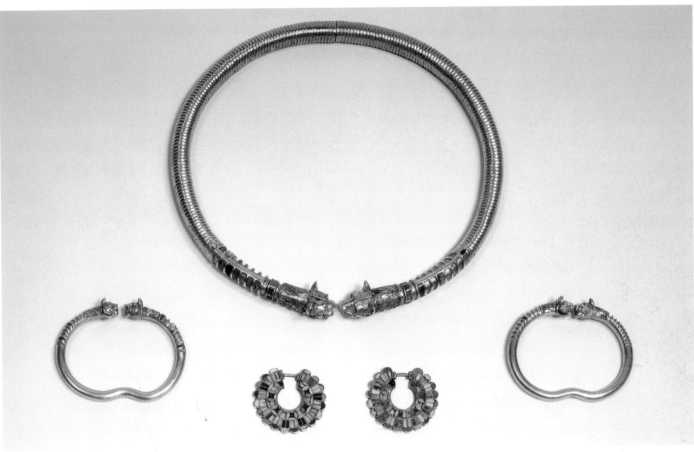

268–70

271

271 Pair of gold roundels

The roundels have cloisonné decoration on the upper convex surfaces and a ring fastener on the underside. There is granulation work around the edge. The inlays are of turquoise, lapis lazuli and carnelian. The decoration shows six circles each containing the bust of a human figure in a crescent moon. The figures are very schematic but seem to be wearing a crown and to have one hand upraised. Comparisons have been made with the figure in the winged disc. These roundels were found close to each other on one side of the skeleton's chest.

Susa Acropolis
Excavations of J. de Morgan, 1901
Diam 2.1 cm
Louvre, Sb 2766
Harper, Aruz and Tallon 1992: no. 179

272 (bottom), 273 (top), 274 (centre)

272 Necklace of gold and inlaid beads with pendants

The inlaid gold beads, which are spaced throughout the necklace, have longitudinal grooves inlaid with turquoise and lapis lazuli. There are eighteen pendants consisting of hook-shaped gold sheets to which have been attached inlays of turquoise, lapis lazuli and carnelian. The pendants are also decorated with granulation. The plain gold beads are melon-shaped.

Susa Acropolis
Excavations of J. de Morgan, 1901
L 70 cm
Louvre, Sb 2763
Harper, Aruz and Tallon 1992: no. 174

273 Necklace of gold beads and semiprecious stones

The gold beads are plain barrels or granulated rings, while the stone beads are in turquoise, lapis lazuli and carnelian, some with gold caps. There are two pendants, one carnelian and one agate, that are disc-shaped and semicircular respectively.

Susa Acropolis
Excavations of J. de Morgan, 1901
L 32 cm
Louvre, Sb 2768
Harper, Aruz and Tallon 1992: no. 175

274 Necklace of gold beads and semiprecious stones

The necklace consists of 400 gold beads and 400 stone beads arranged in four strands (one illustrated). The gold beads are decorated with granulation while the stone beads are made of turquoise, lapis lazuli, carnelian, emerald, agate, jasper, feldspar, flint, quartz, amethyst, hematite, marble and breccia.

Susa Acropolis
Excavations of J. de Morgan, 1901
Each strand: L 124 cm
Louvre, Sb 19355
Harper, Aruz and Tallon 1992: no. 176

275

275 Necklace of agate beads

The excavator J. de Morgan suggested that these sixty-five beads were meant to be sewn onto garments rather than threaded on a necklace, but this seems unlikely, particularly as the two largest beads were found close to the neck of the skeleton.

Susa Acropolis
Excavations of J. de Morgan, 1901
L 26.5 cm; largest beads: L 3.2 cm, W 2.1 cm
Louvre, Sb 12070
Harper, Aruz and Tallon 1992: no. 177

276

276 Head ornament

This ornament consisted of eight large gold beads decorated with granulation. The identification as a head ornament is suggested by Francoise Tallon (in Harper *et al.* 1992, under no. 176) because of the position of the beads in the grave.

Susa Acropolis
Excavations of J. de Morgan, 1901
Each bead L. 1.8 cm, Diam 0.6 cm
Louvre, Sb 19364
De Morgan 1905: 52–4, figs 81–2, pl. IV/4

277, base

277 Silver bowl

The bowl is of carinated form with flared rim and central omphalos. The bowl has been cast. The decoration, visible only from the underside, consists of a rosette in the centre surrounded by the radiating petals of a lotus flower. The shape and decoration of this bowl are typical of the Achaemenid period.

Susa Acropolis
Excavations of J. de Morgan, 1901
H 4.3 cm, Diam 18.4 cm, Wt 562 g
Louvre, Sb 2756
Harper, Aruz and Tallon 1992: no. 170

277

278 (right), 279 (left)

279 Alabaster vessel (alabastron)

Similar to the above.

Susa Acropolis
Excavations of J. de Morgan, 1901
H 16.5 cm, Diam 7.3 cm
Louvre, Sb 537
De Morgan 1905: 42, fig. 68

280 Silver coin of Aradus, 350–332 BC

Obv. Head of Melqart
Rev. Galley
Susa Acropolis
Excavations of J. de Morgan, 1901
max. Diam 2.1 cm
Bibliothèque nationale de France, Suse, 508 1

281 Silver coin of Aradus, 350–332 BC

Incomplete
Obv. Head of Melqart
Rev. Galley
Susa Acropolis
Excavations of J. de Morgan, 1901
Bibliothèque nationale de France, Suse, 508 2

278 Alabaster vessel (alabastron)

With ovoid body, flat rim and ledge-shaped handles. These vessels were for oil or cosmetic products and are well known throughout the Achaemenid Empire. They sometimes bear inscriptions in up to four languages (see cats 140–45), but this example is plain.

Susa Acropolis
Excavations of J. de Morgan, 1901
H 21 cm, Diam 9.1 cm
Louvre, Sb 524
Harper, Aruz and Tallon 1992: no. 180

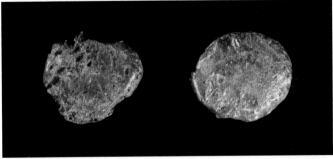

280 obv. (right), 281 obv. (left)

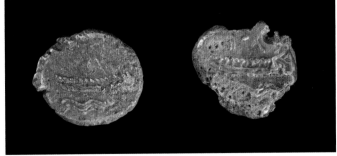

280 rev. (left), 281 rev. (right)

A CAUCASIAN GRAVE

The following four objects are said to have been 'found together in a grave at Karabakh, Erivan, Caucasus'. They were presented to the British Museum in 1898 by Sir Hercules Read, Keeper of the Department of British and Medieval Antiquities and Ethnography, 1896–1921. Unfortunately, we do not know how reliable this information is, so there can be no certainty that the objects were all found together, but if they were, then a date in the Achaemenid period seems most likely for the grave. The carinated bronze bowl, cat. 284, is of classic Achaemenid shape, and the iron spearhead, cat. 285, belongs to a type found both during the Achaemenid period and a little earlier. Bronze pendants as cat. 282 are known from sites in Azerbaijan and Armenia where they are generally dated between the eleventh and seventh centuries BC, though perhaps the type continued into the Achaemenid period. The combination of bowl, spear and pendants is typical for a grave of a male warrior at this date.

282

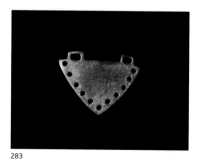

283

284

285

282 Bronze pendant

In the form of three concentric crescents with a serrated projection in the centre and a loop fastener at the top. In a burial at Mingechaur in Azerbaijan the corpse was covered with a cloth to which six pendants of this type had been attached. The significance of the form of this pendant is unknown.

H 10.68 cm, W 9.5 cm, Wt 135 g
ICP-AES analysis: leaded bronze (Ag 0.02%,
   As 0.17%, Au <0.007%, Bi <0.02%, Cd <0.005%,
   Co 0.005%, Cu 78.4%, Fe 0.157%, Mn <0.0009%,
   Ni 0.019%, P <0.04%, Pb 11.27%, S 0.06%,
   Sb 0.02%, Sn 8.64%, Zn <0.020%)
British Museum, ANE 1898-6-16, 2
Curtis and Kruszynski 2002: no.159, fig. 38, pl. 12

283 Bronze ornament

Triangular shape with holes at the sides and two rectangular loops at the top. Unknown purpose but possibly a belt-fitting.

H 4.32 cm, W 5.88 cm, Wt 18.4 g
Surface XRF analysis: leaded bronze
British Museum, ANE 1898-6-16, 3
Curtis and Kruszynski 2002: no. 160, fig. 38, pl. 12

284 Bronze bowl

Carinated in shape with an area of tin on the surface probably applied in modern times.

H 5.5 cm, Diam 14 cm, Wt 223.5 g
Surface XRF analysis: bronze, with area of tin
   on surface
British Museum, ANE 1898-6-16, 1
Curtis and Kruszynski 2002: no. 161, fig. 38

285 Iron spearhead

Leaf-shaped with mid-rib and folded socket.

L 28.6 cm, max. W 4.65 cm, Wt 139.2 g
Surface XRF analysis: iron
British Museum, ANE 1898-6-16, 4
Curtis and Kruszynski 2002: no. 162, fig. 38

9

THE ADMINISTRATION OF THE ACHAEMENID EMPIRE

Andrew R. Meadows

I am Darius, the great king, king of kings,
king of Persia, king of lands.[1]

Many of us today will be familiar with the idea that the democracies imposed upon or adopted by modern states descend by circuitous routes from the democracy of fifth-century BC Athens. Fewer, perhaps, will be aware of the debt we owe the Persian Empire, the contemporary of democratic Athens. Here, at the dawn of observable imperialism, lies one of its great ironies. Democratic Athens developed an empire based on conformism and exclusion. Democratic governments were imposed upon member states, and the penalty for dissent could be the wholesale slaughter of a male population, the enslavement of women and children and the confiscation of land. And in origin, the empire of Athens was a device to exclude the barbarian from Greek-speaking lands. By contrast, the Persian Empire had at its heart a severe, autocratic and self-conscious monarchy. Yet the empire this monarchy created was in many ways the inverse of that of Athens. It was politically, religiously and linguistically inclusive. Such habits did not necessarily originate with the Persians, but they were embodied in their empire and transmitted by later powers over these regions to the modern world. This chapter examines how it was that such flexibility could develop in so vast an empire, and suggests that this underlying tolerance was among the reasons why the Persian Empire survived for two and half centuries, and the Athenian barely a half.[2]

How to comprehend the vastness of the Achaemenid Empire? In modern terms it encompassed for much of its history all or most of Iran, Iraq, Syria, Israel, Lebanon, Egypt, Turkey and Cyprus, along with parts of Afghanistan, Pakistan, Turkmenistan, Uzbekistan, Armenia and Greece (see map p. 11). The territories ruled by the Achaemenid kings constituted the largest empire the world had ever seen, having absorbed the kingdoms and empires of Babylonia, Assyria, Egypt and Lydia. Indeed, few empires since have exceeded this in terms of land mass or variety of peoples.

But what do we mean when we talk of the Achaemenid Empire? At the centre, of course, lay the great king and his court, seasonally established in one of the palaces at the heart of his domain: Pasargadae and later Persepolis, Susa, Babylon and Ecbatana. But beyond this in all directions lay vast tracts of wilderness and civilization inhabited by humanity whose habits varied from tribal nomadism to regulated civic democracy. What if anything did these subject peoples regard as their place in the empire? Why did the great kings of Persia take such trouble to win and retain such a vast territorial space? How was this empire held together?

These are not easy questions to answer. The sheer scale and variety of the empire's inhabitants suggest that no one answer will apply for all regions. And at a remove of some two and a half thousand years what hope can there be of recovering the ancient 'reality'? We are not helped in the act of recovery by the Persians themselves. Despite their obvious embrace of the symbolism of eastern autocracy in the form of monumental art and epigraphy, they were a remarkably unselfconscious imperial power when it came to the practicalities of empire. No Persian treatises survive on the nature of imperial power, no handbooks on the rights and wrongs of government, not even a narrative account of the overall conquest and development of the empire. Indeed, there is little evidence that such works ever existed. Nonetheless, the empire was at certain levels a bureaucracy, and chance has preserved administrative documents from certain key areas. There is a variety of clay tablets from the archives of the royal centre at Persepolis (cats 308–11) and more from further west in Babylonia. From Egypt a limited number of documents survive on papyrus, while excavation of the administrative centre at Daskyleion in northwest Turkey has yielded a number of clay *bullae*, apparently the seals of official documents, if not the documents themselves.[3] And from the

Achaemenid lands around the shores of the Mediterranean there exists a substantial body of evidence in the form of coinage.

Rich though these sources are in the administrative detail of the empire, their potential for reconstructing the overall ethos of the Persian Empire is frankly limited. To attempt to answer the big questions about the nature of Persian administration and rule on the basis of these fortunate documentary survivals is not unlike trying to determine a modern political administration's predilection for large or small government from the contents of half a dozen filing cabinets chosen at random from a civil servant's office in London, Paris or Washington DC. Without the theoretical underpinning, whether in the form of elaborate rhetoric or dry handbook, we have no skeleton on which to hang the evidential scraps that happen to survive. All is not completely lost, however. For while the Persians themselves have left us no literature dealing with their empire, that is not to say that no one else was watching. Indeed the Persian Empire is a fascinating phenomenon today, not just for its size or place in the narratives of African, Asian and European history, but precisely because it was being watched by the nosiest of neighbours – the ancient Greeks.

By the early fourth century BC the Greeks had developed a number of literary forms, which shed light on the Achaemenid Empire in a way that Persian and Near Eastern sources could not. In the person of Herodotus (*fl. c.* 440 BC) the Persian Empire finds its first historian. Persian rule over parts of the Greek world and continued conflict with other Greeks throughout the fifth and fourth centuries BC would ensure that Persia remained in the accounts of Greek historians until the conquest by Alexander the Great. But also throughout this period, the Greeks began to develop a technical literature dedicated to the nature of political entities and their proper administration. Naturally, the Greeks had a word for it: *oikonomika*. Literally meaning 'household-management', it is the word from which the English term 'economics' derives, and provides a clear indication of how the ancient Greeks viewed, metaphorically speaking, the administration of any state. One such treatise, written probably in the late fourth century BC, reveals how the Persian example had influenced the development of Greek technical thinking. Once attributed (erroneously) to Aristotle, it suggests that

> There are four main types of administration (all others may be classified as subtypes of these): Royal, Satrapal, Civic and Personal. The biggest and yet simplest of these is the Royal administration. Satrapal administration is both wide-ranging and complex. Complex too, but easy to manage, is Civic administration. Personal administration is the smallest, but also exceedingly complex.
>
> Royal administration, while potentially all-powerful, is in fact divided into four areas: standards, imports, exports and expenditure. By standards I mean such activity as the seasonal adjustment of prices. Import and export involves the profitable distribution of the revenues sent by the satraps. Expenditure requires decisions on what expenditure should be cut and when, as well as whether payment should be made in money or in goods instead.
>
> Satrapal administration is concerned with six types of revenues deriving from the following areas: general agricultural, specific local production, markets, taxes, cattle and miscellaneous others. The first and most important of these is general agricultural revenue (variously known as the 'produce tax' or 'tithe'). Second is that deriving from specialized local production (gold, silver or copper mining, for example). Third is revenue from markets, and fourth that from tax on land and sales. Fifth comes revenue from cattle (known as 'first-fruits' or 'tithe'). The sixth category includes such revenues as the poll tax and tax on manufacturing.
>
> The third type of administration, Civic, has as its most important revenue that arising from local products. Next come the revenues from commerce and tolls, and finally those from farmed-out taxes.
>
> Fourthly and finally comes Personal administration. This is the most difficult to define because of the necessity to administer to more than one aim, but it is the least significant category because the revenues and expenditures are so small. Most important of these is the revenue from agriculture, next comes revenue from tax-collecting, third comes profit from money-lending.
>
> (Ps. Aristotle, *Oikonomika* II.1)

This remarkable text was written probably soon after the fall of the Achaemenid Empire, but the fact that it defines one area of administration by the title of the Persian regional governor, the satrap, suggests that it was heavily influenced by Persia in the structure it adopted. It offers a hierarchy of the free individual at the bottom and the king at the top, with the civic body and the regional governor between them. The author suggests, moreover, that while such a rigid definition may not apply everywhere, all varieties of administrative entity may find analogies in these broad definitions. Given that these are the views of a near contemporary of the Persian Empire – albeit anonymous – and that he has imported Achaemenid elements to his structure, it is worth seeing how this model of administration fits the other evidence for the working of the empire.

Among the most important sources for the empire are

the writings of the Athenian nobleman Xenophon (*c.* 430–360 BC). An acquaintance of Socrates and a hardened soldier, Xenophon had served in the army of a pretender to the Persian throne (Cyrus the Younger), and ended up leading it, before returning to his homeland to write history, philosophy, an economic handbook of his own (the *Oikonomikos*) and a fictionalized account of the education of Cyrus the Great, known as the *Cyropaedia*. Xenophon was well versed in the practices of Achaemenid administration, and his account of Cyrus the Great's arrangements for the new empire, while fictional in form, are likely to be based on Xenophon's own appreciation of the workings of the empire. He describes the origins of the satrapal system thus:

> When he was in Babylon once more, he thought it would be well to appoint satraps and set them over the conquered tribes ... So it was that Cyrus called a council and spoke as follows: 'Gentlemen and friends of mine, you are aware that we have garrisons and commandants in the cities we conquered, stationed there at the time. I left them with orders simply to guard the fortifications and not meddle with anything else. Now I do not wish to remove them from their commands, for they have done their duty nobly, but I propose to send others, satraps, who will govern the inhabitants, receive the tribute, give the garrisons their pay, and discharge all necessary dues ... We must choose for the satraps who are to go abroad persons who will not forget to send us anything of value in their districts, so that we who are at home may share in all the wealth of the world. For if any danger comes, it is we who must ward it off.'

(*Cyropaedia* VIII.6)

In this narrative of the transition from conquest and occupation to administration we find confirmation of the basic relationship between royal and satrapal administration proposed by the Aristotelian *Oikonomika*. Satrapal administration was concerned with the gathering of revenues and the upward transmission of these to the king.[4] The king and his court (to whom Cyrus's words are notionally addressed), that is to say the Persian core of the empire, would be the beneficiaries of the wealth generated by the empire, though a reciprocal obligation is also acknowledged. The first satraps were chosen from the court of Cyrus – the friends and extended family of the great king. In this respect we can see how the metaphor of administration as extended household management can apply to something as large as the Achaemenid Empire.

That the satraps were responsible, like sons working away from home, to remit their profits to the royal house is confirmed by actual events. The fifth-century-BC Greek historian Thucydides records that the satrap Tissaphernes was issued by the king with a demand for the tribute from his province when he was late remitting it (VIII.5).

Herodotus, our other great source for fifth-century BC Persia, provides a list of what he regarded as the twenty financial districts of the empire and the amount of tribute each sent back to King Darius I (*History* III.89–95):[5]

Financial district	Talents	Kg of silver
1. Ionia, Aeolis, Caria, Lycia, Milyas, Pamphylia	400	13,600
2. Mysia, Lydia, Lasonians, Cabalians, Hytennians	500	17,000
3. Hellespont, Phrygia, Thrace, Paphlagonia, Mariandynians, Syrians	360	12,240
4. Cilicia	360	12,240
5. Phoenicia, Palestine, Cyprus	350	11,900
6. Egypt, Libya	700	23,800
7. Sattagydae, Gandarii, Dadicae, Aparytae	170	5,780
8. Susa	300	10,200
9. Babylonia, Assyria	1000	34,000
10. Media, Paricanians, Orthocorybantians	450	15,300
11. Caspii, Pausicae, Pantimathi, Daritae	200	6,800
12. Bactrians	360	12,240
13. Pactyica, Armenia	400	13,600
14. Sagartii, Sarangeis, Thamanaei, Utii, Myci	600	20,400
15. Sacae, Caspii	250	8,500
16. Parthians, Chorasmians, Sogdi, Arii	300	10,200
17. Paricanii, Ethiopians of Asia	400	13,600
18. Matieni, Saspiri, Alarodii	200	6,800
19. Moschi, Tibareni, Macrones, Mossynoeci, Mares	300	10,200
20. Indians	360 (gold) =	122,399
Total amount of tribute per annum (expressed as kg of silver)		380,799

The backbone, then, of Achaemenid administration is easily laid bare. The king at the centre controlled a network of governors dedicated to the transfer of wealth from the peoples of the empire to their great king. But we must beware of oversimplification. Xenophon, in the same chapter of the *Cyropaedia*, informs us that satraps were not dispatched to certain peoples (Cilicia, Cyprus and Paphlagonia), in apparent recognition of past services rendered to the great king. Elsewhere Cyrus explains that he relied instead on local kings to maintain control, while nonetheless exacting tribute from these areas (*Cyropaedia* VII.4). While the author of the Aristotelian *Oikonomika* would no doubt insist that this was satrapal administration in all but name, it is important to note the potential that was realized here for flexible modes of administration within the empire. Different modes were available within the overall framework. Whereas the thinking of the Aristotelian *Oikonomika* is clearly influenced by the political milieu of the Greek city states, the great king was also compelled to find ways to deal with other types of political structure, such as, in the case of Cyprus, Cilicia and Phoenicia, monarchies. He was king of kings, not just king of lands.

In this structural flexibility, arguably, lies one of the reasons for the Achaemenid Empire's success, and also one of its most powerful legacies. The Persian Empire was able to accommodate existing political habit, without the need to enforce change. This *laissez-faire* attitude extended into other areas too. Recent studies have tended to highlight the extent to which local cultures continued to flourish under Persian rule.[6] The Persians were tolerant of religions other than their own. They were realistic, too, in their approach to the languages and scripts of the empire. While Elamite remained the administrative language in the Persian heartland, further west Aramaic was the lingua franca and remained so, and in Egypt the use of Egyptian and the demotic and hieroglyphic scripts were taken up. Greek remained the language of communication between the western satraps and the Greek cities. And within certain areas local languages such as Carian and Lycian survived until they were supplanted by Greek, rather than a Persian-imposed language.

Viewed from the bottom, then, the Persian Empire perhaps did not look so intrusive as some modern empires and federations have been with their insistence on religious, linguistic and administrative conformity. Nonetheless, there existed the constant need to provide for the requirements of a central power and its often unpredictable agents. Two anecdotes concerning the dynast Mausolus illustrate the reality nicely. Mausolus was a member of the dynasty that ruled Caria (and later Lycia) for the Persians in the fourth century BC. He may not have held the title 'satrap', but he nevertheless maintained a similar relationship as a satrap both to the king above and the subjects below. The Aristotelian *Oikonomika* preserves the details of two ruses that Mausolus perpetrated on those whom he ruled:

Mausolus, the ruler of Caria, receiving from the great king a demand for tribute, gathered together the wealthiest men in his land and told them that the great king was demanding tribute but that he could not afford to pay it. He had previously primed a few men to come forward immediately and offer to help as much as they could. Faced with their example, the wealthier men in the gathering, through a combination of shame and fear, promised and paid far larger sums.

When he was again short of funds, Mausolus gathered together the population of the town of Mylasa, pointed out to them that their home city was unwalled and then told them that the great king was marching on them with an army. So he ordered the Mylasanas to bring as much money as they could, telling them that what they spent now would provide security for the rest of their possessions. And when many men contributed he took the money, but then announced that, for the moment, god forbade the building of city walls.

(*Oikonomika* II.2.13)

A number of features emerge clearly from these stories. First we see once again the extent to which the relationship between king and subjects was financial, and how there was scope for an unscrupulous governor to manipulate the basic tributary nature of the empire to his own advantage. Second, we see how the military reality of the empire played on the minds of those who lived in it. As we have already noted, the Achaemenid Empire was a vast space. The king could not rule from Persia and make financial demands on his subjects in all its corners without backing up his demands for money with military force. The relationship between financial demand and military presence worked, of course, at two levels. As we see in the case of the city of Mylasa the threat of military action on the part of the king was a powerful incentive for a city or any other group to act, whether to defend themselves or to conform with his wishes. But we should not forget the other fact that this story reveals: the city of Mylasa had no walls. It had none because it didn't need them. Membership of the Achaemenid Empire, as of any other, brought with it the guarantee of security. As Xenophon makes Cyrus say in justifying his claims to tribute, 'For if any danger comes, it is we who must ward it off' (*Cyropaedia* VIII.6, quoted above), and Cyrus himself boasts of the benefits brought to Babylon when his 'extensive army marched peacefully through' (Cyrus Cylinder §24). The reciprocity of this relationship is implicit, too, in Herodotus's account of the satrap Artaphernes' settlement of Ionia following a revolt at the beginning of the fifth century BC:

Artaphernes, satrap of Sardis, summoned representatives from the cities and compelled the Ionians to make agreements with each other, so that they might seek legal redress from one another rather than attacking and plundering. He compelled them to do this and then he measured their lands in *parsangs* ... and according to these measurements he established the tribute that each should pay.

(*History* VI. 42)

Note the order of events: Artaphernes (the king's brother) establishes the benefit to the cities of Ionia, and then imposes the charge.

But such compulsion and protection can only be produced by a strong military presence. Herein lay the second principal administrative challenge that faced the Achaemenid kings. The Aristotelian *Oikonomika* is preoccupied with financial administration and has nothing to say of the military organization of the empire, but

Xenophon in both his *Cyropaedia* and *Oikonomikos* presents a relatively coherent picture of how the empire was organized in this respect. For him, the two elements of administration – financial and military – were closely intertwined at a number of levels. His *Oikonomikos* is presented as a dialogue between Socrates and an interlocutor named Critoboulos. Socrates explains that the great king is equally concerned with matters agricultural and military:

> We are agreed that he takes strong interest in military matters; since in all the lands from which he receives tribute every governor has orders from the king what number of cavalry, archers, slingers and infantry it is his duty to support, as adequate to control the subject population, or in case of hostile attack to defend the country. Apart from these the king keeps garrisons in all the citadels. The actual support of these devolves upon the governor, to whom the duty is assigned.
>
> (*Oikonomikos* IV.5)

Beneath the governor, Socrates goes on to explain,

> the governors appointed to preside over these two departments of state are not one and the same. But one class governs the inhabitants, the residents and labourers, and collects the tribute from them, another is in command of the military and the garrisons. If the military commander protects the country insufficiently, the civil governor of the population, who is in charge also of the productive works, brings a charge against the commandant to the effect that the inhabitants are prevented from working through lack of protection. Or if again, in spite of peace being secured for the working of the land by the military governor, the civil authority still presents a territory sparse in population and unworked, it is the military commander who brings charges against the civil ruler. For you may take it as a rule that a population tilling their territory badly will fail to support their garrisons and be quite unequal to paying their tribute. Where a satrap is appointed he has charge of both departments.
>
> (Ibid. IV.9–11)

The picture presented by the literary sources (principally Xenophon) is one of an empire closely observed by a combination of civil and military officials; they were responsible for maintaining a balanced society in which the necessary peace was provided to allow agricultural productivity to be maximized. The evidence from other sources to support this picture is patchy in the extreme. It consists, as we have already noted, of fragmentary archival material from disparate provinces of the empire, as well as incidental mentions of the workings of the Achaemenid state in the Greek literary sources.[7] Nonetheless, the picture of an active and pervasive military structure and civil administration seems well borne out, even if the precise details remain unclear. The only doubt that must remain is over how consistent the pattern was across the empire. Given the flexibility we can observe in other areas of Achaemenid interaction with the different constituent lands and peoples, it would come as no surprise to discover that a similarly flexible approach obtained in the realm of administration. Indeed, Xenophon's recognition that not all provinces had a satrap indicates precisely such flexibility at the highest level.

Yet *quis custodiet ipsos custodes?* We must be struck once again by the sheer size of the Achaemenid Empire. This size brought with it two fundamental administrative problems that may be summarized in two simple words: communication and loyalty.

In a normal year the king himself may not have travelled far from the royal palaces at the centre of the empire. As Xenophon suggests (*Oikonomikos* IV.6 and 8), this gave the king himself the opportunity to inspect both the military forces and the state of the land in those regions closest to the centre of the empire. But he could not be everywhere. Moreover, the system of provincial administration that Cyrus put in place and that his successors adapted vested vast amounts of power in an individual (the satrap) who might be many days (or even months) travel from the great king. It gave the satrap a source of revenue and an army, and while the decision to appoint friends and family members to these possessions might on the one hand seem prone to guarantee loyalty to the king, on the other hand it placed members of the royal family and the Iranian elite in the way of considerable temptation. On a number of occasions such men would prove themselves unable to resist (Cyrus the Younger, with whom Xenophon marched, is a prime example).

Cyrus the Great, if Xenophon is to be believed, was aware of this problem from the start.

> And here I may notice another custom, also instituted by Cyrus, it is said, and still in force today: every year a progress of inspection is made by an officer at the head of an army, to help any satrap who may require aid, or bring the insolent to their senses; and if there has been negligence in the delivery of tribute, or the protection of the inhabitants, or the cultivation of the soil, or indeed any omission of duty whatsoever, the officer is there to put the matter right, or if he cannot do so himself, to report it to the king, who decides what is to be done about the offender. The announcements so often made, such as 'the king's son is coming down', or 'the king's brother', or 'the king's eye', refer to these inspectors, but sometimes no one appears, for at any moment the officer may be turned back at the king's command.
>
> (*Cyropaedia* VIII.6.16)

In addition to keeping a close eye on their provinces, the

great kings seem also to have tried to impose checks on their senior administrators by insuring the loyalty of their subordinates. We hear from Xenophon that the king personally appointed the citadel garrison commanders throughout the empire, and the commanding officers of garrisons throughout the land (*Cyropaedia* VIII.6.9). Furthermore, the king was also responsible for the maintenance of the troops themselves in the citadel garrisons (*Oikonomikos* IV. 6).

But there was still the vastness of the empire to contend with. This was at once a strength and a weakness. The paradox was noted in antiquity. As Xenophon put it,

> any intelligent man could see that while the king's empire was strong in terms of its physical area and population, it was weakened by the great distances between his scattered forces in the face of a sudden swift attack.
>
> (*Anabasis* I.5.9)

Communication across the great distances was an economic as well as military imperative, of course. Large quantities of tribute traversed the empire on a regular basis, but at a lower level there was considerable movement of caravan trade across the empire. And even in a relatively devolved administrative structure of provincial administration, there was nonetheless a need for a regular flow of communication and staff from the royal centres to the local administrative centres. Again, Xenophon credits Cyrus the Great with the origins of the solution, though in reality he may simply have been drawing on the practices of earlier empires such as the Assyrian:

> We hear of another arrangement, devised to meet the huge size of the empire and enable the king to learn with great celerity the state of affairs at any distance. Cyrus first ascertained how far a horse could travel in one day without being over-ridden, and then he had a series of posting stations built, one day's ride apart, with relays of horses, and grooms to take care of them, and a proper man in charge of each station to receive the despatches and hand them on, take over the jaded horses and men, and furnish fresh ones. [18] Sometimes, we are told, this post does not even halt at night: the night messenger relieves the day messenger and rides on. Some say that, when this is done, the post travels more quickly than the crane can fly, and, whether that is true or not, there is no doubt it is the quickest way in which a human being can travel on land. To learn of events so rapidly and be able to deal with them at once is of course a great advantage.
>
> (*Cyropaedia* 17–18)

These posting stations were strung out along a network of royal roads servicing the length and breadth of the empire. Modern estimates suggest a total of 8,000 miles or more for the road system as a whole.[8] We are best informed about two particular elements of the system.

Herodotus (*History* V.52–3) describes the road from Sardis at the western end of the empire to the royal capital at Susa, a distance of approximately 1,600 miles. His list of the posting stations suggests that a journey that normally required ninety days could be cut to a week or two by the express post. From the clay tablets unearthed in excavations at Persepolis – the so-called Fortification Tablets (see p. 197) – we possess the records of numerous journeys carried out on official business along the royal road system as the travellers passed through the region. The documents preserve accounts of the rations issued to the men who made the journeys, such as,

> Abbatema received 110 quarts of flour. As his daily ration he receives 70 quarts. 20 men each receive 2 quarts. He carried a sealed document from the king. They went forth from India. They went to Susa. Month 2, year 23.
>
> (PF 1318; Brosius 2000: no. 187)

Excavations at Persepolis in the 1930s yielded some 30,000 clay tablets in this one particular deposit (perhaps an ancient archive), covering a period of just sixteen years (509–494 BC). Much remains unpublished, but the sheer volume from a single administrative centre, and in so short a period, gives a vivid impression of the bureaucratic reality of the royal administration.[9]

Another striking feature of the Persepolis texts is the near complete absence of money. The payments made to everyone from the chief administrator down to the lowliest worker were all in terms of commodities:

> Parnaka [the head of administration at Persepolis] received as rations 90 quarts of wine, entrusted to Karkiš. For a period of one day, at a village named Hadarakkaš. Hišbeš wrote the text. Mannunda communicated its message. Year 23, month 2, day 25, the sealed document was delivered.
>
> (PF 665, Brosius 2000: no. 141)

> Ziššawiš received as rations 90 quarts of wine supplied by Muška. For a period of 3 days, at Parmadan and Pirradaše(?). Month 9, year 18.
>
> (PF 673, Brosius 2000: no. 145)

> Bakabada the law officer of Parnaka received 20 quarts of beer. He carried a sealed document of Parnaka. The rations were for 20 days. Year 23, month 9.
>
> (PF 1272, Brosius 2000: no. 149)

A hierarchy is clear here, and there is plainly more to it than differing levels of thirst.

The absence of money from these texts is clearly significant, and undoubtedly reflects another important aspect of the administration of the eastern portion of the empire: there was no coinage produced here.

Coinage in fact provides one of the starkest examples of the adaptability of, and lack of homogeneity in, the Achaemenid Empire. The Persian administration first came into contact with coinage when Cyrus conquered the kingdom of Lydia in 547/6 BC. The defeated king Croesus had probably been the first to produce coinage in gold and silver (see cats 316–17). The production of these coins continued after the Persian conquest until, under Darius I, a new type of gold and silver coinage was introduced with the clear royal design of the archer king. With variations, these gold darics and silver sigloi (cats 318–26) would be produced at one or two mints in western Asia Minor until the loss of the region to Alexander the Great, and for all but one brief episode within this period, darics and sigloi were the only coins produced by the Achaemenid administration in western Asia Minor.[10] But they were never produced any further east than Sardis, and seem rarely to have circulated outside Asia Minor.

In addition to the royal issues, however, another category of coinage was produced. Often referred to as 'satrapal', this consisted of a series of issues, beginning in the early fourth century BC with non-royal types, and struck in the names of satraps, and military or regional governors.[11] The phenomenon seems to have begun in the northwest of Asia Minor with a coinage of the satrap Pharnabazus (cats 330–31); but it flourished most spectacularly in southern Anatolia in the province of Cilicia, where a variety of designs were produced and signed by a sequence of senior Persian commanders and administrators (cats 348–61). Towards the middle of the fourth century BC this phenomenon bled over slightly into neighbouring Phoenicia (cats 365–6), Samaria (cat. 361) and ultimately Egypt (cats 370–72). In parallel with these 'satrapal' coins, royal coinage also took on a more flexible appearance and form around the middle of the fourth century. A royal mint in western Asia Minor began to produce a new form of royal coinage on a Greek weight standard rather than the Persian (cat. 327), while in Egypt issues were produced in the name of Artaxerxes III that imitated the design and adopted the weight standard of Athens (cat. 329). Underlying this pattern of relatively consistent royal and sporadic 'satrapal' coinages we should not forget that there existed a continuum of local civic and royal coinages, produced by the Greek cities and local kings and dynasts of Anatolia, Phoenicia and Cyprus.

What can this picture of coinage tell us about the administration of the empire? First and foremost there is the negative picture: vast areas of the great king's realm existed without coinage. Many of his subjects, indeed, would not have recognized a coin. There is a very small amount of evidence that some coinage travelled eastwards from the Mediterranean during the fifth century BC, including the remarkable hoard from Malayer in Media (cat. 382) and two other broadly contemporary finds from Afghanistan, but we cannot say whether such finds represent official or personal initiative. In any case, such a small amount of evidence from so vast an area serves only to reinforce the picture of an essentially coin-less eastern portion of the empire.

In the west the picture is more complex, but seems to fit the broad pattern that emerges from the literary sources. The Persian authorities produced coins in order to make payments. That the payments in the satrapies of the western empire should be made in royal coinage, that is to say in the name of the king, is entirely in line with what we hear, for example, about the king's maintenance of the citadel garrisons, or his selection of their commanders. Viewed in this light, royal coinage was a constant reminder to those who received it of the king's position as ultimate owner of the empire's resources.

The 'satrapal' coinage, by contrast, bears the names of satraps and other senior officials. The existence and nature of this coinage has often worried modern commentators, but unnecessarily so. It is clear that the production of these issues was linked to specific, extraordinary military circumstances. Payments had to be made in certain areas, away from the main royal mint(s), and it is clear that certain officials outside the normal administration of the imperial coinage were required to take charge of its production. These were the men who signed it: satraps, military commanders, governors or other high level administrators. To the king the fact of its production will have been of little consequence in itself. So long as the money was accounted for, and the net result to the empire was security and prosperity, Achaemenid practice was, as we have seen, to allow the high-level functionaries to get on with their jobs. Coinage was merely an administrative tool, one among many applied by the satrap and others. More surprising, perhaps, is the appearance of much of this 'satrapal' coinage. While certain designs clearly have Persian elements to them, the badges of the cities that produced them are regularly also apparent. There are two potential explanations for this. Since the coins were undoubtedly produced in the civic mints of the towns whose badges they carried, the badges might have been an administrative device to identify place of production. Yet royal coinage carried no such device, and even if necessary, it certainly did not need to be so prominent. Alternatively, we may see the choice of design as more economically motivated. The Persian administration was in these cases issuing coins in areas where it had not previously made large-scale payments on its own behalf. In this respect Cilicia provides an interesting case. According to Herodotus (*History* III.90), in the fifth century the Cilicians had provided 360 white horses and money for their riders to guarantee the military security of the region. During the early fourth century, by contrast, commanders in the region obviously had to make large-scale payments in their own names. But whereas, when the daric and siglos were created in the early sixth century, they were introduced into a world where gold and silver coinage was a new phenomenon, the administrators behind the satrapal coinages of the fourth century had to insert new coinages into existing traditions. They chose to make their coins look more local and less royal in order to make them more acceptable to their recipients. Even the royal coinage, in the name or with the designs of the king, was forced to adapt in the middle of the fourth century by changing its weight standards from Persian to Greek, and borrowing the designs of Athens.

Again, in the evidence of its coinage, we see the inherent flexibility of the Persian administration. And we should not forget that within the Greek cities, Phoenician and Cypriot kingdoms and Anatolian dynasties of the empire, civic, royal and dynastic coinages flourished as these peoples went about the business of administering themselves and their lands. Here were administrative entities that made their own payments to meet their own needs. This is the real contrast between the western and eastern portions of the empire; here is Achaemenid flexibility. We can conclude by noting again the contrast in this respect between Persia and the Athenians. In the 420s BC Athens had famously made an attempt to impose its own coinage and weight standards on all of its empire. The attempt, like the Athenian Empire itself, soon failed.

The Achaemenid Empire was far from an ideal political system: its kings were far from perfect, and often far from their subjects; its governors were perforce vested with considerable power, and it seems often to have corrupted them; the systems necessary to ensure loyalty, generate revenues and spend them appropriately generated a prodigious bureaucracy. Nonetheless, by virtue of the basic insight that people are most productive if left to their own habits, beliefs, customs and politics, the empire survived and flourished. This should be its legacy.

1 *DB* I.1 (Brosius 2000: no. 44): the first line of the Bisitun inscription, but the formulation recurs in numerous other royal documents.

2 There exists a vast modern bibliography on the administration and ethos of the Persian Empire. The newcomer is best served by the excellent brief account in Kuhrt 1995: 676–701. More detail and full bibliography can be found in the nonpareil Briant 2002. A useful collection of sources in translation from the many languages of the Persian Empire are collected in Brosius 2000. In the notes that follow I have tried to provide pointers to more detailed and more recent studies where relevant.

3 For discussion of these see now Kaptan 2002.

4 For an account of the development of the satrap and satrapy see Petit 1990.

5 Figures in the second column are the amounts in talents of silver cited by Herodotus for each district. The Babylonian talent weighed approximately 34 kg. The resulting figure in kilograms of silver produced in tribute per annum is given in the third column. The exception is the figure for the Indians, whose tribute is listed by Herodotus in terms of talents of gold dust. As Herodotus notes (*History* III.94), 'The Indians seem to me to be the most populous nation of all mankind, and they pay a greater tribute than any other.' It should be noted, however, that Herodotus's list of districts is problematic. It is clearly not a list of satrapies (as he claims), nor does it bear immediate relation to the lists of nations that the great kings claim for themselves in their monumental texts. Over the figures he cites we have no control at all, although we can compare the tribute that was paid to Athens by her empire during the fifth century BC. According to Thucydides this was originally assessed at 460 talents (*c.* 11,960 kg of silver) per annum.

6 Note the discussion in Briant 1987.

7 For full discussions of the evidence for administration in general and military control in particular see Tuplin 1987a and 1987b respectively.

8 For discussion of the royal road system see Graf 1994.

9 For some important caveats on the use of this evidence see now the comments of Garrison and Root 1996/8.

10 For an overview of the royal coinage see Carradice 1987b.

11 For an overview of the satrapal coinage see Mildenberg 2000; sensible discussion can be found in Le Rider 1997.

ACHAEMENID SEALS AND ADMINISTRATION

During the reign of Darius I the Achaemenid administration was transformed. The use of the cylinder seal was revived for sealing royal documents. This distinctive Mesopotamian sealing device had been in use for almost three thousand years and had been adopted at various periods throughout the Near East, including Iran. It had, however, been largely replaced by stamp seals in Assyria and Babylonia during the sixth and fifth centuries BC. Although stamp seals continued to be used under the Achaemenids, the revival of the cylinder seal was probably for reasons of prestige, with the Achaemenids claiming to have inherited the great empires that had preceded them. Indeed, many of the dockets found in the Fortification archive at Persepolis are copies of Assyrian designs of the seventh century BC. However, most of the designs are distinctively Achaemenid. The seals were rolled out on the clay of the dockets, along one end (between the string holes) and on a side. These dockets, perhaps surprisingly, were inscribed in Elamite. Inscriptions on the seals were generally in cuneiform, sometimes trilingual (as on the famous Darius seal, cat. 398); they give the names of fifth-century BC kings and high officials. The royal seals were probably not personal seals but seals of the royal administration. By the mid-fifth century BC, however, cuneiform on clay had been replaced by the alphabet on perishable materials. The use of the cylinder seal and our knowledge of day-to-day administration disappear together.

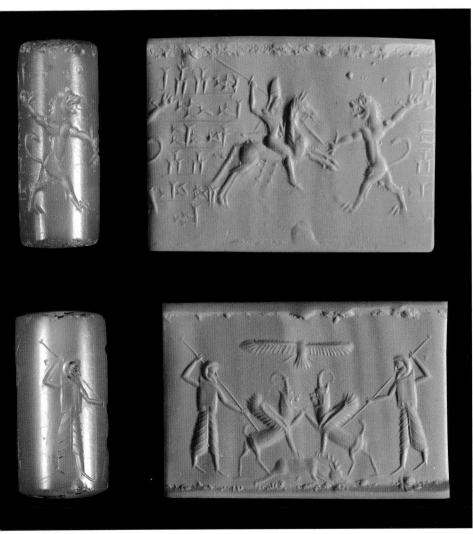

286–7

SEALS AND SEALINGS

286 Cylinder seal in grey-blue chalcedony showing a rider in Median dress

The rider gallops to the right and aims a spear at a rampant lion. There is a six-line inscription in Elamite, reading 'Ainakka son of Fraitish'.

Provenance unknown
Acquired in 1841 from the Claude Scott-Stewart
  Collection
H 3.5 cm, Diam 1.4 cm
British Museum, ANE 89009
Pope 1938: IV, pl. 124C; Merrillees 2005: no. 4

287 Cylinder seal in pale grey chalcedony showing two figures in Persian dress

The figures wear hoods or rounded helmets and possibly cuirasses with high-backed collars. They are striking two winged lion-griffins with their spears. The griffins seem to be fighting over the body of a stag (?) beneath a winged disc.

Said to come from Babylonia
Purchased from Prof. E. Herzfeld in 1936
H 3.15 cm, Diam 1.6 cm
British Museum, ANE 128842
Merrillees 2005: no. 58

288

288 Cylinder seal showing an ibex and lion

A winged ibex runs to the left and is attacked by a leaping lion. There are small motifs of a bird in flight and a star. A large stylized tree frames the scene on the left. The seal is made of dark grey limestone.

Persepolis, Treasury, Room 83 (PT6 673)
H 1.9 cm, Diam 1 cm
Tehran, 771
Schmidt 1957: 42–3, pl. 15; Seipel 2000: 212, no. 125

289 Cylinder seal showing a zebu cow

The zebu cow on this white-grey chalcedony seal suckles her calf.

Acquired by A.H. Layard in Mesopotamia between 1845 and 1851
H 3.35 cm, Diam 1.6 cm
British Museum, ANE 89574 (N 1063)
Layard 1853: fig. on p. 604; Merrillees 2005: no. 91

290 Cylinder seal showing a naked woman and a figure

A naked woman, with her hair in a plait down her back, approaches a figure seated on a chair. Both figures raise a hand towards a round object they hold between them. Behind the seated figure is a zebu. The execution is crude. The meaning of the Aramaic inscription above the figures is unclear. The seal is made of carnelian.

Oxus Treasure
Bequeathed in 1897 by A.W. Franks
H 3.9 cm, Diam 1.3 cm
British Museum, ANE 124016
Dalton 1964: 32, no. 115, fig. 63; Pope 1938: IV, pl. 124C; Merrillees 2005: no. 76

291 Cylinder seal showing a winged animal and an ibex

The winged animal with a human protome wearing a crown leaps towards the right and aims an arrow at a retreating rampant ibex that looks back at its assailant. Above is a winged disc. A stylized tree and a large bird perching on it have been incongruously added to the scene. This might indicate that the chip at the bottom of the seal led to its subsequent use as a trial piece. The seal is in banded brown and white stone.

Provenance unknown
Acquired from the Southesk Collection in 1945 with the assistance of the National Art Collections Fund, previously in the collection of R.P. Greg until 1895
H 1.15 cm, Diam 1.25 cm
British Museum, ANE 129565
Merrillees 2005: no. 61

292 Barrel-shaped cylinder seal with animal designs

This etched agate seal has a white surface and blue banding. The design has been carved in three registers, separated by horizontal lines, on what may have been a large bead, originally about 4.7 cm high, now broken. The upper register is missing. The middle register shows pairs of rampant lions attacking a stumbling bull facing right and a fallen gazelle facing left. Over their backs are Egyptianizing hieroglyphs, possibly with an apotropaic purpose. The bottom register shows confronted pairs of winged creatures sitting on their haunches: the lions look back over their shoulder, and the sphinxes wear flat caps and raise a forepaw.

Provenance unknown
Acquired from the Southesk Collection in 1945 with the assistance of the National Art Collections Fund, previously in the collection of W.T. Ready until 1896
H 3.5 cm, D 1.0–1.6 cm
British Museum, ANE 129596
Boardman 2000: 164, fig. 5/22; Merrillees 2005: no. 85

293 Stamp seal engraved with a design of three bull protomes

On this conoid, veined blue chalcedony seal, the bull protomes rotate to the left around a central circle. For a similar seal, cf. cat. 19.

Provenance unknown
Acquired before 1930
H 2.9, Diam 2.0 cm (base)
British Museum, ANE 115604
Pope 1938: IV, pl. 124K

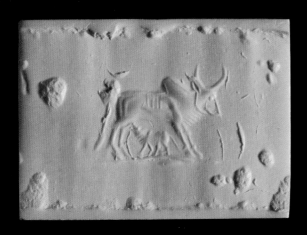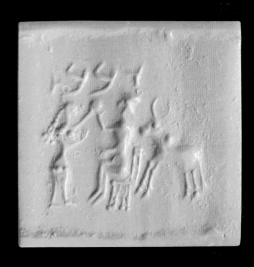

289

290

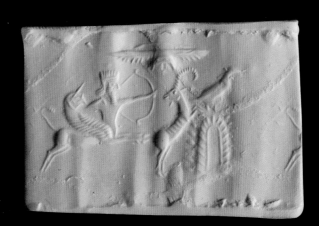

291

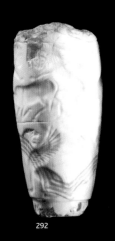

292

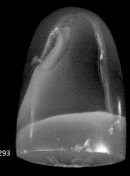

293

294 Stamp seal showing a robed figure

The figure faces left and grasps two lions. Above is a winged disc. The seal, made of translucent blue glass, is of conoid shape.

Provenance unknown
Presented by G.D. Hornblower in 1940
H 1.8 cm, Diam 1.6 cm (base)
British Museum, ANE 130816
Barag 1985: 84, no. 100, pl. 12

295 Stamp seal showing two bulls

The heavily chipped design shows two rearing crossed bulls with a crescent above and a lotus flower on the ground between them. A garland of alternating lotus blossoms and buds surrounds them. The seal, in grey-brown chalcedony, is of conoid shape.

Provenance unknown
Bequeathed by Miss M.F.T. Ready in 1959
H 3.5 cm, Diam 3.2 cm (base)
British Museum, ANE 132507

296 Gold finger-ring with a stirrup-shaped hoop

The flat oval bezel is engraved with a winged bull, which has a crowned and bearded human head, and is walking to the left. Above is an Aramaic inscription, reading 'Pahashp' or 'Zahashp'. In front of the bull is an emblem that is also found on fifth-century BC seals from Lydia.

Oxus Treasure
Bequeathed in 1897 by A.W. Franks
Diam 2.25 cm (hoop), L 1.7 cm (bezel), Wt 11.5 g
British Museum, ANE 124006
Dalton 1964: 28, no. 105, pl. XVI, fig. 54

297 Clay impression from a conoid stamp seal showing the Persian hero

The impression shows the Persian hero grasping the feathered crowns of two Bes-headed rampant sphinxes on a base-line. The square object in front of the hero may be a chip in the seal.

From Ur, found in a coffin of the Persian period
Excavations of C.L. Woolley, 1931–2 (U.18124)
L 2.5 cm, W 2.2 cm
British Museum, ANE 1932-10-8, 198
Collon 1996: 69, fig. 3, pl. 13/c

296

294–5

297

PYRAMIDAL WEIGHTS

298

299

300

298 Pyramidal weight
in grey-green diorite

With a trilingual inscription of Darius I in Old Persian, Elamite and Babylonian. The Old Persian inscription reads '120 *karsha*. I [am] Darius the great king, king of kings, king of countries, king in this earth, son of Hystaspes, an Achaemenian.' The Elamite version also starts with 120 *karsha*, but the Babylonian version starts with 20 *mina*. The form of this kind of weight is Mesopotamian in origin.

Persepolis, Treasury, Room 3 (PT3 283)
H 20.3 cm, 17.7 cm x 13 cm (at base), Wt 9,950 g
Tehran, 122
Schmidt 1957: 105–6, pl. 82/2a–c; Seipel 2000:
  no. 126

299 Fragment of pyramidal weight
in grey diorite

With the ends of four lines of an Elamite inscription similar to above.

Persepolis, Treasury, Room 15 (PT4 972)
H 5.6 cm, W 5.3 cm, Th 6.5 cm, Wt 269.94 g
Tehran, 26
Schmidt 1957: 105–6

300 Pyramidal weight
in polished diorite

With a trilingual inscription of Darius I in Old Persian, Elamite and Babylonian. The Old Persian inscription reads '2 *karsha*. I [am] Darius, the great king, the son of Hystaspes, an Achaemenian.' Two *karsha*s equal one third of a Babylonian *mina*.

Said to come from Hillah, Iraq
Acquired in 1888
H 5.1 cm, 4.4 cm x 4.1 cm (at base), Wt 166 g
British Museum, ANE 91117
Kent 1953: Wa; Schmidt 1957: 105; Walker 1980:
  81

LION WEIGHTS

301

301 Bronze lion weight in the form of a recumbent lion

The lion has a ring on its back, and sits on a rectangular plinth. The style of the lion, with the tear-shaped folds under its eyes, is typically Achaemenid. The weight of 121 kg is equivalent to 4 talents. At an earlier period, bronze lion weights are known in Assyria. A.H. Layard found a set of sixteen bronze lion weights of the eighth century BC at Nimrud (Curtis and Reade 1995: nos 192–3).

Susa Acropolis
Excavations of J. de Morgan, 1901
H 30 cm, L 53 cm, Wt 121 kg
Louvre, Sb 2718
Harper, Aruz and Tallon 1992 : no. 154

302 Bronze lion weight

Similar to cat. 301 above. There is an Aramaic inscription of uncertain meaning on the side of the base, and a single inscribed letter at the base of the spine.

Said to be from Abydos on the Dardanelles,
    western Turkey
Acquired in 1877
H 19 cm, L 35.5 cm, Wt 31.808 kg
XRF analysis: Cu 72%, Sn 25%, As 2.6%, Pb > 0.5%
British Museum, ANE 32625
Mitchell 1973

303 Lion's-head weight (?)

In the form of a cylindrical block of green chert ending in a lion's mask. The object is solid, and the back is well finished with no indication that it was fixed to something else. Ernst Herzfeld considered this to be a furniture foot, but the identification as a weight seems more likely.

Frataraka Temple, near Persepolis
L 23 cm, W 13 cm, Wt 4.513 kg
Tehran, 121
Herzfeld 1941: 263–4, fig. 366; Schmidt 1957: 55,
    n. 57; Porada 1965: pl. 46

DUCK WEIGHTS

304 Duck weight in white stone

This form of duck weight was popular in Mesopotamia.

Persepolis (R166)
H 9.5 cm, W 11.8 cm, L 16.5 cm
Tehran, 419

304

302

303

DOCUMENTS

305 Cuneiform tablet

Sealed contract for the exchange of land in the vicinity of Babylon. Dated in the sixth year of Cambyses (524 BC). The tablet is part of the personal archive of Itti-Marduk-balatu, a member of the Egibi family who were prominent in international trade during the Neo-Babylonian and Achaemenid period.

Babylon
L 10.3 cm, W 7 cm
British Museum, ANE 33973

306 Cuneiform tablet

Litigation in the presence of witnesses. Gubaru, the governor of Babylonia, is mentioned. Dated to the fifth year of Cyrus II (534 BC).

From Babylon, Iraq
L 5.4 cm, W 4 cm
British Museum, ANE 26643

307 Cuneiform tablet

Receipt of silver for the sale of oxen dated to the first year of Cambyses, King of Babylon, and Cyrus, King of the Land (538 BC). Cambyses appears as king of Babylon only in Cyrus's first years of rule.

From Borsippa, Iraq
L 5 cm, W 4.3 cm
British Museum, ANE 29455

305 obv. (left), 306 obv. (right bottom), 307 obv. (right top)

305 rev. (left), 306 rev. (right bottom), 307 rev. (right top)

THE PERSEPOLIS ARCHIVES

Two archives of clay tablets were discovered at Persepolis in the 1930s by the archaeological expedition of the University of Chicago Oriental Institute. Although found at Persepolis, many of the tablets originated from the surrounding regions, and some were written in Susa. The first archive, of some 30,000 tablets and fragments, was found between 1933 and 1934 in the area of fortifications at the northeastern corner of the site, and has since been known as the Persepolis Fortification Tablets (PF). They are mainly written in Elamite, although there are also texts in Babylonian, Phrygian and Greek; they are dated from the thirteenth to twenty-eighth years of Darius I (509–494 BC). The 2,120 texts translated so far are administrative records largely dealing with the management of farm produce and herds, and the provisioning of state workers and official travellers. The latter include long-distance messengers carrying official correspondence throughout the empire.

The second archive, of 753 tablets and fragments, was found in a northeastern room of the Treasury (Persepolis Treasury Tablets, PT). These date from the thirtieth year of Darius I to the seventh year of Artaxerxes I (492–458 BC), and 128 have been published. This archive deals with payments to state employees, of varied nationality (including Thracians, Lydians, Ionians, Egyptians, Babylonians, Sogdians and Bactrians) in the vicinity of Persepolis.

309 Cuneiform tablet with a text in Elamite concerning mothers' rations

The rext reads '12 marriš [of] wine, supplied by Makuku, Irdumartiya received, and gave [it] to 9 women [who bore] male children [and] 6 [women] who bore female [children]. In the 23rd year.' The tablet has a cylinder seal impression of a figure in Persian dress in combat with a lion.

Persepolis, Fortifications (PF 1208)
H 2.7 cm, W 3.5 cm, Th 1.5 cm
Tehran
Hallock 1969: 345

308

309

310

308 Cuneiform tablet with a text in Elamite concerning allocation of cattle

The text reads '8 cattle supplied by Irdumatra were dispensed on behalf of the king. At 4 villages. In the 22nd year.' The cylinder seal impression (left) also occurs on other Persepolis tablets (type PFS 93) and shows a spearman on a horse, attacking three enemies, two of whom lie dead under the horse, the third transfixed by an arrow or javelin. An inscription on this seal (visible to the left of the impression) reads 'Kurash, the Anshanite, son of Teispes.' The Cyrus (Kurash) referred to in this inscription was probably an ancestor of Cyrus the Great.

Persepolis, Fortifications (PF 694)
H 2.2 cm, W 4.7 cm, Th 3.6 cm
Tehran
Hallock 1969: 214–15; Stronach 1997: 39–41, fig. 15

310 Cuneiform tablet with a text in Elamite concerning travel rations for a 'fast messenger'

The text reads '1.5[?] QA of flour supplied by Bakadušda, Muška received, as a fast messenger [pirradaziš]. He went from the king to Ziššawiš. He carried a sealed document of the king. In the 10th [Elamite] month.'

Indistinct cylinder seal impression on the reverse
Fortifications (PF 1285), Persepolis
H 1.9 cm, W 4.3 cm, Th 3.5 cm
Tehran
Hallock 1969: 365

311 Cuneiform tablet recording payments

The tablet records a payment to the *magus* Ukpiš for the *lan* ceremony for Mitra, Mount Ariaramnes and the river Ahinharišda, plus notice of ration payments to workers (including Skudrians and women).

The tablet has indistinct seal impressions and an Aramaic inscription in ink, reading, 'copied' (*nsḫ*). This may indicate that records were also archived in another form, perhaps as scrolls of leather in Aramaic.

Persepolis, Fortifications (PF 1955)
H 10.3 cm, W 7.9 cm, Th 1.6 cm
Tehran
Hallock 1969: 559–60

312 Pottery ostracon with a painted Aramaic inscription on both sides

On the concave side the inscription reads 'Greetings to Micaiah from Nathan son of Gemariah. Now, come, enter tomorrow without fail! Lo, it is wages for me/him for tomorrow. Now do not fail to come tomorrow.' On the convex side it reads 'Greetings [to] Micaiah from Jedaniah. Now, lo, I sent [word] to you yesterday in the name of Hodaviah son of Zechariah, saying, "Come this day," but you did not come. In[to] the hand of [i.e. through] my daughters send [word] to me [or, I sent to you].'

According to the handwriting it was written by the same person who composed some thirty other ostraca around 475 BC (Naveh 1970: 36–7). These messages seem to concern travel of goods, people, or messages by boat between Syene and Elephantine in Egypt. Syene and Elephantine were garrisoned, respectively, by regular units of Aramaean and Judean soldiers of the Persian army, who lived there with their families. The boats were known by the names of their Egyptian owners.

Provenance unknown, but probably from
    Elephantine, Egypt
Acquired in 1907 from W.T. Ready who purchased
    it at Sotheby's from Robert de Rustafjaell in 1906
H 6.7 cm, W 13.7 cm
British Museum, AES 45035
Porten and Yardeni 1991: 207–17, figs 1–2, pls 1–2

311

312

313

314, surface

314, inside

313 Pottery ostracon with a painted Aramaic inscription on one side

The inscription originally gave a short list of five Jewish names, four of which are complete: 'Zaccur son of Zephania[h], Meshullam son of Hodo, Shelomam son of Hodo,...] Jaazan son of Zecharia[h], 'y[...'

Provenance unknown, but probably from
  Elephantine, Egypt
Acquired in 1907 from W.T. Ready who purchased
  it at Sotheby's from Robert de Rustafjaell in 1906
H 6.2 cm, W 6.4 cm
British Museum, AES 45036
Porten and Yardeni 1991: 207–27, pls 1–3

314 Pottery ostracon with painted Aramaic inscriptions

The inscriptions are on the convex surface (in six lines) and on the inside (in seven lines, much worn). The interpretation of the texts is obscure, but it perhaps contains instructions to a tax collector.

Provenance unknown, but probably from
  Elephantine, Egypt
Transferred from the British Library in 1962
British Museum, ANE 133028
Segal 1969: 173–4, pl. XXXVIIb–c

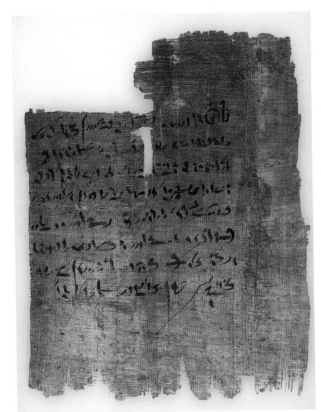

315

315 Papyrus bearing a legal text in the Egyptian cursive script demotic

The text records the divorce of Pati[pa]rewy from his wife Takhet[-...], and is dated to 'year 31, first month of the season of *achet* under Pharaoh Darius (I)' (492/491 BC).

Thebes, Egypt
Purchased from the Revd J.G. Chester and acquired
  before 1883
L 35 cm, W 25 cm
British Museum, AES 10449
Cruz-Uribe 1984: 43/6

THE ROYAL COINAGE
OF THE ACHAEMENID KINGS

The great kings of Persia first came into contact with coinage as a result of Cyrus's conquest of the kingdom of Lydia in the mid-sixth century BC. Coinage had by that time existed as a monetary phenomenon for over a century, but had not spread beyond the western coast of Asia Minor. Cyrus's capture of the Lydian capital of Sardis gave him control of the royal mint of the Lydian kings. Initially, the Persian response to the production and existence of coinage seems to have been to leave well alone. Lydian coinage under the last king, Croesus, had developed into a parallel gold and silver coinage with distinctive types of the facing foreparts of lion and bull (see cat. 316). The same designs were maintained by the Persian administration until the reign of Darius; under him a reform of the coinage took place which fixed the designs and weight standard of the royal coinage for much of the remainder of the dynasty. There were two principal denominations: the gold 'daric' (cats 319, 321, 323, 325), named after the king who introduced it, and the silver 'siglos' or 'shekel' (cats 318, 320, 322, 324, 326). The basic design consisted of an image of the great king, depicted in a variety of poses over time, but consistently portrayed with a bow. During the course of the fourth century BC the royal mint seems to have come under the influence of contemporary Greek practice, and adapted its weight standard to produce heavier silver coinage on a Greek model prevalent in the area of western Asia Minor, the so-called Chian standard. The types (cats 327, 328) remained recognizably royal, however.

One important but perhaps unexpected feature of Achaemenid royal coinage should be stressed. Despite its obvious usefulness as an economic tool and as a vehicle for official iconography, the royal coinage was not produced outside one or perhaps two centres in western Asia Minor, and did not, so far as we can tell, circulate beyond the satrapies of Asia Minor. Behind this curious numismatic fact must lie a profound difference in the workings of the Achaemenid administration in the Persian Empire, as well as a difference in the monetary economies of the different areas of the empire. In the west the Persian administration found itself acting against an economic background that required monetary payments for certain activities and commodities. In the eastern satrapies this plainly was not the case to the same extent.

The one exception to this basic pattern of royal coin production is provided by some rare issues produced in Egypt in the name of Artaxerxes III. These pieces, like some of the coins produced by the Persian governors of Egypt (cats 370, 371) were clearly intended to be acceptable to users of Greek coinage. They copied the designs of the famous 'owls' of Athens. The specimen issued by Artaxerxes (cat. 329) bears the Egyptian legend 'Artaxerxes Pharaoh. Life, Prosperity, Health'.

316 Gold croeseid stater,
c. 560–540 BC

Obv. Foreparts of lion r. and bull l.
    face to face
Rev. Two incuse punches
Wt 8.03 g
British Museum, CM 1841-0726-522;
    BMC Lydia: 6, 33

317 Silver croeseid stater,
c. 540–520 BC

Obv. Foreparts of lion r. and bull l.
    face to face
Rev. Two incuse punches
Wt 5.33 g
British Museum, CM 1866-1201-
    3804; *BMC Lydia*: 8, 47

318 Silver siglos,
c. 520–500 BC

Obv. Great king in *kidaris* and *kandys*,
    half figure, with bow
Rev. Oblong incuse
Wt 5.33 g
British Museum, CM 1852-0902-110;
    BMC Persia: 175, 197

319 Gold daric,
c. 520–500 BC

Obv. Great king in *kidaris* and *kandys*,
drawing bow
Rev. Oblong incuse
Wt 8.31 g
British Museum, CM 1897-0305-78;
BMC Persia: 173, 184

320 Silver siglos,
c. 520–500 BC

Obv. Great king in *kidaris* and *kandys*,
drawing bow
Rev. Oblong incuse
Wt 5.4 g
British Museum, CM 1852-1027-2;
BMC Persia: 173, 185

321 Gold daric,
c. 500–480 BC

Obv. Great king in *kidaris* and *kandys*,
with bow and spear
Rev. Oblong incuse
Wt 8.37 g
British Museum, CM 1919-0516-15;
BMC Persia: 153, 40

322 Silver siglos,
c. 500–480 BC

Obv. Great king in *kidaris* and *kandys*,
with bow and spear
Rev. Oblong incuse
Wt 5.37 g
British Museum, CM 1845-1217-272;
BMC Persia: 158, 74

323 Gold daric,
c. 400–375 BC

Obv. Great king in *kidaris* and *kandys*,
with bow and spear
Rev. Oblong incuse
Wt 8.32 g
British Museum, CM 1915-0108-28;
BMC Persia: 156, 58

324 Silver siglos,
c. 420–375 BC

Obv. Great king in *kidaris* and *kandys*,
with bow and spear
Rev. Oblong incuse
Wt 5.44 g
British Museum, CM 1918-1104-4;
BMC Persia: 154, 45

325 Gold daric,
c. 375–340 BC

Obv. Great king in *kidaris* and *kandys*,
with bow and dagger
Rev. Oblong incuse
Wt 8.29 g
British Museum, CM; *BMC Persia*:
171, 171

326 Silver siglos,
c. 375–340 BC

Obv. Great king in *kidaris* and *kandys*,
with bow and dagger
Rev. Oblong incuse
Wt 5.35 g
British Museum, CM 1919-0516-17;
BMC Persia: 171, 176

327 Silver stater
of Persian royal mint,
c. 340–330 BC

Obv. Great king kneeling, drawing bow
Rev. Great king with spear on
horseback; behind, Herakles head
Wt 15.04 g
British Museum, CM 1919-1120-114

328 Silver stater
of Persian royal mint?,
c. 410–370 BC

Obv. Great king kneeling, with bow
and spear
Rev. Granulated incuse
Wt 14.78 g
British Museum, CM; *BMC Ionia*: 323, 1

329 Silver tetradrachm of
Artaxerxes III (Memphis?),
c. 343/2–338/7 BC

Obv. Head of Athena r. wearing
earring and crested helmet
decorated with olive leaves
Rev. Owl r. within incuse square;
to l. olive-spray and crescent; *3rthš
sš pr-c3*; *ankh, wedj, seneb.*
Wt 16.93 g
British Museum, CM 1990-0121-1

COINAGE OF THE ROYAL ADMINISTRATION

WESTERN ASIA MINOR
PHARNABAZUS (CATS 330–31)

Pharnabazus was the satrap in northwestern Asia Minor at the end of the fifth and early fourth centuries BC. A remarkable and relatively large coinage (cats 330–31) was produced with his name on it, perhaps around 398–395 BC when he was responsible for funding the Persian fleet in the area. This was not a straightforward satrapal issue, however. The coins were clearly produced at the mint of the city of Cyzicus, which marked the coins with its badge, a tunny fish. This would normally indicate that the coins were issued by the city. Moreover, the decision to place what appears to be a portrait of the Persian on the obverse of the coin was a bold innovation. This is one of the earliest instances of the portrayal of a living individual in the position on coins that was usually reserved for the depiction of a god or goddess, which may explain why it was felt necessary to label the portrait with Pharnabazus's name.

TISSAPHERNES (CATS 332–7)

Tissaphernes, like Pharnabazus, is relatively well known from the Greek historical sources. He was satrap at Sardis in the last decade of the fifth century BC and again following his defeat of the rebellious Cyrus the Younger in 401 BC. A number of coinages have been attributed by modern scholars to this famous and colourful Persian governor. Three different silver issues (cats 332–4), all with a 'satrapal' head on the obverse, have been given to Tissaphernes, and the 'portraits' have been regarded as depictions of the satrap himself. None of these coins were signed by Tissaphernes, however, and their legends all seem to be abbreviations of the Greek word for 'of the King': ΒΑΣΙΛΕΩΣ. The reverse designs of two of the issues were surely influenced by Greek coinage: the owl (cat. 332) is borrowed from the coinage of Athens; the lyre (cat. 333) is present on a number of civic coinages of western Asia Minor. The running king on the third of these issues is reminiscent of the royal coinage, and it is probably valid to ask whether all three of these coins, given that they are signed in the name of the king, are not royal issues, too. If so, this raises the interesting possibility that the 'portraits' (if such they are) are in fact intended to represent the king himself. Similar considerations must apply to the bronze coinage that has been attributed to Tissaphernes and, because of its reverse type of an owl, the mint of Sigeion in the Troad (cat. 335). Again, the legend appears to read ΒΑΣ(ΙΛΕΩΣ), and this could be interpreted as a coinage in the name of the great king. Two other bronze issues find more explicit links to Tissaphernes. One of these (cat. 336) is a coin of the mint of Astyra in northwest Asia Minor with a bearded portrait on the obverse that is labelled ΤΙΣΣ or ΤΙΣΣΑ on some issues. This label recalls that on the silver issues with the portrait of Pharnabazus (above, cats 330–31). And we should note here, too, that these are not issues 'of' Tissaphernes, but rather of a city which for some reason chose to adorn its coinage with a satrapal portrait. The other bronze (cat. 337) has as its reverse type a depiction of a horseman hurling a spear, with the legend ΤΙΣΣΑ. The attribution of this coin to a mint is unclear; it is also unclear whether the reverse legend is another label or should be interpreted as identifying the authority behind the coin. Despite this impressive assemblage, there is not one issue that with confidence can be attributed to Tissaphernes as a coinage in his own name.

AUTOPHRADATES, ORONTAS AND SPITHRIDATES (CATS 338–44)

A number of other coinages are known from fourth-century BC western Asia Minor which were apparently signed by Persian officials. Unfortunately the chronology of these issues is generally unclear, and the literary sources for this period do not allow us to assign them unequivocally to a particular individual or occasion. Silver and bronze coins with the name Orontas (cats 338–40) were probably issued by a famous and powerful satrap in Asia Minor who is best known for his activities in revolt from the great king in the 360s. However, Orontas had a long career and is recorded as having served as satrap both in Armenia and in northwestern Asia Minor. Coins produced in the name of Spithridates (cats 341–3) share a design with some of Orontas's issues (the forepart of Pegasus) and may have been produced at the same mint. This may have been the Spithridates who was satrap of Lydia and Ionia prior to Alexander's invasion, but a commander of the same name is also known to have served under Pharnabazus and these may have been his coins. A small issue of coins (cat. 344) with what appears to be a satrapal head on the obverse and the legend OATA, has been interpreted as the issues of a Persian governor named Autophradates. However, the precise identity of Autophradates remains unclear.

THE HECATOMNIDS OF CARIA (CATS 345–7)

The exact position of the Hecatomnids within the hierarchy of Persian administration remains unclear, despite the wealth of evidence for their activity. They may have been satraps or, perhaps more probably, have come nominally under the control of the satrap of Sardis. It is clear, however, that they served the great king, and that their continued control over the land of Caria throughout the fourth century BC until the crisis precipitated by Alexander's arrival was essentially hereditary. During the second half of the century they were able, no doubt with the tacit approval at least of their Achaemenid masters, to extend their control into Lycia. In purely monetary terms they behaved more like the kings and dynasts of the south coasts of Asia Minor and Phoenicia than the satraps of the remainder of the empire. From the reign of Hecatomnus onwards (cat. 345) they issued a plentiful supply of silver coinage, the designs of which soon became standardized (cat. 346), in their own names. Under Pixodarus some gold was also produced (cat. 347).

CILICIA: TIRIBAZUS, PHARNABAZUS AND TARKUMUWA (CATS 348–57)

Perhaps the most remarkable series of coinages that can with certainty be attributed to Persian commanders are those produced during the fourth century BC in Cilicia. The earliest of these was that of the *karanos* (military commander) Tiribazus, who had been charged by the great king with the suppression of the revolt of Egypt in the 380s BC. The principal denomination of this coinage, the stater, appears to have been minted at four different cities but had the same design at all of them (cats 348–51). Tiribazus's post was subsequently taken up by Pharnabazus, the erstwhile satrap of northwestern Asia Minor. His coins present new types, and were produced at perhaps just two mints in the area, Tarsus (cats 353–4) and Nagidos. A third group of coins (cats 355–7) was produced by an individual named Tarkumuwa, who is otherwise unknown. The name is local rather than Persian, and it has been suggested that he was a subordinate military commander who perhaps succeeded Pharnabazus. Certainly one of their coin types overlapped (cf. cats 353, 355).

MAZAIOS (CATS 358–66)

The largest numismatic legacy of all the Persian governors has been left by Mazaios. He had initially been appointed governor of Cilicia some time in the period 361–351 BC by Artaxerxes II or III. As governor of Cilicia he produced an impressive series of coins, including a small gold issue (cats 358–61). At least some of this productivity may have been associated with Mazaios's role in the suppression of a revolt in Egypt, and a concomitant rebellion in Phoenicia centred on the city of Sidon and its king, Tennes. By 353 BC Sidon had been recaptured for Persia, and from this date the coinage of Sidon, while still bearing the traditional types of the city, began to be signed by Mazaios (see cats 365–6). These issues are dated and ran for twenty-one years, from 353 to 333 BC. It is thus clear that Mazaios had some sort of authority over the city until shortly before the arrival there of Alexander of Macedon. The nature of this authority becomes apparent from another series of coins, probably produced at the city of Tarsus, on which Mazaios is given the title 'ruler over Transeuphratene and Cilicia' (cat. 360). Other coins from Samaria (for example, cat. 362) attest to the breadth of his command in this area. It is generally assumed that this extension of Mazaios's power over two districts of the empire came as a result of his role in the suppression of the revolt in the 350s, although there is no firm evidence. What is clear is that Mazaios was a survivor. The invasion of Alexander of Macedon found Mazaios ultimately involved in the unsuccessful defence of Babylon. It is to this city that Mazaios's last series of coins have sometimes been attributed. Characterized by a lion on the obverse (cat. 363, cf. cat. 364), these 'lion staters' may, ironically, be the first coinage that had been produced by a Persian official in Mesopotamia. If so, they were certainly the last. It is fitting that they, like their issuer who continued in charge at Babylon after its surrender to Alexander, survived into the new regime. Lion staters would be minted subsequently under Alexander and his successor Seleucus I.

NORTHERN ASIA MINOR (CATS 367–9)

A number of issues are known from the area of Paphlagonia on the northern, Black Sea coast of Asia Minor, which are signed by individuals who appear to have been Persian officials. The best known of these individuals is Datames, the satrap of Capadocia. His coins (see cat. 367) borrowed the designs of the Greek city of Sinope, and it is generally assumed that they were produced there following his conquest of the city. This would be another interesting example, as at Sardis in the sixth century BC, of the Persians simply adapting an existing coin tradition to their own uses. Other issues are known with the same types but signed in Aramaic with what appear to be Persian names (see cats 368–9). It has been suggested that these issues may belong to the period of crisis around the time of Alexander's invasion, but their chronology remains unclear.

EGYPT (CATS 370–72)

Prior to the arrival of the Persian administration, no silver coinage had ever been produced in Egypt. This process began, most probably, in the reign of Artaxerxes III following his re-conquest of the province in *c.* 343/2 BC (above, cat. 329). Thereafter, two Persian governors of the province issued coins in their names: Sabakes (cat. 370), who was satrap down to his death in 333 BC, and Mazakes (cat. 371), who succeeded him. Like the issues of Artaxerxes, the silver coins produced by these two men were imitations of Athenian coinage and produced on the Athenian weight standard, rather than the Persian. It seems clear that this decision must have reflected monetary habit in the area where the coins were intended to be used. The bronze of Sabakes (cat. 372), almost predictably, bears on the reverse the figure of the great king as archer.

330

331

332

333

334

335

336

337

338

332 Silver tetradrachm of uncertain mint (Tissaphernes), *c.* 420–395 BC

Obv. Head of 'satrap' r.
Rev. Owl r. within incuse square; to l. olive-spray and crescent; ΒΑΣ
Wt 16.96 g
British Museum, CM 1947-0706-4

333 Silver tetradrachm of uncertain mint (Tissaphernes), *c.* 420–395 BC

Obv. Head of 'satrap' l.
Rev. Lyre with seven strings; ΒΑΣΙΑ
Wt 15.31 g
British Museum, *BMC Ionia*: 325, 13

334 Silver coin of uncertain mint, *c.* 420–395 BC

Obv. Head of 'satrap' r.
Rev. Great king running r. with spear and strung bow; ΒΑΣΙ
Wt 3.42 g
British Museum, CM 1866-1201-4124; *BMC Ionia*: 325, 14

335 Bronze coin of Sigeion (Tissaphernes), *c.* 420–395 BC

Obv. Head of 'satrap' r.
Rev. Owl r.; ΒΑΣ
Wt 3.28 g
British Museum, CM 1979-0101-292; *SNG von Aulock* 7636

336 Bronze coin of Astyra (Tissaphernes), *c.* 400–395 BC

Obv. Bearded head r.; below, ΤΙΣΣ
Rev. Cult statue of Artemis seen from front; ΑΣΤΥΡΗ
Wt 1.76 g
British Museum, CM 2002-10-28-1

337 Bronze coin of uncertain mint (Tissaphernes), *c.* 400–395 BC

Obv. Head of Athena r. in crested Attic helmet
Rev. Horseman riding r. and hurling spear; around, ΤΙΣΣΑ
Wt 1.12 g
British Museum, CM 2002-10-28-2

338 Silver coin of uncertain mint (Orontas), *c.* 380–330 BC

Obv. Head of Athena l. in Athenian helmet
Rev. Forepart of Pegasus r.; ΟΡΟΝ
Wt 2.56 g
British Museum, CM 1883-0402-26; *BMC Ionia*: 326, 15

330 Silver tetradrachm of Cyzicus (Pharnabazus), *c.* 410–390 BC

Obv. Head of 'satrap' r.; ΦΑΡΝΑΒΑ.
Rev. Prow of ship l.; on either side, dolphin; tunny beneath
Wt 14.68 g
British Museum, CM 1892-0703-1

331 Silver tetradrachm of Cyzicus (Pharnabazus), *c.* 410–390 BC

Obv. Head of satrap r.; ΦΑΡΝΑΒΑ.
Rev. Prow of ship l.; on either side dolphin; tunny beneath
Wt 14.81 g
British Museum, CM 1875-0701-24; *BMC Ionia*: 325, 12

339

340

341

342

343

344

345

346

339 Bronze coin of uncertain mint (Orontas), *c.* 380–330 BC

Obv. Head of Zeus r.
Rev. Forepart of Pegasus r.; [OP]ONTA
Wt 1.79 g
British Museum, CM 1868-0406-20;
  BMC Ionia: 326, 16

340 Silver coin of uncertain mint (Orontas), *c.* 390–340 BC

Obv. Hoplite or Apollo(?) kneeling
  with spear and shield
Rev. Forepart of winged boar r.;
  [OP]ONTA
Wt 2.79 g
British Museum, CM 1840-1226-97;
  BMC Ionia: 326, 17

341 Silver coin of uncertain mint (Spithridates), *c.* 400–330 BC

Obv. Head of 'satrap' l.
Rev. Forepart of Pegasus r.; ΣΠΙΘΡΙ
Wt 2.88 g
British Museum, CM 1887-0606-29;
  BMC Ionia: 327, 18

342 Silver coin of uncertain mint (Spithridates), *c.* 400–330 BC

Obv. Head of 'satrap' r.
Rev. Forepart of Pegasus r.; ΣΠ
Wt 0.96 g
British Museum, CM 1979-0101-
  373; *SNG von Aulock* 1823

343 Silver coin of uncertain mint (Spithridates), *c.* 400–330 BC

Obv. Head of 'satrap' l.
Rev. Forepart of horse r.; ΣΠΙΘΡΙ
Wt 2.90 g
British Museum, CM 1900-1204-4

344 Silver coin of uncertain mint (Autophradates), *c.* 380–320 BC

Obv. Head of 'satrap' l.
Rev. Head of horse l.; OATA
Wt 1.0 g
British Museum, CM 1874-0716-236

345 Silver tetradrachm of Hecatomnus (?), *c.* 395–377 BC

Obv. Great king shooting bow r.
Rev. Zeus Labraundos r. with double
  axe and sceptre
Wt 15.15 g
British Museum, CM 1981-0220-1

346 Silver tetradrachm of Mausolus, *c.* 377–353 BC

Obv. Head of Apollo facing, laureate
Rev. Zeus Labraundos standing r., clad
  in chiton and himation, holding
  double-axe (*labrys*) over r. shoulder
  and long spear in l., point
  downwards; ΜΑΥΣΣΩΛΟ
Wt 15.16 g
British Museum, CM 1929-0602-32

347 Gold coin of Pixodarus, *c.* 340–334 BC

Obv. Head of Apollo laureate r.
Rev. Zeus Labraundos standing r., clad
  in chiton and himation, holding
  double-axe (*labrys*) over r. shoulder
  and long spear in l., point
  downwards; ΠΙΞΩΔΑΡΟ
Wt 4.15 g
British Museum, CM 1877-0303-1;
  BMC Caria: 184, 1

348 Silver stater of Tiribazus, mint of Issus, *c.* 387–380 BC

Obv. Ahuramazda facing; AMI
Rev. Baal standing l. with eagle and
  sceptre; TRIBZW
Wt 10.30 g
British Museum, CM Bank 1157;
  BMC Cilicia: 91, 3

347

348

349

350

351

352

353

349 Silver stater of Tiribazus, mint of Mallus, c. 387–380 BC

Obv. Ahuramazda facing
Rev. Baal standing l. with eagle and sceptre; *TRIBZW*
Wt 10.46 g
British Museum, CM 1985-1114-1

350 Silver stater of Tiribazus, mint of Soli, c. 387–380 BC

Obv. Ahuramazda facing
Rev. Baal standing l. with eagle and sceptre; *TRIBZW*
Wt 10.30 g
British Museum, CM *BMC Cilicia*: 148, 26

351 Silver stater of Tiribazus, mint of Tarsus, c. 387–380 BC

Obv. Ahuramazda facing
Rev. Baal standing l. with eagle and sceptre; *TRIBZW*; T
Wt 10.11 g
British Museum, CM *BMC Cilicia*: 164, 12

352 Silver fraction Tiribazus, mint of Mallos, c. 387–380 BC

Obv. Bearded head r. in crown
Rev. Baal standing l.
Wt 0.36 g
British Museum, CM 1920-0422-5

353 Silver stater of Pharnabazus, mint of Tarsus, c. 379–373 BC

Obv. Female head facing
Rev. Bearded head in crested helmet l.; *FRNBZ*
Wt 10.67 g
British Museum, CM 1979-0101-992; *SNG von Aulock* 5922

354

355

356

357

358

359

360

354 Silver stater of Pharnabazus, mint of Tarsus, c. 380–375 BC

Obv. Baal seated l.
Rev. Bearded head in crested helmet l.; *FRNBZ*; *HLK*
Wt 10.74 g
British Museum, CM 1979-0101-995; *SNG von Aulock* 5928

355 Silver stater of Tarkumuwa, mint of Tarsus, c. 378–372 BC

Obv. Female head facing
Rev. Bearded head in crested helmet l.; *TRKMW*
Wt 10.99 g
British Museum, CM 1987-0649-461

356 Silver stater of Tarkumuwa, mint of Tarsus, c. 378–372 BC

Obv. Baal seated r.; *B'LTRZ*
Rev. Great king seated r. holding bow; *TRKMW*
Wt 10.33 g
British Museum, CM 1888-1208-6; *BMC Cilicia*: 167, 32

357 Silver stater of Tarkumuwa, mint of Tarsus, c. 378–372 BC

Obv. Baal seated r.; *B'LTRZ*
Rev. Ana standing r. facing Tarkumuwa; *ANA*; *TRKMW*
Wt 10.78 g
British Museum, CM 1979-0101-1003; *SNG von Aulock* 5946

358 Gold stater of Mazaios, c. 361–333 BC

Obv. Baal seated l.; *B'L*
Rev. Lion attacking stag l.
Wt 8.41 g
British Museum, CM 1937-0606-18

359 Silver stater of Mazaios, c. 361–333 BC

Obv. Baal seated l.; *B'LTRZ*
Rev. Lion attacking stag l.; *MZDI*
Wt 10.91 g
British Museum, CM *BMC Cilicia*: 169, 38

361

362

363

364

366

369

360 Silver stater of Mazaios, *c. 361–333* BC

Obv. Baal seated l.; B'LTRZ
Rev. Lion attacking bull above two
  lines of city walls; *MZDI ZI'L*
  BRNHRA
Wt 10.67 g
British Museum, CM 1920-0422-11

361 Silver stater of Mazaios, *c. 361–333* BC

Obv. Baal seated l.; B'LTRZ
Rev. Lion attacking bull l.; *MZDI*
Wt 10.72 g
British Museum, CM 1848-0819-51;
  BMC Cilicia: 171, 52

362 Silver fraction of Mazaios, uncertain mint in Samaria, *c. 361–333* BC

Obv. Great king seated r. on throne,
  holding sceptre in l. hand and flower
  in r.; ŠN
Rev. Winged, bearded and crowned
  deity with bird's tail holding flower
  and uncertain object; MZ
Wt 0.74 g
British Museum, CM 1971-5-10-1

363 Silver stater of Mazaios, uncertain mint (Babylon?), *c. 361–333* BC

Obv. Baal seated l.; B'LTRZ
Rev. Lion walking l., star and crescent;
  MZDI
Wt 10.78 g
British Museum, CM 1896-0601-105;
  BMC Cilicia: 172, 59

364 Silver fraction of Mazaios, uncertain mint (Babylon?), *c. 361–333* BC

Obv. Baal seated l.
Rev. Lion walking l.; above, winged
  disc
Wt 0.57 g
British Museum, CM 2003-11-7-3

365 Silver double shekel of Sidon issued in the name Mazaios, *c. 352* BC

Obv. War galley above zigzag waves
Rev. Sidonian deity in a chariot drawn
  by four horses; *MZDY*
Wt 25.66 g
British Museum, CM *BMC Sidon* 81

366 Silver fraction of Sidon issued in the name Mazaios, *c. 335* BC

Obv. War galley above zigzag waves
Rev. King slaying lion; *MZ*
Wt 0.68 g
British Museum, CM *BMC Sidon* 84

367 Silver stater of Sinope (Datames), *c. 370s–359/8* BC

Obv. Head of nymph Sinope wearing
  earring
Rev. Eagle above dolphin; ΑΠΟ;
  ΔΑΤΑΜΑ
Wt 5.89 g
British Museum, CM *SNG Black Sea*
  1447

368 Silver stater of Sinope (Hydarnes?), *c. 330s* BC?

Obv. Head of nymph Sinope wearing
  earring
Rev. Eagle above dolphin; *WDRN?*
Wt 5.28 g
British Museum, CM *SNG Black Sea*
  1451

369 Silver stater of Sinope (Tiryana?), *c. 330s* BC?

Obv. Head of nymph Sinope wearing
  earring
Rev. Eagle above dolphin; *TYRYN*
Wt 4.96 g
British Museum, CM *SNG Black Sea*
  1452

370 Silver tetradrachm of Sabakes (Memphis?), *c. 335–333* BC

Obv. Head of Athena r. wearing
  earring and crested helmet
  decorated with olive leaves
Rev. Owl r. within incuse square;
  to l. olive-spray and crescent; *SWYN*
Wt 16.19 g
British Museum, CM 1920-0805-370

371 Silver tetradrachm of Mazakes (Memphis?), *c. 333–330* BC

Obv. Head of Athena r. wearing
  earring and crested helmet
  decorated with olive leaves
Rev. Owl r. within incuse square;
  to l. olive-spray and crescent; *MZDK*
Wt 16.45 g
British Museum, CM 1909-0105-12

372 Bronze coin of Sabakes (Memphis?), *c. 335–333* BC

Obv. Horse
Rev. Persian or king with strung bow;
  SWYN
Wt 1.32 g
British Museum, CM 1925-0105-129

370

371

372

PERSIAN INFLUENCE ON LOCAL COIN DESIGN

The coinages of the Persian officials in Asia Minor, Phoenicia, Samaria and Egypt present a mixture of iconographic influences. These result from a variety of factors. On the one hand there is the imperative of royal iconography. Coins of the great king or his representatives should in some sense look royal or at least present some representation of the ruling elite. This is the preconception with which the modern eye tends to approach the ancient coinage, and to a certain extent the coins do not disappoint. Whoever the 'satrapal' figures really are on the various 'satrapal' coinages (for example, cats 330–31, 332–5, 341–4), they are identifiably Persian and of high status. The king as archer or as a slayer of beasts is also a common feature (for example, cats 334, 345, 356, 366, 372). Beyond this, the 'satrapal' coinages of Cilicia display clear references to Iranian religious practice and belief (for example, cats 348–51, 357). Yet at the same time, a number of the satrapal, and even royal coinages are also heavily influenced by Greek coin design (for example, cats 329, 330–31, 332–3, 335–7, 338–352, 367–9, 370–71). In this respect coins differ, perhaps, from other media in the suitable and available repertoire of available images, as a result of their monetary function. While a certain amount of innovation in coin design is tolerable, coins must remain recognizable, with a broadly understood framework of design, in order for them to be recognizable and accepted in payment. Behind this simple fact lies the explanation, for example, of the preference of the Persian administration in Egypt for coins that looked like those of Athens.

It is important to bear in mind this constraining factor when examining the evidence for Persian influence on coins other than their own. Despite the potential clear and strong presence of royal power and ideology throughout the western satrapies, there was also a powerful disincentive from changing existing, successful coin designs. There is, moreover, little evidence that the Persian administration required any changes to or standardization of coin design. The resulting picture of Persian influence over coin design beyond that produced by the administration is to a certain extent haphazard, and the result of local pressures, rather than centralized dictate. Cilicia and Lycia seem to have been particularly susceptible to influence, perhaps for two different reasons. In Cilicia, the tradition of coinage was not old. The earliest local coinages belong to the late fifth century BC, and thus to a period when the area was already firmly under Achaemenid control. Thus no independent tradition of coin design had had a chance to develop. Early on, we find examples of coin design that remind us immediately of the sculpture of the palaces at Persepolis and Susa (cat. 373) or other Persian royal iconography (cat. 375), or that clearly draw on an Iranian tradition, albeit that we cannot quite pin it down (cat. 374). Lycian coinage, by contrast, did extend back into the late sixth century BC, and thus to around the time of the Persian conquest, and had developed a distinctive local repertoire of designs by the mid-fifth century. Here the impetus towards the uptake of Persian influence perhaps came rather as a result of local political conditions. Unlike Cilicia with its civic approach to coinage, Lycia's coinage was issued by dynasts who could develop and adapt a received royal iconography to their own needs. Thus the 'satrapal' head appears surprisingly frequently on the dynastic coinages (for example, cats 376–8). Whether these designs were intended or received as portraits of the Lycian dynasts themselves, or were intended rather to advertise their personal relationships with the satraps and king who stood above them in the hierarchy is unclear, however. Elsewhere the areas of Samaria and Phoenicia, which again were late to adopt the use of coinage, saw a relatively high uptake of coin designs recognizable from Achaemenid royal art. Depictions of the great king in various poses are common (see, for example, cats 362, 364, 379–80). Even at the far east of the empire in Afghanistan, where coinage existed only on a sporadic basis during the period of Persian control, the influence of the great Persian palaces can be seen. Cat. 381 bears the image of a distinctive double-headed Persian capital. Of all the lands encompassed by the Persian Empire in the fifth and fourth centuries BC, those least affected by the monumental art of the Achaemenid kings were those inhabited by the Greeks. Here the strong, self-confident civic traditions of coin design were all but impervious to the influence of royal iconography. Their coinage functioned perfectly well without it, and the Persian rulers were shrewd enough to realize that one should not fix what is not broken.

373 Silver stater of Tarsus, *c*. 410–400 BC

Obv. Horseman riding l.
Rev. Two Persian guards facing each other holding spears and wearing quivers
Wt 10.61 g
British Museum, CM 2000-0508-1

374 Silver stater of Tarsus, *c*. 425–400 BC

Obv. Cow and calf beneath winged disk
Rev. 'Satrap' ploughing l. with yoke of oxen; *TRZ*
Wt 10.35 g
British Museum, CM 1982-0511-1

375 Silver stater of Mallus, *c*. 380–330 BC

Obv. Great king running r. with spear and bow
Rev. Herakles fighting the Nemean lion; ΜΑΛ
Wt 10.35 g
British Museum, CM 1888-1103-4; *BMC Cilicia*: 99, 24

376 Silver stater of Kherei, Lycia, *c*. 425–400 BC

Obv. Head of Athena r. in crested Athenian helmet, adorned with floral volute and three olive leaves; necklace and circular earring; below neck, uncertain symbol
Rev. Head of bearded 'satrap' r., in Persian headdress, tied with diadem knotted behind; before face, symbol: the whole in dotted incuse circle
Wt 8.37 g
British Museum, CM 1877-0508-1; *BMC Lycia*: 22, 102

377 Silver stater of Artumpara, Lycia, *c*. 400–360 BC

Obv. Head of Athena r., in crested Athenian helmet: border of dots
Rev. Head of bearded 'satrap' r. in Persian headdress: the whole in dotted incuse circle; *ARTUMPAR[I]*
Wt 8.06 g
British Museum, CM 1845-0705-; *BMC Lycia*: 25, 111

378 Silver stater of Ddänävälä, Lycia, *c*. 400–360 BC

Obv. Head of bearded 'satrap' r., in Persian headdress: border of dots
Rev. Head of Athena r. in crested Athenian helmet, decorated with floral volute and olive leaves; to l., symbol countermark: the whole in dotted incuse circle; *DDENEWE*
Wt 8.40 g
British Museum, CM 1899-0401-86

379 Silver half shekel of Abdeshmun, Sidon, *c*. 410–400 BC

Obv. War galley before city walls; beneath, two lions
Rev. Great king fighting lion
Wt 6.97 g
British Museum, CM *BMC Sidon* 9

380 Silver fraction of uncertain mint, Samaria, *c*. fourth century BC

Obv. Head of 'satrap' l.
Rev. King fighting winged animal; *ŠMRYN*
Wt 0.75 g
British Museum, CM 1993-11-6-7

381 Silver stater from Kabul hoard, *c*. 500–450 BC

Obv. Double-headed Persian column capital
Rev. Circular incuse punch
Wt 11.48 g
British Museum, CM 1957-0107-1

373

374

375

376

377

378

379

380

381

THE MALAYER HOARD OF GREEK COINS

382 Malayer hoard, *c.* 440–430 BC

This remarkable group of silver coins was discovered in 1934, near the town of Malayer some thirty miles to the south of Hamadan, the site of the Median and later Achaemenid capital of Ecbatana. The precise location of discovery is not recorded. A large number of coins, 306 according to contemporary accounts, were confiscated by the police in 1935 in Malayer itself. These coins were transferred to the National Museum in Tehran where they are now housed in the Department of Coins and Seals. However, at least a hundred more escaped the authorities and passed into commerce.

Apart from the coins found together in the foundations deposits of the Apadana at Persepolis (see cat. 4), this is the only known hoard of silver coins from Iran deposited in the period of the Achaemenid Empire. From the composition of the hoard it seems likely that this collection of money was formed at the eastern end of the Mediterranean, perhaps in Tyre or Sidon, whose coins dominate the hoard, and then travelled eastwards across Mesopotamia and perhaps then up the Khorasan road towards the capital at Ecbatana. From the dates of the Greek coins included in the hoard it is possible to deduce that it was buried in the period *c.* 440–430 BC, but the precise circumstances of burial, like those of its discovery, are unrecoverable.

What makes the hoard remarkable is precisely its unique status. From the relative dearth of such finds from the Iranian and Mesopotamian heartlands of the empire, it becomes clear that coinage was rarely used there. The pattern confirms that offered by the Achaemenid coinage (see cats 330–72), which was produced largely in Asia Minor and around the shores of the Mediterranean. Also remarkable is the fact that the Malayer hoard seems to have included few or no coins produced by the great kings or their satraps. The coins that are included form a representative sample of coinage from around the Mediterranean, from as far west as Sicily and Cyrene, from Greek cities, notably Athens and Aegina, and from the cities and peoples of Asia Minor and Phoenicia. In total the hoard represents perhaps four or five years pay for a manual worker. If this was the property of a private individual, he was wealthy beyond the dreams of many of his contemporaries.

Said to have been found near Malayer, Iran
Tehran

382

10

TRANSPORT AND WARFARE

Nigel Tallis

The Persians teach their sons, between the ages of five
and twenty, only three things: to ride a horse, use the bow,
and speak the truth.

(Herodotus, *History* I.136.2)

The vast Achaemenid Empire could not have functioned without effective systems of communication and transport.[1] Although power was
devolved to provincial governors or satraps, the political
oversight of the periphery from the centre, the movement and operations of royal armies, and the flow of
resources in tribute and trade to support these activities
all demanded efficient communications. Herodotus's
statement that Babylonia alone provided a third of the
total supplies for the court and the army, if in any sense
accurate, would be meaningless unless these supplies, or
their value in other materials, could be transported
beyond the local areas of production. The nature and
structure of the army, economy and state were therefore
directly related.

The overall nature and general organization of the
Achaemenid army, and to a lesser extent the navy,
were deeply rooted in the administrative and military
traditions of the ancient Near East. This was unavoidable as the structure and deployment of the forces were
at least partly determined by the way the empire's
resources were harnessed, and how the empire was
administered.

Land transport in the ancient world relied on the
muscle power of humans and animals. Transport was
difficult and extremely expensive over long distances, a
situation only partially alleviated by water transport.
Utilization of the horse was central to rapid transit on
land, and so it is not surprising that the Achaemenid
Persians, and the Medes before them, were renowned as
consummate horsemen, or that skilled horsemanship
should have remained a matter of great interest in Iran
into modern times.

One of the most revealing examples of the difficulties inherent in the study of Achaemenid transport –
and the Persian military system in particular – is illustrated through the quote from Herodotus which opens
this chapter. It is often cited as encapsulating the
quintessential nature of a specifically Persian attitude
to civil and military horsemanship. Although it most
likely refers only to the education of the court elite, if
not primarily to the king himself, it probably applied
more widely, if only through imitation of the court. It
is only one of several allusions to the education of Persian youths in Classical sources. Clearly drawing upon
the same tradition available to Herodotus, yet providing additional detail, is Strabo's description of the education of young Persians: 'From five years of age to
twenty-four they are trained to use the bow, to throw
the javelin, to ride, and to speak the truth; and they
use as teachers of science the wisest men, who also
interweave their teachings with the mythical element,
thus reducing that element to a useful purpose ...'
(Strabo XV.3.18).

The elite nature of this education is also revealed in
the terse statements of Darius I (522–486 BC), which in
essence agree with Herodotus and Strabo, and must at
least partly underlie their comments: 'As a horseman I
am a good horseman. As a bowman I am a good
bowman both on foot and on horseback. As a spearman
I am a good spearman both on foot and on horseback'
(Darius DNb). Remarkably, however, the closest comparison is to be found in the summary of the military and
scholarly education of Ashurbanipal, King of Assyria
(668–627 BC), as recounted in his annals:

> The art of master Adapa I learned – the hidden treasure of
> all scribal knowledge ... I mounted my horse ... I held the bow,
> I shot the arrow, the sign of my valour. I threw unwieldy
> *azmaru*-spears like arrows. Holding the reins like a driver I
> made the wheels go round. I learned to handle the *aritu* and
> heavy *kababu* shields like a fully-equipped bowman.

(ARAB II; 986; Streck 256.I.22)

Clearly there are many layers of complexity in the relationships between these apparently straightforward accounts, and the manner in which they may reflect an ancient tradition of elite culture. Viewed in isolation, these ancient texts, whether Greek, Persian or even Assyrian, give a misleading, or at best only a partial insight into the realities of the Persian Empire.

HORSES AND HARNESS

Achaemenid art, especially the fine reliefs at Persepolis, supported by a limited amount of oesteological evidence, appears to show the same type of Persian draught and riding horses. This suggests that they are the famous

58 Stone relief from Palace H at Persepolis showing a tribute horse and the typical harness elements of an Achaemenid-period bridle. *Persepolis Museum 821.*

'Great Nesaean' horses, said by Classical writers to have been bred on the Median plain.[2] They are depicted as long-bodied and ram-headed, with thick necks and heavy crests, and were the primary mounts of elite Persian horsemen. Greys seem to have been reserved for the king, senior commanders and the horses of the sacred chariot.[3]

The Medes and Armenians were also said to have supplied large numbers of tribute horses (Strabo XI.13.8; XI.14.9). The tribute chariot horses depicted on the Apadana reliefs at Persepolis appear much smaller than Nesaeans, the size of large ponies, and are clearly a different breed. However, it is possible that they have been reduced in scale slightly to fit the composition; the wheel diameters of the attendant vehicles also seem to have been reduced accordingly. The wheels of the Persepolis

chariots are noticeably small in comparison to other representations (compare cats 20, 399).

Draught and riding horses are shown with a distinctive design of headstall (usually formed of cheekstraps dividing at the lower ends and joined by a band over the nose), with a throatlash secured with a toggle and sometimes a browband. The strap-crossings are often decorated with strap-dividers in the form of birds' beaks, boars' tusks (cats 387–8) or simple discs (cat. 393). The straps of headstalls can also be decorated with roundels or discs (cat. 20). The horses are shown being controlled by a bridle and a simple snaffle bit (cats 383–6), of which contemporary examples have been found widely throughout the Near East – many at Persepolis. This type, first attested in this period, is usually made of bronze but also of iron, and has a jointed mouthpiece. Its canons, which are often studded or barbed, are cast in one piece together with the bar cheekpieces and their rectangular or circular rein attachments. The cheekpieces usually have two holes to take the ends of the headstall's divided cheekstraps, and are curved or angular, sometimes with figured terminals (most commonly in the form of a hoof and phallus; fig. 58).

Other animals attested for riding and draught are asses, and dromedary and Bactrian camels (Oxus Treasure cat. 257 and Apadana cat. 20).[4] The development of camel transport in the first millennium BC was probably a major factor in the growth of long-distance caravan trade. Bovids, an essential part of agricultural life, are sometimes depicted in representations of ploughing scenes on seals.[5] Pack animals were also employed in large numbers by the army; the Macedonians captured 7,000 donkeys and camels at Damascus (Curtius III.13.16; III.3.24). Human porters were a similarly unglamorous mode of transport largely neglected in the arts, but mentioned, if only rarely, in other sources (Curtius III.13.16).

VEHICLES
WAGONS AND CARTS

Evidence for Achaemenid wheeled vehicles is provided by finds of actual vehicles, and by representations in the major and minor arts and Arabian rock-art. Relevant textual sources from within the empire are limited largely to cuneiform material from Babylonia, but this can be supplemented by extensive references in Classical literature.[6]

It is often difficult to distinguish between two-wheeled light carts and chariots in representations, even assuming that such a simple distinction actually existed in antiquity. It is easy to forget that a bewildering variety of horse-drawn vehicles existed worldwide, with many local variations, well into modern times.[7] Four-wheeled wagons are hardly ever depicted but in the Achaemenid period might be included together with two-wheelers under the Persian term *harmamaxa*, or 'covered carriage', preserved in Greek texts: 'It was thus that Xerxes rode out of Sardis; but when he was so minded he would alight from the chariot into a *harmamaxa*' (Herodotus, *History* VII.41); 'Cyrus inspected the barbarians first, and they marched past with their cavalry formed in squadrons and their infantry in companies; then he inspected the Greeks, driving past them in a chariot [*harma*], the Cilician queen in a covered carriage [*harmamaxa*]' (Xenophon, *Anabasis* I.2.16). These vehicles, possibly covered or tilted, are attested as being used by the king, by royal officials such as ambassadors, and by royal women, children and staff of the court.[8]

CHARIOTS AND LIGHT CARTS

In the ancient Near East light two-wheeled carts, or chariots, drawn by two or more horses or asses, and carrying between two and four occupants, were vehicles of high status and prestige used for transport, warfare, hunting and display. The chariot retained most of these roles in the Achaemenid period, although its use in warfare declined. Representations of Achaemenid-period chariots are known from stone reliefs on the Apadana at Persepolis (cat. 26); seals (cat. 398); coinage from Sidon in the Levant (cat. 365); Graeco-Persian gems (cat. 407) and reliefs; and tomb paintings from Anatolia. The chariot of Darius III forms the centrepiece of the Alexander Mosaic found at Pompeii, which is thought to have derived from a lost near-contemporary Hellenistic painting. It illustrates the battle of Issus (333 BC) between the Persian and Macedonian armies in terms of a personal combat between Darius and Alexander.

There are two detailed gold models of Achaemenid-period chariots from the Oxus Treasure (cats 399–400); a bronze model from the Levant (cat. 401); and numerous stone and terracotta models of chariots from Cyprus. There is a small but significant amount of archaeological material, particularly wheels, from Egypt, Anatolia and the Caucasus.[9]

The chariot boxes or cabs from this period have rectangular floor plans, and 'sprung' floors of interlaced thongs (as represented on one of the Oxus gold models and on a Cypriot stone model).[10] The decorated solid sides, often shown with crossed outer braces, may have either a horizontal upper edge or one sloping towards either the front or rear of the vehicle (cat. 20). Handholds are situated at the upper rear of the cabs, while the chariot on the Alexander Mosaic uniquely shows a strap across the side, indicating it was closed by a shield –

otherwise shown only by the highly detailed lion hunt chariot reliefs of Ashurbanipal (although this detail may in fact be decoration on the box).

The Oxus models clearly show that the central partition in the cab – dividing it from front to rear, and known from earlier and contemporary Cypriot chariot models (cat. 402) – could be used as a seat (also suggested on Achaemenid-period seals). On a Graeco-Persian relief from Xanthos the seat appears to run across the cab from side to side; this is more likely to be one of the rare examples of an identifiable variant form of light cart specially made for civil use.

Depictions of two-wheeled funerary vehicles carrying coffins on Graeco-Persian and Levantine stelae and sarcophagi appear to be partially dismantled chariots of Persian type, or hearses in chariot style.[11] Other Graeco-Persian monuments also show chariots with an open-framed cab of east Greek type, and this would appear to be the design of excavated funerary vehicles.

In terms of the undercarriage and draught, the axle is depicted in various positions. The most common and practical location is at the rear of the cab, as unless the occupants remained seated, the vehicle would rock back and forth endangering both crew and draught-team. Actual linchpins from Persepolis match those shown on vehicles on Persepolis reliefs (cat. 20) securing the wheels to the axle (fig. 59). Wheels are shown with between six and twelve spokes, the latter possibly reflecting an Elamite tradition, usually with ferrules or carved decoration about the mid-point of the spoke. As mentioned above, it seems that the wheels on the Persepolis vehicles may have been slightly scaled down to fit the artistic composition, as the large wheels on both the Oxus Treasure chariot model and the Alexander Mosaic are nearly identical to earlier Assyrian examples. Fragments of wheel from Uplistsikhe in Georgia match the evidence for Achaemenid construction, revealing that they were made with an inner and an outer felloe, the latter partially encased in a metal tyre of channel section, and with the tread studded with large, oval-headed, hobnails (as on earlier Assyrian royal chariots).

The so-called Y-pole form of draught pole was still in use, and is shown on a bronze model from the Levant (cat. 401), but the gold models of the Oxus Treasure and most Cypriot chariot models show the use of two draught poles with traction provided by a team of four horses under either a pair of two- or a single four-horse yoke (cat. 399). This is also the arrangement found in chariot A7 that was buried with draught team and harness at Salamis in Cyprus.[12] Although seemingly a very unwieldy design, modern experiments with this type of draught have demonstrated that the turning circle of

59 An anthropoid linchpin holding in place the spoked wheel of a royal chariot on the east side of the Apadana at Persepolis. The form of the spokes is distinctive of the Achaemenid period.

two-pole chariots was only 'a sweep of about 10 metres'.[13] Harnessing was limited to a neck-strap, to keep the yoke in place, and a 'backing element' in the form of a strap passing under the belly and probably joined to the yoke. These straps are sometimes highly decorated, and, on royal chariot horses, a bell-shaped, fringed ornament hangs at the withers, probably derived from the earlier 'menat'-inspired collar counterpoises of earlier vehicles. Fan-shaped yoke ornaments, again continuing an earlier tradition, are shown at Persepolis (cats 25, 26) and four originally decorated the yoke of an Oxus model (cat. 399). Reins were passed through terrets on the yoke.

RIDING

Horses were ridden astride, although the infirm and women may have ridden in a side saddle on asses. This was the method of riding adopted by Assyrian kings, presumably at a time when riding on horseback, rather than in a chariot, was still not entirely respectable. It is revealing that the most basic techniques of horsemanship, even mounting, could benefit from Persian expertise, as when Xenophon advised his Greek readership that: 'It is well for the groom to know how to give a leg-up in the Persian fashion, so that his master himself, in case he is indisposed or is getting old, may have someone to put him up conveniently' (Xenophon, *Horsemanship* VI.1.12). Persian saddle cloths, fastened with girths and breastband, were recognized as highly distinctive, with rich decoration and edged with a fringe or characteristic stepped tabs.[14] A saddle cloth of this type, made of felt, was found in barrow 5 at Pazyryk in southern Siberia (fig. 60). Simple pad saddles, as found at Pazyryk, may possibly have been used, concealed by the saddle cloth, but hard stirrups at least were a much later invention.[15]

POST SERVICE

There is nothing in the world which travels faster than these Persian couriers … It is said that men and horses are stationed along the road, equal in number to the number of days the journey takes – a man and a horse for each day. Nothing stops these couriers from covering their allotted stage in the quickest possible time – neither snow, rain, heat, nor darkness.

(Herodotus, *History* VIII.98)

Horsemen, runners and express messengers were employed in the royal post service along the network of roads – semi-paved in part, at least – within the Achaemenid Empire, one messenger for each daily stage, according to Herodotus.[16] Texts from Persepolis give information about the officials and other travellers using the royal roads often to travel over long distances

60 A rider in Median dress walking beside his mount shown on a woollen pile carpet from barrow 5 at Pazyryk in Siberia. *State Hermitage, St Petersburg.*

throughout the empire (cat. 310). These texts, which note the rations issued to travellers, preserve the titles in Elamite or Persian for a sophisticated organization of specialists under the direction of officials called *astandes* (preserved in Greek sources). These included 'road controller' (*datimara*; mentioned by Herodotus under the name *hodophylakai*), 'travelling companions' (*barrišdama*), 'caravan leader' (*karabattiš*) and the elite 'express messenger' (*pirradaziš*), known from Greek sources as *aggaros*, whose speed of travel so fascinated Greek authors. A similar system, on a lesser scale but using some of the same routes, is known from eighth-century Assyrian sources (this seems to have made extensive use of light mule carts rather than horsemen). According to Herodotus, the main Achaemenid royal road linked Sardis in western Anatolia with Susa, but this was only part of a substantial network of roads and tracks, 'safe to travel by, as it never leaves inhabited country', apparently marked at regular intervals with 'milestones' and furnished with guards and regular royal staging posts with inns.

A vivid account of the practicalities of heavy road transport in the empire is preserved in an anecdote by Xenophon; this aside over the baggage train of Cyrus the Younger's army neatly encapsulates Greek obsessions with Persian appearance, organization and discipline:

Once in particular, when they came upon a narrow, muddy place which was hard for the wagons [*amaxa*] to get through, Cyrus halted with his train of nobles and dignitaries and ordered Glus and Pigres to take some of the barbarian troops and help to pull the wagons out. But it seemed to him that they took their time with the work; accordingly, as if in anger, he directed the Persian nobles who accompanied him to take a hand in hurrying on the wagons. And then one might have beheld a sample of good discipline: they each threw off their purple cloaks [*porphurous kandus*] where they chanced to be standing, and rushed, as a man would run to win a victory, down a most exceedingly steep hill, wearing their very costly tunics and many-coloured trousers [*poikilas anaxuridas*], some of them, indeed, with necklaces [torcs?] around their necks and bracelets on their arms; and leaping at once, with all this finery, into the mud, they lifted the wagons high and dry and brought them out more quickly than one would have thought possible.

(Xenophon, *Anabasis* I.5.7)

SHIPS AND BOATS

Most long-distance commerce would have been by river or sea[17] – Darius I is said to have constructed the first Suez canal expressly for this purpose. The general peculiarities and cargoes of riverine transport in Mesopotamia and Egypt are amply documented by

Herodotus (*History* I.194), and in a more detailed, day-to-day level in cuneiform and Aramaic texts (cat. 312).[18] The movement of materials for the construction of Persepolis records the transportation of wood by Assyrians, presumably as logs and in a similar manner to the movement of logs for Sargon II's palace at Khorsabad. The unique vessels of these rivers are also depicted in Assyrian reliefs, engaged on building projects, and, indeed, remained little changed into modern times. As pontoons, boats also provided the basis of probably the majority of bridges, most famously the temporary structures over the Hellespont for Xerxes' punitive expedition against the Greeks (Herodotus, *History* VII.36), but also for all manner of more permanent water crossings (Herodotus, *History* I.193; Xenophon, *Anabasis* I.2.5, II.4.13).

WEAPONRY AND WARFARE
THE ACHAEMENID ARMY

The Greek and Persian wars have inspired innumerable studies of the warfare of the period. There is not space here to discuss in detail the many recent works on Greek warfare, but they invariably treat the Persian army in isolation (if at all) without knowledge of, or any reference to, the 2,500 years of Near Eastern military tradition of which the Persians were the direct inheritors.[19]

The army was firmly under the command of the king, his family and his closest companions.[20] The armed might available to the king is a significant topic in Achaemenid art. It is represented, for example, on palace reliefs in glazed brick from Susa (cat. 51), and in stone at Persepolis (cat. 33) in the form of the Persian guardsmen possibly to be identified as the so-called 'Immortals'. They made up a 10,000-strong corps, according to Greek sources, and were depicted in the minor arts, for example as the guardsmen and cavalry featured on seals (cat. 414). It is significant that Achaemenid palace reliefs do not, unlike their Assyrian predecessors, depict actual warfare, but focus instead on soldiers in court dress. Thus direct military force is not celebrated in itself, but is hinted at subliminally as the ultimate sanction of the great king against the transgressor and the rebellious.

ORIGINS OF THE ARMY

No race is so ready to adopt foreign ways as the Persian; for instance, they wear the Median costume as they think it handsomer than their own, and their soldiers wear the Egyptian corselet [fig. 61].

(Herodotus, *History* I.135)

As noted in the introduction to this chapter, there are many threads of cross-cultural influences in the Achaemenid Empire. In the military sphere they include the use of divine insignia carried in chariots as an army standard;[21] the adoption of pieces of equipment such as the Elamite *akinakes* and Elamite 'court' dress or items of armour; the adoption of a possible Elamite tradition of massed infantry archery; the use of so-called 'dipylon', figure-of-eight or 'waisted' shields;[22] the adoption of the 'Egyptian corselet' (described in Herodotus, *History* II.182 and III.47.2, worn also by Assyrians IX.63); the wearing of 'Saka' armour and Kurgan-style helmets (the latter also known earlier in Elam); and, perhaps most significantly, aspects of military drill and ritual known from Assyrian sources and also preserved in Herodotus.

Given the long military dominance of Assyria in the Near East it has sometimes been suggested that the formidable Neo-Assyrian military was likely to have been a formative influence on the Medes and Persians, but, until recently, there has been little direct evidence.[23] A relief fragment from the North Palace at Nineveh (fig. 62), showing Elamite and other archers, and Assyrian guard spearmen marching towards a group of priests, has long been identified (on the basis of the feather or floral crowns matching the fluted caps on guardsmen from the Persepolis reliefs) as perhaps showing auxiliary archers from Persia.[24] The Assyrian guards do not wear garlands in this fragment, but similar guardsmen do in other surviving fragments. The scene depicted is likely to be a ceremonial parade at Arbela following the return of the victorious Assyrian army from their great victory over the Elamites at the River Ulai in 653 BC. The much-abraded surface of the relief has until now concealed a vital detail: the guard spearmen are depicted marching with reversed spears. If we substitute 'garlands' for 'crowns' to describe the headgear it becomes clear that this fragment is actually a vital piece of evidence not only for military continuity in the ancient Near East, but also for the astonishing accuracy of at least some of the sources woven together by Herodotus to create the vivid account of Xerxes and his army marching across the bridge of boats into Europe in 480 BC:

They crossed over, the foot and horse all by the bridge nearest to the Pontus, the beasts of burden and the baggage train by the bridge towards the Aegean. The ten thousand Persians, all wearing garlands [*stephanos*], led the way, and after them came the mixed army of diverse nations. All that day these crossed; on the next, first crossed the horsemen and the ones who carried their spears reversed; these also wore garlands. After them came the sacred horses and the sacred chariot, then Xerxes himself and the spearmen and the thousand horse, and after them the rest of the army.

(*History* VII.55.1)

61 Composite drawing of the king's weapon-bearer shown on the central panels from the two sides of the Apadana at Persepolis. He carries an axe, a bow-case (*gorytus*) and short sword (*akinakes*), and wears Median dress.

Note the careful planning: baggage is separated from the main body and has its own bridge for operational reasons.

ARMY ORGANIZATION

The Assyrian and Achaemenid military systems also had much in common in their use of large professional guards' formations bolstering units of conscripts who were performing their obligations to the state in person or in kind. Both employed a decimal organization, with sections of ten men, companies of 100 and larger formations of 1,000 (the largest Persian body attested is the division of 10,000 men, possibly also known in Assyria); both used paid 'mercenaries', and both established small provincial forces.

It has been suggested that the name 'Immortals' (*athanoi* in Greek) for the famous corps of Persian infantry guardsmen is actually due to a Greek mistaking of the Old Persian word *anushiya* ('attendants' or 'retainers') for the Old Persian *anausha* ('immortals'). This would certainly accord more with the terminology in Assyrian and Neo-Babylonian texts where royal guards were also known as 'attendants' (*qurbute*). However, the similarity of the words in Old Persian may well have suggested the name of *anausha* for the guards as a Persian

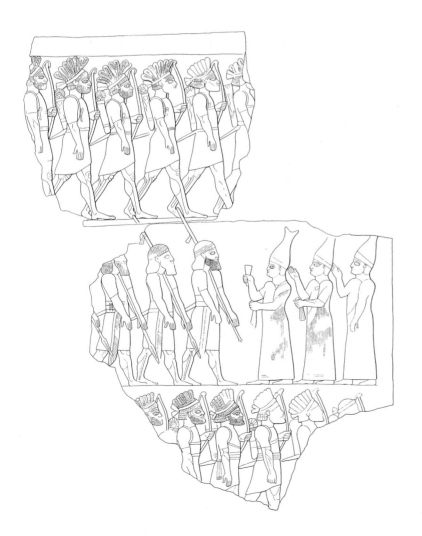

62 Drawing of two fragments of an Assyrian stone relief from the North Palace of Ashurbanipal at Nineveh showing a military parade matching Herodotus's description of the 'Immortals'. *British Museum, ANE 124923 and ANE 135204.*

nickname. Herodotus's statement that 'the Persians whom the king called Immortals/attendants' (*History* VII.211.1) is significant, since Assyrian kings could also refer to their elite troops using epithets commonly applied to divine heroes (as found in the usage of the term *huradu*, for example).

Persian written sources can give us information on ration lists and some technical terms, but not on how these armies fought. It is difficult to assess the capabilities of the Persian armies through the more ample Greek written sources because of their inherent bias, and the ubiquitous use of literary topoi (see Villing in this volume, pp. 236–43). For example, most scholars now dismiss the idea that Persian armies massively outnumbered their Greek opponents, based on logistical considerations and the need to garrison lines of communication; indeed by the time of Xerxes' offensive in Greece numbers must have been evenly matched.

CHARIOTS IN WARFARE

Modern views of the military role of chariots in the ancient Near East are especially confusing and contradictory. According to some scholars, chariots were primarily a 'mobile firing platform', and a flanking and pursuit arm which evolved into largely stationary command and prestige vehicles with the development of cavalry in the first millennium BC. There are, however, many problems with this view of chariot warfare. For example, it ignores the very large numbers of chariots attested in textual sources for the Late Bronze and early Iron Age (and the attendant difficulties of manoeuvring many hundreds of vehicles in any sort of primarily 'skirmishing' role), and, indeed, the distant origins of fighting vehicles in the third millennium BC. It also fails to take account of the evidence that Babylonian charioteers were still being mustered for military service in Egypt in the reign of Darius I.

It seems more likely that the rapid evolution of the cavalry resulted in Near Eastern military chariots abandoning a multi-purpose role to concentrate on their strengths in an area to which the inherently more flexible cavalry were as yet poorly suited, namely as a close-combat 'threat' weapon. This was a process that finally culminated in the famous scythed chariot developed in the Achaemenid period:

> From each of these there projected out beyond the trace horses scythes three spans long [*c.* 70 cm] attached to the yoke, and presenting their cutting edges to the front. At the axle housings there were two more scythes pointing straight out with their cutting edges turned to the front like the others, but longer and broader. Curved blades were fitted to the ends of these.

> (Diodorus XVII.53.2)

Diodorus's mention of trace horses reflects Greek, not Persian draught. Curtius (IV.9.5) adds that a spear projected forward from the end of the chariot pole and that blades below the chariot reached towards the ground.

Deployed in hundreds, rather than in the thousands of the period of classic chariot warfare, the Achaemenid scythed chariot was probably specially adapted to compensate for the effect of fewer chariots by exaggerating the weaponry that they carried. As a seminal modern work has it: 'Carrying only a driver, and with iron scythes attached to the axle ends and under the floor, with a high armoured box, said to be "like a turret", it was designed to terrify the enemy and break up his battle formation, thus enabling the mounted troops and infantry that followed to charge and decide the battle.'[25] But these chariots were deployed in too few numbers to have any significant effect (as recognized by Xenophon).

CAVALRY

> There was no more javelin-throwing and no manoeuvring of horses, as usual in cavalry engagements.
>
> (Arrian, *Anabasis* III.15.2)

Persian pictorial sources and Greek texts show that the bow and javelin were the chief weapons of Persian horsemen (cats 420, 421), while cuneiform sources provide more details of equipment. A text of 423/2 BC from the Murashu archive lists the armour and weapons of a cavalryman, including a horse with girth and reins, a saddle cloth, an iron corselet, helmet, what may be a neck-protector, a bronze-faced shield, 130 arrows and two *azmaru* throwing/thrusting spears.[26] Such spears were called *palta* by Xenophon, who recommended them over the long Greek lance, together with Persian forms of cavalry armour:

> Since the rider is seriously imperilled in the event of his horse being wounded, the horse also should be armed, having head, chest, and thigh pieces: the last also serve to cover the rider's thighs. But above all the horse's belly must be protected; for this, which is the most vital part, is also the weakest. It is possible to make the cloth serve partly as a protection to it. The quilting of the cloth should be such as to give the rider a safer seat and not to gall the horse's back.

> Thus horse and man alike will be armed in most parts. But the rider's shins and feet will of course be outside the thigh-pieces. These too can be guarded if boots made of shoe-leather are worn: there will thus be armour for the shins and covering for the feet at the same time.

Herodotus notes that the Persian, Median and Elamite cavalry of Xerxes' punitive expedition against Greece were armed like the infantry, except that some wore bronze or iron helmets (*History* VII.84). Achaemenid cavalrymen on cylinder seals and in some Anatolian monuments appear to wear items of armour adopted from the Saka, in the form of protective shields fitted to the back or arm, high collars and domed helmets known from Central Asian burials. Other armours – combined rider-and-horse leg and thigh defences – are also known from Greek and Anatolian sources. Greek historians of the Persian Wars tended to downplay the role of cavalry in battle, and therefore it is somewhat overlooked that the decisive battle of Plataea only came about following the Greek army's near collapse from the highly successful skirmishing attacks of the Persian horsemen. The Persians seem to have perceived the ragged Greek retreat to a stronger position to be a rout and advanced too hurriedly in pursuit.

INFANTRY

Although often represented in court or Persian dress, military battle-dress was based upon the Median dress, or riding costume, also observed in battle by Herodotus and Xenophon:

> The nations of which the army [Xerxes' army] was composed were as follows: First the Persians themselves: the dress of these troops consisted of the tiara, or soft felt cap [*kidaris*], embroidered tunic with sleeves, a coat of mail looking like the scales of a fish, and trousers [*anaxyrides*]; for arms they carried light wicker shields, quivers slung below them, short spears, powerful bows with cane arrows, and daggers swinging from belts beside the right thigh … The Median contingent … was equipped in the same way as the Persians … that armour is originally Median and not Persian.
>
> (*History* VII.6 1.1, 7.62)

The basic description is quite accurate, and matches in general appearance, if not in detail, for example the Persepolis Apadana reliefs (fig. 63).

Persian infantry were seemingly formed into formations of mixed archers and shieldbearers with spears, as also attested in earlier Assyrian sources. Spearbearers,

63 Drawing of a Persian infantryman shown on a Greek cup (Berlin 3156) with a shield made of wooden rods inserted through a leather sheet. Such shields are also illustrated at Persepolis and have been found in excavations at Pazyryk, Siberia.

arštibara, are known from Persian sources; and *sparabarai*, defined by the Greek lexicographers as 'troops bearing wicker shields', are derived from an assumed Persian form *sparabara*, or 'shieldbearer'. In earlier Assyrian texts similar terms are used interchangeably for 'soldiers'. It is likely that a battle array of this kind would be highly effective when facing the large mounted forces known in the Near East since at least the second millennium BC. A horse is a large and vulnerable target for archery; well-equipped infantry is less vulnerable – as the Persians were to discover. It is probable that Achaemenid formations followed the Elamite tradition of maximizing the number of archers in the infantry units, unlike the Assyrians who seem to have maintained a 50:50 ratio of archers to shielded spearmen.

THE PERSIAN NAVY

The trireme, or fast, three-banked ship designed for ramming, was the standard warship of the Achaemenid period. Persia had created a trireme fleet in the Mediterranean as early as 525 BC (Herodotus, *History* III.19). Indeed, according to Thucydides (I.13.2), Corinth was

first *amongst the Greeks* to use the trireme; Clement of Alexandria (late second to early third century AD) attributed its invention to the Sidonians (*Stromateis* I.16.36). It is even possible that an early form of the three-banked ship was invented by the Phoenicians in the eighth century BC under pressure from the Assyrians; similarly the true trireme may have been developed to serve Persian imperial needs.[27] Ephorus of Cyme refers to the Persian fleet as the royal navy (*basilikos stolos*) and states that the king furnished the ships, and that the Ionian Greeks (and other seafaring peoples), primarily the Phoenicians, supplied the crews (Diodorus Siculus XI, 3.7).

Herodotus gives a total for the Persian fleet mustered against the Greeks as 1,207 triremes (*History* VII.89.1) and nearly 2,000 other vessels. However, this is possibly inspired by the 'catalogue of ships' in Homer, and, if true, would have required more than a quarter of a million men as crew! As with the land forces, if the figure has any basis in reality, then it might reflect the total skilled manpower available in the coastal provinces, of which only a fraction might practically be mustered at any one time.

1 The frontiers of the huge Central Asian hinterland make estimates of size difficult. At around 7,500,000 square kilometres (2,900,000 square miles) the Achaemenid Empire was the same size or larger than the Roman and Han Chinese Empires at their peak.
2 'The horses are called Nesaean because there is in Media a wide plain of that name, where the great horses are bred' (Herodotus, *History* VII.40.3). Arrian (*Anabasis* VII.13.1) claims that 150,000 mares were pastured there.
3 Mardonius rode a grey at Plataea (Herodotus, *History* IX.63); 'The sacred chariot of Zeus was drawn by eight white horses' (VII.40.4). Ordinary mounts were apparently usually black (Aeschylus, *Persae* 318).
4 For camels used as paired draught in a seemingly ritual context see Calmeyer 1975: 13/3.
5 Delaporte 1923: A791.
6 For example, there were supposedly at least 400 food wagons in the baggage train of Cyrus the Younger's army (Xenophon, *Anabasis* I.10).
7 Sturt 1923: 17ff.
8 Arrian, *Ach.* 70; Xenophon, *Cyr.* III.1.40, VI.4.11; Curtius III 3, 14–25; 13, 10–11.
9 For vehicle finds from Georgia see Kipiani 1999:

7–18; Kipiani 2000: 74–95.
10 Studniczka 1907: no. 32.
11 Littauer and Crouwell 1979: 146–7.
12 Karageorghis 1973: 73.
13 Crouwell 1987: 113.
14 Goldman 1984.
15 For soft stirrups see Littauer 1981.
16 Plutarch (*Vit. Alex* XVIII.7) says that the royal messenger service were dressed in distinctive cloaks.
17 For travel costs overland in the late Roman empire doubling in only 150 miles see Garnsey *et al.* 1983: 104, n. 46.
18 Abraham 2004: 84–118.
19 Postgate 2000 summarizes the state of research of ancient Near Eastern armies. Recent studies on ancient Greek warfare: Hanson 1989, Van Wees 2004, Hanson (ed.) 1991, to cite only a few.
20 Herodotus lists the Persian commanders of the army corps, nearly all connected in some way to the royal family.
21 Persian examples described variously, but apparently a winged disc: Herodotus, *History* VII.40; Xenophon, *Anabasis* I.10.
22 Possibly of Anatolian origin. A bronze element similar to the shield boss of a waisted shield, as depicted at Persepolis, has been found on Samos

(Jantzen 1972: pl. 56/B1681).
23 Dandamayev 1997; Liverani 1995.
24 Not least because it has sometimes been dismissed as completely fictional: Sekunda 1992: 12–13.
25 Littauer and Crowell 1979: 152.
26 Ebeling 1952.
27 Morrison 1995: 55. Perhaps these early three banked ships were the origin of the early Egyptian 'triremes' of Necho.

HORSES AND HARNESS

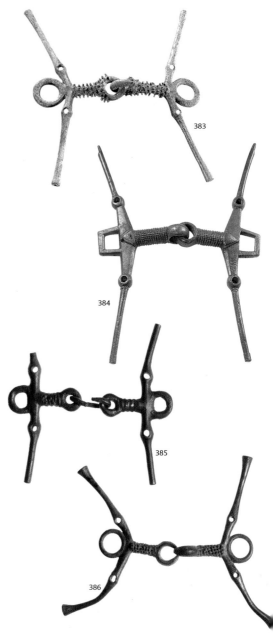

383

384

385

386

According to pictorial and archaeological sources, Achaemenid Persian draught and riding horses were both controlled by a simple bitted bridle. The commonest form known is a bronze snaffle with jointed canons, or mouthpiece, cast in one piece together with the usually curved or angular, rod- or bar-like cheekpieces and rein attachments. The attachments are ring-shaped or rectangular, while the cheekpieces, often with decorated terminals, have two holes to take the ends of the bifurcated cheekstraps.

Significantly, the canons are usually studded or barbed, which is a device to improve a rider's control (by increasing the effect of the bit on the horse's mouth). This arrangement particularly suggests a military context, where a horse will be operating in an unusual and frightening environment and where an extra emphasis on coercive control is required.

Fifteen bits of this type were found at Persepolis in the Treasury and the Garrison Quarters, and examples are also known beyond Persia from Georgia, Iraq, Turkey, the Levant, Egypt and Greece. Iron examples have been discovered, but are rare, while earlier inscribed examples are also known from Urartu. The cheekpieces of this form of bit are easily identifiable on the Persepolis reliefs on both Persian and tribute horses.

Interestingly, while the Alexander Mosaic chariot horses have this type of bit, the Persian cavalry horses are shown with Greek forms. This suggests that either the artist had only imperfect access to authentic references or, perhaps less likely, that some Persian cavalry had adopted the more extreme forms of Greek bitting (perhaps in addition to Greek lances, although this is also uncertain: Arrian, *Anabasis* III.15.2).

383 Bronze snaffle-bit

This bit has curved cheekpieces with plain, slightly swollen terminals. Each cheekpiece has double circular perforations for the ends of the cheekstrap, and integral round rein-attachments. It has a jointed mouthpiece and the canons are barbed.

This is the commonest type of Persian bit, a development of an earlier form with separate, straight bar cheekpieces. Fifteen examples were found by Schmidt in the Treasury at Persepolis (and others in subsequent excavations); horse bits of this type have also been discovered throughout the Near East, as well as in Georgia and even on the Acropolis at Athens.

Persepolis, probably from the Treasury or Garrison
  Quarters
L 25 cm (cheekpiece), W 21.5 cm (canons),
  max. Th 4 cm
Tehran, 204
Cf. Schmidt 1957: pl. 78/4; Tadjvidi 1976: 96–7,
  205, figs 151, 165; Moorey 1980a: 69–72

384 Bronze snaffle-bit

The bit has angular cheekpieces, each with double circular perforations for the ends of the cheekstrap. These are decorated with ridges forming a triangle at the junction with the canons, below the integral square rein-attachments. The terminals are flattened and plain; one end has a cylindrical thickening while the other end is cut away. It has a jointed mouthpiece and the canons are lightly studded.

Persepolis, found in Hall 38 of the Treasury
  (PT5 819)
L 37 cm (cheekpiece), W 31 cm (canons),
  max. Th 5 cm
Tehran, 334
Schmidt 1957: pls 78: 3, 79: 8

385 Bronze snaffle-bit

This example has slightly curved bar cheekpieces, swollen around double perforations for the cheek-strap, and slightly swollen terminals. The canons are joined by a separate ring, a rare variant of the standard type, and are barbed.

Found at Warka, Iraq
Excavated by W.K. Loftus and acquired in 1856
L 15.24 cm (cheekpiece)
British Museum, ANE 91187
Potratz 1966: 117, pl. LII/122

386 Bronze snaffle-bit

This has curved cheekpieces with plain, flattened, slightly swollen terminals. Each cheekpiece has double circular perforations for the ends of the cheekstrap, and integral round rein-attachments. It has a jointed mouthpiece and the canons are barbed.

Probably from Deve Hüyük, Syria
Acquired in 1913
L 21.6 cm/25.4 cm (cheekpieces), W 21.59 cm
  (canons)
British Museum, ANE 108759
Potratz 1966: pl. LII/124b; Moorey 1980a: no. 228,
  fig. 10/228

BRIDLE-HARNESS ATTACHMENTS

The Persepolis reliefs show that bridle ornaments in the shape of boars' tusks were mounted on horses' headstalls in sets of four and were used to align and divide the straps of the harness. They are depicted both on horses belonging to the Persians and on horses being led by tributaries (see fig. 58). Actual examples in stone and in bone, as well as three pierced boar's tusks, have been found at Persepolis (Tadjvidi 1976: 198, fig. 152; Schmidt 1957: 100, pl. 79/3-5; Herzfeld 1941: 271) and Babylon, and there are examples in stone from Susa. These bridle ornaments are thought to have developed from bone attachments that are linked with the nomadic people of the steppes, and it has been argued that they should be associated with Iranian tribes such as the Cimmerians and the Scythians.

389

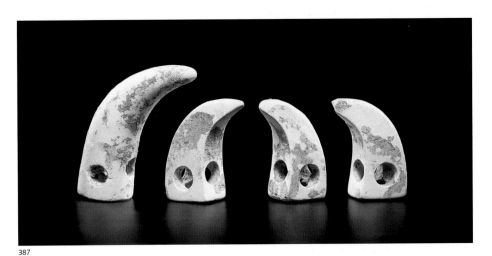
387

390

387 Four horse-harness strap-dividers

Made of white stone in the shape of boar's tusks. The three smaller dividers are pierced with interconnecting holes at right angles to each other and have an incised line along the outside face. The larger example is closed at the top and has no groove.

Persepolis, from Room 1 in the Fortifications
Excavations of A. Tadjvidi
H 5.2 cm, Diam 2.05 cm (base); H 3.65 cm,
   Diam 2 cm (base); H 3.6 cm, Diam 1.95 cm (base);
   H 3.6 cm, Diam 1.9 cm (base)
Tehran, 4525
Tadjvidi 1976: 198, fig. 152

388

388 Horse-harness strap-divider

Made of bronze, in the form of a boar's tusk. It is square in section and tapers to a point. The other end is hollow and is pierced on four sides with interconnecting holes. The end is closed.

Provenance unknown
Acquired in the nineteenth or early twentieth
   century
H 3.33 cm, W 3 cm, 1.58 cm x 1.53 cm (base),
   Wt 32.4 g
British Museum, ANE 1999-12-1,17
Curtis and Kruszynski 2002: no. 180, fig. 44, pl. 17

389 Horse-harness strap-divider

Made of copper-gold alloy with gold inlay, in the form of a griffin head. It has been deliberately given a dark patina in antiquity to enhance the surface contrast with the inlay.

Provenance unknown
Purchased from Messrs Rollin & Feuardent in 1891
H 3.2 cm
British Museum, ANE 1891-5-13, 3
Walters 1899: no. 2875

390 Horse-harness strap-divider

Bronze, in the form of a goat or ibex.

Said to have been acquired in the Troad
Purchased from Revd John Greville Chester in 1888
H 3.14 cm, W 3.18 cm, max. Th 1.55 cm, Wt 23.5 g
British Museum, GR 1888.5-12.12
Curtis and Kruszynski 2002: no. 185, fig. 45, pl. 18

391 Horse-harness strap-divider

In the form of a bronze plaque showing a recumbent goat or ibex in low relief. Two loop-fasteners are mounted on the back, which is flat.

Provenance unknown
Purchased in 1956 from Mrs Margarette Burg
H 2.94 cm, W 3.35 cm, max. Th 1.76 cm, Wt 33.5 g
British Museum, ANE 132120
Curtis and Kruszynski 2002: no.186, fig. 45, pl. 18

392 Horse-harness strap-divider

A bronze plaque showing a recumbent boar in low relief facing left. On the back, which is flat, is a hollow 'junction box' pierced by four lateral holes.

Provenance unknown
Purchased from Messrs Rollin & Feuardent in 1891
H 2.25 cm, W 4.1 cm, Th 1.7 cm, Wt 43 g
British Museum, GR 1891.5-13.2
Walters 1899: no. 2876; Curtis and Kruszynski 2002: no. 187, fig. 45, pl. 18

393 Gold strap-divider, probably a bridle-fitting

A plain disc with a flat top, at the back of which is a hollow 'junction box' with four openings at right angles to each other.

Oxus Treasure
Bequeathed in 1897 by A.W. Franks
Diam 2.4 cm, Wt 6.5 g
British Museum, ANE 124049
Dalton 1964: no. 146, fig. 69; Curtis and Kruszynski 2002: no. 174, fig. 41, pl. 16

394 Hemispherical gold disc

Embossed with a pair of recumbent boars placed head to tail, each facing a goat's head. There is a stout loop for attachment on the reverse.

Oxus Treasure
Bequeathed in 1897 by A.W. Franks
Diam 4.3 cm, Wt 23.3 g
British Museum, ANE 123944
Dalton 1964: no. 43, fig. 50; Curtis and Kruszynski 2002: no. 175, fig. 42, pl. 16

395 Circular gold plaque

With embossed decoration showing the head of a roaring lion facing front. There is a cable pattern border and a thick gold wire loop for attachment on the back. This was probably a harness ornament.

Circular rings made of gold wire form part

391

392

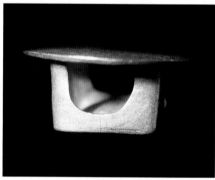

393

of the frontlet of the Oxus gold horse model (cat. 400) and are probably intended to represent circular plaques, or *phalerae*. A wooden disc from a tomb at Pazyryk in Siberia with a similarly stylized lion's mask is classified as a harness ornament (Rudenko 1970, pl. 138A) as are similar elements from barrow 4 at Pazyryk (Rudenko 1970: pls 111D and F).

Oxus Treasure
Bequeathed in 1897 by A.W. Franks
Diam 4.15 cm, Wt 10.2 g
British Museum, ANE 123941
Dalton 1964: no. 40, pl. XII; Curtis and Kruszynski 2002: no. 176, fig. 42, pl. 16g

396 Horse-harness ornament or silver shield-boss

With gold overlay, consisting of a circular disc with embossed centre pierced by five holes.

There is a guilloche pattern around the edge, and between the rim and the central boss is a hunting scene involving three riders on horseback. They are wearing Median dress with caps and ornate trouser-suits. They ride without stirrups, which were not known at this time. The horses wear patterned saddle-cloths secured with a breaststrap and fringed at the back, and their tails are tied in mud-knots with bows. The ornate saddlecloths may be compared with those shown on the pottery horses (cats 410–12). Two of the horsemen converge on a pair of ibexes, one of which has already been struck by a spear. One of these horsemen is armed with a spear and the other with a bow and arrow. The third horseman, again armed with a spear, pursues two deer, one of which has a broken spear sticking into

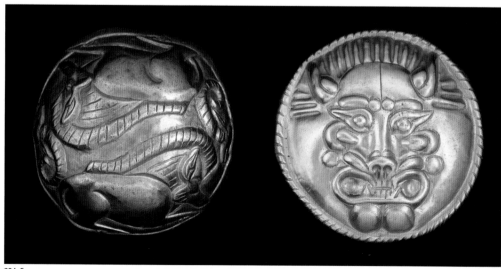

394–5

CHARIOTS AND CARTS

it. In front of the ibexes is a hare, but as Professor B.A. Litvinsky has pointed out, Dalton was mistaken in thinking that one of the riders was aiming an arrow at the hare.

Dalton pointed out that the figure-of-eight or waisted-shield types at Persepolis are sometimes represented with similar circular fittings in the centre (Dalton 1964: fig. 47), but the similarities are not close. Instead, the Persepolis representations are best paralleled by a circular bronze disc from Samos (Jantzen 1972: 60, pl. 56 B 1681). So it is more likely that this piece is a harness ornament, or *phalera*, in which case the central holes could be for attachment of a tassel, or to secure the disc to harness.

Oxus Treasure
Bequeathed in 1897 by A.W. Franks
Diam 9.65 cm, Wt 29 g
British Museum, ANE 123925
Dalton 1964: no. 24, pl. X; Litvinsky 2001: 157–8, fig. 9

398

398 Cylinder seal in green and grey-brown clouded chalcedony

The king stands in a chariot driven towards the right, and aims a third arrow at a rampant wounded lion. The two horses are leaping over the body of a fallen lion. Above is a figure in a winged disc. The scene is flanked by palm trees, between which is a trilingual cuneiform inscription in Old Persian, Elamite and Babylonian (SDa): 'I [am] Darius, great king' (the word 'great' only occurs in Babylonian). This was probably a seal of office (cf. Garrison and Root 2001: pl. 281).

Said to have been found in Lower Egypt
Acquired from the Salt Collection in 1835
H 3.7 cm, Diam 1.7 cm
British Museum, ANE 89132
Pope 1938: IV, pl. 123A; Boardman 2000: 161, fig. 5.9; Merrillees 2005: no. 16

396–7

397 Gold disc

The disc is convex, with embossed decoration showing an eagle in the centre, surrounded by a band of lotus-flower decoration. There is a scalloped border around the edge and at the back is a ring for attachment. This was possibly a harness ornament.

Oxus Treasure
Bequeathed in 1897 by A.W. Franks
Diam 9.8 cm, Wt 39 g
British Museum, ANE 123926
Dalton 1964: no. 25, pl. XI

399

399 Gold model four-horse chariot

The chariot box or cab is open at the back. It has an irregular square front, wider at the top than the bottom, ornamented with two incised bands in saltire, probably representing diagonal bracing struts as shown on the seal above and the copper-alloy model from the Louvre, cat. 401 (also on a seal of possibly Neo-Elamite date: Schmidt *et al.* 1989: pl. 233, no. 43). These bands are decorated with triangles and have a Bes head at the intersection. The floor is covered with cross-hatching, most probably representing a flooring of interlaced leather thongs. The two large wheels each have eight or nine spokes, and the running surfaces are studded with small pellets to represent the bulbous heads of large stud-like nails which in the full-size original would have secured a tyre and felloe-sheathing of bronze. A seat, in the form of a narrow strip of gold, runs from the front to back of the interior. On this is seated the principal

figure. He wears a long robe reaching to the ankles, the sleeves of which appear to be empty like those of the *kandys*. On his head is a hood or cap and around his neck is a gold wire torc.

The driver wears a similar cap without a fillet, a short girded tunic and a wire torc; his legs are also formed of wires. The two human figures are fixed to the chariot by wires.

The chariot is pulled via a pair of draught-poles fixed to four horses under a single four-bay yoke, as in an excavated chariot from Salamis B in Cyprus. On the yoke, above each horse, is a large loop, representing the terrets, through which the wire reins pass; alternating with these loops were originally four crescentic fan-shaped yoke ornaments (found full-size made of sheet-bronze on the Salamis B chariot). The bits have large rings at the sides as rein attachments, and each animal has duplicate representations of the neck-strap and backing-element, the former with a pendant tassel, punched into the metal.

The horses are small, pony-sized animals, but otherwise have the appearance of ram-headed Nesaeans. Their tails are tied up in mud-knots and the hair of the forelock is pulled back, as shown on the Darius seal (cat. 398), and horse vessel (cat. 410), but not tied in a splayed tuft as shown on the Persepolis reliefs and elsewhere. Only nine legs of the horses survive and the spokes of one wheel are imperfect.

The profile of the cab or box and the general appearance of the wheel match representations of Achaemenid chariots on the sculptured façades of the Apadana at Persepolis, on the so-called Darius seal above, and the Alexander Mosaic. These do not show the fronts of the chariots, although the Alexander Mosaic and the scaraboid seal (cat. 407) suggest that, other than band decoration, they were plain. The royal chariots depicted at Persepolis on the eastern stairway of the Apadana have a different decorative scheme;

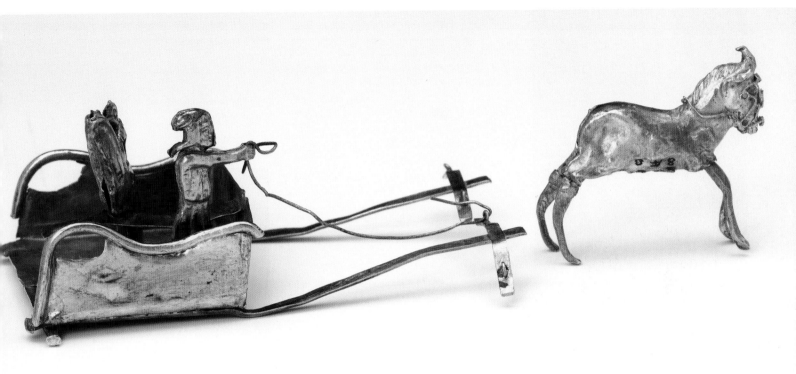

400

the box is edged with a frieze of striding lions and decorated with a lattice pattern. They are also equipped with quivers. The use of a Bes head on the Oxus chariot model is compatible with it having been made for a child or as a votive offering, as Bes was regarded as being a protective deity of the young, and his popularity throughout the Persian Empire is demonstrated by the discovery of amulets (for example, in a hoard at Babylon) and on gold jewellery.

Oxus Treasure
Bequeathed in 1897 by A.W. Franks
L 18.8 cm
British Museum, ANE 123908
Dalton 1964: no. 7, fig. 20, pl. IV
Cf. Karageorghis 1973: 79, figs 10–11, pls CCL–I; Littauer and Crouwel 1979: 145–52, fig. 82; Abdi 1999: fig. 8/4; Kipiani 1999: 7–18; Kipiani 2000: 74–95

400 Gold model chariot

The chariot has no wheels, and contains a driver and a now-headless seated figure. There is only a single surviving gold model horse. The vehicle has a long body with a central box-divider and seat, and added wire stiffening for the top edge of the sides forming two open loop handgrips at the rear of the box. The axle is formed by gold wire and is placed at the rear edge of the box. There are two draught-poles, as the model above, but made of flat gold strip. Unlike that model, there are two two-horse yokes, each originally fitted with two terret rings for reins (only one of which survives).

The horse has a highly detailed headstall made of gold wire, which includes a frontlet consisting of a central diamond joined to two upper and lower rings, probably intended to represent circular plaques or *phalerae* as found on a bridle from barrow 5, Pazyryk (Rudenko 1970: pl. 114; see also pls 73A–B, 90G–H).

Oxus Treasure
Bequeathed in 1897 by A.W. Franks
L 8.4 cm, W 4.7 cm; L 4.3 cm (horse)
British Museum, ANE 132256 (chariot), 123909 (horse)
Dalton 1964: 4, fig. 21 and unnumbered pl.

401

401 Bronze model chariot with figures of two divinities in Egyptian style

The chariot has a rectangular cab or box with external cross-braces in saltire on the front and sides, and raised bands on the upper edges and front angles. There are looped, round-topped handgrips at the top rear. Two six-spoked wheels are set under the middle of the cab and the two draught-poles run underneath the length of the floor. Each pole has an upper support secured to the front of the box (as also shown on the Darius seal, cat. 398, and on earlier Neo-Assyrian chariots).

Certain elements of the group are known prior to the first millennium BC, but the vehicle's combination of features indicates an Achaemenid date.

Said to come from 'Phoenicia'
Acquired in Beirut for the de Clerq Collection
H 6.5 cm (vehicle, excluding handgrips), W 10.8 cm,
  L 6.75 cm
Louvre, AO 22265
De Ridder 1905: 129ff., no. 209, pl. XXXII; Littauer,
  Crouwel and Collon 1976

402 Limestone model four-horse chariot with traces of red paint

There are two figures in the cab or box and both heads are now missing. There is a clear cab-divider/seat and the vehicle has two draught-poles and two two-horse yokes. It dates to the late sixth century BC.

From Idalion, Cyprus
Purchased from Sir Robert Hamilton Lang in 1873
H 19.5 cm
British Museum, GR 1873.3-20.93
Smith 1900: no. C84

403

403 Linchpin from a wheeled vehicle, probably a chariot

The upper part is of bronze cast on an iron core, in the form of a beardless man in an apparently sleeveless belted tunic and wearing a plain round, flat-topped Persian cap. His arms are flexed and his hands are shown resting on his chest. A ring on each wrist, made of metal strip and representing a bracelet, was probably intended to make a jingling noise as the vehicle moved.

Persepolis, from Hall 41 (PT6 206) of the Treasury
H 8.95 cm, max. W 7.7 cm, Th 2.75 cm
Tehran, 332
Schmidt 1957: 68, pl. 31/8; Calmeyer 1980b:
  100–101, no. A1, fig. 1

402

404

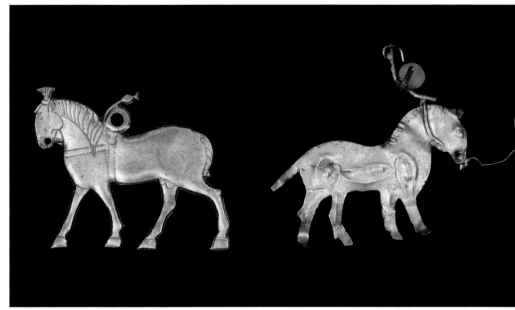

405 (right), 406 (left)

404 Linchpin from a wheeled vehicle, probably a chariot

Similar to cat. 403 above, in bronze with an iron core, but representing a female figure in a robe with her hands clasped below her breasts. Linchpins of this form, showing figures with clasped hands, are depicted in use on reliefs of chariots at Persepolis (Calmeyer 1980b: pls 21/13, 22/1–2, 23/1).

Persepolis
H 9.5 cm, max. W 4.1 cm
Persepolis Museum
Calmeyer 1980b: 100–101, no. A2, pl. 23/2, 24/1–3

405 Gold sheet cut-out figure of a horse

With punched and embossed details. There are the remains of an attached yoke with a circular yoke-standard and a short length of rein. This must originally have been a draught horse for a model chariot, possibly also made of metal sheet.

Oxus Treasure
Bequeathed in 1897 by A.W. Franks
H 3.4 cm, L 5.25 cm, Wt 5.5 g
British Museum, ANE 123946
Dalton 1964: no. 45, pl. XIV

406 Gold sheet cut-out figure of a horse

The horse, possibly intended to be a Nesaean, is more finely finished than the above, with punched and incised details of harness, mane (though not dressed in typical Persian style) and tail. The mouth is pierced, probably for wire reins now missing. The forelock is shown tied into a splayed tuft on the poll and there is a loop on the horse's back, probably for a wire yoke. If so, then this is a draught horse for another chariot model.

Oxus Treasure
Bequeathed in 1897 by A.W. Franks
H 4.2 cm, L 5.5 cm, Wt 9.5 g
British Museum, ANE 123947
Dalton 1964: no. 46, pl. XIII

407 Scaraboid stamp seal in carnelian

The seal is engraved in 'Graeco-Persian' style on the convex face with a mounted figure in Median dress, wearing a cap or hood and a cloak. He is seated on a tufted saddlecloth, and aiming a spear at two figures in a fleeing two-horse chariot. The charioteers wear rounded helmets or caps and long-sleeved tunics. The main figure appears to have a crest to his helmet and carries a small double-recurved bow. The chariot is superficially of Persian type, with an eight-spoke wheel (with decorative ferrules or turnings on the spokes) and a studded tyre. The front of the box, however, is open at the top with a double fenestration; this possibly owes more to East-Greek styles of vehicle. The reverse is engraved with a seated dog.

Many of the so-called Graeco-Persian seal stones produced during the fourth century BC were probably made in Asia Minor. They may have been commissioned by the local ruling satraps.

Said to be from Mesopotamia
Purchased from I Élias Géjou in 1911
L 2.4 cm, W 1.8 cm
British Museum, GR 1911.4-15.1
Walters 1926: no. 435, pl. 7; Boardman 1970: no. and pl. 864, col. pl. 307/3

407

RIDING

408

409

408 Gold figure of a male rider

The rider is wearing a high, stiff cap, trousers and a tunic with edge-decoration. He was probably originally holding reins and mounted on a horse.

Oxus Treasure
Purchased from the 2nd Earl of Lytton in 1931
H 7.6 cm, Wt 69 g
British Museum, ANE 124098
Dalton 1964: after pl. XL

409 Cast bronze figurine of a horse and rider

The rider is wearing Median riding dress with a soft cap and an *akinakes* suspended from a waist belt on his right thigh. His tunic has edge decoration and he wears bracelets. The horse has a rectangular saddle blanket with edging tufts along the lower edge and stepped lappets at the rear. There is a strap below the blanket to secure either it or a pad-saddle and a breaststrap. The mane is pulled but has long strands on the lower neck and a forelock tied up into a splayed crest on the poll – all of which are distinctively Achaemenian features. The horse is shown in a fast gallop, and the pairs of fore and hind hooves are joined together for attachment to an ele-

ment now missing (perhaps a vessel). Similar riders are shown as border decoration in a pile hanging or carpet from barrow 5, Pazyryk (Rudenko 1970: pls 174–6); a decorated saddle blanket of felt with stepped lappets in Achaemenid style was recovered from the same barrow (see fig. 38) (Rudenko 1970: pl. 160).

Provenance unknown
Purchased from W. Talbot Ready in 1890
H 8.5 cm, L 10.1 cm
British Museum, ANE 117760
Ghirshman 1964: fig. 315; Curtis 2000:
   fig. 65

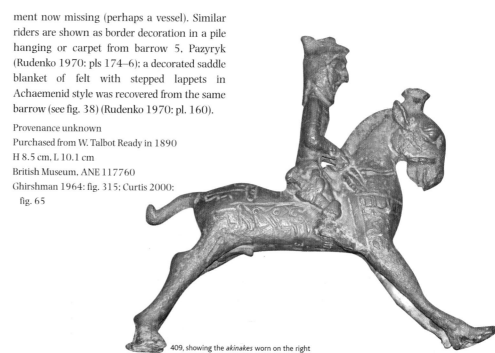

409, showing the *akinakes* worn on the right

410 Horse-shaped vessel

A 'horse rhyton' in yellow ceramic, with details of horse and harness added in red, yellow and black paint. It has a saddlecloth with stepped lappets.

Said to be from Maku, Azerbaijan
Found in 1924
H 21 cm, W 11 cm, L 31.5 cm
Tehran, 6700
Ghirshman 1964: 287–8, pl. 467, figs 347–8;
    Stronach 1974: 243ff., pl. LIII: 2; Moorey 1985:
    30, fig. 6a; Seipel 2000: no. 101

411 Horse-shaped vessel

In a buff ceramic with details of horse and harness added in purplish-red paint. It has a tufted saddlecloth. It can be dated to the fifth century BC.

Susa, Achaemenid Village I (Susa 1329/3179)
H 22.8 cm, W 10.5 cm, L 30 cm
Tehran, 8485
Ghirshman 1964: 289–91; Stronach 1974: 243ff., pl.
    LIII/1; Moorey 1985: 30, fig. 6b; Seipel 2000: no. 42

410

411

412

412 Fragmentary horse-shaped vessel

In a buff ceramic with added painted harness details, and tufted saddlecloth. It was found in a bathroom with other vessels and was perhaps used for perfumes or cosmetics, or in washing. Dated to the late fifth century BC.

Persepolis, from bathroom F6
A. Tadjvidi excavations (72/III/13)
H 6 cm, W 5.7 cm, L 9.7 cm
Tehran, 4181
Stronach 1974: 243ff., pl. LIII/4; Tadjvidi 1976:
    175, fig. 126

WEAPONRY, HUNTING AND WARFARE

413 Cylinder seal in blue chalcedony

The seal is engraved with two battle scenes divided by vertical lines, showing a figure in Persian dress, probably the king, fighting opponents who wear nomadic-style dress. This consists of a long-sleeved, thigh-length, cut-away coat, with double borders, with a girdle tied in front and high boots coming to a point at the knee, fastened with tassel-ended cords. The king has a quiver on his back with three tassels (probably with a practical use for cleaning arrows as well as for decorative effect) and containing a bow and arrows. In his right hand he grasps a long spear with a spherical terminal at the butt. The standing nomad in the wider scene wears a cap or hood with ribbon-like attachments which is falling off. In the space above the combatants is a version of the figure in the winged disc, and on the other a winged disc and a bust inside a circle.

Oxus Treasure

Bequeathed in 1897 by A.W. Franks

H 3.7 cm, Diam 1.1 cm

British Museum, ANE 124015

Dalton 1964: 31–2, no. 114, pl. XVI, fig. 114; Pope 1938: IV, pl. 124X; Boardman 2000: 160, fig. 5.5; Merrillees 2005: no. 66

414 Cylinder seal of red and pale brown limestone

An archer in Persian dress aims an arrow at a figure armed with a prominent battle-axe (cf. cat. 436), which he holds upright in both hands. This figure has a short pointed beard and wears a pointed hood or cap, with nomadic-style dress of a jacket and kilt or belted tunic and leggings – or possibly trousers – with folds. As well as the axe he is equipped with a large *gorytus* bow-case.

Between these figures are two animals facing right: a semi-crouching, snarling lion above, and a dog-like creature with bull's hooves below. To the side, facing left, is a monkey (?) with a staff and above it is a crescent. There is a small letter-like sign beneath the elbow of the figure on the left.

Provenance unknown

Acquired in 1945, with the assistance of the National Art Collections Fund, from the Southesk Collection, having been acquired for that collection in 1902 from J.J. Naaman

L 3 cm, Diam 1.3 cm

British Museum, ANE 129569

Carnegie 1908: 107–108, no. Qc32; Merrillees 2005: no. 38

415 Cylinder seal of pale blue chalcedony

The seal shows a battle scene, with the Persian royal hero preparing to stab an enemy dressed in nomad style with a distinctive pointed hat, tunic and leggings, and carrying an axe and a *gorytus*. Between them lies the body of a similarly dressed enemy which is being attacked by a rearing lion. Behind the royal hero, and attached to his waist by a rope around the neck, is a captive. A crowned figure in a winged disc is shown above a palm tree. This scene resembles that showing Darius's victory over his enemies on the rock relief at Bisitun. Two of the enemies may be 'pointed hat Scythians' who are depicted on reliefs from Persepolis.

Provenance unknown

Bequeathed by Miss M.F.T. Ready in 1959

H 2.15 cm, Diam 1.1 cm

British Museum, ANE 132505

Merrillees 2005: no. 65

416 Scaraboid stamp seal in greyish-blue chalcedony

The seal is set in a silver mount which may be modern. A rider in Median dress gallops towards the right and spears a boar that leaps towards him. The rider sits on a saddlecloth, with tufts along the rear edge, secured by a breaststrap.

Provenance unknown

Acquired before 1930

H 1.3 cm, Diam 2.0 x 2.8 cm (base)

British Museum, ANE 120325

Boardman 1970: 354, pl. 905

417 Cylinder seal of mottled blue and grey-blue chalcedony

A horse stands facing right. The dismounted rider in Median dress spears an advancing boar. The reading of the name, written in Aramaic above the horse, is uncertain, but it is probably of Iranian origin.

Provenance unknown

Purchased from J.R. Steuart in 1846

H 3.3 cm, Diam 2.2 cm

British Museum, ANE 89144

Pope 1938: IV, pl. 123R; Merrillees 2005: no. 12

418 Cylinder seal in grey, translucent sparry calcite

A rider in Median dress gallops from the right and aims a spear at a rampant lion.

Acquired by A.H. Layard in Mesopotamia between 1845 and 1851

H 2.5 cm, Diam 1.1 cm

British Museum, ANE 89583 (N1082)

Merrillees 2005: no. 9

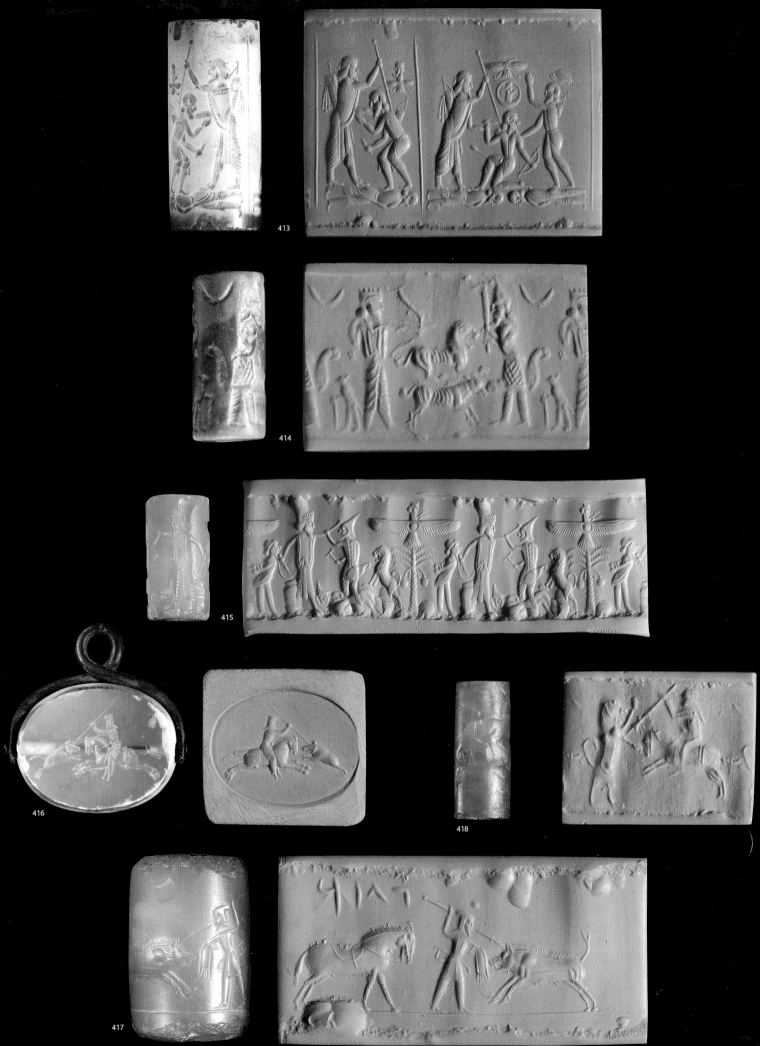

413

414

415

416

417

418

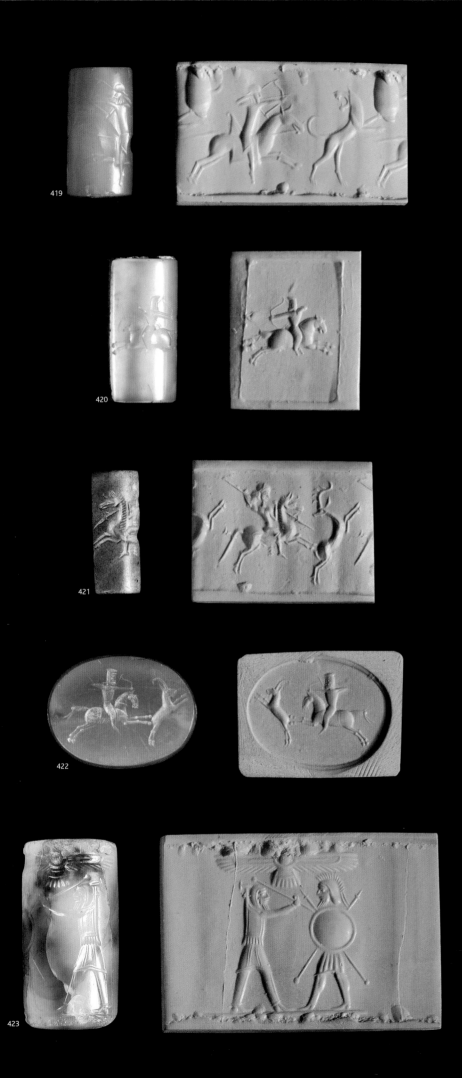

419 Cylinder seal of pale white-grey chalcedony

A rider in Median dress, with a *gorytus* at his waist, gallops towards the right and aims an arrow at a retreating rampant lion that turns its head to look back at him. The seal is late Elamite–Early Achaemenid.

Provenance unknown
Presented by G.D. Hornblower in 1940
H 2.35 cm, Diam 1.2 cm
British Museum, ANE 130808
Merrillees 2005: no. 6.

420 Cylinder seal in pale blue chalcedony

Only half of the seal remains. A rider in Median dress gallops towards the right and turns back in the saddle to aim an arrow from a double-recurved bow at a leaping lion, of which only the nose and forepaws survive. This is an example of the so-called 'Parthian shot', first known in the Near East from ninth-century Assyrian depictions: a skirmishing technique of the highly skilled horse-archer later made famous by the Parthians in the wars against Rome. The rider sits on a saddlecloth, with tufts along the rear edge, secured by a breaststrap.

Provenance unknown
Acquired in 1869
H 2.6 cm, Diam 1.4 cm
British Museum, ANE 89816
Merrillees 2005: no. 14

421 Cylinder seal of red and brown limestone

The seal shows a rider galloping towards the right and aiming a spear at a retreating, leaping stag that looks back at him.

Provenance unknown
Acquired from J.J. Naaman in 1909
H 2.2 cm, Diam 0.9 cm
British Museum, ANE 103013
Merrillees 2005: no. 3

422 Scaraboid stamp seal in greyish-blue chalcedony

A rider in Median dress gallops towards the left and aims an arrow at a retreating wild goat.

Provenance unknown
Acquired before 1930
H 1.3 cm, 2.0 x 2.8 cm (base)
British Museum, ANE 120326
Boardman 1970: 354, pl. 927

423 Cylinder seal in streaked grey chalcedony

There are remains of an iron pin in the perforation. Two soldiers face each other beneath a winged sun disc. On the left a soldier in Median dress, wearing a cuirass with a fringe (*pteruges*) and with an axe apparently carried in its high collar, aims a spear at a Greek hoplite who wears a crested Attic helmet and kilt, and carries a round shield and two crossed spears.

Provenance unknown
Purchased in 1859 at Sotheby's from J. Mayer via
    G. Eastwood, originally part of the Hertz Collection
H 3.3 cm, Diam 1.75 cm
British Museum, ANE 89333
Pope 1938: IV, pl. 124A; Merrillees 2005: no. 64

424

424 Impression of a cylinder seal

The seal shows a soldier in Persian dress aiming his spear at a vanquished Greek hoplite wearing a crested, possibly Corinthian, helmet. In the complete design, not present here, three further hoplites are in a line to the left with their hands tied behind their backs (Schmidt 1957: pl. 9, seal no. 28).

Persepolis
Excavations of A. Tadjvidi
L 2.6 cm, W 2.5 cm
Tehran, 6580
Tadjvidi 1976: pls 140–42

425 Athenian red-figured *hydria* (water-jar) with two Greeks fighting a mounted Persian

On the right a bearded Persian is mounted on a rearing white horse and aims a spear at a Greek warrior on foot. The Persian wears a soft skin hat (*kidaris*) with its long ear-flaps hanging down, an oriental trouser-suit, and soft shoes. The young warrior is equipped with a white *pilos*-style helmet, circular shield and a *chlamys* round his back. He thrusts up with his long spear at the Persian. On the left a wavy-haired archer, wearing a short *chiton* and with a quiver at his hip, aims his bow at the Persian.

This is one of the latest red-figured Athenian vases to show a fight between Greeks and Persians, dating to about 360–330 BC.

From Cyrenaica (Libya, north Africa)
Gift of George Dennis in 1866
H 29.5 cm
British Museum, GR 1866.4-15.244
Smith 1896: 183, no. E 233; Beazley 1963: 1471,
    no. 3 (near Group G); Raeck 1981: 120–21, 327,
    no. P 659

425

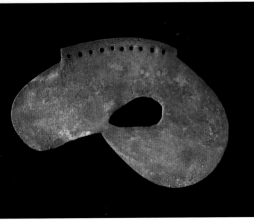

426

426 Copper *gorytus*-fitting

This thin metal plate with a row of ten holes along one edge was originally stitched onto the tip of a combined quiver/bow-case known as a *gorytus*. Its shape mimics that of a bird's beak and wattles, most probably that of a cockerel because of the resemblance of the neck of the *gorytus*, stretched when carrying a bow, to a cockerel when crowing. Quiver covers decorated to resemble a crowing cockerel are earlier shown used by horsemen, perhaps even Medes or Persians in Assyrian service, on a few seventh-century Assyrian reliefs (for example, Barnett *et al.* 1998: no. 351b, pls 258–9, 261).

Deve Hüyük, Syria
L 8.9 cm
British Museum, ANE 108681
Moorey 1980: 66–7, no. 218, fig. 10/218

427

427 Gold *gorytus*-fitting

Gold cut-out plaque in the shape of a stylized bird's head with a large curved beak and a coiled serpentine neck. At the back of the plaque are five loops for attachment. This plaque was evidently attached to cloth or leather, and most probably decorated the top of a *gorytus* or bow-case as shown on the Persepolis reliefs (see fig. 61) (Moorey 1985: 27).

Plaques for fixing to clothes, textiles and horse harness are well known from Scythian contexts, and stylized bird's heads with round bulging eyes and hooked beaks are a characteristic feature of Scythian art.

Oxus Treasure
Bequeathed in 1897 by A.W. Franks
L 3.35 cm, Wt 3.9 g
British Museum, ANE 123940
Dalton 1964: no. 39, pl. XIII

428 Arrowheads

Thirteen cast bronze tripartite socketed arrowheads and one large bronze bipartite arrowhead. Small, light arrowheads of this type, ideal for use by mounted archers, and quick and easy to manufacture, are the standard Persian form and are found throughout the empire. The type appears in the Near East around the seventh century BC in association with the Cimmerians and Scythians. It thereafter remained the commonest form of arrowhead until the Parthian period.

Persepolis, Fortifications
Excavations of A. Tadjvidi
L 2.5–4.25 cm, W 0.7–1.35 cm (tripartite)
L 6.01 cm, W 1.5 cm (bipartite)
Tehran 4193; 4194; 4196; 4198; 4199; 4202; 4204; 4209; 4223; 4237; 4265; 4289; 4299; 7184
Tadjvidi 1976: 209, fig. 172

429 Tripartite bronze javelin head or large arrowhead

Persepolis, from Room 5 in the Fortifications
Excavations of A. Tadjvidi
L 9.6 cm, W 3.15 cm, Diam 1.65 cm (socket)
Tehran, 4331
Tadjvidi 1976: 199, fig. 156

429

428

430 Gold dagger

Gold dagger with the handle ending in addorsed lions' heads. The hilt at the top of the blade is decorated with ibex heads.

Said to be from Hamadan
L 41.27 cm, W 10.47 cm, Wt 817 g
Illustrated London News, 21 July 1956, pl. on p. 107;
    Ghirshman 1964: fig. 328

431 Gold scabbard for an *akinakes*

With embossed decoration of hunting scenes. It was originally overlaid onto a wooden or leather sheath with a double-convex profile, with a separate chape, now missing. The reverse was plain. The wide upper part shows four riders on horseback, armed with long spears and attacking lions, within herring-bonepattern and serpentine borders. There is a winged disc above one pair of horsemen. The riders wear belted decorated dresses and tall hats, and are apparently barefoot. They are seated on rounded saddlecloths, the surfaces covered with small punched circles, the edges

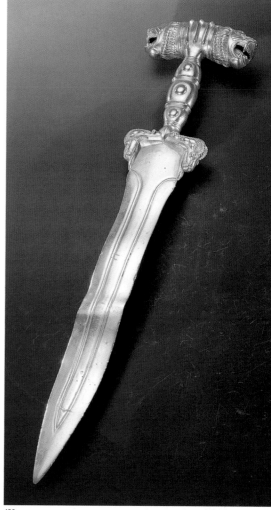

430

finished with decorative borders or fringes. The long narrow part of the scabbard has a further five horsemen and lions arranged in a line. At the top of scabbard on the back is a strap-fitting by which the scabbard was partly suspended. It has been restored from seven fragments.

This scabbard has sometimes been compared with Assyrian art of the seventh century BC because of the lion hunt theme and the tall fez-like hats of the riders; however, the horse harness is not Assyrian and has Scythian parallels, particularly with the rounded saddlecloths. David Stronach believes, partly because of the form of the winged disc, that this scabbard cannot be earlier than the reign of Darius and possibly dates from the reign of Artaxerxes II (404–359 BC).

Oxus Treasure
Bequeathed in 1897 by A.W. Franks
L 27.6 cm, Wt 160 g (with perspex support)
British Museum, ANE 123923
Dalton 1964: 9–11, no. 22, pl. IX; Moorey 1985:
    26–7; Stronach 1998; Curtis 2000: fig. 67

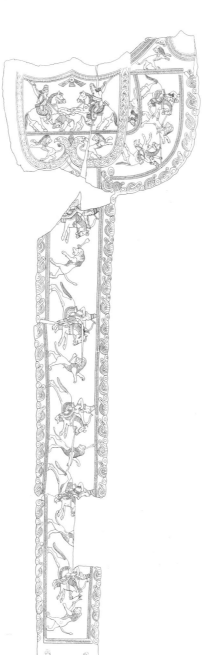

431

432

432 Scabbard for a small *akinakes* made of tamarisk wood

Made in two pieces and joined lengthways, this was originally decorated with gilded stucco, traces of which still survive.

Acquired in Egypt and purchased from Joseph Sams
  in 1834
L 28 cm, W 8.9 cm
British Museum, AES 5428
Barnett 1962: 95 n. 2, pl. IIc

433 Ivory or bone pommel for an *akinakes*

With ram's-head terminals.

Provenance unknown
Acquired in 1906. Formerly ex Clot Bey Collection
H 1 cm, W 4.5 cm, Th 1 cm
Louvre, N8331/MN 1373
Stucky 1985: no. 15, pl. 8; Moorey 1988a: fig. 75

434 Ivory or bone scabbard chape for an *akinakes*

The chape shows a lion attacking a goat.

Said to be from Egypt
Acquired in 1906. Formerly Clot Bey Collection
H 3 cm, W 4.5 cm, Th 1 cm
Louvre, N8336/MN 1376
Herzfeld 1941: fig. 367; Stucky 1985: no. 17, pl. 8

435 Ivory or bone scabbard chape

With carved relief decoration showing part of a stylized ram.

Provenance unknown
Purchased in 1961
H 4.4 cm, W 6.6 cm
British Museum, ANE 132925
Barnett 1962: 79, n. 4, pl. IIb

436 Bronze axehead

With a vertical socket and a long, thin blade. There is a modelled ram's head at the front of the junction of the blade with the socket. Rudenko suggests that the warrior from Pazyryk barrow 2 and all the sacrificed horses were killed by blows from axes of this type, which left distinctive wounds on the skulls (Rudenko 1970: 219). Cf. fig. 61.

Persepolis, found on the floor of the Hall
  of 100 Columns (PT4 1094)
H 4.9 cm, L 24 cm
Tehran, 2052
Schmidt 1957: pls 78/1, 79/1a–1b

437 Axehead

This axehead has a vertical bronze socket, closed at the top, and a long, thin iron blade. There is a stylized bird's head on the front of the socket beneath the blade and a projection at the back with a square hole. There are two circular holes at the bottom of the socket, presumably for attachment of the axehead to a haft.

Provenance unknown
Purchased in 1969
H 7.9 cm, L 20.25 cm, Wt 297.5 g
British Museum, ANE 135142
Curtis and Kruszynski 2000: no.178, fig. 43, pl. 17

438 Iron axehead

The axehead has a vertical socket and long, thin blade with a tubular projection at the back, and a carefully modelled sheep's head at the junction of socket and blade. It is made of wrought iron.

Provenance unknown
Purchased in 1969
H 5.7 cm, L 23.9 cm, Wt 532.5 g
British Museum, ANE 135855
Curtis and Kruszynski 2000: no.179, fig. 43, pl. 17

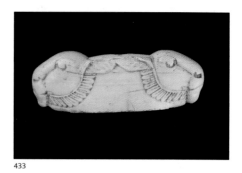

433

434

435

436

437

438

SHIPS AND BOATS

439 Amphora

With a stamp impression on the shoulder showing a galley of Phoenician type.

Susa, 'Donjon'
Excavations of R. de Mecquenem, 1928
Louvre, Sb 9278
Cf. de Mecquenem 1934 : 223; de Mecquenem
  1947 : 90, fig. 48

440 Clay sealing

Showing a galley of Phoenician type with a long conical ram. Warships of this distinctive type are first shown on Assyrian palace reliefs of the seventh century BC. At this early date the exact rowing arrangements are disputed, but by the Achaemenid period warships of this form are almost certainly 'three-banked' ships. This sealing was originally attached to another object with cord, burnt traces of which still survive. It has four other impressions apart from the galley, showing the king and a priest in a ritual ceremony, a male figure in a crescent moon, a scene of heroic encounter and a mythical combat scene.

Persepolis, Treasury (PT4 704)
L 6.3 cm, W 5.6 cm
Tehran, 1921/58
Schmidt 1957: pl. 9, no. 32

439

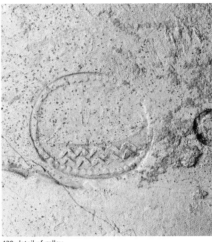

439, detail of galley

440

11

PERSIA AND GREECE

Alexandra Villing

INTRODUCTION

It is a commonplace that the ancient Greeks despised the Persians, following the destruction inflicted on Greece in the cataclysmic Graeco-Persian Wars of 490–480/79 BC. The Greek victory against all odds is the background against which Classical Greece entered its greatest period: the 'Greek miracle', the moment of the birth of modern western civilization. Ever since, we have tended to think of the Greek spirit as being in fundamental opposition to Eastern culture: western democracy versus eastern monarchy; freedom and accountability versus oppression and absolute rule; the free-spirited art of the Parthenon versus the rigid, monotonous processions of Persepolis.

This is the Classical view, an 'ideology of difference', that for a long time dominated the western, European perception of Persia, having been first constructed by the fifth-century-BC Greeks themselves.[1] Yet much has changed in recent decades. Increased study of ancient Near Eastern texts and archaeological data, along with critical scrutiny of Greek texts and their ideological agenda, have been central to the rewriting of the history of Persia and its relations with Greece. Crudely Helleno-centric views looking merely for signs of a Hellenization of the east have given way to analyses of the Persian Empire's impact on the cultures of its subject populations and models of two-way cultural interactions. We have seen the picture of the evil Persian versus the good Greek dissolve into a more balanced assessment of the two great cultures and their various encounters over the 220 years of Achaemenid rule.

CONTACTS BETWEEN PERSIANS AND GREEKS IN THE ARCHAIC AND CLASSICAL PERIODS

Greeks and Persians first came into contact with each other on the west coast of Asia Minor, where Greek cities had prospered for hundreds of years in close proximity to their eastern neighbours, the kingdoms of Phrygia and Lydia. By the mid-sixth century BC Lydia was in con-trol of most of western Anatolia, including several Greek coastal cities. Lydian rule, once submission was assured, could be generous. Overall, the Greek cities prospered and the culture of Greeks and Lydians entered what might almost be called a successful symbiosis.[2]

The Lydian kingdom came to an end in 546 BC when it was conquered by Persia under King Cyrus. The story is well known: King Croesus of Lydia decided to embark on a war against Persia after the Delphic oracle had told him that, if he crossed the River Halys, he would destroy a great empire – it turned out to be his own. Cyrus besieged and conquered the Lydian capital Sardis, the Greek cities which had refused to revolt against Croesus were subjugated, and a Persian satrap was installed at Sardis. Soon most of western Anatolia, including Lycia and Caria, was under Persian rule, and the Greek cities in Ionia, Aeolis and Caria became subjects of the Persian Empire, liable to pay tribute to the great king.[3]

What did the Achaemenid Persians actually know of the Greeks and what did they think of them? From what precious little is preserved, it seems that to the Persians the Greeks were all 'Ionians': there were 'Ionians of the land', 'Ionians who are on the sea and the people beyond the sea', and 'petasos-wearing Ionians'.[4] Ionians also appear in Achaemenid art, most notably among the groups of gift-bearing delegations of subject peoples on the Apadana reliefs in Persepolis (cat. 20). We recognize them first by their typical Ionian dress: a fine, pleated tunic under a thicker mantle, which is closely matched by contemporary Greek representations. The tribute, or gift, they carry is balls of wool, folded cloth and precious metal vessels: Ionia was famous for its production of fine wool, and Ionian and Lydian silversmiths were renowned for their work.

The characterization of the Ionians is thus quite accurate, as it is also for the other nationalities on these reliefs, and betrays a familiarity both with the outward appearance of Ionian Greeks and with the principal goods their lands produced. Of course, the Greeks were situated very much at the fringes of the Persian Empire, and the Greek fifth-century-BC historian Herodotus may well have a point in assuming that his own people were not at the forefront of the Persians' minds, or for that matter, esteem:

> After their own nation they [the Persians] hold their nearest neighbours most in honour, then the nearest but one – and so on, their respect decreasing as the distance grows, and the most remote being the most despised.

(*History* I.134)

Yet this did not prevent an ongoing interaction between 'heartland' and 'periphery'. The Persian Empire was characterized by a relatively tolerant rule, which usually did not interfere unduly in matters of local religion or custom, though obviously a firm hold was maintained on politics and administration, if necessary with merciless force.[5] Greeks could hold posts of importance and their cities generally prospered. Contact with Persia was mostly indirect, for instance through the satrap and Persian administrative staff in Sardis. Yet at times Greek objects and Greek people also travelled right into the Persian heartland.[6] Some of the objects would have arrived there by trade (Attic pottery, for example), while others would have been loot, such as a massive bronze hucklebone once dedicated to Apollo at Didyma and taken from there to Susa (cat. 445). A bronze figured cauldron (cat. 446) and the fragment of an early Classical Greek statue of Penelope also made their way to Persepolis (cat. 441), as loot or otherwise.[7] Some pieces of booty are known only from literary sources, such as the bronze statue of Apollo Philesios by Kanachos from Didyma, taken to Ecbatana (Pausanias VIII.46.3), and the statue group of the Tyrannicides, taken from Athens to Susa by Xerxes in 480 BC (Pausanias I.8.5).

Greek literary accounts also relate tales of personal human contact. Herodotus (*History* I.153), for example, recounts that Cyrus, having sacked Sardis, took the Lydian King Croesus back with him to Persia where he served as an adviser. Perhaps Cyrus also took along other dignitaries, as well as artisans – a certain Telephanes, for example, supposedly worked for Darius and Xerxes (Pliny, *Natural History* XXXIV.68). In addition, archaeological evidence and Persian sources clearly suggest that foreign craftsmen and foreign supplies played a major role in Persia.[7] Darius's so-called Foundation Charter for Susa lists as sources of materials places from Ionia to Egypt and Central Asia, and mentions different peoples responsible for the construction and decoration (cat. 1). The 'painted wall decoration' was brought from Ionia – perhaps this refers to pigment such as *miltos*, since stone reliefs and plastered walls would have been painted. The Akkadian version mentions 'Ionians from Babylon' working on unbaked brick for walls or foundations, and as masons there were Ionians and Lydians. In addition, the Persepolis Treasury Tablets from the first half of the fifth century BC mention Carian masons, as well as Ionians and Lydians.

More immediate physical evidence for the presence of Greeks in the heart of Persia comes in the shape of graffiti and caricatures.[8] In a quarry at Persepolis two Late Archaic graffiti were left behind by Greeks who may well have worked there, Pytharchos (an Ionian name) and Nikon. A representation of Herakles stealing the tripod from Apollo survives scratched into a stone plaque from the treasury at Persepolis, an unmistakably Greek scene that attests the presence of a Greek artist in the area around 500 BC. A Greek may also have worked as a scribe in the Persepolis secretariat, since one of the Treasury Tablets dealing with wine transactions is written in Greek.

Ionian Greeks, though few in number, are thus attested in Persia particularly in the context of building projects. Many may not have chosen their fate, but were possibly forced to make their way east, never to return home.[9] What was their influence on the material culture of Persia?

Recent studies have revealed numerous foreign, notably Egyptian, technical and formal influences in Achaemenid buildings in Pasargadae and Persepolis. Greek features[10] include the use of the claw chisel, clamps and cramps that are exactly matched only in Lydia and Ionia. A Greek bead-and-reel ornament has been found both at Susa and Persepolis. The column bases in Palace P at Pasargadae (dating to around 510 BC) are horizontally fluted in the Greek manner, and the workmanship and cutting of bases and drums is Ionic. The classic Persian column type used from the beginning of the fifth century BC onwards has fluted shafts, as do Greek columns. Also for 'bell' bases (cats 8–9) some have suggested a Greek origin. The royal Tomb of Cyrus, finally, seems to have been built using Lydo-Ionian techniques.

Sculpture, too, may reveal some Greek influence.[11] The distinctive pattern of splaying overlapping folds, and the zigzag hems on figures carved from at least the period of Darius are reminiscent of late Archaic Greek art. But in their formal and stylized conception, lacking obvious anatomical forms beneath the dress, the figures are essentially un-Greek and more reminiscent of Assyrian types.

Greek influence on Persian art and architecture, then, is undeniable, yet seems confined to stoneworking and building techniques, and possibly some patterns in sculpture. Otherwise, there seems to be little connection, especially in subsequent decades. Whilst in the case of sculpture, for example, Greece went through a revolution in the course of the fifth century BC, Persian sculptural style, once it had been established under Darius, persisted virtually unaltered to the end of the empire.

Similarly, Persian influence on the arts of the Greek cities on and off the coast of Asia Minor, and even more so further away on the Greek mainland, appears to have been minimal, if virtually non-existent. The situation is different for the regions further inland in Anatolia, which had close connections with both Greek and Achaemenid cultures. Sardis (Sparda) is a case in point.[12] An important bastion on the empire's western edge and governed by Persians of highest rank, Sardis developed something of a 'polyethnic' elite. Finds from Sardis and the burial mounds around it reveal Anatolian, Greek and imperial Persian elements. This new social identity could even extend right down into the material culture of average Lydians, illustrated by the spread of Achaemenid *phialai* as preferred drinking vessels in plain pottery.

A certain Graeco-Persian *koine* is also attested by seals in the western satrapies.[13] Seals were used by both Greeks and Persians, even though in Persia they played a far greater role in official administration. They were produced in various centres of the Persian Empire, and from the early fifth century BC onwards a group of Graeco-Persian seals emerged that combined Greek style with Achaemenid subjects. Their iconography includes scenes of Greek myths and of fighting (cat. 449), but also of Persians hunting and of Persian women (cat. 416). Finally, a similar and perhaps even more pronounced fusion of Greek and Persian art is also apparent in funerary monuments in northern and northwest Anatolia, around the satrapal seat of Daskyleion.[14]

THE GRAECO-PERSIAN WARS AND THEIR AFTERMATH

In 499 BC the Greek cities on the west coast of Asia Minor, led by Miletus, revolted against Persia, following internal Greek discord in which the Persian satrap had become involved (Herodotus, *History* V.30–38).[15] The Athenians and Eretrians sent ships in support, but they were ultimately defeated and in 494 BC Miletus was razed to the ground. Incensed not least by the destruction of the satrapal capital Sardis and its temples at the hands of the Athenians and Eretrians (Herodotus, *History* V.97), in 491 BC Darius despatched heralds to Greece asking for submission. The island of Aigina yielded, but both Athens and Sparta responded by killing the heralds. The following year, 490 BC, Darius sent Datis

to invade Greece; his army succeeded in destroying the city of Eretria and its temples but was later defeated by the Athenians and Plataeans at the battle of Marathon. In 480/79 BC Xerxes, son of Darius, set off against Greece with an even larger army and fleet. Athens was occupied and the temples on its Acropolis razed to the ground. Ultimately, however, those Greek cities which rallied around Athens and Sparta were successful in beating the Persians in the sea battle off Salamis in 480 BC and the land battle at Plataea in 479 BC. Some further clashes ensued, but they were minor, and at least in part driven by the Greeks themselves.

It was during the Persian Wars and the years following them that the Greek image of the Persians was shaped. The experience of war had been shattering, and the victory thorough and seemingly miraculous; Greeks now tried to make sense of it all. In this process, the projection of the Persians as a barbarian 'other' was a convenient foil against which Greek values and norms could be set. The victory was seen as an ideological one, Greek discipline overcoming eastern weakness, democracy defeating despotism, civilization triumphing over barbarity. Official Athenian rhetoric, plays and imagery all served to construct an ideology of difference between Greeks and Persians.[16]

One of the first and already very powerful manifestations of this development was Aeschylus's *Persians*, the oldest extant Greek tragedy, first performed in Athens in 472 BC. The play is set in the Persian capital Susa and tells of how the news of the Persian defeat in Greece was received there. It used to be seen primarily as an extraordinary display of empathy for the Persian plight and an expression of common humanity even with the enemy – and this is certainly one aspect of it. But recent analysis[17] has shown that the play's main emphasis is its highlighting, and relishing, of the heroic Athenian victory and the devastation wrought on Persia.

Throughout the play the choir of Persian elders, for example, is represented as indecisive, lamenting and pathetic. Xerxes' mother Atossa, by contrast, is prominent and influential. Both features together paint a picture of the Persians as weak and effeminate. Athens, on the other hand appears as the heroic defender of Greece. It is Athenian values of freedom and equality that are presented as the cause for the Greeks' victory, and Athenian democracy is shown to justly defeat Persian tyranny. This defeat is represented as a massive disaster that affects the whole of the Persian empire, heralding its impending demise. Of course, this was just Athenian wishful thinking. In fact, the Persian defeat at the hands of the Greeks was but a brief inconvenience in the history of the Persian Empire. It was an unexpected defeat by an enemy who proved stronger than had been anticipated, but in the wider scheme of things it was of no consequence.

Many of the contrasts between Asia and Greece contained in the play are further developed by later authors, such as the Greek historian Herodotus,[18] one of the main Greek sources on ancient Persia: the unaccountable monarchy of the Persians versus the accountable democracy of Athens; the slavish masses of the king's vast flotilla versus the small band of pious, disciplined and courageous Greeks; the empty pomp of the Persian court versus the masculine simplicity of the Athenians. Continuing to propagate such a negative yet still dangerous image of the Persians was in Athens' interest, not least since it sustained the further existence of the league of Greek states which had been formed against a

by Greeks, helpless, or fleeing in fear; face and body language often express a lack of control (fig. 64). Often, Greek heroic nudity also contrasts with the elaborate patterned dress of the Persians – their unnecessary, almost feminine finery.

Soon, battle scenes are joined by genre scenes and more caricature-like figures. An example is a representation on an Athenian red-figure jug[20] of about 470 BC (fig. 65), which clearly plays a joke on the image of the peasant-like, weak Persians by equating them with Hephaistos, the lame god of blacksmiths and least glamorous of the Greek gods. Just as Hephaistos in Greek myth had once been made drunk by the god of wine Dionysos and packed on to a mule – the rustic animal of peasants – so a Persian soldier, a battle axe over his shoulder, here rides a mule side-saddle like the god.[21]

64 (below left) Athenian red-figure *kalyx-krater*, *c.* 470/60 BC, showing a combat between a Greek and a Persian. *Basel, Antikenmuseum BS 480.*

65 (above right) Two sides of an Athenian red-figure *oinochoe* depicting two Persians in retreat. The representation probably dates from the time of the defeat of the Persians at the battle of the Eurymedon in the 460s BC. *British Museum, GR 1912.7-9.1.*

continued potential Persian threat and which proved increasingly profitable for Athens.

A similar stereotyped image of Persians was developed in Athenian art from their first appearance in about 490 BC.[19] Their physical form clearly shows that Athenians did know Persians well enough from personal observation: what is represented is the 'Median' dress (to the Greeks the Medes, another Iranian people in the Persian Empire, were one and the same), which was also described in battle by Herodotus (*History* VII.61–2). At first, they are mostly shown in battle, being struck down

Another Persian, carrying a battle axe, bow, quiver and whip, walks behind. Persian warriors, then, were lame, drunk, weak, womanish, unrestrained and mere peasants or craftsmen rather than fighters.

Greek *andreia* (manliness) as set against Persian *anandreia* (cowardice) is particularly striking on a head vase (cat. 448) dating to the late fifth century BC. It takes the shape of the head of a Persian, wearing the Persian soft cap and sporting a moustache. What would have stared the Greek consumer handling this drinking vessel directly in the face was the effect that he, himself, had on others –

with open mouth, aghast, eyes wide open in terror, the Persian is mortified, because he finds himself suddenly confronted with his vanquisher, the ordinary Athenian citizen. In this vase the Greek victory is thus forever cast in clay, to be relished by the Greek user every time he picks up the cup. And on the neck of the vase a Persian slave girl is serving her Athenian mistress: the consequences of Greek victory, if perhaps not in reality then at least in imagination.

Also beyond the realm of the individual, the Greek victory lived on for all to see in the decoration of public buildings and temples: in the Marathon painting of the Stoa Poikile in the Agora, in the Parthenon metopes that allude to the defeat of the Persians through mythical battles of Greek civilization against barbarian disorder, and on the Athena Nike temple and its friezes of Greeks in battle against Persians.[22]

66 Athenian pottery *phiale* with horizontal polychrome fluting, imitating Achaemenid metal vessels. Signed by the potter Sotades, *c.* 460 BC. *British Museum, GR 1894.7-19.2 (Vase D8).*

From all of this evidence one gets the impression that everything Persian would have been anathema to the Athenians. But in fact the picture is more complex. Paradoxically, some Persian objects were highly fashionable in Classical Athens. Athenians would have been quite familiar with Persian luxury objects already in the sixth century BC, as aristocratic guest-friendships and rivalries extended across a wide network as far as east Greece and its Anatolian hinterland. In addition, rich spoils were taken from the Persian army after its defeat.[23] Some objects were dedicated directly in sanctuaries as trophies and thank-offerings, such as an Achaemenid bronze bit and short sword (*akinakes*) on the Acropolis; similarly, a bronze helmet of Near Eastern type was dedicated at Olympia by 'the Athenians, to Zeus, having seized it from the Medes'. Spoils paid for several expensive victory monuments (cf. Herodotus, *History* IX.80).

Persian garments were also adopted, but in the process were often subverted. In Persia, for example, the *kandys* jacket was worn – sleeves unused – by men of rank as a mark of status. In Athens it occasionally appears in art from the end of the fifth century BC, but now worn by women, especially by maids, servants and by mythological figures considered barbarians; a more common adaptation of the *kandys*, in which the sleeves were used, was popular with women and children. The

cap with long sidepieces that was part of the Median dress also occasionally puts in an appearance in Athenian art, though when it is worn by the Athenian city goddess Athena underneath her helmet, one might suspect it to be a symbol of the city's victory.[24]

Mostly, however, the Persian elements that Athenian elites incorporated into their lives were not so much demonstrations of triumph as of wealth and power. This is the case with the parasol and fly whisk, common at the Neo-Assyrian and later the Achaemenid court (cf. cat. 38). They very occasionally appear in Greek art from the late sixth century BC onwards, but in Athens became popular only in the later fifth century, when servant maids carry them for their mistresses. That their eastern origin was clearly appreciated in Athens is obvious when one looks at representations of eastern kings in pottery.[25] It was probably less the memory of the Persian Wars that was evoked through them than the conspicuous consumption and leisure that only the elite could afford.

Finally, Persian influence was also felt in Attic pottery, for some shapes of plain black-glazed pottery seem to adapt Achaemenid metalware.[26] Most notable among them is the *phiale*, or shallow bowl with everted offset rim. In Attica, it appears in pottery from the late sixth century BC onwards as a ritual vessel, thus deviating from its Persian use as a drinking vessel. Some examples even feature the horizontal fluting that is characteristic of Persian types but had been previously unknown in the Athenian ceramic tradition (fig. 66). Similarly, cylindrical beakers with horizontal fluting reflect Achaemenid prototypes, and a *pyxis* with horizontal fluting from the last quarter of the fifth century BC closely resembles an Achaemenid silver *pyxis* in the British

67 Athenian red-figure lion-head cup belonging to a type adapted from Achaemenid animal-head vessels, *c.* 480–470 BC. *British Museum, GR 1873.8-20.276 (Vase E796).*

Museum (cat. 151). Deep round-bottomed bowls were adopted from the second quarter of the fifth century BC onwards, sometimes with stem and handle attached. What are probably the most recognizable Achaemenid shapes – animal-head cups and rhytons – found their way into Attic pottery from around 500 BC (fig. 67), at first with added handle and/or foot, but later also without.

On a personal and political level, links with Persia also continued in various ways throughout the Classical period, both in Ionia and on the mainland, including Athens.[27] Financial support by the Persians, for example, was crucial in deciding the Peloponnesian War in favour of Sparta at the end of the fifth century BC, and throughout the fourth century BC the Persian king continued to serve as the guarantor of settlements between the cities of Greece. The Persian Empire also remained a haven for refugees from Greece and for those looking for a fortune overseas. Even the great fifth-century BC democratic statesman and Persian War general Themistokles, having been banished from Athens, saw out his final days as a landed gentlemen on an estate given to him by Artaxerxes I (Plutarch, *Themistokles* 29–31). And in 401 BC over 10,000 Greeks, mostly from the Peloponnese, followed Cyrus as mercenaries in his campaign against his brother Artaxerxes II. Respectively, the presence of at least a handful of high-ranking Persians is attested in Classical Athens,[28] including a Persian student of Plato (Diogenes Laertes III.25). They appear to have left behind a number of monuments such as the striking fourth-century BC Kamini stele, representing the Persian king with two lion-griffins.[29]

To some degree, then, contacts between Greeks and Persians persisted throughout the time of the Achaemenid Empire, in terms of material culture as well as on a political and personal level – facts that may easily be forgotten in the face of Athenian rhetoric. Also with regard to values and attitudes, it is only recently that closer connections between Classical Athenians and Achaemenid Persians have been considered a possibility; this becomes apparent particularly when looking at Persian documents alongside Greek ones.

Not surprisingly, scholars have found that Persian sources easily contradict the Greek image of the uncontrolled, cowardly, weak, slavish and blasphemous Persians ruled by a whimsical king. The Achaemenid Empire presents itself as highly efficient yet not overly repressive (if this can ever be said of any empire), and in official texts Persians clearly have the same claim to justice, valour and piety as is asserted by the Greeks, although this may be expressed in different ways.[30] In terms of self-perception and self-representation, then, differences are hardly fundamental.

A comparison between the two principal architectural monuments epitomizing Classical Athens and Achaemenid Persia – the Parthenon and the Persepolis palaces – from the perspective of empire opens up further vistas. Traditionally, one might view Persian palaces with their reliefs of tribute-bearers and of kingly glory as embodiments of imperial power, asking for allegiance and submission, intended to inspire awe for the almighty power of the Persian king. By way of contrast, the Parthenon apparently stands as a symbol of piety for the gods, of democracy, a monument to Greek freedom and to victory over imperial oppression. But at the time it was built, Athens, too, was head of an empire. Originally established as a league of free Greek states to ward off any further Persian threats, by the mid-fifth century BC these states, many in Ionia and on the east Greek islands, were reduced to being Athenian subjects. So the supposed opposition with Persepolis is dissolved at least in part when we consider that the Parthenon was built from funds appropriated from the treasury of the league headed by Athens, as a monument to Athenian glory, and that the 'allies' must have felt their impotence very clearly when confronted with this monument – and they were confronted with it regularly, since their delegations were forced to attend the religious celebrations in Athens and bear gifts to the city goddess, Athena.[31]

Just how close the Athenians themselves, when under pressure, could come to the abhorred image of 'barbarian' cruel inhumanity is revealed in 415 BC. When the people of Melos refused to submit to the Athenian Empire, their women and children were enslaved and the men executed (Thucydides V.84.1–116.4). Sparta, Athens' rival, who was called on for help by many of Athens' 'allies', proved little less oppressive, and by the time of the Peace of Antalkides (or King's Peace) in 386 BC, when the east Greek cities were finally returned to Persian rule, it may have appeared to many quite an improvement by comparison.[32] In fact, the following period in western Asia Minor proved to be one of unprecedented stability, peace and growth.

THE FOURTH CENTURY BC IN WESTERN ASIA MINOR

In the western satrapies of the Persian Empire, particularly the Anatolian regions of Lydia and Lycia, elements of Achaemenid material culture and iconography had been adopted by the local elites (and sometimes the wider population at large) ever since their conquest by Persia in 546/5 BC. We have discussed this earlier with regard to Sardis and Daskyleion. To these we may add Cyprus, which had also become Persian at this time. The culture of this

68 Two gold spiral earrings from Cyprus terminating in Achaemenid-style crested griffins' heads, c. 425–400 BC. *British Museum, GR 1894.11-1.450-1 (Jewellery 1646).*

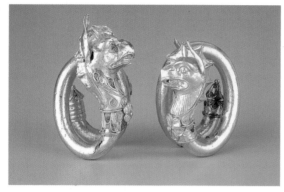

69 A relief from the Nereid Monument at Xanthos showing an audience scene inspired by Achaemenid models. The Lycian dynast Arbinas, wearing a Median-style cap and shaded by an umbrella, receives elders surrendering a city, c. 390–380 BC. *British Museum, GR 1848.10-20.62 (Sculpture 879).*

important trading centre had for long been fed by native Cypriot, Phoenician, Greek, Egyptian and Assyrian elements. Under the umbrella of the Persian Empire, these were joined by Achaemenid features.[33] Cypriot earrings of a common Greek spiral-shaped type, for example, in the later fifth century BC acquired terminals that are clearly Achaemenid in their choice of griffin and lion-griffin heads (fig. 68), while the splendid pair of bracelets found at Pasargadae (cat. 152) may possibly, on grounds of technique, form and style, be Cypriot rather than Achaemenid.[34]

Yet nowhere is the phenomenon of the impact of empire more pronounced than in fourth-century-BC Lycia and Caria, where native traditions merged with Greek style and Persian iconography. Following the King's Peace of 387/6 BC, Persia had replaced the single satrapy of Lydia with the triad of Lydia, Ionia and Caria, over which Caria's Hekatomnid dynasty proved dominant. Achaemenid objects found in Halikarnassos as well as the architecture and decoration of the Mausoleum (cat. 444) are prime examples of a cultural amalgamation of the highest artistic order.[35]

However, it is the Nereid Monument of Xanthos in Lycia – a region mostly under Persian control but for a period also part of the Athenian Empire – that remains the most quintessential example of this process.[36] Built

in the early fourth century BC by the Lycian dynast Erbbina, or Arbinas, the Nereid Monument in structure is basically a Lycian pillar tomb like many in the region. Its style is essentially Greek, both in its temple shape and the carving of its sculpture, while its iconography employs both Greek and royal Achaemenid elements. The latter are most pronounced in representations of the dynast himself: in one case wearing a 'Median' cap, he appears several times on the building, including an audience scene (fig. 69) that clearly imitates Persian royal audience scenes, such as those on the Apadana at Persepolis. The aristocratic hunt as well as the siege and battle scenes are equally of eastern inspiration in composition and theme, if Greek in style.

Persian, Greek and Anatolian/east Greek elements are evident also in the *symposion* scene on the north cella frieze (cat. 123).[37] Unlike at a Greek *symposion* where all participants would be equal, the central figure – obviously the dynast – is set apart from his fellow diners. Most crucially, however, the diners on the Nereid Monument do not use Greek drinking cups but rhytons, quintessentially Achaemenid pouring vessels with animal foreparts. The dynast himself holds a spouted rhyton of classic Achaemenid type (cf., for example, cat. 119), and other diners use an Anatolian horn-shaped version or a Greek version with handle derived from Achaemenid prototypes. Achaemenid rhytons, along with other precious plate or jewellery from the Achaemenid court repertoire, functioned as emblematic status symbols that were part of a system of royal gift-giving between the king, his officials and regional elites.[38] By displaying these gifts, the Xanthian dynast thus advertised his wealth and good standing with the Persian king.

To conclude, Greeks and Persians encountered each other in many different ways throughout the 220 years of the Achaemenid Empire: in aristocratic guest-friendships and exchanges, in war and hatred, in rule and dependence, and above all in every aspect of political power play. Greeks always remained on the fringes of the Persian horizon and may have had little impact on Persian culture, yet for the Greeks their war with Persia seems to have been vital in accelerating their culture's unparalleled flourishing in the fifth century BC. Classical Athenian democracy found itself opposed to Persian autocracy, yet Archaic Greece had been dominated by monarchies and oligarchies, too; and the aristocratic elements, which even in the most radical democratic systems never entirely vanished or lost their grip on power, often retained a link with Persia if opportune. Persia continued to play a role not just as overlord of the Greek cities in western Asia Minor, but also as a continued force in mainland Greek politics. Though perhaps in some ways fundamentally opposed, Greek and Persian cultures also had their points of contact. As has been pointed out, even empire could be one of them.[39] The Persian Empire was ruled by an autocratic king, the Athenian one by a democratic assembly, but both – Athens perhaps more so than Persia – had a tendency to encourage, if not impose, their own type of government, and both king and *demos* were able to use force ruthlessly to maintain power and financial gain. The main difference, at least from a modern perspective, may indeed lie in the Athenian democratic system allowing for some public reflection, debate and criticism of its imperial policies.

Art and material culture, too, could be a point of contact and even of successful symbiosis – not in Athens or Sparta, nor in Susa or Persepolis, but in those areas of the Mediterranean world that lay on the fringes of both their areas of influence. Here, local rulers forged from Greek and Persian art and iconography their own language of cultural and political statement and allegiance. One such area, not mentioned so far, was Macedonia. This kingdom on the northern edge of the Greek world had already been enmeshed in the Achaemenid Empire for a period in the late sixth and early fifth centuries BC, and Persian luxury arts had been appreciated by the Macedonian aristocracy.[40] Two hundred years later Alexander the Great set out from here to found his own empire that was to conquer and succeed the Persian Empire.[41] Once more, and for one final time, Greek and Persian culture were thus joined to serve a new master: neither Greek nor Persian but Macedonian.

1 Cf. Gehrke 2000; Georges 1994; Hall 1989; Hartog 1988; cf. also Harrison (ed.) 2002. For a recent survey of relations between Persia and Greece see also Cawkwell 2005.

2 Boardman 1999: 84–102; DeVries 2000.

3 On the east Greek cities under Persian rule see Briant 2002: 493–505; Austin 1990; Boardman 1999: 102–9; Balcer 1984 and 1991; Cook 1962: 98–120.

4 See Kuhrt 2002 and Briant 2002: 178–83, for a summary of the Persian perception of (Ionian) Greeks.

5 On the tight grip of the empire's administration see Fried 2004: esp. 108–55 (on Asia Minor).

6 On Greeks in Persia see Boardman 2000; Miller 1997: 97–133; Hofstetter 1978.

7 Discussed by Boardman 2000: 128–34; Curtis, forthcoming.

8 Boardman 2000: 131–3.

9 Cf. the account by Diodorus Siculus (XVII.69.2–9) of how Alexander encountered a large group of mutilated Greek craftsmen who had been deported to Persepolis. On deportation cf. also Briant 2002: 505–6.

10 Boardman 2000: 44–84; Curtis, forthcoming.

11 Boardman 2000: 102–22; Curtis, forthcoming.

12 Dusinberre 2003; cf. also Briant 2002: 700–5.

13 Boardman 2000: 152–74; Dusinberre 2003: 158–71, 246–83.

14 Boardman 2000: 181–2; cf. also Summerer 2003; Briant 2002: 697–700.

15 On the Graeco-Persian Wars see Green 1996.

16 Cf. Harrison 2002; Georges 1994; Hall 1989; Hartog 1988.

17 Harrison 2000.

18 On Herodotus see Hartog 1988.

19 On Persians in Greek art see Bovon 1963; Raeck 1981: 101–63; Miller 2003.

20 British Museum GR 1912.7-9.1: Attic red-figure *oinochoe* by the Painter of the Brussels *Oinochoai*, c. 460 BC; cf. Raeck 1981: 109, 135–6, 327, no. P573, figs 47–8. The jug is of the same date and shape as what is probably the most extreme caricature of Graeco-Persian relations, the 'Eurymedon *oinochoe*': cf. Wannagat 2001; Smith 2001; Miller 1997: 13, fig. 1–2. D. Wannagat is also currently preparing a study of the head vase, cat. 448.

21 See, for example, *LIMC* IV (1988), 641 Hephaistos 149, pl. 396, for a very similar side-saddle.

22 Cf., for example, Castriota 1992.

23 On spoils see Miller 1997: 29–62, esp. 42, figs 5–6.

24 Knauer 1992.

25 British Museum GR Vase E 447; Attic red-figured *stamnos* by the Midas Painter, c. 440 BC; cf. DeVries 2000: 346–50.

26 For a thorough discussion see Miller 1997: 135–52.

27 On Ionian cities and their relations with Persia see Briant 2002: 493–505; Hornblower 1994; Balcer 1984 and 1991; Corsaro 1991; Baslez 1986; Cook 1961. Cf. also Starr 1974.

28 Bäbler 1998: 101–14.

29 Bäbler 1998: 109–11, 233, no. 41. For a late fourth-century tomb of a Persian or Phoenician envoy (?) at Athens see Scholl 2000.

30 As argued by Castriota 2000.

31 Cf. Root 1985. Her thesis of the Parthenon sculptures having been inspired by the Persepolis Apadana reliefs, however, is not convincing.

32 Hornblower 1994; Castriota 2000. It should be noted, however, that Persian dealings with the Greek cities could also be ruthless: the territory of Kyme was ravaged and the city besieged by the satrap Tissaphernes when the Ionian cities refused to pay tribute in the early fourth century (Diodorus Siculus I.27, 35; Xenophon *Hellespont* III.1); cf. Briant 2002: 493–4.

33 Petit 1991.

34 Williams, forthcoming.

35 Cf. Curtis in this volume (pp. 44–5).

36 On Lycia see Keen 1998; on the Nereid Monument see Childs and Demargne 1989; Bruns-Özgan 1987; Jacobs 1987.

37 Discussed extensively by Ebbinghaus 2000.

38 Paspalas 2000. A later Lycian monument shows that furniture, too, could be a part of this process. On the Tomb of Payava, a ruler (probably the satrap Autophradates) is shown seated on a throne featuring typically Persian legs; their type can be traced from royal Persepolis to the Levant, Egypt, the Caucasus, the Troad and even Macedonia: Paspalas 2000.

39 For a comparison of the Persian and Athenian Empires, see esp. Castriota 2000 and Balcer 1984.

40 Cf. Paspalas 2000; Paspalas, forthcoming.

41 Briant 2002: 866–76; Badian 1985; Bosworth 1980.

441 Statue of Penelope in white marble

This fragmentary statue of a woman, lacking its head, arms and lower legs, has traditionally been identified as Penelope because of its pose that signifies her despair at her husband Odysseus's absence. Other than this, however, there are no firm grounds for the identification. The statue is wearing a Greek *chiton* and was represented resting her head on her right hand. The statue is early Classical in style, dating from the mid-fifth century BC. The circumstances in which it was brought to Persepolis from the Greek world is unknown.

Persepolis, Treasury. Found in Corridor 31
(a fragment of the right hand from the same statue was also found in Hall 38) (PT4 1166)
H 83 cm, W 60 cm, Th 35 cm
Tehran, 4111
Schmidt 1957: 66–7, pls 29–30; Seipel 2000:
220–21, Boardman 2000: 111, fig. 3.32

441

442

442 Cypriot limestone head of a male statue of the Achaemenid period with Persian influence

He wears a wreath with beads or acorns. The stylized treatment of the hair and beard is characteristically Persian. Made in Cyprus *c.* 475–450 BC.

Found in the Sanctuary of Apollo, Idalion, Cyprus,
   by Sir Robert Hamilton Lang and acquired in 1873
H 33 cm
British Museum, GR 1873.3-20.9
Pryce 1931: no. C155

443 Cypriot stone statue with Persian influence of a female figure wearing a crown

The statue may either represent a worshipper holding an offering of a flower, or a goddess, probably Aphrodite. The figure can be compared with the seated females wearing crowns and holding flowers on the two gold rings from the Oxus Treasure (cats 180, 210) and the figures on the Oxus plaques holding flowers (cats 242–3). Made in Cyprus *c.* 450 BC.

Found in the Sanctuary of Apollo, Idalion, Cyprus,
   by Sir Robert Hamilton Lang and acquired in 1873
H 37 cm
British Museum, GR 1873.3-20.51
Pryce 1931: no. C323

443

444 Marble head of a Persian wearing a *kyrbasia* (headdress)

Persians featured heavily in the sculptural decoration of the Mausoleum of Halikarnassos, the tomb of King Mausolus of Caria, *c.* 350 BC. Although Caria was a region under Persian control, the sculptural decoration of the Mausoleum included Persian iconography. This head comes from a group showing Greeks and Persians at war, a popular theme in Greek art. Elsewhere on the building, sculptured images of Persians stood in a more peaceful attitude alongside members of the Carian court.

From the Mausoleum at Halikarnassos
 (modern Bodrum), Turkey
H 34 cm
British Museum, GR 1857.12-20.263
Smith 1900: no. 1057; Waywell 1978: 119–20,
 no. 49, pl. 23

444

445

445 Large bronze weight in the form of a hucklebone

With a dedication to Apollo of Didyma in archaic Greek. This was probably made *c.* 550–525 BC and brought back to Susa after the Persian sack of Miletus in 494 BC. It was found with the lion weight (cat. 301).

Susa Acropolis
Excavations of J. de Morgan, 1901
H 27.5 cm, W 39 cm, Th 24.5 cm, Wt 93.7 kg
Louvre, Sb 2719
De Morgan 1905: 155–65, pl. XXIX; Boardman
    1999: 108, fig. 125

446 Archaic Greek bronze crater-rim fragment

In the form of a pair of chariot horses. Cast in one piece with grooves and holes for attachment.

Persepolis, Hall of 100 Columns (PT5 175)
H 15 cm, L 26.2 cm, Th 4 cm
Tehran, 2207
Schmidt 1957: 70, pls 38, 39: 1; Boardman 2000:
    137, fig. 4.8

446

447

448

447 Athenian red-figured plate signed by the painter Epiktetos, *c.* 520–510 BC

A single figure in oriental costume – trousers (*anaxyrides*), tight-fitting sleeved coat (*kandys*) and soft skin hat (*kidaris*) with long ear-flaps hanging down – fills the circular field of this plate. This outfit, which resembles the Median costume, was most commonly used in Athenian art for Scythians, but since the figure is not bearded, it is most likely in this case to be intended to depict an Amazon archer. Later representations of Persians, Scythians and Amazons lose much of their individual identity. She draws an arrow from her quiver (here a *gorytos*) as she turns back to shoot at the enemy, her composite bow at the ready in her left hand.

From Vulci (Etruria, central Italy)
Purchased in 1837 from the collection of Lucien
  Bonaparte, Prince of Canino and Musignano
Diam 19.5 cm
British Museum, GR 1837.6-9.59
Smith 1896: 136, no. E 135; Beazley 1963: 78, no. 93

448 Athenian drinking cup in the form of the head of a bearded Persian, *c.* 420–410 BC

The bearded head wears a Persian soft skin hat (*kidaris*), properly tied under the chin. There is also a broad fillet tied around the head, the ends knotted at the rear. His forehead is furrowed, eyebrows contracted and mouth open, all suggesting anger, fear or pain. The head was mould-made and the clay was covered first with a white slip, over which other colours were added.

Above the head there is on the mouth of the vase a red-figure scene of a mistress and maid. The elegant mistress sits on a chair, gazing at her image in a mirror, while the servant stands holding a closed box before her. This servant is dressed in an oriental trouser-suit (probably made up of an *anaxyrides* and a *kandys*), with a sleeveless patterned *ependytes* over the top, and a soft hat with ear-flaps hanging down (*kidaris*). She is presumably intended to be a Persian slave. In Persia the *ependytes* was worn by men, but in Athens it was taken over as an item of female dress. There are traces of a preliminary sketch for this red-figured scene: the painter originally thought to show two standing figures confronted.

From Nola (Campania, central Italy)
Purchased from W. Hope, via H.O. Cureton, in 1849.
  Originally from the collection of E.A. Durand
H 23.5 cm
British Museum, GR 1849.6-20.12
Smith 1896: 375–6, no. E 791; Beazley 1963: 1550,
  no. 3 (Class W, the Persian Class): Raeck 1981:
  160, 327, no. P571; *Corpus Vasorum Antiquorum
  London, British Museum* 4: III.Ic.8, pls (230, 231),
  7.6A-B, 8.4

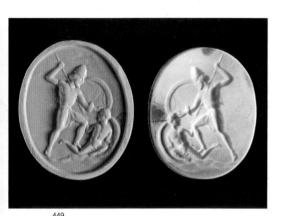

449

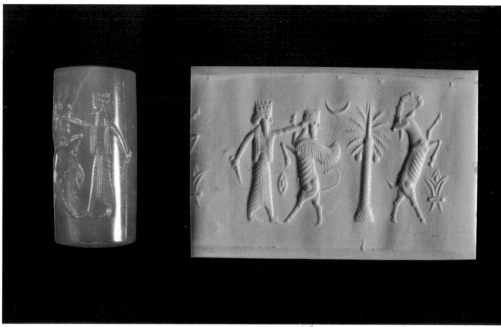

450

449 Scaraboid stamp seal in blue chalcedony, pierced lengthways

A soldier wears a Greek crested *pilos* helmet, a short, belted tunic draped over his left shoulder, and sandals. He carries a Greek hoplite shield on his left arm, and tramples a naked fallen enemy at whom he aims a spear.

Oxus Treasure
Bequeathed in 1897 by A.W. Franks
L 2.45 cm
British Museum, ANE 124014
Dalton 1964: no. 113, fig. 62

450 Cylinder seal in dark grey-blue chalcedony

The seal shows the Persian royal hero in combat with a confronting monster. The hero wears a crown, Persian dress, and shoes with two or three ties or straps (usually royal figures have shoes without straps). He holds a short sword at his side, and seizes by the back of the head a winged, rampant, crowned human-headed bull. To the side is a palm-tree and there is a crescent above to the left. To the right is a goat or ibex.

Acquired in 1772 from the collection of Sir William Hamilton. The seal is often described as from the plain of Marathon, probably due to its illustration with other seals in an unpublished manuscript by Cullum of *c.* 1834, where he mentions that seals probably lost in the battle were found at Marathon inscribed in the Persian style
H 3.1 cm, Diam 1.45 cm
British Museum, ANE 89781
Merrillees 2005: no. 62

451 Head of a bearded man wearing a Persian or Phrygian cap

This bronze relief comes from a series of horse-trappings. They are of Greek workmanship although some show figures in oriental attire, such as this roundel. In Greek art there are many depictions of figures wearing head-dresses such as this, and it is almost impossible to determine whether they are Amazons, Phrygians, Persians or other peoples.

Said to have been found in a tomb in Elis, Peloponnese, Greece
Purchased from G. Nikolaos through Messers Rollin & Feuardent in 1906
Diam 10.4 cm
British Museum, GR 1906.4-25.2
Marshall 1909: 157

451

12

THE LEGACY OF ANCIENT PERSIA

Vesta Sarkhosh Curtis

After the collapse of the Achaemenid Empire in 330 BC the legacy of ancient Persia – its splendour and the geographical extent of its empire – remained alive in the minds of succeeding dynasts. But already in the fifth to sixth centuries AD Sasanian historiography had produced a royal history and genealogy that left no place for the rule of the Achaemenid kings. Some sources in Arabic and Persian soon after the Islamic conquest *do* refer to the ancient Persian empire, but generally in the Islamic period the ruins of ancient Parsa (known to the Greeks as Persepolis) were associated with mythological figures: Persepolis became the abode of Jamshid, hence the Persian name for it, Takht-i Jamshid, and the ruins of Pasargadae and Cyrus's tomb were linked with the legendary King Solomon of the Old Testament and the Quran. In Iran there was no precise knowledge about the Achaemenid period until increased interest in the ancient past was combined with a growing sense of nationalism in the nineteenth century. Meanwhile, in Europe it had been known since the end of the sixteenth century that the ruins at Takht-i Jamshid were in fact Persepolis.

After the destruction of Persepolis by Alexander in 330 BC the kings of Persis, who came from around Persepolis and were under the yoke of the Seleucids, minted coins in the second century BC using an iconography which is closely related to that of ancient Persian coins of the fifth and fourth centuries BC. These early coins from Persis show on the reverse a ruler who is seated on a throne holding a long staff. This motif is strikingly similar to royal reliefs from Persepolis. On some Persid coins a figure, probably the local ruler, is shown worshipping in front of a building, which may be a representation of Persepolis. Above the building we find a symbol similar to the Achaemenid winged figure, the *farnah* or 'kingly glory', and at the side is the royal Persian standard.

In the middle of the third century BC the Arsacid Parthians from northeastern Iran appeared on the political scene and gradually conquered western Iran and Mesopotamia. By the first century BC this dynasty had once again established Iranian rule over former Achaemenid territories. Early coins of these rulers from the third to second centuries BC bear a resemblance to Persian coins of the fifth to fourth centuries BC. The portrait of the Arsacid Parthian king on the obverse and the seated archer on the reverse recall Persian prototypes. There is also a similarity between the royal throne with bulbous legs, as shown on early Parthian coins, and the throne of the Persian kings as seen on the reliefs from Persepolis. The revival of the ancient Persian tradition under the Parthians shows itself in the reappearance of the royal title 'king of kings' in the early first century BC. Roman sources also mention the significance of ancient Persia for the Parthian kings. When in the first century AD Rome and Parthia quarrelled over Armenia and the appointment of a Parthian prince as king of Armenia, the Parthian king Artabanus II (AD 10–38) informed Rome 'that whatever was possessed by Cyrus, and afterwards by Alexander, was his undoubted right, and he was determined to recover the same by force of arms'.[1]

With the collapse of the Parthian Empire at the beginning of the third century AD, a Sasanian dynasty from Persis, the former Achaemenid heartland, came to power. The Sasanian king Ardashir and his father Papak were closely attached to the region around Persepolis. Graffiti from the so-called harem building at Persepolis dating from the early third century AD show representations of Ardashir, his father Papak, and his elder brother Shapur.[2] These indicate that the early Sasanians regarded the ruins as significant and therefore left their images there. When Ardashir defeated the Parthians and established himself as the new 'king of kings of Iran', he placed the Achaemenid platform throne, which he must have copied from the reliefs at Persepolis, on the reverse of his coins. The throne with its lion paws is combined with a Zoroastrian fire altar.

Ardashir, his son and grandsons also chose the nearby site of Naqsh-i Rustam, where the Achaemenid kings had cut their tombs into the rock, for their monumental reliefs (fig. 70). Shapur I (AD 240–71) celebrated his victory over the Roman kings Valerian and Philip the Arab below the tomb of Darius. Furthermore, Shapur's trilingual inscription in Pahlavi, Parthian and Greek is carved on a square stone building, the Kaba-i Zardosht, which faces the Achaemenid tombs and the Sasanian rock reliefs. In fact, it is suggested by some scholars that the text of Shapur's inscription shows some similarity to the early sixth-century BC inscription of Darius at Bisitun in western Iran.[3] This is not impossible as Aramaic versions of ancient Persian inscriptions were sent to different parts of the Persian Empire.

70 The tomb of Artaxerxes I (465–424 BC) at Naqsh-i Rustam with two Sasanian reliefs at the foot of the cliff showing Shapur II (AD 309–79) leaning on his sword (above) and a jousting scene involving Hormuzd II (AD 302–9, below). The relief showing the victories of Shapur I (AD 240–71) over the Roman emperors Valerian and Philip the Arab is further to the right. See also figs 4 and 22.

71 Pahlavi (Middle Persian) inscriptions from the reign of the Sasanian king Shapur II (AD 309–79) carved on a pillar of the south portico of the Palace of Darius at Persepolis.

The *Karnamak-i Ardashir-i Papakan*, which was written down in the sixth century AD, but goes back to the time of Ardashir I and his sons in the third century, describes how after the death of Alexander and the rule of the feudal kings – i.e the Arsacid Parthians – Eranshahr, the empire of Iran, and kingship in Iran were restored. The restoration of kingship is attributed to Ardashir, who was descended from Dara (Darius), the son of Dara (Darius). The *Letter of Tansar*, which also dates in its original form from the reign of Ardashir, but was amended in the sixth century AD, refers to Alexander's conquest and describes how the king of kings – Ardashir – avenged Dara (Darius III).[4]

In AD 311 the Sasanian king Shapur II (AD 309–73), visited Persepolis and had a Pahlavi inscription carved inside the ruins of the Palace of Darius (fig. 71):

> In the month of Spendarmad, in the second year of the Mazda worshipping Lord, Shapur, the king of kings of Eran and An-Eran, whose origin is of the gods. At that time when Shapur, the king of the Sakae, king of Hindustan, Sakistan and Turan down to the seashore ... travelled on this road, the road from Istakhr to Sakistan, and graciously came here to *sad-stun*, he ate bread in this building ... And he organised a great feast, and he had divine rituals performed, and he prayed for this father and his ancestors, and he prayed for Shapur, the king of kings, and he prayed for his own soul, and he also prayed for the one who had this building constructed.[5]

Shapur II refers to Persepolis not by its Old Persian name of Parsa, but as *sad-stun* (New Persian *sad situn*), meaning 'one hundred columns'. The term 'one hundred' to this day signifies a large number in the Persian language, as does forty. Although he talks in his inscription about 'the one who had the buildings constructed', the names of the ancient Persian kings and their connection with the site of Persepolis are not mentioned. On the other hand, the Roman historian Ammianus Marcellinus, who describes Emperor Julian's conflict with Shapur II, refers to the Persian kings Cyrus, Darius and Xerxes, and mentions Persepolis by name.[6]

Under Shapur II the growing threat from other religions, for example, Christianity and Judaism to the west and Buddhism to the east, created the need for an Iranian state religion. It was therefore at this time that Zoroastrianism became the state religion. The Sasanian kings, who saw themselves as the legitimate possessors of the 'divine and kingly glory', the *farr-izadi*, had to have a religiously acceptable genealogy. In the fifth to sixth centuries AD an official national history, the *Xwaday-namag*, was written down under the influence of Zoroastrian priests. Here Avestan kings, who derived from an east Iranian tradition, were presented as the first Iranian dynasties. The Achaemenid kings were therefore ignored.

Knowledge about the ancient Persian kings Cyrus and Darius, albeit rather blurred, comes from historians of the early Islamic period.[7] Tabari in the ninth and tenth centuries lists the ancestors of the Sasanian king Ardashir I as Sasan, the son of Dara the Great (Darius III), the son of Ardashir Bahman (Artaxerxes?). He goes on to say that at the time of Dara, Alexander attacked the country and 'destroyed all the towns, fortresses and fire temples of the Persians, he killed the priests and burnt their books'. Dinawari of the ninth century AD, when describing the early history of Iran, refers to both Kay Khusrow, one of the mythological kings of the Avestan

tradition, and to Solomon as the kings of Fars. He names Bahman as the king who allowed the Jews to return to their homeland; presumably this is Cyrus. Dinawari also states that the conquest of Alexander happened at the time of Dara, the son of Dara. Hamzeh Isfahani writes that according to Jewish writings and traditions Bahman is the same as 'Kurush', that is Cyrus. Biruni's *Athar ul-baqiya* makes many references to Cyrus/Kurush and his kingship, and also lists all the other Achaemenid kings. Biruni also equates Cyrus with Kay Khusrow. A Persian source dating from the middle of the tenth century AD discusses Tabari's commentary in Arabic on the Holy Quran and describes an ancient site which is very similar to Persepolis. There is also a reference to the winged figure above the enthroned king as a symbol of 'kingly fortune', the *farnah*.

The official Sasanian history, together with other sources and a vivid oral tradition, are all preserved in Firdowsi's *Shahnameh*, or *Book of Kings*. This early eleventh-century epic in 55,000 double verses not only revived the Persian language after the Arab conquest in the middle of the seventh century AD, but also brought alive the pre-Islamic heritage of Iran. As the poet Firdowsi from Tus, Khorasan, in northeastern Iran, himself writes, the Sasanian *Book of Kings* served as one of his sources. The early and mythological part of the *Shahnameh* describes the kings of the Pishdadi and Kiyanid dynasties, who appear in Zoroastrian books as the Paradata and Kavi kings. Amongst these, the mythological Jamshid/Yima of the Avesta, who cannot otherwise be identified, is the most virtuous and prominent of all Iranian kings, the ruler par excellence, who possesses the *farr-izadi*, the divine glory. When he sins, the glory abandons him and the usurper Zahhak seizes the throne. In the story of Jamshid the terms *takht-i Jamshid*, the 'platform/throne or abode of Jamshid', and *sad situn*, 'one hundred columns', are used by Firdowsi.[8] These are, then reflections of Persepolis, but the site or its kings are not mentioned. Instead, the site is associated with Jamshid.

One of the heroes of the *Shahnameh*, whose name is also linked with the ancient past, is Rustam, the King of Sistan, whose legendary skills and bravery were unequalled. This has prompted Iranians to associate images of victorious kings with him. The relief of the Sasanian king Shapur I (AD 240–71) celebrating his victory over the Roman kings, for example, has traditionally been regarded as the triumph of the hero Rustam, and the site is known by Iranians as Naqsh-i Rustam, the 'image of Rustam'.

There are a number of inscriptions by prominent visitors to Persepolis during the Islamic period. Two in the Tachara Palace of Darius refer to a visit to the site in AH

344/AD 955 by the local Dailamite ruler, Azadud Dawla, on his return to Shiraz from a victorious campaign against the Samanids in northeastern Iran.[9] A third inscription, also in Arabic, dates to the year AH 392/AD 1001 and describes how another Dailamite ruler Baha Dawla, 'king of kings', and his entourage came to Marv-dasht for the hunt. They used Persepolis as their base. The same local rulers had a palace called Abu Nasr built in Shiraz and took some architectural fragments from the northern gateway of the Tachara Palace for the new building. These fragments have now been returned to their original site.

In the early twelfth century AD the historian Ibn Balkhi wrote in his *Farsnameh* (*The Book of Fars*) that Istakhr was built by King Jamshid, who constructed three fortifications and a palace. The latter, at the foot of a mountain, was according to him unique in the world. This seems to be the site of Persepolis. The description of the bull-men figures protecting the Gate of All Nations is particularly interesting. Their

> face is as the face of a man with a beard and curly hair, with a crown set on the head, but the body, with the fore and the hind legs, are those of a bull, and the tail is a bull's tail. ... Everywhere and about may be seen the sculptured portrait of Jamshid, as a powerful man with a well-grown beard, a handsome face, and curly hair. In many places his likeness has been set so that he faces the sun. In one hand he holds a staff, and in the other a censer ... In other places he is represented with his left hand grasping the neck of a lion ... while in his right hand he holds a hunting-knife, which he has plunged into the belly of the lion ...[10]

Here Darius, Xerxes and Artaxerxes are seen as images of the legendary King Jamshid. Also mentioned are 'on the upper part of the hill ... many great tomb chambers'.

Ibn Balkhi also writes about the healing powers of these ancient stones and how they were taken away by people, who when they were injured applied the stone powder to the wounds. In connection with Pasargadae he mentions the tomb 'of the mother of Solomon', which is clearly the Tomb of Cyrus the Great.[11] In the thirteenth century AD during the reign of the Atabaks of Fars, the tomb of Cyrus in Pasargadae was turned into a mosque. This indicates that this pre-Islamic site had a religious significance in the Islamic period. Some of the columns, which were brought from the nearby palaces for the construction of the mosque, were returned to their original positions in 1971.

A reference to Qasr-i Jamshid, the palace of Jamshid, and its thousand columns, the carved stone figures and half-bull, half-man figures is also found in the *'Ajayib nameh, The Book of Marvels*, of the late twelfth century AD.[12]

Many more inscriptions have been carved on the stone walls, door and window jambs at Persepolis, particularly the ruins of the Tachara Palace of Darius. One of these, in Persian, dates to AH 773/AD 1371 and mentions 'the great Lady ... of astonishing beauty, the Queen of the great and august Amir ... Bahram Shah ... She visited this eminent place, and this wonderful building'.[13] Another inscription in the portico of the Tachara Palace by the Timurid prince, Ibrahim Sultan, son of Shahrukh, dating to AH 886/AD 1481, includes a poem by the famous poet Sa'di (died 1292) from Shiraz, who associated the ruins with King Jamshid:

> Whom knowest thou of rulers of 'Ajam [Persia]
> Of Faridun, of Zahhak, and of Jam [Jamshid],
> Who did not lose his throne and rule at last,
> Deposed and overthrown by fate's strong blast?[14]

A reference to the palace of Jamshid is also made by another Shirazi poet, Hafiz (d. 1389):

> Pursuit of wine and secret pleasure is ill-starred;
> Whate'er it be, to reckless rogues I this discard.
> Who knows to where Jamshid and Kayumars have gone?
> Who knows when Jamshid's palace met a fate so hard?[15]

The fifteenth-century historian Hafiz Abru describes in his *Geography of Fars* a number of ancient sites near Shiraz, and says that they were visited by the kings of Iran once a year. The following seems to be a reference to Persepolis: 'They said that from the time of Jamshid there was a temple in that place, and the ancients regarded it as a good augury. And in the plain there was the imperial palace of Estakhr ...'[16]

The seventeenth-century historian Mahmud Haravi writes in his *Jam'eh Mufidi* that 'in a mountain cleft near Estakhr a temple has been made ... And the building of the *chihil minar* [The Forty Columns] is one of the wonders of the age. Its builder was Jamshid, and Homa, the daughter of Bahra, while reigning, added other buildings, and Eskandar-e Rumi [Alexander], when he came to Fars, ordered its demolition.'[17] In the Safavid period the terms *chihil situn* ('forty columns') and *chihil minar* ('forty columns') are used for Persepolis.

The European[18] rediscovery of Persepolis dates to the early fourteenth century, when a Franciscan monk, Odoric of Pordenone, visited the site on his way to China. In a short account he called the site Comum. Early travellers who made significant contributions include Don Garcia de Silva Figueroa, who visited the site in 1617 and correctly identified it as Persepolis, and Pietro della Valle, a Venetian merchant, who arrived there in 1621 and was the first to copy the Old Persian cuneiform inscriptions. Both Jean Chardin, a Frenchman who spent four years in Persia (1673–7), and the Dutchman Cornelis de Bruijn who visited Persepolis in 1704–5 recorded many of the standing monuments. In the spring of 1765 Carsten Niebuhr, a member of the Royal Danish Arabia Expedition, interrupted his voyage in the Persian Gulf to join a caravan travelling from Bushire to Shiraz. Niebuhr called Persepolis 'the jewel of his journey'. At Persepolis, Naqsh-i Rustam and nearby Naqsh-i Rajab Niebuhr copied the inscriptions of the Achaemenid and Sasanian kings, which were then used by scholars such as Grotefend to begin deciphering the Old Persian cuneiform script in 1802. By now, knowledge in Europe about ancient Persia was not just restricted to the Old Testament and Classical sources, as the Iranian epic the *Shahnameh* or *Book of Kings* had been translated into French by Jules Mohl in 1771. In addition, Anquetil du Peron, another Frenchman, had translated the Avesta, the holy book of the Zoroastrians.

With the beginning of the nineteenth century and growing British interest in Persia, first of a commercial and then a political nature, the number of British travellers increased considerably, and visits were made to Shiraz and Persepolis. James Morier travelled to Persia twice, once with Harford Jones's mission in 1809, and then as First Secretary with Sir Gore Ouseley in 1811. The latter mission also included Robert Gordon, brother of the 4th Earl of Aberdeen, and William Ouseley, a distinguished Orientalist, who had studied at Paris and Leiden. It was during this period that James Morier and Robert Gordon dug briefly at Persepolis, but their activities were stopped by the governor and local people. Some reliefs which were discovered were shipped to Britain via Bombay, and ended up in stately homes. Most were later presented to the British Museum. Both Morier and William Ouseley made correct identifications of some of the monuments and sites, and produced valuable sketches of them.[19]

Claudius James Rich, East India Company Resident in Baghdad, first visited Persia in 1820 while escaping the summer heat of Baghdad. Then in 1821 he visited Persepolis and Pasargadae, as well as Naqsh-i Rustam, Naqsh-i Rajab and the ruins of Istakhr. At Persepolis he left his name and date of visit on the inside of the winged *lamassu* protecting the Gate of All Nations, and wrote that his 'sensation on approaching Persepolis can hardly be described'. At Pasargadae he copied the Old Persian inscription over the winged genie and described the tomb of Cyrus as 'the tomb of the best, the most illustrious, and the most interesting of Oriental Sovereigns'. Rich died in a cholera epidemic at Shiraz in 1821.[20] While Resident in Baghdad, Rich met the artist Robert Ker Porter, who had been sent to Persia by the Russian Academy of Fine Arts in 1817 to record the monuments and reliefs of ancient Persia.[21] Ker Porter's drawings and watercolours are a magnificent contribution to the recording of ancient Persia. He was also regularly in touch with other scholars of his time, particularly his newly acquired friend Charles Bellino, whom he had met in Baghdad. Both Bellino and Rich believed that Ker Porter's drawings were much more accurate than those of earlier travellers:

> Apart from the fact that they frequently differ from those of early travellers, even Niebuhr, we have here no doubt that Sir Robert has made truthfulness in his drawings his main objective, for most of those he has drawn ... are uncommonly accurate.[22]

In western Iran Ker Porter recorded the rock relief of Darius at Bisitun near Kermanshah, but he thought it too difficult and risky to copy the trilingual inscriptions on the rock face. Instead, these inscriptions and those at Mount Alvand, near Hamadan, were copied by Henry Creswicke Rawlinson, a British officer who had come to Persia from British India to organize the shah's army. His copies of the Bisitun inscriptions contributed to the decipherment of Babylonian cuneiform.

In the mid-nineteenth century archaeological travellers to Iran included Austen Henry Layard, the famous excavator of Nimrud and Nineveh in Mesopotamia, who left Baghdad for western Iran in the summer of 1840 in local dress. Layard believed he 'could ... pass very well' as a Persian but must have been regarded with suspicion and amusement by the local inhabitants.[23] At Taq-i Bustan near Kermanshah he met Eugène Flandin and Pascal Coste, two Frenchmen who recorded the monuments of Persia in exemplary fashion.

Then in 1850–52 William Kennet Loftus undertook at Susa (Shush) the first and only major British excavation in Persia in the nineteenth century, after having dug at Warka in southern Mesopotamia.[24] Despite the discovery of a fair number of objects, coins, architectural remains and the correct identification of Susa with biblical Shushan, as mentioned in the Old Testament, Loftus was forced by the Trustees of the British Museum, in particular Rawlinson, to terminate the excavations. It is interesting to note here that not all British archaeological work in Iran in the nineteenth century had as its purpose the acquisition of antiquities for the British Museum. Colonel Ephraim Stannus, the British Political Resident at Bushire, made casts of Persepolis sculptures in 1825,[25] and the Weld Blundell expedition made many more casts in 1892. Some of these are in the present exhibition.

Interest in ancient Persia amongst the Qajar rulers,[26] a tribe from northeast Iran, can be traced back to the time of the founder of the dynasty, Agha Muhammad Khan (1785–97), who is reported to have enjoyed reading Firdowsi's *Shahnameh*. When a new royal crown was designed for him, this royal headgear was named the Kiyanid crown (*taj/kolah-i kiyani*), which, according to

Qavam al-Mulk completed in 1885, and the Kakh-e Eram in the Bagh-e Eram. Achaemenid themes are also found on glazed tiles, for example in the late nineteenth-century Mo'avenolmolk at Kermanshah (fig. 73).

Nasir ed-Din Shah (1846–96) was also interested in antiquities, which he combined with an enthusiasm for photography. He himself took photographs of the excavations at Khorheh, a Hellenistic-Parthian site near Isfahan, and he would like to have been able to read ancient scripts, including cuneiform. He wrote in his memoirs that he 'was very angry and disturbed about being unable to read those inscriptions'.[27]

From the time of Nasir ed-Din Shah there are two informative Persian inscriptions at Persepolis, both in the Tachara Palace (fig. 74).[28] One of these dates to AH 1294/AD 1877 and describes how his uncle, Farhad

72 Marble reliefs decorated in the Achaemenid style at the Naranjistan in Shiraz, a nineteenth-century house belonging to the Qavam family.

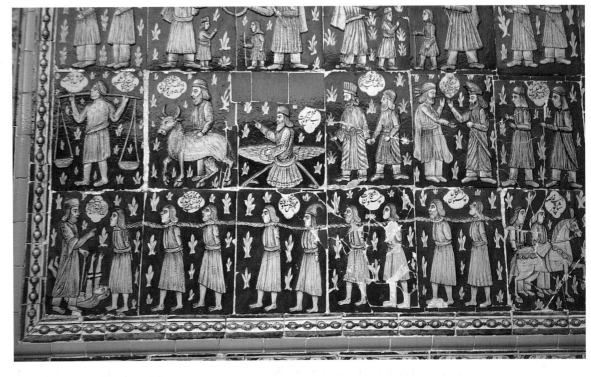

73 Glazed tile decoration in the late nineteenth-century *Takiyeh* of Mo'avenolmolk at Kermanshah with scenes from Achaemenid art, including the relief of Darius at Bisitun showing captured rebel kings in front of Darius.

the tradition of the *Shahnameh*, was worn by the ancient kings of Iran. Fath 'Ali Shah, Agha Muhammad Khan's nephew and successor, shared his uncle's interest in the *Shahnameh* and liked to identify himself with the legendary heroes of ancient Iran, particularly Rustam and Isfandiyar. Under Fath 'Ali Shah a series of rock reliefs was carved around the capital Tehran and in the provinces, which were clear imitations of pre-Islamic Parthian and Sasanian but not Achaemenid themes.

Later in the Qajar period, however, Achaemenid motifs were imitated in the stone and plaster decoration of grand houses, particulary in Shiraz. There are examples in the Naranjistan (fig. 72), the town house of the

Mirza, the Governor-General of Fars, 'came to Persepolis, and commissioned several thousand workmen to clear away the earth which had been heaped up through countless centuries on this platform, so that foreign and national travellers might view the carvings...' The second inscription records that in AH 1296/AD 1878 Farhad Mirza's brother and entourage 'came to this ancient site in order to view and examine some of the monuments, and stayed several nights'.

The excavations referred to in the first inscription were conducted by an official from nearby Marvdasht, and Farhad Mirza joined him and his workmen for a few days. Between 14 March and 14 May they found

74 Inscriptions in the Palace of Darius at Persepolis dating from the reign of Nasir ed-Din Shah, recording visits to Persepolis by his uncle Farhad Mirza and his brother in AH 1295–6 (1877–8 AD).

'antique objects', and 'sculptures in stone, the site of a lofty building, a bridle and an iron plate the pattern of which was not visible'.[29]

The end of the reign of Nasir ed-Din Shah saw a growing interest in ancient Iran and its monuments. In 1879 Mirza Fursat Shirazi had begun to put together information about the most important monuments of Persia. His *Asar-e 'Ajam* was published in Bombay in AH 1314/AD 1896, and contained plans of the site of Persepolis and drawings of the reliefs. He also recorded Naqsh-i Rustam, Naqsh-i Rajab, Istakhr and Pasargadae in Fars, as well as important Achaemenid and Sasanian monuments elsewhere. His identifications of the ruins of Persepolis and the reading of the cuneiform inscriptions are in general correct: Cyrus, who is equated with Kay Khusrow of the *Shahnameh*, is dated to 559 BC; Cambyses, Cyrus's son, is identified with Kay Kavus of the *Shahnameh*; Darius is dated to 425 BC; and Xerxes, who is not mentioned by his Persian name Khashayar, is equated with the invincible hero of the *Shahnameh*, Isfandiyar. The ancient history of Iran is seen here within the framework of the *Shahnameh*, and Jamshid, the mythological king, is regarded as the ruler who first built Persepolis. This was before the Achaemenids. Fursat Shirazi also refers to European travellers, whose work he used for an understanding of the monuments and their history. He mentions the German Iranologist, Friedrich Spiegel, as his main source for the reading and understanding of the Old Persian cuneiform inscriptions.

In AH 1313/AD 1895 the *Fars-nama Nasiri* by Haji Mirza Hasan Fasai gave a detailed account of Fars and its monuments. He describes how in 1811 Hussein Ali Mirza, the Governor of Fars, opened the stone coffins in the tombs at Persepolis but found only dust.[30] When describing the monuments of Pasargadae, he wrote that Solomon and the legendary Jamshid were one and the same person.

Around this time (1884–6) the French under Marcel and Jane Dieulafoy started digging at Susa, and in 1895 France was granted a monopoly of excavations in Iran for the sum of FF 55,000. This concession, arising from the royal family's pro-French sympathies, was regarded critically by some Iranians, who felt that 'those ancestral treasures our motherland has preserved for us Iranians in her bosom for ages ... are lost to a *farangi* [foreigner]'.[31] On the other hand, it has to be said that with growing British and Russian interest in Iran in the nineteenth century, the Qajar rulers perhaps thought it would be better for Iran's sake to side with the French, who were less of a threat after the defeat of Napoleon.

With the collapse of the Qajars and Reza Khan's appearance on the political scene in 1921 various patriotic movements emerged and the Society for National Heritage (*anjoman-e asar-e melli*) was set up to protect the cultural heritage and to produce histories of both pre-Islamic as well as Islamic Iran. In 1934, to mark the millennium of the poet Firdowsi, a mausoleum was built at Tus in Khorasan that received its inspiration from the architecture of the Tomb of Cyrus at Pasargadae.

In 1924 Reza Khan visited Susa and was dismayed by what he saw.[32] Soon after, in 1927, the French monopoly on all excavations in Iran was abolished. An Antiquities Service was established in 1929, and in 1930 an Antiquities Law was passed which made it possible for other foreign missions to engage in archaeological activities. Reza Shah visited Susa again in 1928 and 1937. It was during his last visit that he found out about the fate of objects discovered by the French excavators and remarked 'those thieves took all those objects to the Louvre and left the cement for Iran'.[33]

In 1931 the Oriental Institute of Chicago began excavations at Persepolis under the directorship of Ernst Herzfeld, who had already excavated at Pasargadae in 1928. The excavations were wholeheartedly supported by Reza Shah, who after his second visit in 1928 remarked that the 'ruins speak for themselves and tell you the glory of ancient Iranian monarchs'.[34] On his last visit in March 1937, he urged Erich Schmidt, who had replaced Herzfeld as director in 1934, to 'work faster'.[35]

Persepolitan motifs were now very popular amongst the Iranian elite and educated people. Banknotes were decorated with columns and images of Persepolis (fig. 75), and public buildings, such as banks and police headquarters, were built in the Persepolitan style. Reza

Shah's passion for ancient Iran showed itself also in his adopted family name Pahlavi, 'called after an ancient form of our Persian language'.[36] It was also during this time that the term 'Persia', which had long been used by non-Iranians for Iran, and had also become associated with Iran's ancient past in the west, was banned by the imperial government of Iran. According to the national-

75 Iranian 100-rial banknote from the reign of Mohammad Reza Pahlavi (1941–79) showing on the back the 'audience scene' from Persepolis featuring Xerxes, the crown-prince Darius and officials. This relief was originally set up on the north side of the Apadana, but was removed in antiquity. It is now in the National Museum in Tehran.

ists, the term should only be used to refer to the province of Fars, and not the country. The Iran Bastan Museum was founded in 1937 to house the country's national antiquities and in the same year Tehran University received its Department of Archaeology.

After the abdication of Reza Shah in 1941 and Mohammad Reza Pahlavi's accession to the throne, ancient Persian culture and history continued to play an important role, partly as it had done for the earlier Qajar rulers, to give credibility to their dynasty. After 1945 and the end of occupation of north Iran by the Russians and of south Iran by the British, there was a period of national reawakening, which produced a greater desire amongst educated Iranians to glorify ancient Iran and to produce an accurate history of it. During the reign of Mohammad Reza Pahlavi the ancient past was enthusiastically promoted and Cyrus became the icon of the Pahlavi regime. The Shah added the title Aryamehr ('Light of the Aryans') and became King of Kings. He also adopted the Cyrus Cylinder as one of the emblems of the Pahlavi dynasty. The culmination of this ancient Iranian revival took place in October 1971 when the Shah celebrated the 2,500th anniversary of the foundation of the Persian Empire by Cyrus. In the presence of hundreds of eminent guests and to the embarrassment of many ordinary Iranians he stood in front of the Tomb of Cyrus at Pasargadae and, moved to tears, said: 'Sleep in peace forever, for we are awake and we remain to watch over your glorious heritage.'[37] At Persepolis hundreds of Iranians dressed in copies of ancient costumes marched in files to the sound of trumpets and music before the eyes of the royal family and their international guests. Despite the collapse of the regime and the Revolution in 1979, Persepolis and ancient Persia continue to play an important role in the lives of modern Iranians, who identify closely with their ancient heritage.

1 Tacitus, *Annals* VI.31.

2 Herzfeld 1941: figs 401–2; Shahbazi 1976: fig. 24.

3 Sims-Williams 1995–6: 83; Huyse 1999; Shahbazi 2001: 67.

4 Boyce 1984: 103–11; Shahbazi 2001: 61.

5 Wiesehöfer 2001: 223. For a detailed study of the history of Persepolis see Mousavi 2002.

6 xxxiii.6, 7–8, 42; Shahbazi 1977: 201.

7 Tabari: 484, 486, 487; Dinavari: 38, 47–9, 51–2, 54–5; Hamzeh Isfahani: 38, 91; Biruni: 23, 26, 29, 152, 296; see also Daryaee 1995: 133–4.

8 *Shahnameh*, vol. I, 33, line 199: 'suy-i takht-e jamshid benhad ruy' and 37, line 54: 'le larzan shod an khane-ye sad sotun'.

9 Mostafavi 1978: 217 (inscriptions 3, 4, 5); Shahbazi 1379/2000b: 114–15.

10 Mostafavi 1978: 21–2; Rajabi and Mahmudi Aznaveh 1378/2000: 1; Razmjou 2003: 90.

11 Sami 1338/1959; 21; Shahbazi 1979/2000b: 114–16.

12 Shahbazi 1977: xx.

13 Mostafavi 1978: 225, no. 17.

14 Mostafavi 1978: 227, no. 20.

15 Mostafavi 1978: xxiii.

16 Mostafavi 1978: ix.

17 Mostafavi 1978: xi.

18 Budge 1920: 1, 22; Curtis 2000: 84–9; Wiesehöfer 2001: 223–42; 2002: 271–3; 278; Errington and Curtis, forthcoming.

19 Curtis 1998: 45–8.

20 Rich 1836, I: 199–222, II: 219–20; Alexander 1928: 303–4, 307, 309.

21 Ker Porter 1821–2, vols I and II.

22 Barnett 1974: 11.

23 Layard 1887, I: 203.

24 Loftus 1857; Curtis 1993.

25 Simpson 2000.

26 Diba 1999: 34, 36–7; Amanat 2001: 373; Luft 2001: 43–5.

27 Adle 2000: 16.

28 Mostafavi 1978: 228–9, nos 23 and 24.

29 Adle 2000: 16.

30 Lerner 1998: 165.

31 Abdi 2001: 55.

32 Abdi 2001: 54, 59.

33 Abdi 2001: 54, no. 46.

34 Abdi 2001: 60.

35 Abdi 2001: 60.

36 Pahlavi 1960: 27.

37 Shawcross 1989: 47.

452

the two distances mentioned on the stone are equal to ⅔ and 2 parasangs respectively. The script is difficult to date, but is possibly *c.* fifth to fourth centuries BC.

Persepolis
H 46 cm, W 28 cm, Th 22 cm
Persepolis Museum, 3410

454 Silver tetradrachm of Bagadates

Bagadates was a local ruler of Persis in the second century BC. The obverse shows the head of the bearded king with earrings and a Median-style cap, with tucked-in ear-flaps and a neckguard. The reverse shows a seated king holding a long staff, similar to royal images at Persepolis, and wearing a Median-style coat (*kandys*) slung over his shoulders.

Wt 16.62 g
British Museum, CM *BMC Persia*: 195, 1

455 Silver tetradrachm of Bagadates

Bagadates was a local ruler of Persis in the second century BC. The obverse shows the head of the bearded local ruler with earrings and a Median-style cap, with tucked-in ear-flaps and a neckguard. The reverse shows a building, perhaps Persepolis, with the symbol of the winged disc and the royal standard.

Wt 16.91 g
British Museum, CM *BMC Persia*: 196, 2

452 Clay tablet

A fragment of a Babylonian astronomical diary with a mention of the defeat of Darius III by Alexander of Macedon at Gaugamela on 1 October 331 BC, and of Alexander's later entry into Babylon.

Babylon
H 8.7 cm, W 8.1 cm
British Museum, ANE 36761
Sacks and Hunger 1988: no. 330

453 Stone merlon

With an added inscription in Greek on two sides, probably indicating re-use as a milestone or boundary marker.

Front: ΣΤΑ[ΔΙΟΙ] ΕΙΚΟΣΙ
'Twenty stades'

Reverse: ΣΤΑΔΙΟΙ ΕΞΗΚΟΝ-ΤΑ
'Sixty stades'

The Greek stade consisted of 600 feet. The Persian parasang was equated to 30 stades, so

453, front

453, back

456 Silver drachm of Mithradates II (*c.* 123–88 BC)

The obverse shows the bearded Arsacid/Parthian king wearing a bejewelled tiara. The reverse depicts the seated royal archer. The title 'king of kings' is that previously used by the Achaemenid kings.

Wt 4.06 g
British Museum, CM *BMC Parthia*: 34, 108

457 Silver drachm probably of Arsaces I (*c.* 238–211 BC)

The obverse shows the Arsacid/Parthian king wearing a Median-style cap, with ear-flaps and neckguard. The reverse depicts the seated royal archer wearing a Median-style coat slung over the shoulders.

Wt 4.1 g
British Museum, CM 1968-0212-1

458 Silver tetradrachm of Artabanus II (*c.* AD 10–38)

The obverse shows the frontal head of the bearded and long-haired Arsacid/Parthian king. The reverse depicts the king, who is wearing the Median-style jacket and trousers, on horseback and in the presence of a standing goddess.

Wt 12.98 g
British Museum, CM 1848-0803-97

454

455

456

457

458

459

459 Gold dinar of Ardashir I (AD 224–40)

The obverse shows the bearded Sasanian ruler wearing a bejewelled tiara similar to that of the Parthian king Mithradates II. The reverse shows a Zoroastrian fire altar and a royal throne with lion's-paw legs. The throne is similar to Achaemenid platform thrones at Persepolis.

Wt 8.47 g
British Museum, CM
Thomas 1853: 180, fig. 1

460 Engraving showing delegations on the Apadana frieze

The delegations are shown from the two lower registers on the west wing of the north side of the Apadana at Persepolis (see cat. 20). Cornelis de Bruijn (1652–1727) was at Persepolis between 1704 and 1705.

From *Voyages de Corneille le Brun par la Moscovie, en Perse, et aux Indes Orientales*. Freres Wetstein, Amsterdam, 1718 (2 vols), pl. 126 (after the original edition of 1711)
H 23 cm, L 94 cm
British Museum, ANE

460

461

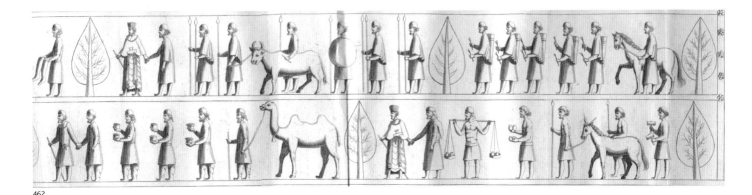

462

461 Engraving showing a view of the ruined buildings on the terrace at Persepolis

From *Voyages de Corneille le Brun par la Moscovie, en Perse, et aux Indes Orientales*. Freres Wetstein, Amsterdam, 1718 (2 vols), pl. 119 (after the original edition of 1711)
H 30 cm, L 64 cm
British Museum, ANE

462 Engraving showing delegations on the Apadana frieze

The delegations are shown from the two lower registers on the west wing of the north side of the Apadana at Persepolis (see cat. 20). Jean Chardin (1643–1713) was at Persepolis between 1673 and 1677 and these views show that the north side of the Apadana had already been cleared in the seventeenth century.

From *Voyages du Chevalier Chardin, en Perse, et autres lieux de l'Orient*. De la Normant, Paris, 1811, detail of pl. 58 G (after the original edition of 1686)
H 30 cm, L 98 cm
British Museum, ANE

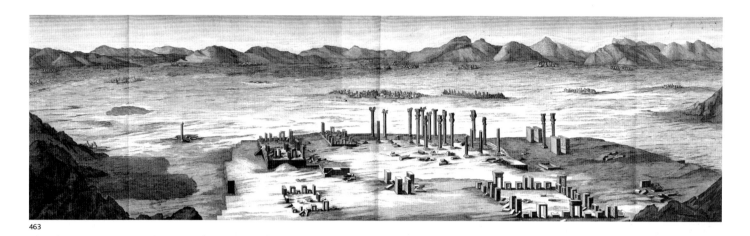

463

463 Engraving showing a view of the ruined buildings on the terrace at Persepolis

From *Voyages du Chevalier Chardin, en Perse, et autres lieux de l'Orient*. De la Normant, Paris, 1811, pl. 53 (after the original edition of 1686)
H 24.5 cm, L 74.5 cm
British Museum, ANE

464 Sir Robert Ker Porter, drawing of a colossal bull in the 'Gate of All Nations' at Persepolis

Reproduced in Ker Porter 1821–2: I, pl. 31
Pen and ink on paper
H 41.9 cm, W 26.2 cm
British Museum, ANE

465 Sir Robert Ker Porter, drawing of some defeated rebels from the Bisitun relief

A drawing of the complete relief is in Ker Porter 1821–2: II, pl. 60
Pen and ink on paper
H 35.2 cm, W 18.5 cm
British Museum, ANE

466 Sir Robert Ker Porter, drawing showing part of the decoration on the tomb of Xerxes at Naqsh-i Rustam

A drawing of the complete façade of the tomb is in Ker Porter 1821–2: I, pl. 17
Pen and ink on paper
H 41.7 cm, W 26 cm
British Museum, ANE

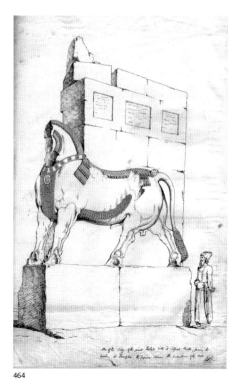

464

465

466

467 Sir Henry Creswicke Rawlinson, framed copy of *Inscription of Xerxes at Mt. Alwand near Hamadan*

In the spring of 1835 Henry Rawlinson (1810–95), then a military advisor stationed at Kermanshah, was able to visit Mount Alvand, southwest of Hamadan, and copy its two Old Persian inscriptions. Knowing only that the German scholar G.F. Grotefend had identified the names of some of the Achaemenid Persian kings, Rawlinson analysed one of the Alvand inscriptions as containing the names of Darius (522–486 BC) and his father Hystaspes, and the other as containing the names of Xerxes (486–465 BC) and Darius. His large original coloured drawing of the latter part of the Xerxes inscription has the two royal names, Xerxes and Darius, underlined, with word-dividers coloured red. The decipherment of these royal names was the beginning of Rawlinson's decipherment of the whole Old Persian script. The enlarged copy, cat. 467, and cat. 468 below were possibly produced for lecturing purposes.

Pen and coloured ink on paper
H 105 cm, W 150.5 cm
British Museum, ANE

468 Sir Henry Creswicke Rawlinson, framed copy of *Paragraphs of the Persian cuneiform inscriptions cut into rock at Mt. Elwend near Hamadan*

This smaller copy of the two Old Persian inscriptions at Mount Alvand, of Darius on the left and Xerxes on the right, underlines the names of Darius and Hystaspes, and of Xerxes and Darius.

Pen and ink on paper
H 35.2 cm, W 61.8 cm
British Museum, ANE

467

468

469 Frederick Stacpoole (1813–1907) after Briton Riviere (1840–1920), *Persepolis* (1880)

This picture, showing lions in the ruins of Persepolis, combines two of Riviere's favourite and most successful genres: animal studies and 'Classical' subjects. Published by Thomas Agnew & Sons in 1880, the print reproduces Riviere's untraced oil painting first exhibited at the Royal Academy of Arts in 1878 (no. 201). The exhibition catalogue appended a quote from Omar Khayyam's *The Rubaiyat*: 'they say

the lion and the lizard keep the courts when Jamshyd gloried and drank deep'.

Presented by Thomas Agnew & Sons, London
Mezzotint engraving with roulette on *chine collé*
H 56 cm, W 86 cm
British Museum, PD 1885-11-29, 80

470 Gold coin struck to commemorate 2,500 years of Persian monarchy in 1971

The denomination is 1 pahlavi, named after the ruling dynasty which came to power in 1921. On the obverse is Muhammed Reza

Shah Pahlavi (1941–79), and on the reverse is the Cyrus Cylinder.

Wt 9 g
British Museum, CM 1972-0816-1

471 Banknote of 50 Rials, issued 1974–5, showing on the reverse the Tomb of Cyrus at Pasargadae

H 6.3 cm, L 13.6 cm
Private Collection

469

470

BANK MARKAZI IRAN

50   50

50 RIALS

471

472

472 Postage stamp with a face value of 5 Rials, showing the Cyrus Cylinder

This is one of a set of four stamps issued on the 12 October 1971 to celebrate the 2,500-year anniversary of the foundation of the Persian Empire. Altogether 8 sets of stamps (of which this is the last) were issued to commemorate the anniversary.

H 4.2 cm, L 5.75 cm
Private Collection

473 Gold medal issued to commemorate 2,500 years of Persian monarchy in 1971, showing on the reverse the Cyrus Cylinder

Presented to Dr R.D. Barnett, Keeper of the Department of Western Asiatic Antiquities at the British Museum (1955–74), who attended the festival at Persepolis on behalf of the British Museum.

Diam 3.6 cm
British Museum, CM 1972-0614-1

473

KING LIST AND GLOSSARY

LIST OF ACHAEMENID KINGS

550–530 BC	Cyrus II (the Great)
530–522	Cambyses
522	Bardiya
522–486	Darius I
486–465	Xerxes
465–424	Artaxerxes I
424–423	Xerxes II
423–404	Darius II (Ochus)
404–359	Artaxerxes II (Arsaces)
359–338	Artaxerxes III (Ochus)
338–336	Artaxerxes IV (Arses)
336–330	Darius III

SELECT GLOSSARY

Achaemenid – the dynasty of Cyrus and his successors, named after the legendary king Achaemenes

Ahuramazda – the supreme god of the Zoroastrian religion. He is frequently invoked by the Achaemenid kings in their official inscriptions. He is probably shown in the winged disc symbol.

akinakes – a short sword with a characteristic scabbard. There is an Elamite form that is shown with Persian dress (stuck in a waist band) and a Median form that is shown with Median dress (hanging from a belt).

Anahita – the goddess of all waters and fertility in the Zoroastrian religion.

apadana – a columned hall with corner towers and porticoes on three sides.

Aramaic – a north-west semitic language written in a script related to Hebrew that was commonly used for administrative purposes in the Achaemenid Empire.

Arrian – a Greek writer (*c.* AD 95–175) who wrote a *History of Alexander* in *c.* AD 150.

Assyria – an empire based in northern Mesopotamia (Iraq) that flourished between the ninth and seventh centuries BC. The Assyrians were a semitic-speaking people, and their main capital cities were at Nimrud and Nineveh.

Avesta – the sacred book of the Zoroastrian religion.

Babylonian – a semitic language that was used in Babylonia (modern southern Iraq), written in cuneiform.

barsom – a bundle of sticks or twigs that is carried by a priest or by others as a sign of piety.

Bes – an Egyptian god who is shown as a bandy-legged dwarf with a lion's face. He looked after the household. Representations of Bes are common in the Achaemenid Empire, but his significance at this time is not properly understood.

cuneiform – a wedge-shaped script, different forms of which were used for writing Old Persian, Elamite and Babylonian.

daric – a gold coin showing a royal archer issued from the time of Darius onwards.

Egyptian blue – a blue frit produced by firing a mixture of quartz, calcite and copper with a small amount of alkali.

Elamite – a language that was used in southwest Iran from at least 3000 BC onwards and written in a form of the cuneiform script. The clay tablets from Persepolis are written in Elamite.

faience – an artificial composition of powdered quartz originally with a glazed surface.

glazed bricks – the polychrome glazed bricks of the Achaemenid period are made from coarse quartz faience and the glazes are retained within black cloisons. Earlier glazed bricks are made of mud with straw temper.

gorytus – a protective case for a composite bow and its arrows.

Herodotus – a historian writing in Greek who was born in Halicarnassus in southwest Turkey *c.* 484 BC and died in Italy *c.* 425 BC. His *Histories* are the most important source for the Graeco-Persian wars and have earned him the posthumous title of 'Father of History'.

magus - the name for a priest in the Achaemenid period, reflected in the modern English word 'magic'. The three *magi* in the New Testament were kings from the east.

Medes – people speaking an Indo-European language who, like the closely related Persians, migrated onto the Iranian plateau from the north. They were well established in western Iran from at least the ninth century BC onwards, principally around Hamadan. They joined forces with the Babylonians to overthrow Assyria in 612 BC.

Median dress – a belted tunic worn with trousers, sometimes with the addition of an overcoat (*kandys*). This costume might be worn with a cap that has a neck-guard and ear-flaps tied under the chin (*kyrbasia* or *bashlik*), or with a domed hat (*kolah*).

Mithra – the sun god in the Zoroastrian religion.

Old Persian – an Iranian language belonging to the Indo-European family that was used for monumental inscriptions from the time of Darius onwards. It was written in a cuneiform script that was specially adapted for the purpose.

Oxus Treasure – a collection of gold and silver objects and coins that was found between 1876 and 1880 on the north bank of the River Oxus, perhaps at the site of Takht-i Kuwad.

Persians – people speaking an Indo-European language who migrated onto the Iranian plateau from the north. They are attested in Assyrian sources in the ninth century BC and by the sixth century BC were established in Parsa (modern Fars) in Iran.

Persian dress – a full-sleeved and pleated robe reaching down to the ankles, usually worn either with a fluted crown or with a turban.

satraps – governors in charge of major administrative provinces (satrapies). The Old Persian (*xšaçapāvan*) means 'protecting the kingdom'.

winged disc – where there is the bust of a human figure in the winged disc he is probably to be identified either as Ahuramazda or the divine glory (*khvarnah* or *farr*). It is sometimes suggested that the figure is that of a deceased king, but this seems unlikely.

Xenophon – a Greek historian born in Athens *c.* 430 BC. His *Anabasis* describes the failed attempt by Cyrus the Younger to seize the throne from his brother Artaxerxes II, and the retreat to the Black Sea of Cyrus's 10,000 Greek mercenaries after the Battle of Cunaxa in 401 BC. His *Cyropaedia* is a treatise on the career of Cyrus the Great.

Zarathustra – the prophet of the Zoroastrian religion. He is traditionally dated to around 600 BC but probably lived around 1000 BC or earlier.

Zoroaster – the Greek form of Zarathustra

Zoroastrianism – a religion that believes in a single supreme god, Ahuramazda, who created all things. He is supported by divine helpers known as *yazatas*. Ahuramazda stands for everything Good, in contrast to Ahriman, who represents Evil. Fire symbolizes Truth and is an important element in Zoroastrian temples.

CONCORDANCE OF BRITISH MUSEUM OBJECT NUMBERS

BM NUMBER	CAT. NUMBER
ANE 26643	306
ANE 29455	307
ANE E 30755	67
ANE E 32625	302
ANE 33973	305
ANE 36761	452
ANE 89009	286
ANE 89132	398
ANE 89144	417
ANE 89324 (N 1069)	208
ANE 89333	423
ANE 89337	72
ANE 89352	205
ANE 89422	202
ANE 89528	200
ANE 89549	68
ANE 89574 (N 1063)	289
ANE 89583 (N 1082)	418
ANE 89585	73
ANE 89781	450
ANE 89816	420
ANE 89852 (N 1065)	203
ANE 89891	69
ANE 89893	66
ANE 90854	10
ANE 90855	11
ANE 90920	6
ANE 91117	300
ANE 91187	385
ANE 91453	142
ANE 91454	143
ANE 91455	144
ANE 91456	145
ANE 91459	141
ANE 91895	206
ANE 92253	31
ANE 103013	421
ANE 108681	426
ANE 108759	386
ANE 115523	209
ANE 115604	293
ANE 116410	134
ANE 116411	120
ANE 117760	409
ANE 117840	132
ANE 118014	135
ANE 118462	133
ANE 118837	30
ANE 118838	33
ANE 118839	23
ANE 118840	37
ANE 118841	37
ANE 118843	25
ANE 118844	27
ANE 118845	28
ANE 118847	24
ANE 118848	22
ANE 118851	26
ANE 118855	198
ANE 118857	36
ANE 118864	21
ANE 118866	29
ANE 118868	40
ANE 118869	35
ANE 120325	416
ANE 120326	422
ANE 120450	129
ANE 123255	108
ANE 123256	106
ANE 123258	107
ANE 123259	109
ANE 123263	136
ANE 123264	137
ANE 123265	151
ANE 123901	260
ANE 123902	258
ANE 123903	259
ANE 123905	261
ANE 123906	262
ANE 123908	399
ANE 123909	400
ANE 123911	127
ANE 123917	150
ANE 123918	125
ANE 123919	100
ANE 123920	105
ANE 123921	99
ANE 123922	98
ANE 123923	431
ANE 123924	194
ANE 123925	396
ANE 123926	397
ANE 123927	186
ANE 123928	187
ANE 123929	183
ANE 123933	184
ANE 123934	185
ANE 123936	188
ANE 123939	189
ANE 123940	427
ANE 123941	395
ANE 123944	394
ANE 123946	405
ANE 123947	406
ANE 123949	213
ANE 123950	236
ANE 123951	214
ANE 123952	216
ANE 123953	215
ANE 123954	218
ANE 123955	219
ANE 123956	217
ANE 123957	220
ANE 123958	222
ANE 123959	241
ANE 123960	221
ANE 123961	224
ANE 123962	232
ANE 123963	229
ANE 123964	230
ANE 123965	233
ANE 123966	226
ANE 123967	252
ANE 123968	252
ANE 123969	235
ANE 123970	228
ANE 123971	227
ANE 123972	245
ANE 123973	231
ANE 123974	250
ANE 123975	249
ANE 123976	251
ANE 123977	234
ANE 123978	237
ANE 123979	240
ANE 123980	239
ANE 123981	223
ANE 123982	244
ANE 123983	254
ANE 123984	238
ANE 123985	253
ANE 123986	225
ANE 123990	243
ANE 123991	246
ANE 123992	247
ANE 123993	248
ANE 123994	242
ANE 123995	255
ANE 123996	254
ANE 123999	257
ANE 124000	256
ANE 124004	180
ANE 124005	210
ANE 124006	296
ANE 124007	18
ANE 124012	182
ANE 124013	181
ANE 124014	449
ANE 124015	413
ANE 124016	290
ANE 124017	153
ANE 124018	154
ANE 124019	155
ANE 124021	160
ANE 124025	162
ANE 124026	161
ANE 124027	156
ANE 124034	163
ANE 124035	157
ANE 124036	164
ANE 124037	166
ANE 124038	167
ANE 124040	168
ANE 124041	158
ANE 124042	159
ANE 124043	165
ANE 124044	169
ANE 124045	170
ANE 124047	171
ANE 124048	171
ANE 124049	393
ANE 124059	178
ANE 124081	119
ANE 124082	104
ANE 124098	408
ANE 127400	19
ANE 128842	287
ANE 128849	201
ANE 128851	204
ANE 128865	207
ANE 129381	46
ANE 129565	291
ANE 129569	414
ANE 129571	74
ANE 129596	292
ANE 130808	419
ANE 130816	294
ANE 132103	193
ANE 132104	193
ANE 132105	193
ANE 132106	193
ANE 132107	193
ANE 132108	192
ANE 132111	191
ANE 132114	140
ANE 132120	391
ANE 132256	400
ANE 132353	195
ANE 132505	415
ANE 132507	295
ANE 132525	51
ANE 132620	196
ANE 132925	435
ANE 133028	314
ANE 134385	49
ANE 134740	111
ANE 134761	70
ANE 135125	197
ANE 135142	437
ANE 135571	101
ANE 135855	438
ANE 135953	116
ANE 136050	94
ANE 136209	9
ANE 1882-12-20, 25	179
ANE 1891-5-13, 3	389
ANE 1898-6-16, 1	284
ANE 1898-6-16, 2	282
ANE 1898-6-16, 3	283
ANE 1898-6-16, 4	285
ANE GR 1912-7-11, 1	176
ANE 1932-10-8, 192	75
ANE 1932-10-8, 198	297
ANE 1932-10-8, 226	124
ANE 1994-1-27, 1	103
ANE 1996-9-28, 1	93
ANE 1998-1-17, 1	102
ANE 1999-12-1, 17	388
CM 1840-1226-97	340
CM 1841-0726-522	316
CM 1845-0705	377
CM 1845-1217-272	322
CM 1848-0803-97	458
CM 1848-0819-51	361
CM 1852-0902-110	318
CM 1852-1027-2	320
CM 1866-1201-3804	317
CM 1866-1201-4124	334
CM 1868-0406-20	339
CM 1874-0716-236	344
CM 1875-0701-24	331
CM 1877-0303-1	347
CM 1877-0508-1	376
CM 1883-0402-26	338
CM 1887-0606-29	341
CM 1888-1103-4	375
CM 1888-1208-6	356
CM 1892-0703-1	330
CM 1896-0601-105	363
CM 1897-0305-78	319
CM 1899-0401-86	378
CM 1900-1204-4	343
CM 1909-0105-12	371
CM 1915-0108-28	323
CM 1918-1104-4	324
CM 1919-0516-15	321
CM 1919-0516-17	326
CM 1919-1120-114	327
CM 1920-0422-11	360
CM 1920-0422-5	352
CM 1920-0805-370	370
CM 1925-0105-129	372
CM 1929-0602-32	346
CM 1937-0606-18	358
CM 1947-0706-4	332
CM 1957-0107-1	381
CM 1968-0212,1	457
CM 1971-0510-1	362
CM 1972-0614-1	473
CM 1972-0816-1	470
CM 1979-0101-1003	357
CM 1979-0101-292	335
CM 1979-0101-373	342
CM 1979-0101-992	353
CM 1979-0101-995	354
CM 1981-0220-1	345
CM 1982-0511-1	374
CM 1985-1114-1	349
CM 1987-0649-461	355
CM 1990-0121-1	329
CM 1993-1106-7	380
CM 2000-0508-1	373
CM 2002-1028-1	336
CM 2002-1028-2	337
CM 2003-1107-3	364
CM Bank 1157	348
CM BMC Persia: 195, 1	454
CM BMC Cilicia: 148, 26	350
CM BMC Cilicia: 164, 12	351
CM BMC Cilicia: 169, 38	359
CM BMC Ionia: 325, 13	333
CM BMC Sidon: 81	365
CM BMC Sidon: 84	366
CM BMC Sidon: 9	379
CM BMC Persia: 196, 2	455
CM BMC Parthia: 196	456
CM SNG Black Sea 1447	367
CM SNG Black Sea 1451	368
CM SNG Black Sea 1452	369
CM Thomas NC XV 180.1	459
CM BMC Ionia: 323, 1	328
CM BMC Persia: 171, 171	325
AES 1697	267
AES 1719	267
AES 5428	432
AES 10449	315
AES 12963	122
AES 37496	266
AES 45035	312
AES 45036	313
GR 1837.6-9.59 (Vase E 135)	447
GR 1849.6-20.12 (Vase E 791)	448
GR 1857.12-20.263 (Sculpture 1057)	444
GR 1866.4-15. 244 (Vase E 233)	425
GR 1870.6-6.7	114
GR 1873.3-20.51 (Sculpture C323)	443
GR 1873.3-20.9 (Sculpture C155)	442
GR 1873.3-20.93	402
GR 1888.5-12.12	390
GR 1891.5-13.2 (Bronze 2876)	392
GR 1906.4-25.2	451
GR 1911.4-15.1	407
GR 1848.10-20.97	123
PD 1885-11-29, 80	469

Abdi, K., 1999. 'Bes in the Achaemenid empire', *Ars Orientalis* XXIX: 111–40.

Abdi, K., 2001. 'Nationalism, politics, and the development of archaeology in Iran', *AJA* 105: 51–76.

Abdi, K., 2002a. 'An Egyptian *cippus* of Horus in the Iran National Museum, Tehran', *Journal of Near Eastern Studies* 61: 203–10.

Abdi, K., 2002b. 'Notes on the Iranianization of Bes in the Achaemenid empire', *Ars Orientalis* XXXII: 133–62.

Abraham, K., 2004. *Business and Politics under the Persian Empire: The Financial Dealings of Marduk-nasir-apli of the House of Egibi (521–487 B.C.E.)*, Bethesda.

Adkins, L., 2003. *Empires of the Plain: Henry Rawlinson and the Lost Languages of Babylon*, London.

Adle, C., 2000 (SH 1379). 'Khorheh: The dawn of Iranian scientific archaeological excavation', *Tavoos* 3–4: 4–43 (in Persian), 226–65 (in English).

Akishev, K.A., 1978. *Kurgan Issik*, Moscow.

Akurgal, E., 1966. 'Griechisch-Persische Reliefs aus Daskyleion', *Iranica Antiqua* VI: 147–56.

Alexander, C.M., 1928. *Baghdad in Bygone Days*, London.

Al-Qaddumi, G. al-Hijjawi, 1996. *Book of Gifts and Rarities (Kitab al-Hadaya wa al-Tuhaf): Selections Compiled in the Fifteenth Century from an Eleventh-Century Manuscript on Gifts and Treasures*. Cambridge, Mass.

Amanat, A., 2001. 'The Kayanid crown and Qajar reclaiming of royal authority', *Journal of the Society of Iranian Studies* 34: 17–30.

Amandry, P., 1956. 'Vaisselle d'argent de l'époque achéménide (collection Hélène Stathatos)', *Memorial Festschrift of G.P. Ekonomu*, vol. AE 1953/4, Athens:12–19.

Amandry, P., 1958. 'Orfèvrerie achéménide', *Antike Kunst* I: 9–23.

Amandry, P., 1959. 'Toreutique achéménide', *Antike Kunst* II: 38–56.

Ambers, J., and Simpson, St J., 2005. 'Some pigment identifications for objects from Persepolis', *Arta* 2005.02 (Achaemenet): 1–13.

Amigues, S., 2003. 'Pour la table du grand roi', *Journal des Savants*, January–June: 3–59.

Amiet P., 1988. *Suse, 6000 ans d'histoire*, Paris.

Austin, M.M., 1990. 'Greek Tyrants and the Persians, 546–479 B.C.', *Classical Quarterly* 40: 289–306.

Babelon, E., 1893. *Catalogue des monnaies grecques de la Bibliothèque nationale. Les Perses achéménides*, Paris.

Bäbler, B., 1998. *Fleissige Thrakerinnen und wehrhafte Skythen: Nichtgriechen im klassischen Athen und ihre archäologische Hinterlassenschaft*, Stuttgart and Leipzig.

Badian, E., 1985. 'Alexander in Iran', *Cambridge History of Iran* II: 420–501.

Balcer, J.M., 1984. *Sparda by the Bitter Sea: Imperial Interaction in Western Anatolia*, Chico.

Balcer, J.M., 1991. 'The East Greeks under Persian Rule: A reassessment', *Achaemenid History* VI: 57–65.

Barag, D., 1968. 'An unpublished Achaemenid cut glass bowl from Nippur', *Journal of Glass Studies* 10: 17–20.

Barag, D., 1975. 'Rod-formed kohl-tubes of the mid-first millennium BC', *Journal of Glass Studies* 17: 23–36.

Barag, D., 1985. *Catalogue of Western Asiatic Glass in the British Museum*, vol.1, London.

Bare_, L., 1999. *Abusir IV: The Shaft Tomb of Udjahorresnet at Abusir*, Prague.

Barnett, R.D., 1957. 'Persepolis', *Iraq* 19: 55–77.

Barnett, R.D., 1960. 'Ancient Oriental goldwork', *The British Museum Quarterly* XXII: 29–30.

Barnett, R.D., 1962. 'Median Art', *Iranica Antiqua* 2: 77–95.

Barnett, R.D., 1963–4. 'A review of Western Asiatic Antiquities, 1955–62 (II)', *The British Museum Quarterly* XXVII: 79–88.

Barnett, R.D., 1974. 'Charles Bellino and the beginnings of Assyriology', *Iraq* 36: 5–28.

Barnett, R.D., 1976. *Sculptures from the North Palace of Ashurbanipal at Nineveh (668–627 BC)*, London.

Barnett, R.D., et al. 1998. *Sculptures from the Southwest Palace of Sennacherib at Nineveh*, London 1998.

Barnett, R.D. and Curtis, J.E., 1973, 'A review of acquisitions 1963–70 of Western Asiatic Antiquities (2)', *The British Museum Quarterly* XXXVII: 119–37.

Baslez, M.-F., 1986. 'Présence et traditions iraniennes dans les cités de l'Egée', *Revue des Etudes Anciennes* 87: 137–55.

Beazley, J.D., 1963. *Attic Red-Figure Vase-Painters* (2nd edn), Oxford.

Benveniste, E., 1929. *The Persian Religion according to the Chief Greek Texts*, Paris.

Berger, P.-R., 1975. 'Der Kyros-Zylinder mit dem Zusatzfragment BIN II Nr. 32 und die akkadischen Personennamen im Danielbuch', *Zeitschrift für Assyriologie* 64: 192–234.

Bernard, P., and Inagaki, H., 2000. 'Un torque achéménide avec une inscription grecque au Musée Miho (Japon)', in *Treasures of Ancient Bactria*, Miho Museum, Japan: 207–210.

Bettles, E., 2003. 'Carinated-shoulder amphorae from Sarepta, Lebanon', *National Museum News* 17: 60–79.

Bienkowski, P. (ed.), 1991. *The Art of Jordan*, Liverpool.

Bienkowski, P., 2001. 'The Persian period', in MacDonald, B., Adams, R., and Bienkowski, P. (eds), *The Archaeology of Jordan*, Sheffield: 347–65.

Bingöl, F.R.I., 1999. *Museum of Anatolian Civilizations: Ancient Jewellery*, Ankara.

Biruni, Abu Rayhan. *Athara al-baqiyah*, translated into Persian by A. Daneshseresht, Tehran 1984 (SH 1363).

Bivar, A.D.H., 1988. 'The Indus Lands', *Cambridge Ancient History*, 2nd edn, IV: 194–210.

BMC Caria = Head, B.V., 1897. *Catalogue of the Greek Coins of Caria, Cos, Rhodes, &c*, London.

BMC Cilicia = Hill, G.F., 1900. *Catalogue of the Greek Coins of Lycaonia, Isauria, and Cilicia*, London.

BMC Ionia = Head, B.V., 1892. *Catalogue of the Greek Coins of Ionia*, London.

BMC Lydia = Head, B.V., 1901. *Catalogue of the Greek Coins of Lydia*, London.

BMC Parthia = Wroth, W., 1903. *Catalogue of the Coins of Parthia*, London.

BMC Persia = Hill, G.F., 1922. *Catalogue of the Greek Coins of Arabia, Mesopotamia and Persia*, London.

BMC Sidon = Hill, G.F., 1910. *Catalogue of the Greek Coins of Phoenicia*, London.

Boardman, J., 1970. 'Pyramidal stamp seals in the Persian empire', *Iran* VIII: 19–45.

Boardman, J., 1988. 'The Greek World', in *Cambridge Ancient History Plates to Volume IV*: 95–178.

Boardman, J., 1994. *The Diffusion of Classical Art in Antiquity*. London.

Boardman, J., 1999. *The Greeks Overseas: Their Early Colonies and Trade*, 4th edn, London.

Boardman, J., 2000. *Persia and the West: An Archaeological Investigation of the Genesis of Achaemenid Art*, London.

Bosworth, A.B., 1980. 'Alexander and the Iranians', *Journal of Hellenic Studies* 100: 1–21.

Boucharlat, R., 1997. 'Susa under Achaemenid rule', in Curtis, J.E. (ed.) 1997: 54–67.

Boucharlat, R., 2005. 'La période achéménide en Iran: données archéologiques', in Briant, P.(ed.) 2005 (forthcoming).

Boucharlat, R., and Shahidi, H., 1987. 'Fragments architecturaux de type achéménide: découvertes fortuites dans la ville de Shoush 1976–1979', *Cahiers de la Délégation Archéologique Française en Iran* 15: 313–27.

Bowman, R.A., 1970. *Aramaic Ritual Texts from Persepolis*. Oriental Institute Publications 91, Chicago.

Bovon, A., 1963. 'Le representation des guerriers perses et la notion de barbare dans la première moitié du Ve siècle', *Bulletin de Correspondance Hellénique* 87: 579–602.

Boyce, M., 1975. *A History of Zoroastrianism* I, Leiden.

Boyce, M., 1979. *Zoroastrians: Their Religious Beliefs and Practices*, London.

Boyce, M., 1982. *A History of Zoroastrianism* II: *Under the Achaemenians*, Leiden-Köln.

Boyce, M., 1984. *Textual Sources for the Study of Zoroastrianism*, Manchester.

Brandenstein, W., and Mayrhofer, M., 1964. *Handbuch des Altpersischen*, Wiesbaden.

Bregstein, L.B., 1993. 'Seal Use in Fifth Century B.C. Nippur, Iraq: A Study of Seal Practices in the Murashû Archive', unpublished Ph.D. thesis, University of Pennsylvania.

Briant, P., 1987. 'Pouvoir central et polycentrisme culturel dans l'empire Achéménide. Quelques réflexions et suggestions', *Achaemenid History* I: 1–31.

Briant, P., 1988a. 'Le nomadisme du Grand Roi', *Iranica Antiqua* 23: 253–73.

Briant, P., 1988b. 'Ethno-classe dominante et populations soumises dans l'empire achémenide. Le cas de l'Égypte', *Achaemenid History* III: 137–74.

Briant, P., 1989. 'Table du roi, tribut et redistribution chez les achéménides', in Briant and Herrenschmidt: 35–44.

Briant, P., 2001. *Alexander the Great: The Heroic Ideal*, London.

Briant, P., 2002. *From Cyrus to Alexander: A History of the Persian Empire*, Winona Lake, Indiana.

Briant, P. (ed.), 2005. *L'Archéologie de l'Empire Achéménide*, Proceedings of a colloquium at the College de France, 21–2 November 2003 (forthcoming).

Briant, P., and Descat, R., 1998. 'Un registre douanier de la satrapie d'Égypte à l'époque achéménide', in Grimal, N., and Menu, B. (eds) *Le commerce en Égypte ancienne*, Bibl. d' étude 121, Cairo: 59–104.

Briant, P., and Herrenschmidt, C. (eds), 1989. *Le Tribut dans l'empire perse*, Paris.

Britton, J., and Walker, C., 1996. 'Astronomy and Astrology in Mesopotamia', in Walker. C. (ed) *Astronomy: Before the Telescope*, London.

Brosius, M., 1996. *Women in Ancient Persia: 559–331 BC*, Oxford.

Brosius, M., 2000. *The Persian Empire from Cyrus II to Artaxerxes I*, LACTOR 16, London.

Bruijn, C. de, 1718. *Voyages de Corneille le Brun par la Moscovie, en Perse, et aux Indes Orientales*, 2 vols, Amsterdam.

Bruns-Özgan, C., 1987. *Lykische Grabreliefs des 5. und 4. Jahrhunderts v. Chr.*, Tübingen.

Budge, E.A.W., 1920. *By Nile and Tigris*, 2 vols, London.

Budge, E.A.W., 1925. *The Rise and Progress of Assyriology*. London.

Burchardt, M., 1911. 'Datierte Denkmäler der Berl. Sammlung aus der Achamenidenzeit', *Zeitschrift für Ägyptische Sprache und Altertumskunde* 49: 69–80.

Burkard, G., 1995. 'Literarische Tradition und historische Realität. Die persische Eroburg Ägyptens am Beispiel Elephantine', *Zeitschrift für Ägyptische Sprache und Altertumskunde* 122: 31–7.

Cahn, H.A., 1985. 'Tissaphernes in Astyra', *Archäologischer Anzeiger*: 587–94.

Cahn, H.A., 1986. 'Zwei griechische Miszellen', in Margolis, R., and Voegtli, H. (eds) *Numismatics – Witness to History*, Wetteren: 11–14.

Cahn, H.A., 1989. 'Le monnayage des satrapes: iconographie et signification', *REA* 91: 97–106.

Calmeyer, P., 1972–5. 'Hose', *Reallexikon der Assyriologie und Vorderasiatischen Archäologie* 4: 472–6.

Calmeyer, P., 1975. 'Barsombündel im 8. und 7. Jahrhundert v. Chr.', *Wanderungen – Studien zur antiken und neueren Kunst*: 11–15.

Calmeyer, P., 1980a. 'Textual sources for the interpretation of Achaemenian palace decorations', *Iran* XVIII: 55–63.

Calmeyer, P., 1980b. 'Zur Genese altiranischer Motive VII. Achsnägel in Form von Betenden', *Archäologische Mitteilungen aus Iran* 13: 99–111.

Calmeyer, P., 1993. 'Die Gefäße auf den Gabenbringer-Reliefs in Persepolis', *Archäologische Mitteilungen aus Iran* 26: 147–60.

Calmeyer, P., 1994. 'Metamorphosen Iranischer Denkmäler', *Archaeologische Mitteilungun aus Iran* 27: 1–27, taf. 1–5.

Cameron, G.C., 1948. *Persepolis Treasury Tablets*, Oriental Institute Publications 65, Chicago.

Canby, J.V., 1979. 'A note on some Susa bricks', *Archäologische Mitteilungen aus Iran* 12: 315–20.

Cardascia, G., 1951. *Les archives des Mura_u*, Paris.

Carradice, I. (ed.), 1987a. *Coinage and Administration in the Athenian and Persian Empires*, BAR Int. Series 343, Oxford.

Carradice, I., 1987b. 'The "Regal" Coinage of the Persian Empire', in Carradice 1987a: 73–95.

Casabonne, O., 1996. 'Présence et influence perses en Cilicie a l'époque achéménide – iconographie et representations', *Anatolia Antiqua* 4: 121–45.

Casabonne, O., 2000. 'Conquête perse et phénomène monétaire: l'exemple cilicien', in Casabonne, O. (ed.), *Mécanismes et innovations monétaires dans l'Anatolie achéménide: numismatique et histoire: actes de la table ronde internationale d'Istanbul, 22–23 mai 1997*, Paris: 21–91.

Castriota, D., 1992. *Myth, Ethos and Actuality: Official Art in Fifth-Century B.C. Athens*, Madison: University of Wisconsin Press.

Castriota, D., 2000. 'Justice, kingship and imperialism: rhetoric and reality in fifth-century B.C. representations following the Persian Wars', in Cohen B. (ed.), *Not the Classical Ideal: Athens and the Construction of the Other in Greek Art*, Leiden: 443–79.

Cawkwell, G., 2005. *The Greek Wars. The Failure of Persia*, Oxford.

Chardin, J., 1811. *Voyages du Chevalier Chardin, en Perse, et autres lieux de l'Orient*, Paris.

Chattopadhyaya, S., 1974. *The Achaemenids and India*, New Delhi.

Chevalier, N., 1997. *Une mission en Perse 1897–1912*, exh. cat., Musée du Louvre, Paris.

Childs, W.A.P., and Demargne, P., 1989. *Fouilles de Xanthos 8. Le monument des Néréides: le décor sculpté*, Paris.

Collon, D., 1996. 'A Hoard of Sealings from Ur', in Boussac, M.-F., and Invernizzi, A. (eds) *Archives et sceaux du monde Hellénistique*, BCH Suppl. 29, Athens: 65–84.

Contenau, G., 1934. 'Monuments mésopotamiens nouvellement acquis ou peu connus', *Revue des Arts Asiatiques*: 99–103.

Contenau, G., 1947. *Manuel d'Archéologie orientale*, IV, Paris.

Cook, J.M., 1961. 'The Problem of Classical Ionia', *Proceedings of the Cambridge Philological Society* 187 (n.s. 7): 9–18.

Cook, J.M., 1962. *The Greeks in Ionia and the East*, London.

Corsaro, M., 1991. 'Gli Ioni tra Greci e Persiani: Il problema dell'identità ionica nel dibattito culturale e politico del V secolo', *Achaemenid History VI*: 41–55.

Costa, P.M., 1978. *The Pre-Islamic Antiquities at the Yemen National Museum*, Rome.

Cowley, A., 1923. *Aramaic Papyri of the Fifth Century BC*, Oxford.

Crouwel, J.H., 1987. 'Chariots in Iron Age Cyprus', *Report of the Department of Antiquities, Cyprus*: 101–18.

Cruz-Uribe, E., 1984. 'A Look at Two Early Divorce Documents', in Thissen, H-J., and Zauzich, K-Th. (eds) *Grammata Demotika: Festschrift für Erich Lüddeckens zum 15 Juni 1983*, Wurzburg: 41–6.

Culican, W., 1975. 'Syro-Achaemenian ampullae', *Iranica Antiqua* XI: 100–112.

Curtis, J.E., 1983. 'Late Assyrian bronze coffins', *Anatolian Studies* 33, 85–93.

Curtis, J.E., 1993. 'William Kennet Loftus and his Excavations at Susa', *Iranica Antiqua* XXVIII: 1–56.

Curtis, J.E., 1997. 'Franks and the Oxus Treasure', in Caygill, M., and Cherry, J. (eds) *A.W. Franks: Nineteenth-Century Collecting and the British Museum*, London: 230–49.

Curtis, J.E. (ed.), 1997. *Mesopotamia and Iran in the Persian Period: Conquest and Imperialism 539–331 B.C.*, London.

Curtis, J.E., 1998. 'A chariot scene from Persepolis', *Iran* XXXVI: 45–51.

Curtis, J.E., 2000. *Ancient Persia*, 2nd edn, London.

Curtis, J.E., 2003. 'Oxusschatz (the Oxus Treasure)', *Reallexikon der Assyriologie* 10: 153–7.

Curtis, J.E., 2005. 'The Achaemenid period in Northern Iraq', in Briant (ed.) 2005 (forthcoming).

Curtis, J.E., forthcoming. 'Greek Influence on Achaemenid Art and Architecture', in Villing, A. (ed.), *The Greeks in the East*, British Museum Occasional Paper, London.

Curtis, J.E., and Reade, J.E., 1995. *Art and Empire: Treasures from Assyria in the British Museum*, London.

Curtis, J.E. and Kruszynski, M., 2002. *Ancient Caucasian and Related Material in the British Museum*, British Museum Occasional Paper 121, London.

Curtis, J.E., Cowell, M.R., and Walker, C.B.F., 1995. 'A Silver Bowl of Artaxerxes I', *Iran* XXXIII: 149–53.

Curtis, J.E., Searight, A. and Cowell, M.R., 2003. 'The gold plaques of the Oxus Treasure: manufacture, decoration and meaning', in Potts, T., Roaf, M., and Stein, D. (eds), *Culture through Objects. Ancient Near Eastern Studies in Honour of P.R.S. Moorey*, Oxford: 219–47.

Curtis, V.S., 1993. *Persian Myths*, London.

Dalton, O.M., 1964. *The Treasure of the Oxus with Other Examples of Early Oriental Metal-Work*, 3rd edn, London.

Damerji, M.S., 1991. 'The Second Treasure of Nimrud', in Mori, M. *et al.* (eds), *Near Eastern Studies Dedicated to H.I.H. Prince Takahito Mikasa on the Occasion of his Seventy-Fifth Birthday*, Wiesbaden: 9–16.

Dandamaev, M.A., 1997. 'Assyrian Traditions during Achaemenid Times', in Parpola, S., and Whiting, R.M. (eds), *Assyria 1995: Proceedings of the 10th Anniversary Symposium of the Neo-Assyrian Text Corpus Project, Helsinki, September 7–11, 1995*, Helsinki: 41–8.

Dandamaev, M.A., and Lukonin, V.G., 1989. *The Culture and Social Institutions of Ancient Iran*, Cambridge.

Daniels, P.T., and Bright, W., 1996. *The World's Writing Systems*, New York and Oxford.

Daryaee, T., 1995. 'National history or Keyanid history?: the nature of Sasanid Zoroastrian historiography', *Iranian Studies* 28: 129–41.

Davies, N. de G., 1953. *The Temple of Hibis in el-Khargeh Oasis III: The Decoration*, MMA Egyptian Excavations 17, New York.

DeVries, K., 2000. 'The Nearly Other: The Attic Vision of Phrygians and Lydians', in Cohen, B. (ed.), *Not the Classical Ideal*, Leiden: 306–63.

Diba, L.S., 1999. 'Images of power and the power of images: intention and response in early Qajar painting (1785–1834)', in Diba, L.S., and Ekhtiar, M. (eds), *Royal Persian Paintings: the Qajar Epoch 1785–1925*, Brooklyn, 30–49.

Dieulafoy, M., 1893. *L'Acropole de Suse d'après les fouilles exécutées en 1884, 1885, 1886*, Paris.

Dinawari, Abu Hanifa. *Akhbar al- tiwal*, translated into Persian by M.Mahdavi-Damghani, Tehran, 1989 (SH 1368).

Driver, G.R., 1954. *Aramaic Documents of the Fifth Century BC*, Oxford.

Dusinberre, E.R.M., 1997. 'Imperial style and constructed identity: A "Graeco-Persian" cylinder seal from Sardis', *Ars Orientalis* 27: 99–129.

Dusinberre, E.R.M., 1999. 'Satrapal Sardis: Achaemenid bowls in an Achaemenid capital', *American Journal of Archaeology* 103: 73–102.

Dusinberre, E.R.M., 2003. *Aspects of Empire in Achaemenid Sardis*, Cambridge.

Ebbinghaus, S., 1999. 'Between Greece and Persia: rhyta in Thrace from the late 5th to the early 3rd centuries BC', in Tsetskhladze, G.R. (ed.), *Ancient Greeks West and East*, Leiden: 385–425.

Ebbinghaus, S., 2000. 'A banquet in Xanthos: seven rhyta on the northern cella frieze of the "Nereid" Monument', in Tsetskhladze, G.R., Prag, A.J.N.W., and Snodgrass A.M. (eds), *Periplous: Papers on Classical Art and Archaeology Presented to Sir John Boardman*, London: 98–109.

Ebeling, E., 1952. 'Die Rüstung eines babylonischen Panzerreiters nach Vertage aus der Zeit Darius II', *Zeitschrift für Assyriologie* 50: 203–13.

Elayi, J., and Elayi, A.G., 2004. *Le Monnayage de la Cité Phénicienne de Sidon à l'Époque Perse (V^e–IVe s. av. J.-C.)*, Paris.

Ellis, R.S., 1966. 'A note on some Ancient Near Eastern Linch Pins', *Berytus* XVI: 41–8.

Engels, D., 1978. *Alexander the Great and the Logistics of the Macedonian Army*. London.

Errington, E., and Curtis, V.S., forthcoming. *From Persepolis to the Punjab: Nineteenth-Century Discoveries*.

Fales, F.M., and Postgate, J.N., 1995. *Imperial Administrative Records, Part II: Provincial and Military Administration*, State Archives of Assyria XI, Helsinki.

Fleming, D., 1989. 'Eggshell ware pottery in Achaemenid Mesopotamia', *Iraq* 51: 165–85.

Fol, A., Nikolov, B., and Hoddinott, R.F., 1986. *The New Thracian Treasure from Rogozen, Bulgaria*, London.

Fossing, P., 1937. 'Drinking bowls of glass and metal from the Achaemenian times', *Berytus* 4: 121–9.

Francfort, H.-P., 1988, 'Central Asia and Eastern Iran', *Cambridge Ancient History*, 2nd edn, IV: 165–93.

French, D., 1998. 'Pre- and early-Roman roads of Asia Minor: The Persian road', *Iran* XXXVI: 15–43.

Fried, L.S., 2004. *The Priest and the Great King: Temple-Palace Relations in the Persian Empire*, Winona Lake, Indiana.

Furtwängler, A., 1906. *Griechische Vasenmalerei*, Munich.

Garnsey, P., Hopkins, K., and Whittaker, C.R. (eds), 1983. *Trade in the Ancient Economy*. London.

Garrison, M.B., 1991. 'Seals and the elite at Persepolis: some observations on early Achaemenid Persian Art', *Ars Orientalis* 21: 1–29.

Garrison, M.B., and Root, M.C., 1996/8. *Persepolis Seal Studies: An Introduction with Provisional Concordances of Seal Numbers and Associated Documents on Fortification Tablets 1–2087*, Achaemenid History IX, Leiden.

Garrison, M.B., Root, M.C., and Jones, C.E., 2001. *Seals on the Persepolis Fortification Tablets I: Images of Heroic Encounter*, Oriental Institute Publications 117, Chicago.

Gauer, W., 1990. 'Penelope, Hellas und der Perserkönig. Ein hermeneutisches Problem', *Jahrbuch des Deutschen Archäologischen Instituts* 105: 31–65.

Gehrke, H.-J., 2000. 'Gegenbild und Selbstbild: Das europäische Iran-Bild zwischen Griechen und Mullahs', in Hölscher, T. (ed.), *Gegenwelten zu den Kulturen Griechenlands und Roms in der Antike*, Munich: 85–109.

Georges, P., 1994. *Barbarian Asia and the Greek Experience*, Baltimore.

Ghirshman, R., 1954. *Village perse-achéménide*, Mémoires de la Mission Archéologique en Iran XXXVI, Paris.

Ghirshman, R., 1962. 'Notes Iraniennes XI: le rhyton en Iran', *Artibus Asiae* 25: 57–80.

Ghirshman, R., 1964. *The Arts of Ancient Iran, from Its Origins to the Time of Alexander the Great*. London.

Gitler, H., 2000. 'Achaemenid motifs in the coinage of Ashdod, Ascalon and Gaza from the 4th century BC', *Traneuphratene* 20: 73–87.

Gnoli, G., 1993. 'Dahan-e Golaman', *Encyclopaedia Iranica* VI: 582–5.

Godard, A., 1950. *Le trésor de Ziwiyè* (Kurdistan), Haarlem.

Goldman, B., 1984. 'The Persian saddle blanket', *Studia Iranica* 13: 7–18.

Graf, D.F., 1994. 'The Persian royal road system', *Achaemenid History* VIII: 167–89.

Green, P., 1996. *The Greco-Persian Wars*, Berkeley.

Greenewalt, C.H., Jr., 1997. 'Arms and weapons at Sardis in the mid-sixth century BC', *Arkeoloji ve Sanat* 79: 2–13.

Grenet, F., 1990. 'Burial: ii Remnants of Burial Practice in Ancient Iran', *Encyclopaedia Iranica* IV: 559–61.

Gunter, A.C., 1988. 'The art of eating and drinking in ancient Iran', *Asian Art* 1/2 (spring): 3–54.

Gunter, A.C., 2000. 'Ancient Iranian Ceramics', in Cort, L., Farhad, M., and Gunter, A.C. (eds), *Asian Traditions in Clay: The Hauge Gifts*, Washington: 14–15.

Gunter, A.C., and Cool Root, M., 1998. 'Replicating, inscribing, giving: Ernst Herzfeld and Artaxerxes' silver *phiale* in the Freer Gallery of Art', *Ars Orientalis* 28: 1–38.

Gunter, A.C., and Jett, P., 1992. *Ancient Iranian Metalwork in the Arthur M. Sackler Gallery and the Freer Gallery of Art*, Washington.

Haerinck, E., 1973. 'Le palais achéménide de Babylone', *Iranica Antiqua* X: 108–32.

Haerinck, E., 1978. 'Painted pottery of the Ardabil style in Azerbaidjan (Iran)', *Iranica Antiqua* XIII: 75–91.

Haerinck, E., 1997. 'Babylonia under Achaemenid rule', in Curtis, J.E. (ed.) 1997: 26–34.

Hakemi, A., 1977. *The Art of the Achaemenians, Parthians and Sasanians*, exh. cat., Reza Abbasi cultural and arts centre, Tehran.

Hall, E., 1989. *Inventing the Barbarian: Greek Self-Definition through Tragedy*, Oxford.

Hallock, R.T., 1969. *Persepolis Fortification Tablets*, Oriental Institute Publications 92, Chicago.

Hamzeh Isfahani. *Tarikh muluk al-ard w'-al anbiya*, translated into Persian by J. Shu'ar, Tehran , 1988 (SH 1367).

Hanson, V.D., 1989. *The Western Way of War. Infantry battle in Classical Greece*, Oxford.

Hanson, V.D. (ed.),1991. *Hoplites: The Classical Greek Battle Experience*, London.

Harbsmeier, M., 1992. 'Before Decipherment: Persepolitan Hypotheses in the Late Eighteenth Century,' *Culture and History* 11: 23–59.

Harcourt-Smith, C., 1931. *Catalogue of Casts of Sculptures from Persepolis and the Neighbourhood, with List of prices, Illustrating the Art of the Old Persian Empire, from 550 – 340 BC*, London.

Harcourt-Smith, C., 1932. *Photographs of Casts of Persian Sculptures of the Achaemenid Period mostly from Persepolis*, London.

Harden, D.B., 1981.*Catalogue of Greek and Roman Glass in the British Museum*, vol.1, London.

Harper, P.O., Aruz, J., Tallon, F. (eds), 1992. *The Royal City of Susa: Ancient Near Eastern Treasures in the Louvre*, New York.

Harrison, C.M., 1982. 'Coins of the Persian Satraps', unpublished Ph.D. thesis, University of Pensylvania.

Harrison, T., 2000. *The Emptiness of Asia: Aeschylus' Persians and the History of the Fifth Century*, London.

Harrison, T. (ed.), 2002. *Greeks and Barbarians*, Edinburgh.

Hart, S., 1995. 'The Pottery', in Bennett, C.M. and Bienkowski, P., *et al.* (eds), *Excavations at Tawilan in Southern Jordan*, Oxford: 53–66.

Hartog, F., 1988. *The Mirror of Herodotus: The Representation of the Other in the Writing of History*, Berkeley.

Hassoulier, B., 1905. 'Offrande à Apollon Didyméen', *Mémoires de la Délégation en Perse* VII: 155–165.

Head, D., 1992. *The Achaemenid Persian Army*, Stockport.

Henkelmann, W., 2003. 'Persians, Medes and Elamites: acculturation in the Neo-Elamite period', in Lanfranchi, G.B., Roaf, M., and Rollinger, R. (eds), *Continuity of Empire (?): Assyria, Media, Persia*, Padua: 181–231.

Herzfeld, E., 1935. 'Eine Silberschüssel Artaxerxes I', *Archäologische Mitteilungen aus Iran* VII: 1–8

Herzfeld, E.E., 1941. *Iran in the Ancient East*, London and New York.

Hinnells, J.R., 1985. *Persian Mythology*, New York.

Hinz, W., and Koch, H., 1987. *Elamisches Wörterbuch* (AMI Ergänzungsband 17), 2 vols, Berlin.

Hoffmann, H., 1958. 'Fragment of a Faience Rhyton', *The Brooklyn Museum Bulletin* 19/3 (summer): 10–12.

Hoffmann, H., 1961. 'The Persian Origin of the Attic Rhyta', *Antike Kunst* 4: 21–4.

Hofstetter, J., 1978. *Die Griechen in Persien. Prosopographie der Griechen im Persischen Reich vor Alexander*, Berlin.

Hornblower, S., 1994. 'Asia Minor', *Cambridge Ancient History*, 2nd edn, VI: 208–33.

Hughes, M.J., 1984. 'Analyses of silver objects in the British Museum', in Curtis, J.E, *Nush-i Jan III: The Small Finds*. London: 58–60.

Hughes, M.J., 1986. 'Analysis of silver and gold items found in a hoard at Babylon', *Iran* XXIV: 87–8.

Hussein, M.H., and Suleiman, A., 1999. *Nimrud: A City of Golden Treasures*. Baghdad.

Huyse, P., 1999. *Die dreisprachige Inschrift __buhrs I. an der Ka'ba-I Zardu_t (_KZ)*, 2 vols, Corpus Inscriptionum Iranicarum, Part III, vol. 1, Texts I, London.

Jabak-Hteit, S., 2003. 'Les jarres de l'époque perse du site Bey 010', *National Museum News* 17: 80–94.

Jacobs, B., 1987. *Griechische und persische Elemente in der Grabkunst Lykiens zur Zeit der Achaemenidenherrschaft*, Jonsered.

Jaffar-Mohammadi, Z., and Chevalier, N. (eds), 2001. *Les Recherches Archéologiques Françaises en Iran*, exh.

cat., 20 October to 21 November 2001, National Museum of Iran, Tehran.

Jakob-Rost, L., 1975. *Die Stempensiegel im Vorderasiatischen Museum*, Berlin.

Jamzadeh, P., 1996. 'The Achaemenid throne-leg design', *Iranica Antiqua* XXXI: 101–46.

Jantzen, U., 1972. *Ägyptische und orientalische Bronzen aus dem Heraion von Samos*, Samos VIII, Bonn.

Jidejian, N., 1971. *Sidon through the Ages*, Beirut.

Jidejian, N., 2000. 'Greater Sidon and its cities of the dead', *National Museum News* 10: 15–24.

Johnson, J.H., 1983. 'The Demotic Chronicle as a statement of a theory of kingship', *Journal of the Society for the Study of Egyptian Antiquities* 13: 61–72.

Kagan, J., 1994. 'An Archaic Greek Coin Hoard from the Eastern Mediterranean and Early Cypriot Coinage', *Numismatic Chronicle* 154: 17–52.

Kantor, H.J.,1957. 'Achaemenid jewelry in the Oriental Institute', *Journal of Near Eastern Studies* XVI: 1–23.

Kaptan, D., 2001. 'On the satrapal centre in northwestern Asia Minor: some evidence from the seal impressions of Ergili/Daskyleion', in Bakir, T. (ed.), *Achaemenid Anatolia*, Leiden: 57–64.

Kaptan, D., 2002. *The Daskyleion Bullae: Seal Images from the Western Achaemenid Empire*. Achaemenid History XII, Leiden.

Karageorghis, V. 1973. *Excavations in the Necropolis of Salamis* III, Nicosia.

Karageorghis, V., 2001. *Ancient Art from Cyprus: the Cesnola Collection in the Metropolitan Museum of Art*, New York.

Keen, A.G., 1998. *Dynastic Lycia*, Leiden.

Kellens, J., 1989. 'Avestique', in Schmitt, R. (ed.), *Compendium Linguarum Iranicarum*, Wiesbaden.

Kent, R.G., 1953. *Old Persian: Grammar, Texts, Lexicon*, 2nd edn, New Haven.

Ker Porter, Sir Robert, 1821–2. *Travels in Georgia, Persia, Armenia, Ancient Babylonia, etc.*, 2 vols, London.

Khan, F., *et al.*, 2000. *Akra: The Ancient Capital of Bannu*, Journal of Ancient Civilisations XXIII.

King, L.W., and Thompson, R.C., 1907. *The Inscription of Darius the Great at Behistun*, London.

Kipiani, G., 1999. 'Up'lisc'ixis ganadgurebuli k'vablebi', *Narkvevebi* 5: 7–18 (in Georgian with German summary).

Kipiani, G., 2000. 'Up'lisc'ixis kidovani samarxis inventari (katalogi da senisvnebi)', *Ark'eologiuri Jurnali* 1: 4–95 (in Georgian).

Kleeman, I., 1958. Der Satrapensarkophag aus Sidon, 1st Forsch. 20, 1958.

Knapton, P., Sarraf, M.R., and Curtis, J.E., 2001. 'Inscribed column bases from Hamadan', *Iran* 39: 99–117.

Knauer, E.R., 1986. 'The Persian saddle blanket ... gleanings', *Studia Iranica* 15: 265–6.

Knauer, E.R. 1992. 'Mitra and Kerykeion. Some reflections on symbolic attributes in the art of the classical period', *Archäologischer Anzeiger*: 373–99.

Knauss, F., 2001. 'Persian rule in the north Achaemenid palaces on the periphery of the empire', in Nielson, I. (ed.), *The Royal Palace Institution in the First Millennium BC*, Athens: 125–37.

Konuk, K., 1998. 'The Coinage of the Hekatomnids of Caria', unpublished D.Phil. thesis, University of Oxford.

Korostovtsev, M.A., 1947. 'Un étendard militaire égyptien?', *Annales du Service des Antiquités de l'Egypte* XLV: 127–31.

Krefter, F., 1971. *Persepolis Rekonstruktionen*. Teheraner Forschungen 3, Berlin.

Kroll, S., 2003. 'Medes and Persians in Transcaucasia? Archaeological horizons in North-Western Iran and Trancaucasia', in Lanfranchi, G.B., Roaf, M., and Rollinger, R. (eds), *Continuity of Empire (?): Assyria, Media, Persia*, Padua: 281–7.

Kuhrt, A., 1990. 'Achaemenid Babylonia: sources and problems', *Achaemenid History* IV: 177–94.

Kuhrt, A., 1995. *The Ancient Near East c. 3000–330 BC*, 2 vols, London.

Kuhrt, A., 2002. *'Greeks' and 'Greece' in Mesopotamian and Persian Perspectives*, 21st J.L. Myres Memorial Lecture, Oxford.

Labrousse, A., and Boucharlat, R., 1972. 'La fouille du palais du Chaour à Suse en 1970 et 1971', *Cahiers de la Délégation Archéologique Française en Iran* 2: 61–167.

Lampre, G., 1905. 'La représentation du lion à Suse', *Mémoires de la Délégation en Perse* VIII: 159–76.

Larsen, M.T., 1994. *The Conquest of Assyria: Excavations in an Antique Land*. London and New York.

Layard, A.H., 1853. *Discoveries in the Ruins of Nineveh and Babylon; With Travels in Armenia, Kurdistan and the Desert: Being the Result of a Second Expedition Undertaken for the Trustees of the British Museum*, London.

Layard, A.H., 1887. *Early Adventures in Persia, Susiana, and Babylonia*, 2 vols, London.

Lemaire, A., 1989. 'Remarques à propos du monnayage cilicien d'époque Perse et ses légendes araméennes', *Revue des Etudes Anciennes* 91: 141–56.

Lemaire, A., 2001. 'Les inscriptions araméennes de Daskyleion', in Bakir, T., *Achaemenid Anatolia*, Leiden: 21–35.

Le Rider, G., 1995. 'Histoire économique et monétaire de l'orient hellénistique', *Annuaire du Collège de France* 95: 767–79.

Le Rider, G., 1997. 'Le monnayage perse en cilicie au IVe Siècle', *NAC* 26: 151–69.

Lerner, J., 1998. 'Sasanian and Achaemenid revivals in Qajar art', in Curtis, V.S., Hillenbrand, R., and Rogers, J.M. (eds), *The Art and Archaeology of Ancient Persia*, London: 162–7.

Lewis, D.M., 1994. 'The Persepolis tablets: speech, seal and script', in Bowman, A.K., and Woolf, G. (eds), *Literacy and Power in the Ancient World*, London: 7–32.

Lichtheim, M., 1980. *Ancient Egyptian Literature, III: The Late Period*, Berkeley.

Littauer, M.A., 1981. 'Early stirrups', *Antiquity* 55: 99–105.

Littauer, M.A., and Crouwel, J.H., 1979. *Wheeled Vehicles and Ridden Animals in the Ancient Near East*, Leiden–Köln.

Littauer, M.A., Crouwel, J.H., and Collon, D., 1976. 'A Bronze Chariot Group from the Levant in Paris', *Levant* 8: 71–81.

Litvinsky, B.A., 2000. 'A Finial from the Temple of the Oxus in Bactria', *Parthica* 2: 131–41.

Litvinsky, B.A., 2001. 'The Bactrian ivory plate with a hunting scene from the Temple of the Oxus', *Silk Road Art and Archaeology* 7: 137–66.

Litvinsky, B.A., and Pichikyan, I.R., 2000. *The Hellenistic Temple of the Oxus in Bactria (South Tajikistan)*, vol.1, Moscow.

Liverani, M., 1995. 'The Medes at Esarhaddon's court', *Journal of Cuneiform Studies* 47: 57–62.

Lloyd, A.B., 1982. 'The Inscription of Udjahorresnet. A Collaborator's Testament', *Journal of Egyptian Archaeology* 68: 166–80.

Lloyd, A.B., 1983. 'The Late Period, 664–332 BC' in Trigger, B.G. *et al.* (eds), *Ancient Egypt: A Social History*, Cambridge: 279–364.

Loftus, W.K., 1857. *Travels and Researches in Chaldaea and Susiana*, London.

Lordkipanidze, O., 2001. 'The 'Akhalgori Hoard'. An attempt at dating and historical interpretation', *Archäologische Mitteilungen aus Iran* 33: 143–90.

Luft, J.P., 2001. 'Qajar rock-reliefs', *Iranian Studies* 34: 31–49.

Luschey, H., 1939. *Die Phiale*, Bleicherode am Harz.

Luschey, H., 1983. 'Die Darius-Statuen aus Susa und ihre Rekonstruktion.' *Archäologische Mitteilungen aus Iran* suppl. 10: 191–206.

L'vov-Basirov, O.P.V., 2001. 'Achaemenian Funerary Practices in Western Asia Minor', in Tomris Bakér *et al.* (eds), *Achaemenid Anatolia*, Leiden: 101–7.

Lyonnet, B., 2005. 'La présence achéménide en Syrie du nord', in Briant, P. (ed), 2005.

McLauchlin, B.K., 1989. 'Rock crystal working at Sardis: a local industry', *American Journal of Archaeology* 93: 250 (summary).

Maffre, F., 2004. 'Le monnayage de Pharnabaze frappé dans l'atelier de Cyzique', *NC* 164: 1–32.

Magee, P., 2001. 'Excavations at Muweilah 1997–2000', *Proceedings of the Seminar for Arabian Studies* 31: 115–30.

Mamédova, R., n.d. *Archeologicheskie Pamyatniki, 7: Pamayatniki Materialnoi Kulturi Azerbaidjana*, Baku.

Marshall, F.H., 1909. 'Some recent acquisitions at the British Museum', *Journal of Hellenic Studies* XXIX: 151–67.

Mathieson, I, *et al.*, 1995. 'A stela of the Persian period from Saqqara', *Journal of Egyptian Archaeology* 81: 23–41.

Meadows, A., 2002. 'Royal Achaemenid issues', in Ashton, R., *et al.*, 'The Pixodarus Hoard', *Coin Hoards* 9: 159–243.

Meadows, A., 2003. 'The Apadana Foundation Deposit (IGCH 1789): some clarification', *Numismatic Chronicle* 163: 342–4.

De Mecquenem, R., 1934. 'Fouilles de Suse 1929–1933', *Mémoires de la Mission archéologique de Perse* XXV: 177–237.

De Mecquenem, R., 1943. 'Fouilles de Suse 1933–1939', *Mémoires de la Mission archéologique en Iran* XXIX: 3–161.

De Mecquenem, R., 1947. 'Contribution à l'étude du palais achéménide', *Mémoires de la Mission archéologique en Iran* XXX: 1–119.

Melikian-Chirvani, A.S., 1993. 'The international Achaemenid style', *Bulletin of the Asia Institute* (NS) 7: 111–30.

Mellink, M., 1971. 'Excavations at Karata_-Semayük and Elmali, Lycia, 1970', *American Journal of Archaeology* 75: 245–55.

Merrillees, P.H., 2005. *Catalogue of the Western Asiatic Seals in the British Museum. Cylinder Seals VI: Pre-Achaemenid and Achaemenid Periods*. London (forthcoming).

Meshorer, Y., and Qedar, S., 1991. *The Coinage of Samaria in the Fourth Century BCE*, Jerusalem.

Mildenberg, L., 1990–91. 'Notes on the coin issues of Mazday', *INJ* 11: 9–23.

Mildenberg, L., 1998. 'Money Supply under Artaxerxes IV Ochus', in Ashton, R., and Hurter, S. (eds), *Studies in Greek Numismatics in Memory of Martin Jessop Price*, London: 277–86.

Mildenberg, L., 2000. 'On the so-called satrapal coinage', in Casabonne, O., (ed.), *Mécanismes et innovations monétaires dans l'Anatolie achéménide: numismatique et histoire: actes de la table ronde internationale d'Istanbul, 22–23 mai 1997*, Paris: 9–20.

Miller, M.C., 1993. 'Adoption and adaptation of Achaemenid metalware forms in Attic black-gloss ware of the fifth century', *Archäologische Mitteilungen aus Iran* 26: 109–46.

Miller, M.C., 1997. *Athens and Persia in the Fifth Century BC: A Study in Cultural Receptivity*, Cambridge.

Miller, M.C., 2003. 'Art, myth and reality: Xenophantos' Lekythos re-examined', in Csapo, E., and Miller, M.C. (eds), *Poetry, Theory, Praxis: The Social Life of Myth, Word and Image in Ancient Greece. Essays in Honour of William J. Slater*, Oxford: 19–47.

Mitchell, T.C., 1973. 'The bronze lion weight from Abydos', *Iran* XI: 173–5.

Mitchell, T.C., 2000. 'The Persepolis Sculptures in the British Museum', *Iran* XXXVIII: 49–56.

Mond, R., and Myers, O.H., 1934. *The Bucheum* (3 vols), London.

Moorey, P.R.S., 1975. 'Iranian troops at Deve Hüyük in Syria in the earlier fifth century BC', *Levant* 7: 108–17.

Moorey, P.R.S., 1980a. *Cemeteries of the First Millennium BC at Deve Hüyük, near Carchemish, Salvaged by T.E. Lawrence and C.L. Woolley in 1913*, BAR-S87, Oxford.

Moorey, P.R.S., 1980b. 'Metal wine-sets in the Ancient Near East', *Iranica Antiqua* 15: 182–97.

Moorey, P.R.S., 1985. 'The Iranian contribution to Achaemenid material culture', *Iran* XXIII: 21–37.

Moorey, P.R.S., 1988a. 'The Persian Empire', in *Cambridge Ancient History Plates to Volume IV*: 1–94.

Moorey, P.R.S., 1988b. 'The technique of gold-figure decoration on Achaemenid silver vessels and its antecedents', *Iranica Antiqua* 23: 231–46.

Moorey, P.R.S., 1998. 'Material aspects of Achaemenid polychrome decoration and jewellery', *Iranica Antiqua* XXXIII: 155–71.

Moortgat, A., 1940. *Vorderasiatische Rollsiegel*, Berlin.

De Morgan, J., et al., 1900. *Recherches archéologiques*, Mémoires de la Délégation en Perse I, Paris.

De Morgan, J., 1905. 'Découverte d'une sépulture achéménide', *Mémoires de la Délégation en Perse* VIII: 29–58.

Morrison, J. (ed.) 1995. *The Age of the Galley*, London.

Mostafavi, S.M.T., 1978. *The Land of Pars*, Chippenham.

Motamedi, N., 1995/6. 'Ziwiyeh: a Mannaean/Median fortress', *Proceedings of the Conference on the History of Architecture and Town-Planning in Iran at Bam, Kerman*, Tehran, vol. 1: 320–57.

Mousavi, A., 2002. 'Persepolis in retrospect: histories of discovery and archaeological exploration at the ruins of ancient Passeh', *Ars Orientalis* XXXII: 209–251.

Muscarella, O.W., 1977. 'Unexcavated Objects and Ancient Near Eastern Art', in Levine, L., (ed.), *Mountains and Lowlands: Essays in the Archaeology of Greater Mesopotamia*, Malibu: 153–207.

Muscarella, O.W., 1980. 'Excavated and Unexcavated Achaemenid Art', in Schmandt-Besserat, D. (ed.), *Ancient Persia: The Art of an Empire*, Malibu: 23–42.

Muscarella, O.W., 1988. *Bronze and Iron: Ancient Near Eastern Artifacts in The Metropolitan Museum of Art*, New York.

Muscarella, O.W., 2000. *The Lie Became Great: The Forgery of Ancient Near Eastern Cultures*, Gröningen.

Mysliwiec, K., 2000. *The Twilight of Ancient Egypt: First Millennium BC*, translated by D. Lorton, Cornell.

Naveh, J., 1970. 'The Development of the Aramaic Script', *Proceedings of the Israel Academy of Sciences and Humanities* 5/1: 36–7.

Newell, E.T., 1919 [1920]. 'Myriandros – Alexandria Kat' Isson', *American Journal of Numismatics* 53, pt II: 1–42.

Newton, C.T., 1862–63. *A History of Discoveries at Halicarnassus, Cnidus and Branchidae*, I–II, London.

Nicolet-Pierre, H., 1979. 'Les monnaies des deux derniers satrapes d' Égypte avant la conquête d'Alexandre', in Mørkholm, O., and Waggoner, N.M. (eds), *Greek Numismatics and Archaeology. Essays in Honor of Margaret Thompson*, Wetteren: 221–30.

Oliver, A., Jr., 1970. 'Persian Export Glass', *Journal of Glass Studies* 12: 9–16.

Oppenheim, A.L., 1949. 'The golden garments of the gods', *Journal of Near Eastern Studies* VIII: 172–93.

Ouseley, W.,1821. *Travels in Various Countries of the East, more particularly Persia*, vol.2, London.

Özgen, I., and Öztürk, J., et al., 1996. *Heritage Recovered: The Lydian Treasure*. Istanbul.

Pahlavi, M.R.,1960. *Mission for my Country*, London.

Pallis, S.A., 1954. *The Antiquity of Iraq*. Copenhagen.

Pardee, D., 2004. 'Ugaritic', in Woodard, R.D. (ed.), *The Cambridge Encyclopedia of the World's Ancient Languages*, Cambridge University Press, Cambridge: 288–318.

Parkinson, R., 1999. *Cracking Codes: The Rosetta Stone and Decipherment*, British Museum Press, London.

Parpola, S., 1987. *The Correspondence of Sargon II, Part I. Letters from Assyria and the West*, State Archives of Assyria, I, Helsinki.

Paspalas, S.A., 2000. 'On Persian-type furniture in Macedonia: the recognition and transmission of forms', *American Journal of Archaeology* 104: 531–60.

Paspalas, S.A., forthcoming. 'The Achaemenid empire and the north-west Aegean', *Ancient East and West*.

Pestman, P.W., 1994. *Les Papyrus Démotiques de Tsenhor (P. Tsenhor). Les archives privées d'une femme égyptienne du temps de Darius Ier*, Studia Demotica 4, Leuven.

Petit, T., 1990. *Satrapes et Satrapies dans l'Empire Achéménide de Cyrus le Grand à Xerxès Ier*, Paris.

Petit, T. 1991. 'Présence et influences perses à Chypre', *Achaemenid History* VI: 161–78.

Pope, A.U., 1938. *A Survey of Persian Art* IV, London and New York.

Pope, M., 1975. *The Story of Decipherment: From Egyptian Hieroglyphic to Linear B*. London.

Porada, E., 1965. *Ancient Iran*, London.

Porten, B., 1996. *The Elephantine Papyri in English: Three Millennia of Cross-Cultural Continuity and Change*, Studies in Near Eastern Archaeology and Civilisation 22, Leiden.

Porten, B., and Yardeni, A., 1991. 'Three unpublished Aramaic ostraca', *Maarav* 7: 207–27.

Postgate, J.N., 2000. 'The Assyrian army at Zamua', *Iraq* 62: 89–108.

Potratz, J.A.H., 1966. *Die Pferdentrensen des alten Orient*, Analecta Orientalia 41, Rome.

Potts, D., 1999. *The Archaeology of Elam*, Cambridge.

Price, M.J., 1993. 'More from Memphis and the Syria 1989 hoard', in Price, M., Burnett, A., and Bland, R. (eds), *Essays in Honour of Robert Carson and Kenneth Jenkins*, London: 31–5.

Pritchard, J.B., 1950. *Ancient Near Eastern Texts relating to the Old Testament*, Princeton.

Pryce, F.N., 1928. *Catalogue of Sculpture in the Department of Greek and Roman Antiquities of the British Museum* I.1, London.

Pryce, F.N., 1931. *Catalogue of Sculpture in the Department of Greek and Roman Antiquities of the British Museum* I.2, London.

Raeck, W., 1981. *Zum Barbarenbild in der Kunst Athens im 6. und 5. Jahrhundert v. Chr.*, Bonn.

Rajabi, P., and Mahmudi-Aznaveh, S., 2000 (SH 1378). *Takht-e Jamshid, bargah-e tarikh*, Tehran.

Rawlinson, G., 1871. *The Five Great Monarchies of the Ancient Eastern World*, 3 vols, 2nd edn, London.

Razmjou, S., 2001, 'Des Traces de la deesse Spenta Armaiti à Persepolis et proposition poure une nouvelle lecture d'un logogramme Elamite', *Studia Iranica*, 30 : 7–15.

Razmjou, S., 2002a. 'Assessing the damage: notes on the life and demise of the Statue of Darius from Susa', *Ars Orientalis* 32: 81–104.

Razmjou, S., 2002b. 'Traces of paint on the statue of Darius', *Arta* 2002.003 (Achaemenet): 1–2.

Razmjou, S., 2003. 'Reconstruction of an Unknown Building at Persepolis', MA thesis, Azad University, Tehran.

Razmjou, S, 2004a. 'Unidentified Gods in Achaemenid Calendar', *Name-ye Iran-e Bastan*, vol. 3, no. 1, Iran University Press: 15–34.

Razmjou, S., 2004b. 'Lan Ceremony and other Ritual Ceremonies in the Achaemenid Period: Persepolis Fortification Tablets', *Iran* XLII: 103–17.

Reade, J.E., 1986. 'A hoard of silver currency from Achaemenid Babylonia', *Iran* XXIV: 79–89.

Redmount, C.A., and Friedman, R.F., 1997. 'Tales of a Delta site: The 1995 Season at Tell el-Muqdam', *Journal of the Amercian Research Center in Egypt* 34: 57–83.

Rehm, E., 1992. *Der Schmuck der Achämeniden*, Munster.

Reuther, O., 1926. *Die Innenstadt von Babylon (Merkes)*, WVDOG 47, Leipzig.

Rich, C.J., 1836. *Narrative of a Residence in Koordistan by the late Claudius James Rich Esquire, Edited by his Widow*, 2 vols

Ridder, A. de, 1909. *Collection de Clercq, VI. Les terres cuites et les verres*. Paris.

Roaf, M.D., 1974. 'The subject peoples on the base of the statue of Darius', *Cahiers de la Délégation Archéologique Française en Iran* 4: 73–160.

Roaf, M.D., 1983. 'Sculptures and sculptors at Persepolis', *Iran* 21.

Robinson, E.S.G., 1950. 'A "silversmith's hoard" from Mesopotamia', *Iraq* XII: 44–51.

Root, M.C., 1979. *The King and Kingship in Achaemenid Art*. Acta Iranica IX, Leiden.

Root, M.C., 1985. 'The Parthenon Frieze and the Apadana Reliefs at Persepolis: reassessing a programmatic relationship', *American Journal of Archaeology* 89: 103–120.

Rudenko, S.I., 1970. *Frozen Tombs of Siberia*, London.

Sachs, A.J., and Hunger, H., 1988. *Astronomical Diaries and Related Texts from Babylonia* I, Vienna.

Sami, A., 1955. *Persepolis*, 2nd edn, Shiraz.

Sami, A., 1959 (SH 1338). *Pasargad. Qadmitarin paytakht-e shahanshahi Iran (The oldest capital of the kingdom of Iran)*, Shiraz.

Sami, A., 1970. *Persepolis*, 6th edn, Shiraz.

Sancisi-Weerdenburg, H., 1989. 'Gifts in the Persian Empire', in Briant and Herrenschmidt 1989: 129–46.

Sancisi-Weerdenburg, H., 1995. 'Persian food: stereotypes and political identity', in Wilkins, J., Harvey, D., and Dobson, M. (eds), *Food in Antiquity*, Exeter: 286–302.

Sarianidi, V., 2002. 'The fortification and palace of Northern Gonur', *Iran* XL: 75–87.

Sarre, F., 1922. *Die Kunst des Alten Persien*, Berlin.

__apova, J.L., 2000. 'On the Material and Manufacturing Technique of the Finial from the Temple of the Oxus', *Parthica* 2: 143–5.

Scheil, V., 1929. *Inscriptions des Achéménides à Suse*, Mémoires de la mission Archéologique de Perse XXI, Paris.

Schmidt, E.F., 1953. *Persepolis I: Structures, Reliefs, Inscriptions*, Oriental Institute Publications 68, Chicago.

Schmidt, E.F., 1957. *Persepolis II: Contents of the Treasury and Other Discoveries*, Oriental Institute Publications 69, Chicago.

Schmidt, E.F. *et al.*, 1989. *The Holmes Expedition to Luristan*, Chicago.

Schmitt, R., 1991. *The Bisutun Inscription of Darius the Great: Old Persian Text*, Corpus Inscriptionum Iranicarum, part 1, vol. 1, London.

Schmitt, R., 2000. *The Old Persian Inscriptions of Naqsh-i Rustam and Persepolis*, Corpus Inscriptionum Iranicarum, Part 1, vol. 1, Texts II, London.

Scholl, A., 2000. 'Der "Perser" und die "skythischen Bogenschützen" aus dem Kerameikos', *Jahrbuch des Deutschen Archäologischen Instituts* 115: 79–112.

Segal, J.B., 1969. 'Miscellaneous fragments in Aramaic', *Iraq* XXXI: 170–74.

Seidl, U., 1976. 'Ein Relief Dareios I in Babylon', *Archäologische Mitteilungen aus Iran* 9: 125–30.

Seipel, W. (ed.), 2000. *7000 Ans d'art perse. Chefs-d'oeuvre du Musée National de Téhéran*. Milan/Vienna.

Sekunda, N., 1989. 'The Persians' in Hackett, J. (ed.), *Warfare in the Ancient World*, London: 82–8.

Sekunda, N., 1992. *The Persian Army 560–330 BC*, London.

Shahbazi, A.S., 1975. *The Irano-Lycian Monuments: The Principal Antiquities of Xanthos and its Region as Evidence for Iranian Aspects of Achaemenid Lycia*, Tehran.

Shahbazi, A.S., 1976. *Persepolis Illustrated*, Tehran.

Shahbazi, A.S., 1977. 'From Parsa to Takht-i Jamshid', *Archäologische Mitteilungen aus Iran* 10: 197–207.

Shahbazi, A.S., 1987. 'Astodan', *Encyclopaedia Iranica* II: 851-853.

Shahbazi, A.S., 1999. (SH 1378). 'Kohantarin towsif takht-e jamshid dar zaban-e farsi' ('The oldest description of Persepolis in Persia'), *Iranian Journal of Archaeology and History* 12: 2–5.

Shahbazi, A.S., 2000a. (SH 1379). *Rahnama-ye jam'eh takht-e jamshid (Complete Guide to Persepolis)*, Tehran.

Shahbazi, A.S., 2000b. (SH 1379). *Rahnama-ye jam'e pasargad (Complete Guide to Pasargadae)*, Tehran.

Shahbazi, A.S., 2001. 'Early Sasanians' claim to Achaemenid heritage', *N_me-ye Ir_n-e B_st_n* (The International Journal of Ancient Iranian Studies) 1/1: 61–73.

Shahbazi, A.S., 2004. *The Authoritative Guide to Persepolis*, Tehran.

Shahnameh of Firdausi, translated by A.G. and E. Warner, Jules Mohl Edition, Tehran, 1369/1990.

Shaki, 1996. 'Dez i Nebest', *Encyclopaedia Iranica* VII: 348–50.

Shawcross, W., 1989. *The Shah's Last Ride*, London.

Shefton, B.B., 1993. 'The White Lotus, Rogozen and Colchis: The Fate of a Motif', in Chapman, J., and Dolukhanov, P. (eds), *Cultural Transformations and Interactions in Eastern Europe*. Avebury: 178–209 and corrigenda.

Shefton, B.B., 1998. 'Metal and clay: prototype and re-creation. Zoffany's "Tribuna" and lessons from the Malacena fabric of Hellenistic Volterra (Calyx-krater, stamnos, situla and the Achaemenid rhyton', *Revue des études anciennes* 100: 619–62.

Sherman, E.J., 1981. 'Djedhor the Saviour: statue base OI 10589', *JEA* 67: 82–102.

Simpson, St J., 1996. 'An Achaemenid furniture leg from Egypt', *British Museum Magazine* no.26: 17–18.

Simpson, St J., 1998. 'Late Achaemenid silver bowl from Mazanderan', *British Museum Magazine* no.32: 32.

Simpson, St J. 2000. 'Rediscovering past splendours from Iran', *British Museum Magazine* no.36: 28–9.

Simpson, St J., 2003. 'From Mesopotamia to Merv: reconstructing patterns of consumption in Sasanian households', in Potts, T., Roaf, M., and Stein, D. (eds), *Culture through Objects. Ancient Near Eastern Studies in Honour of P.R.S. Moorey*, Oxford: 347–75.

Sims-Williams, N., 2001. 'The inscriptions on the Miho bowl and some comparable objects', *Studia Iranica* 30: 187–98.

Sims-Williams, N., and Cribb, J., 1995–6. 'A new Bactrian inscription of Karishka the Great', *Silk Road Art and Archaeology* 4: 75–142.

Smirnov, Y.I., 1934. *Der Schatz von Achalgori*, Tbilisi.

Smith, A., 2001. 'Eurymedon and the Evolution of Political Personifications in the Early Classical Period', *Journal of Hellenic Studies* 119: 128–41.

Smith, A.H., 1900. *A Catalogue of Sculpture in the Department of Greek and Roman Antiquities in the British Museum*, vol. II, London.

Smith, C.H., 1896. *Catalogue of the Greek and Etruscan Vases in the British Museum, vol. III, Vases of the Finest Period*, London.

SNG Black Sea = Price, M.J. 1993. *Sylloge Nummorum Graecorum. [Great Britain] Vol. 9, the British Museum, pt. 1, the Black Sea*, London.

SNG von Aulock = *Sylloge Nummorum Graecorum Deutschland Sammlung von Aulock*, Berlin, 1957–68.

Stadtmueller, H. (ed.) 1899. *Anthologia Graeca epigrammatum Palatina cum Planudea*, vol. 2.1, Leipzig.

Starr, Ch.G., 1974. 'Greeks and Persians in the fourth century B.C. A study in cultural contacts before Alexander', *Iranica Antiqua* 11: 39–99.

Stauber, J., and Barth, M., 1996. 'Münzen die Städte in der Bucht von Adramytteion', in Stauber, J. (ed.), *Die Bucht von Adramytteion. Inschriften Griechischer Städte aus Kleinasien Band 51, Teil II*, Bonn: 181–325.

Stern, E., 1982. *Material Culture of the Land of the Bible in the Persian Period 538–332 B.C.*, Warminster.

Stern, E., 2001. *Archaeology of the Land of the Bible, vol. 2: The Assyrian, Babylonian and Persian Periods (732–332 B.C.E.)*, New York.

Stern, E.M., 1997. 'Glass and rock crystal: a multifaceted relationship', *Journal of Roman Archaeology* 10: 192–206.

Steve, M.-J., 1974. 'Inscriptions des Achéménides à Suse (fouilles de 1952 à 1965)', *Studia Iranica* 3: 135–69.

Steve, M.-J., 1987. *Ville royale de Suse, 7: nouveaux mélanges épigraphiques*, Mémoires de la Délégation Archéologique en Iran LIII, Nice.

Stolper, M.W., 1985. *Entrepreneurs and Empire: The Murashû Archive and Persian Rule in Babylonia*, Leiden.

Streck, M., 1916. *Assurbanipal und die letzen assyrischen Könige bis zum Untergange Nineveh's*, Vorderasiatische Bibliothek 7, Leipzig.

Stronach, D.B., 1974. 'Achaemenid Village I at Susa and the Persian Migration to Fars'. *Iraq* 36: 239–48.

Stronach, D.B., 1978. *Pasargadae: A Report on the Excavations Conducted by the British Institute of Persian Studies from 1961 to 1963*, Oxford.

Stronach, D.B., 1985. 'The apadana: a signature of the line of Darius I', in Huot, J.-L., *et al.* (eds), *De L'Indus aux Balkans: Recueil a la memoire de Jean Deshayes*, Paris: 433–45.

Stronach, D.B., 1997. 'Anshan and Parsa: early Achaemenid history, art and architecture on the Iranian plateau', in Curtis 1997: 35–53.

Stronach, D.B., 1998. 'On the date of the Oxus gold scabbard and other Achaemenid matters', *Bulletin of the Asia Institute*, n.s. 12: 231–48.

Stronach, D.B., 2001. 'From Cyrus to Darius: Notes on Art and Architecture in Early Achaemenid Palaces', in Nielsen, J. (ed.), *The Royal Palace Institution in the First Millenium BC* (Monographs of the Danish Institute at Athens 4), Athens: 95–111.

Studniczka, F., 1907. 'Der Rennwagen im syrisch-phonikischen Gebeit', *Jahrbuch des Archäologischen Instituts* 22: 147–96.

Stucky, R.A., 1985. 'Achämenidische Hölzer und Elfenbeine aus Ägypten und Vorderasien im Louvre', *Antike Kunst* 28: 7–32.

Stucky, R.A., 1998. 'Le sanctuaire d'Échmoun à Sidon', *National Museum News* 7: 3–13.

Stucky, R.A., and Mathys, H.-P., 2000. 'Le sanctuaire sidonien d'Échmoun. Aperçu historique du site, des fouilles et des découvertes faites à Bostan ech-Cheikh', *Baal* 4: 123–48.

Sturt, G., 1923. *The Wheelwright's Shop*, Cambridge.

Summerer, L., 2003. 'Achämenidische Silberfunde aus der Umgebung von Sinope', *Ancient Civilisations from Scythia to Siberia* 9: 17–42.

Summers, G.D., 1993. 'Archaeological evidence for the Achaemenid period in Eastern Turkey', *Anatolian Studies* XLIII: 85–108.

Sumner, W., 1986. 'Achaemenid Settlement in the Persepolis plain', *American Journal of Archaeology* 90: 3–31.

Tabari, Abu Ja'far Muhammad. *The History of al-Tabari, Volume V: The Sasanids, the Byzantines, the Lakmids, and*

Yemen, translated and annotated by
C.E. Bosworth, New York 1999.

Tadjvidi, A., 1976. *Danistaniha-yi nuvin dar barah-i hunar va bastanshinasi-i 'asr-i Hakhamanishi bar bunyad-i kavusha-yi panj salah-i Takht-i Jamshid: salha-yi 2527 ta 2532 Shahanshahi*, Tehran (in Persian).

Tadmor, M., 1974. 'Fragments of an Achaemenid Throne from Samaria', *Israel Exploration Journal* 24: 37–43.

Tallon, F., 1995. *Les pierres précieuses de l'Orient ancient des Sumériens aux Sassanides*, Paris.

Thomas, E., 1853. 'Notes on certain unpublished coins of the Sassanidae', *Numismatic Chronicle* XV (1st series): 180–87.

Triantafyllidis, P., 2003. 'Achaemenian glass production', *Annales du 15e Congres de l'Association Internationale pour l'Histoire du Verre (New York–Corning 2001)*, Nottingham: 13–17.

Triantafyllidis, P., 2003. 'Achaemenian glass production', *Annales du 15e Congres de l'Association Internationale pour l'Histoire du Verre (New York - Corning 2001)*, Nottingham: 13–17.

Tuplin, C., 1987a. 'The Administration of the Achaemenid Empire' in Carradice 1987a: 109–58.

Tuplin, C., 1987b. 'Xenophon and the garrisons of the the Achaemenid Empire', *Archäologische Mitteilungen aus Iran* 20: 167–245.

Tuplin, C., 1990. 'Persian decor in *Cyropedia*: some observations', *Achaemenid History V*: 17–29.

Valbelle, D., and Defernez, C., 1995. 'Les sites de la frontiére égypto-palestinienne à l'époque perse', *Transeuphratène* 9: 93–100.

Van Wees, H., 2004. *Greek Warfare: Myths and Realities*, London.

Venedikov, I., and Gerassimov, T., 1975. *Thracian Treasures*, Sofia/London.

Vickers, M., 1972. 'An Achaemenid Glass Bowl in a Dated Context', *Journal of Glass Studies* 14: 15–16.

Vickers, M., 1991. 'Persian, Thracian and Greek gold and silver: questions of metrology', *Achaemenid History VI*: 31–9.

Vickers, M., 1996. 'Rock crystal: the key to cut glass and *diatreta* in Persia and Rome', *Journal of Roman Archaeology* 9: 48–65.

Vickers, M., 2002. '"Shed no tears"? Three studies in ancient metrology', in Clarke, A.J., and Gaunt, J. (eds), *Essays in Honor of Dietrich von Bothmer*, Amsterdam: 333–8.

Vickers, M., and Gill, D., 1994. *Artful Crafts: Ancient Greek Silverware and Pottery*, Oxford.

Von Saldern, A., 1959. 'Glass finds from Gordion', *Journal of Glass Studies* 1: 23–49.

Von Saldern, A., 1963. 'Achaemenid and Sasanian cut glass', *Ars Orientalis* 5: 7–16.

Walker, C.B.F., 1972. 'A recently identified fragment of the Cyrus Cylinder', *Iran* 10: 158–9.

Walker, C.B.F., 1980. 'Elamite Inscriptions in the British Museum', *Iran* 17: 75–81.

Walker, C.B.F., 1987. *Cuneiform*, London.

Walker, C.B.F., 1997. 'Achaemenid chronology and the Babylonian sources', in Curtis 1997: 17–25.

Wallinga, H.T., 1993. *Ships and Sea-Power before the Great Persian War: The Ancestry of the Ancient Trireme*, Leiden.

Walser, G., 1966. *Die Völkerschaften auf den Reliefs von Persepoli*, Teheraner Forschungen 2, Berlin.

Walters, H.B., 1921. *Catalogue of the Silver Plate (Greek, Etruscan and Roman) in the British Museum*, London.

Wannagat, D., 2001. '"Eurymedon eimi" – Zeichen von ethnischer, sozialer und physischer Differenz in der Vasenmalerei des 5. Jahrhunderts v. Chr.', in van den Hoff, R., and Schmidt, S. (eds) *Konstruktionen von Wirklichkeit: Bilder in Griechenland des 5. und 4. Jahrhunderts v. Chr.*, Stuttgart: 51–71.

Waywell, G.B., 1978. *The Free-Standing Sculptures of the Mausoleum at Halicarnassus*, London.

Weissbach, F.H., 1911. *Die Keilschriften der Achämeniden*. Vorderasiatische Bibliothek 3, Leipzig.

Wiesehöfer, J., 2001. *Ancient Persia*, London and New York.

Wiesehöfer, J., 2002. '"... sie waren das Juwel von allem, was er gesehen". Niebuhr und die Ruinenstätten des Alten Iran', in Wiesehöfer, J., and Conermann, S. (eds), *Carsten Niebuhr (1733–1815) und seine Zeit*, Stuttgart: 267–85.

Will, E., 1960. 'Chabrias et les finances de Tachôs', *Revue des études anciennes* 62: 254–75.

Williams, D., forthcoming, 'From Phokaia to Persepolis: East Greek, Lydian and Achaemenid jewellery', in Villing, A. (ed.), *The Greeks in the East*, British Museum Occasional Paper, London.

Winlock, H.E., 1941. *The Temple of Hibis in el-Khargeh Oasis* I, MMA Egyptian Excavations 1, New York.

Winter, F., 1912. *Der Alexander-Sarkophag aus Sidon*, Strasburg.

Woolley, C.L., 1923. 'A drinking-horn from Asia Minor', *Liverpool Annals of Archaeology and Anthropology* 10: 69–72.

Woolley, C.L., 1962. *Ur Excavations IX: The Neo-Babylonian and Persian Periods*, London.

Wuttmann, M., *et al.*, 1998. 'Ayn Manawir (oasis de Kharga). Deuxième rapport préliminaire', *Bulletin de l'Institut Français d'Archéologie Orientale* 98: 367–463.

Yule, P., 2001. *Die Gräberfelder in Samad al Shan (Sultanat Oman)*, Rahden/Westf.

Zournatzi, A., 2000. 'The processing of gold and silver tax in the Achaemenid Empire: Herodotus 3.96.2 and the archaeological realities', *Studia Iranica* 29/2: 241–71.

ILLUSTRATION ACKNOWLEDGEMENTS

British Museum (© British Museum), photography by Lisa Baylis: 6, 9, 10–11, 18–19, 21–31, 33, 35–7, 40, 46, 49, 66–70, 72–4, 93–4, 98–109, 111, 114, 116, 119–20, 122–3, 125, 127, 129, 132–7, 140–45, 150–51, 153–71, 179–89, 191–8, 200–10, 213–62, 266–7, 282–7, 289–97, 300, 302, 305–7, 312–15, 385–6, 388–400, 402, 405–9, 413–23, 425–7, 431–2, 435, 437–8, 442–4, 447–52; Nigel Tallis: 176, 178, 409b, 460–68, 471–2; coins by Richard Hodges

Louvre (© Photo RMN), including photography by Hervé Lewandowski: 1, 91, 128, 401, 434; Michel Urtado: 277; Gérard Blot: 55–7, 59; Christian Larrieu: 52, 301; Phillippe Bernard: 43, 47; Franck Raux: 8, 17, 32, 50, 53, 60–65, 81, 89, 110, 199, 278–81, 401, 439; Lee Oi-Cheong: 54, 76, 58, 268–75; Etienne Revault: 445

Tehran Museum (© National Museum of Iran), all photography by Ebrahem Khadem-Bayat except the following – Goran Vranić, Zagreb: 5, 34, 48, 78, 92, 96–7, 113, 118, 126, 196, 263–4, 288, 298, 441; Catarina Maria Gomes Ferreira, Lisbon: 410–11

Fig. 64 © Antikenmuseum, Basel; figs 53–6 by Barbara Armbruster; figs 31–3, 39, 44–5, 65–9, 75 and figs on pp. 66–7, 77–8 © British Museum; fig. 50 © Brooklyn Museum; figs 1–5, 7–13, 17–18, 24–6, 30, 41–2, 51, 70–72 by John Curtis; fig. 73 by Vesta Curtis; fig. 43 by Sam Moorhead; fig. 59 © Oriental Institute, Chicago; figs on pp. 95, 99, 173 by Shahrokh Razmjou; figs 46–7, 49 by St John Simpson; figs 15–16, 19–22, 52, 58 by Nigel Tallis

All drawings by Ann Searight unless otherwise stated.